The Age of Bismarck

*the text of this book is printed
on 100% recycled paper*

The Age of Bismarck

Documents and Interpretations

Edited by

THEODORE S. HAMEROW

HARPER TORCHBOOKS

Harper & Row, Publishers

New York, Evanston, San Francisco, London

Contents

Introduction

The unification of Germany was the most important single political development of the nineteenth century, altering the diplomatic balance of power on the Continent and shifting the center of economic predominance eastward. For more than four hundred years the states of Western Europe had held the lead in the international race for hegemony. Their geographic position had given them access to the great maritime trade routes and to the wealth created by the commercial capitalism of the early modern period. Their material resources in turn made possible the establishment of a centralized system of government and an efficient organization of the armed forces. By the end of the eighteenth century Englishmen, Frenchmen, or Spaniards could look back with pride on the accomplishments of their nation. But in Central Europe the course of political and economic development had run in the opposite direction. During the Middle Ages the rulers of Germany had possessed greater power and prestige than the monarchs of Western Europe. Even after central authority in the Holy Roman Empire had weakened, the economy continued to prosper from the mercantile and banking activities of the German cities. It was not until the Reformation that the civic and material decline of Central Europe became disastrous, as religious strife aggravated the effect of the shift of the major trade routes to the Atlantic seaboard. The two centuries following the outbreak of the Thirty Years' War marked the nadir in the history of Germany.

The political fragmentation and economic backwardness of the Holy Roman Empire encouraged the development of civic attitudes different from those which prevailed in Western Europe. As central authority declined, the functions of government were increasingly assumed by local notables—dukes, margraves, bishops, abbots, and the wealthy patricians of the free cities. The result was a growing popular attachment to provincial rights and freedoms. While in Western Europe people gradually accepted the sovereignty of the national state, in Central Europe particularistic loyalties began to predominate. The Germans thought of themselves more and more as Prussians, Austrians, Saxons, Bavarians, or Hanoverians rather than as Germans. The princes entered into alliances with foreign monarchs directed against fellow princes and even against the emperor himself. Central Europe became a battleground on which the armies of the Great Powers fought for the advancement of their national interest with the support of the German rulers. Particularism reflected the civic outlook of a country which was politically divided and economically stagnant. In a pre-industrial hierarchical society governed by princely authority, loyalty to local custom and tradition seemed natural. It came to be accepted as a truism that the German spirit, as opposed to the French or the English, had a tendency toward diversity, uniqueness, and localism. The Augustan age of German culture, the age of Goethe, Schiller, Kant, Herder, Mozart, and Beethoven, coincided with a period of political disunity and weakness. The energies which in Western Europe turned to the improvement of man and society were directed in Central Europe to the perfection of the mind and the soul.

The French Revolution transformed the civic attitudes and loyalties of Germany. A nation vegetating in the cozy provincialism of the Holy Roman Empire was suddenly exposed to the ideals of freedom and equality which the armies of France brought with them. After 1792 Central Europe fell under the influence of the government in Paris. The Directory gained possession of the Rhineland, while Napoleon subjugated the region between the Rhine and the Elbe. Under his direction the number of autonomous political units in Germany was drastically reduced. Those principalities which survived the process of territorial consolidation were, moreover, combined by the French to form the Confederation of the Rhine. The Holy Roman Empire came to an end, and even the two largest states of Central Europe, Austria and Prussia, were forced to become allies of the invincible Corsican. As important as the change in diplomacy and politics was the change in values and allegiances. The teachings of benevolent despotism, which had been accepted without question under the old order, were now increasingly challenged by new theories of liberal government and egalitarian society. Seeking to emulate the achievements of the French, the rulers of Germany imitated their example. They completed the abolition of serfdom, they established legal equality for all classes, they removed the disabilities of religious minorities, they introduced local self-government, and they abrogated corporative restrictions on industrial entrepreneurship. For the first time in its history Central Europe began to feel the influence of liberalism.

Even more significant was the birth of German nationalism. The effect of foreign domination in Central Europe was the emergence of a sense of unique political identity among its people. The old order of princely particularism, which had surrendered before the onslaught of the French invaders, could not be expected to undertake the task of civic regeneration. Many of those chafing under the Napoleonic yoke concluded that only the vision of a new Teutonic destiny would provide the strength with which to end alien tyranny. Yet the resentment of French oppression did not transform all inhabitants of Central Europe into ardent nationalists. There were countless Germans who remained loyal to the tradition of particularism, and there were even some who believed that Napoleon's rule benefited the entire Continent. The lower classes, moreover, remained by and large indifferent to the new civic ideals which they found incomprehensible. To be sure, a political movement had now emerged which advocated the creation of a free and united Germany. But the fact that liberalism and nationalism appeared late in the history of Central Europe, not spontaneously, but as a reaction against foreign domination, had a profound effect on the character which they assumed east of the Rhine.

The War of Liberation, by bringing about the defeat of Napoleon, removed the most important motive of civic reform in Germany. The princes, who had been ready to support unity and freedom while the struggle against the French was going on, began to follow more traditional policies under the Restoration. Now that the danger from abroad had been overcome, they became concerned for the preservation of their prerogatives. The result was a half century of conflict between those favoring change and those who believed that the German Confederation formed in 1815 satisfied the political needs of the nation. On one side were businessmen, politicians, publicists, and academics—most of them of middle-class background—whose interests and ideals made them advocates of parliamentarism and unification. On the other side were aristocratic courtiers, bureaucrats, landowners, and army officers who felt that their privileged status would be most secure under legitimism and particularism. The defenders of the old order had the advantage, not only because they occupied a strategic position in government and administration, but also because the masses remained generally loyal to the crown. The reformers were only a small minority whose strength was insufficient to alter the established political system in Central Europe. As long as German society remained static and agrarian, the supporters of the *status quo* could check the forces of liberalism and nationalism.

The weakness of the reform movement became apparent in the

years following the overthrow of Napoleon. Once the French had
been driven out of Central Europe, the princes began to stiffen their
resistance against demands for unity and freedom. The outcome was
a decisive victory for the established order. By the early 1820s the
introduction of constitutional government had been restricted to the
secondary states of the south, and the nationalist agitation of the
university students had been effectively suppressed. Ten years later
there was an outbreak of unrest in Germany inspired by the July
Revolution in France. But after constitutions had been granted in the
secondary states of the north, the established order regained the upper
hand. The most important clash between the forces of tradition and
reform came in 1848, when the entire Continent was swept by a
revolutionary movement. For a time it looked as if the old order
in Central Europe had been defeated once and for all. In one state
after another the liberals came to power, while the task of unification
was entrusted to a popularly elected national assembly meeting in
Frankfurt am Main. But the very magnitude of the victory which the
bourgeois reformers had won revealed their fundamental weakness.
Having finally gained control of the government, they showed themselves incapable of making effective use of their authority. They were
torn by disputes between moderates and radicals as well as between
Austrophiles and Prussophiles. Even more important, they were unable
to retain the support of the lower classes, which were interested in
economic improvement rather than political innovation. The result
was a steady erosion of their strength, until in 1849 the old order returned to power throughout Central Europe. Frederick William IV
of Prussia continued to contemplate the achievement of national
unification under conservative Hohenzollern auspices. But the opposition of Austria and Russia forced him to abandon his visionary schemes.
In 1851 the German Confederation was finally reestablished in all its
familiar inadequacy.

The years which followed were a period of out-and-out reaction.
Never had the prospect for civic reform in Germany appeared dimmer.
Those who had participated in the revolutionary movement were now
discredited, some of them driven into exile or condemned to imprisonment. Legitimism and particularism became enshrined as the official
orthodoxy of the ruling classes of Central Europe. Yet the conservative
1850s were the seedbed of new economic forces which soon led to a
revival of liberalism and nationalism. For the decade beginning with
the defeat of the revolution marked the breakthrough of industrial

capitalism in Germany. The return of political and social stability after the upheaval of 1848 generated an economic boom which established the primacy of urban over rural forms of wealth. To be sure, the process of industrialization had begun much earlier in the period following the defeat of Napoleon. But its final victory over preindustrial handicraft manufacture and anticapitalistic hierarchical agrarianism came during the reaction. The liberal economist Max Wirth described in 1858 the great achievements of the national economy in the preceding decade:

> The stagnation, the utter paralysis of business in the years 1848, 1849, and 1850 had ended after the [revolution]. The totally depleted warehouses had to be filled again, and when at the same time the effects of the introduction of California gold and of the low discount rate made themselves felt by way of England, there gradually developed a spirit of enterprise more powerful than any experienced in Germany up to that time. . . . The steamboat traffic on the rivers, the shipment of goods on the railroads, the construction of ships and machinery grew at an extraordinary rate. Railroads and machine shops, coal mines and iron foundries, spinneries and rolling mills seemed to spring out of the ground, and especially in the industrial regions of Saxony, the Rhineland, and Westphalia smokestacks sprouted from the earth like mushrooms.

The increase in the volume of production encouraged the growth of the system of transportation. The rail network of Germany almost doubled between 1850 and 1860, rising from 5,800 to 11,000 kilometers. The figures for international commerce provided another measure of the economic boom which followed the revolution. The value of foreign trade expanded by 50 percent between 1850 and 1860, from 2,100,000,000 to 3,200,000,000 marks, as German merchants continued to compete with the French for the leading position among the continental states. The world of banking adjusted to the process of industrialization by altering the form of its organization and the character of its investment. First, financial institutions began to change from family firms or limited partnerships to joint-stock companies which would provide a greater volume of credit. Second, they proceeded to shift their funds from government bonds and commercial ventures to the construction of factories, mines, and railroads. In the course of the 1850s important new banks like the Disconto-Gesellschaft and the Darmstädter Bank came into existence to help finance the growth of industrial capitalism in Central Europe. "Each city, each state, however small, wants to have its bank and its lending establishment," reported the French counsul in Leipzig. "It seems as if there is as much deter-mination to cover Germany with a network of credit institutions as there was to cover her with a network of railroads." The abortive civic revolution of the mid-century was followed by a successful material revolution.

Such a fundamental change in the economy was bound to have a profound effect on politics. The process of industrialization rein-forced those groups in society which were seeking to alter the structure of the state. The movement for civic reform, though it drew its followers from all classes, was largely bourgeois in composition. As long as the dominant occupations in Central Europe had remained agrarian, the opponents of the established order had lacked the strength to effect its overthrow. But that began to change during the 1850s. Once the economy entered the stage of industrial capitalism, the middle class acquired the material resources needed to transform the political sys-tem. The intellectuals who had been the leading spokesmen for liberalism and nationalism now found growing support among manufacturers, mineowners, merchants, and financiers. The shift in economic pre-ponderance from the aristocracy to the bourgeoisie encouraged de-mands for a corresponding shift in political preponderance. This was the fundamental reality behind the new civic crisis of the 1860s. The middle class, having established the superiority of industry over agriculture, felt growing dissatisfaction with a form of government in which birth and tradition exercised greater influence than talent and wealth. It wanted to alter the balance of power in politics, coun-tering the prerogative of the crown with the authority of the leg-islature. The manufacturers and financiers of Central Europe, more-over, were the natural enemies of particularism, which placed annoying obstacles in the path of industrial capitalism. They chafed at the multiplicity of weights, measures, currencies, and business regulations in the German Confederation. To them national unification was more than a noble ideal. It was a practical necessity dictated by the require-ments of material progress. The economic boom of the mid-century thus prepared the way for a new conflict between traditional aristo-cratic agrarianism and modern bourgeois industrialism.

The revival of the movement for civic reform at the end of the 1850s came to be called "the new era." As the demands for unity and freedom grew louder, the advocates of national unification under Prussia formed the *Nationalverein*, while the supporters of Austria founded the *Reformverein*. The Prussophile publicists and politicians in the *kleindeutsch* camp began to clash with those in the Austrophile *grossdeutsch* party. But both sides were in agreement that the existing system of authority in the German Confederation must be altered. The princes, realizing that the agitation for reform could no longer be ignored, decided to swim with the current. Some conservative statesmen retired from office, while others suddenly displayed an interest in plans for political reconstruction. The federal diet in Frankfurt am Main, hitherto a bulwark of particularism, opened discussions concerning a closer union of the states of Central Europe. After losing a war in Italy, the Austrian government attempted to appease its domestic opponents by introducing a constitution for the empire. But the most significant change of policy occurred in Prussia, where in 1857 the neurotic Frederick William IV suffered a mental breakdown. The following year, when a regency was established under his brother Prince William, the period of reaction came to an end. The regent was no liberal, to be sure, but neither was he in sympathy with the rigid conservative orthodoxy of his predecessor. He immediately announced his determination to follow a middle-of-the-road policy, and the Hohenzollern kingdom joined in the general movement of the states of the German Confederation toward civic reform.

Yet the hopes of the new era soon began to turn to bitter disappointment. It became apparent that the old order was unwilling to alter the political system of Central Europe to the extent demanded by the reformers. The governments of the secondary states, resolved to retain their sovereignty, refused to go beyond a few hesitant steps in the direction of greater centralization. The federal diet became bogged down in endless deliberations on how to reconcile particularism with nationalism. Austria discovered that the introduction of constitutional government was not enough to end the conflict among the numerous nationalities within her borders. And in Prussia the enthusiasm aroused by the establishment of the regency petered out amid resentments and recriminations. Prince William, who became king on the death of his brother in 1861, was ready to seek an understanding with the opponents of the old order, but he would not agree to a curtailment of the royal prerogative. The outcome was a growing tension between the crown and the legislature, which was controlled by liberals. An open conflict, bound to come sooner or later, arose over the question of military reform. The monarch insisted that he alone had the right to determine the size and the organization of the army. Parliament maintained that it should at least have a voice in policies for which it was expected to provide funds. A total impasse resulted, with each side afraid that retreat would lead to defeat. The king refused to modify his plan for enlarging the armed forces, while the legislature refused to approve the budget until a modification had been made. At one point William I even thought of abdicating, but he finally decided to hold out. In September 1862 he appointed Otto von Bismarck head of the cabinet with the task of defending the position of the crown.

The new prime minister of Prussia proved to be the last of the great conservative statesmen of the Continent. He succeeded in checking the forces of liberalism and maintaining the traditional authoritarian system of government in Central Europe. While west of the Rhine civic institutions responded to the demand for a democratization of politics, to the east they continued to reflect the domination of the landed nobility and state bureaucracy. The man responsible for the preservation of the established order was by background and upbringing indistinguishable from countless other Junkers who flourished amid the aristocratic estates beyond the Elbe. There had been nothing in his early political views and activities to suggest that he was more than a bluff country squire loyal to the monarchical traditions of the Hohenzollern kingdom. He seemed to accept without question the teachings of conservatism, particularism, and legitimism. His only distinctive quality was the tenacity with which he clung to his convictions. In the spring of 1848, when most noblemen had been too frightened or discouraged to oppose the revolution, he had not hesitated to express his hostility to the new order. And as it became apparent that the liberals lacked the strength to carry out their program, he was among the first to advocate a policy of reaction. The boldness which characterized his statecraft in the years to come was apparent from the outset.

His devotion to the crown was rewarded in 1851 with an appointment to the position of Prussian representative at the federal diet in Frankfurt am Main. The eight years which he spent there were the turning point in his political career, converting a narrow-minded Junker into a skilled and subtle diplomat. Bismarck encountered for the first time a social milieu more cosmopolitan than that of the eastern latifundia where he had spent most of his life. He now had an opportunity to observe firsthand the bourgeois society of a municipal republic which was a center of industry, commerce, and banking. Even more important, he gained a clear insight into the effects of the particularism on which the German Confederation rested. The result was a transformation of his philosophy and outlook. He had come to Frankfurt am Main believing that the maintenance of decentralized sovereignty through a balance between Prussia and Austria was in the best interest of the states of Central Europe. He left convinced that the defense of monarchical institutions and aristocratic interests required a fundamental alteration in the system of government. The predominance of crown and nobility could not survive in its existing form. The advance of industrialization and the growth of the bourgeoisie meant that it must either adjust to changing conditions or perish. Since traditional principles could no longer protect authoritarian values, the theoretical justification of conservatism would have to bow to its practical needs.

More concretely, Bismarck came to believe that national unification in Central Europe had become inevitable. The development of industrial capitalism was creating greater economic interdependence among the states of the German Confederation which must sooner or later lead to political consolidation. If the established order did not assume the leadership of the forces of nationalism, the reformers and radicals would. And the result would be the gradual weakening of the dominant position in society which crown and nobility had historically occupied. It was therefore in the interest of the Prussian government to adopt a policy of centralization. The teachings of particularism and legitimism which the aristocracy had defended in the past would have to be abandoned. They had become outworn dogmas incapable of reflecting new civic realities. The established order, instead of fighting for a lost cause, should seek to achieve national unification, but in a form which would perpetuate the ascendancy of throne, aristocracy, bureaucracy, and army. Bismarck thus pursued traditional objectives, although he was prepared to employ radical means in order to attain them. It would be a mistake to regard him as simply an opportunist bent on the acquisition of power. He had firm convictions regarding the proper function of government and the natural relationship of classes. But he was always ready to subordinate ideology to fundamental political and economic forces. "I have never in my life been a doctrinaire," he declared after the establishment of the German Empire.

His conversion to the cause of national unification forced him to alter the civic beliefs he had hitherto espoused. For one thing, he broke with the dogmas of legitimism which taught that the political system established in Central Europe after the downfall of Napoleon, sanctified by solemn treaties, was inviolable. To Bismarck the contractual obligations which a government assumed could not override the dictates of self-preservation. His abandonment of legitimism led logically to his rejection of particularism. The existence of some thirty-five sovereignties in Central Europe, he insisted, was incompatible with the achievement of national unification. It seemed intolerable to him that gingerbread principalities like Schwarzburg-Sondershausen or Reuss-Schleiz-Gera should possess the same dignity and independence as a leading state like Prussia. This indifference to the realities of political life was for him sufficient proof of the incorrigible weakness of the German Confederation. And since the established system of decentralized authority was bound to be altered in any case, Berlin would gain an important advantage by assuming the leadership of the national movement. To be sure, such a policy would lead to a struggle between Hohenzollerns and Habsburgs. The Austrians could not be expected to stand idly by, while the Prussians established their domination over Central Europe. But Bismarck did not shrink from the prospect of war. To him armed conflict was a legitimate instrument of statecraft. The ultimate questions of national destiny, he believed, were settled not at the conference table but on the field of battle.

Bismarck's conversion to the cause of nationalism was disturbing to his superiors in Berlin. The Prussian government hesitated to follow a course which would in all probability result in civil war in the German Confederation. While Berlin admired the skill and boldness with which its representative at the federal diet was defending Hohenzollern interests, it also feared the ruthlessness with which he proposed to bring about the political reconstruction of Central Europe. Some of his aristocratic friends, moreover, began to suspect him of heresy. Hitherto they had regarded him as a believer in the traditional teachings of conservatism. But his sudden rejection of the confederal system, his indifference to the sovereign rights of the secondary states, and his open advocacy of a struggle against Austria disturbed them. They failed to see that he sought the same goals as they, only by different means. Early in 1859 the prince regent, afraid that Bismarck's intransigence would prove an obstacle to the policy of moderation which the government had decided to pursue, shifted him from Frankfurt am Main to the less sensitive post of Prussian ambassador to Russia. He remained in St. Petersburg for three years, while the hopes of the new era were dwindling amid accusations and counter-

accusations occasioned by the struggle over army reform. In the spring
of 1862 Bismarck was transferred from the Russian capital to the
French. But his stay in Paris was to be brief. Four months later the
conflict between king and legislature in Berlin produced a crisis which
led to his appointment as head of the cabinet. The long climb from
country squire to prime minister was now over.

The strategy which Bismarck adopted in the struggle against liberalism appeared at first sight to be nothing more than a stubborn determination to make no concession on the issue of army reform. To the
legislature's refusal to approve the budget he replied by governing
without a budget. He sought to justify this violation of the constitution by maintaining that in the event of a deadlock between crown
and parliament, the ministry had the right to continue to perform
the essential functions of administration. But this argument was mere
sophistry which persuaded no one. The stalemate continued for four
years, the legislature pursuing a policy of passive resistance and the
king ruling without budgetary authorization. Before Prussia lay the
gloomy prospect of an endless war of attrition in which the strength
of both sides would gradually become exhausted. Bismarck, however,
had no intention of allowing domestic discord to weaken the state.
While publicly announcing his determination to resist parliamentary
encroachment on the royal prerogative, he was privately weighing
alternative strategies for putting an end to the constitutional conflict.
At first he thought of enlisting the aid of the lower classes in the battle
against the bourgeoisie. That was when he entered into secret negotiations with the socialist leader Ferdinand Lassalle. He soon discovered,
however, that the price he would have to pay for proletarian support
was high. Uneasy at the thought of social reform which might alter
class relations and restrict property rights, he decided instead to defeat
liberalism through nationalism. The achievement of political consolidation, he reasoned, was so important to his middle-class opponents that in
return they would be willing to compromise their civic principles.

The international situation was favorable to Bismarck's plan for
strengthening the position of Prussia by blood and iron. In the fall
of 1863 a dispute between Denmark and the German Confederation
over the duchies of Schleswig and Holstein gave him an opportunity
to demonstrate once again the toughness with which he pursued his
political objectives. He first induced the Austrians to join him in a war
against the Danish monarchy. The statesmen in Vienna were afraid that
if they refused to collaborate with the Prussians, the latter would go

ahead on their own. The result was a brief military conflict in which the Hohenzollern armies played the decisive role. It was to be expected that Denmark could not hold out for long against the combined might of the two leading states of Central Europe. But the swiftness of the victory surprised even the supporters of Prussia. Equally impressive was the skill with which Bismarck handled the diplomatic problems created by the war. The government in Copenhagen had counted on foreign assistance, and there was in fact considerable pressure from the neutral powers for a negotiated settlement. But since the Danes overplayed their hand, the Prussian prime minister could use their refusal to make substantial concessions as a pretext for continuing the hostilities. The outcome of the struggle was thus determined by the soldiers rather than the statesmen. In the summer of 1864 the Danish king was forced to accept a peace settlement surrendering his rights to Schleswig-Holstein. The two duchies now came under the joint sovereignty of Prussia and Austria.

The war over Schleswig-Holstein proved to be the prelude to a war over Central Europe. For the question of what to do with the duchies led to a test of strength between Prussia and Austria which ended in the overthrow of the German Confederation. To say that Bismarck had from the outset expected the dispute with Copenhagen to produce a reckoning with Vienna would be incorrect or at least exaggerated. He was a gifted statesman, not a prophet. Yet he did recognize early that the struggle against the Danes might prepare the way for a confrontation with the Austrians. He was not bent on provoking a quarrel with Vienna. It would have been enough for him to partition Central Europe into spheres of influence, with Prussia dominating the region north of the Main River. But when Emperor Francis Joseph refused to abandon the system of confederacy which had served the interests of his monarchy so well, a break between the Hohenzollerns and the Habsburgs became inevitable. For two years the adversaries threatened, negotiated, advanced, and retreated, until in the spring of 1866 the last hope of avoiding a civil war in Germany vanished. Public opinion regarded the approach of hostilities with dismay. Legitimists deplored the conflict as a breach of monarchical solidarity. Reformers feared that it would lead to military despotism. Particularists trembled for the sovereignty of the secondary states. And nationalists were appalled at the thought of Germans fighting Germans. The prevalent view was that Bismarck had decided to launch a war of desperation in order to extricate himself from the impasse which the constitutional conflict had produced in Prussia. Most of the governments of the German Confederation supported the Austrians, who appeared to be defenders of legitimate authority against the schemes of aggrandizement emanating from Berlin.

Yet the struggle for political unification in Central Europe was decided neither by popular opinion nor by diplomatic negotiation but by the force of arms. A sense of helplessness seemed to grip the nation, as the opposing armies marched forth to determine its future. But while the civilians agonized, the soldiers resolved the German question on the field of battle. Less than three weeks after the outbreak of hostilities the Prussian troops, directed by the military genius of Helmuth von Moltke, defeated the Austrians at Sadowa. The result was a diplomatic revolution which altered the balance of power on the Continent. Before the statesmen of the neutral countries could fully grasp what was happening, Bismarck succeeded in altering the political structure of Central Europe.

First of all, Austria agreed under the terms of the preliminary peace of Nikolsburg to withdraw from the Teutonic commonwealth of which she had been a part since the days of Charlemagne. Prussia now became the dominant power in Germany. Not only did she annex some of the secondary states which had opposed her, but she forced most of the others to join her in forming the North German Confederation. The region above the Main River thus fell under the domination of Berlin. This brilliant success in foreign policy enabled Bismarck to resolve the constitutional conflict afflicting the Hohenzollern kingdom since the end of the new era. He was in a position at last to propose a compromise which his opponents could not reject. National unification, sought by the reform movement for half a century, was now a reality, at least in the north. Not only had political consolidation been achieved, but Bismarck also promised to establish a parliamentary form of government in the confederation which he was building. Would it not therefore be better to participate in the creation of a united country than to insist on a sterile adherence to abstract principle? The answer was provided by the decision of the Prussian legislature concerning a bill of indemnity which granted the government retroactive approval "with regard to the administration conducted since the beginning of the year 1862 without a legally determined state budget." The measure won approval by a vote of 230 to 75, most of the liberals supporting it.

The founding of the North German Confederation, however, appeared to be the last great achievement of the statecraft of blood and iron which had revolutionized Central Europe. In the years after 1866 admiration for the accomplishments of Prussia began to cool. The states forced to unite under the house of Hohenzollern had no choice but to accept the new order, although even in the north there were complaints about the centralization and authoritarianism fostered by Berlin. But the loudest criticism of Bismarck was heard in the south. Many Bavarians and Swabians, separated from the Prussians by geography, history, and religion, regarded the outcome of Sadowa as a threat to their political independence. Bismarck tried to prepare the way for the union of north and south by encouraging closer economic ties between them. He succeeded in establishing a Zollverein parliament representing all the states of Germany to discuss common trade policies. His hope was that consideration of commercial problems would lead to a consideration of political questions. Yet this strategy failed to overcome the stubborn separatism of the south Germans. In the elections to the Zollverein parliament, the particularists defeated the centralists below the Main. Resistance to the completion of national unification was obviously growing. Those groups in southern society whose interests and traditions favored a decentralized form of authority —the nobility, the bureaucracy, the clergy, and the peasantry—were too strong for the forces of consolidation which derived their support from the middle-class world of businessmen, lawyers, publicists, and academics. Only some unexpected crisis threatening Germany as a whole could revive the feeling of nationalism which had been declining since the victory of the Hohenzollern armies over Austria.

What the ingenuity of Prussian statecraft could not achieve was made possible by the ineptitude of French statecraft. The international dispute in the summer of 1870 arising out of the candidacy of a member of the Hohenzollern family for the throne of Spain led to an armed conflict which most Germans, south as well as north, considered a just war in defense of the fatherland. Although Bismarck deliberately invited hostilities in order to attain his political objectives in Central Europe, the French were not without fault either. The government of Napoleon III, discredited by a succession of foreign and domestic reverses, was eager to regain popularity by some brilliant diplomatic or military success. The result was that a disagreement which could have been settled by reasonable compromise developed into a crisis for which there seemed to be no peaceful solution. While each side sought the struggle for reasons of its own, Berlin maneuvered Paris into the position of the aggressor. Public opinion, not only in the neutral countries but in south Germany as well, tended to sympathize with Prussia. Even many particularists felt that William I had been provoked by Gallic arrogance and that the entire nation must now help him resist Bonapartist greed. The French had hoped to exploit the differences dividing Central Europe, but in fact their blundering diplomacy revived the feeling of nationalism among the Germans. The states below the Main rallied to the defense of Teutonic honor, and the troops of Napoleon III had to face a united and determined enemy.

The outcome was once again an impressive political achievement made possible by a brilliant military victory. The Prussian soldiers demonstrated beyond a doubt that they were the most effective armed force in Europe. They succeeded in beating the French in several important battles along the frontier, and then inflicted on them a disastrous defeat at Sedan which altered the nature of the war. It was now no longer a question of frustrating Gallic designs but of curbing Teutonic ambitions. A bloodless revolution in Paris overthrew the empire and proclaimed a republic in the hope that a democratic government might still be able to turn the tide. But it was too late. Although the new regime fought with desperate courage, the military superiority of the Germans could not be overcome. Early in 1871 France was forced to accept a treaty by which she had to pay a large indemnity, accept an army of occupation, and, worst of all, cede Alsace-Lorraine. It was a peace of vengeance which ensured that the wounds of war would never heal.

But Bismarck was more interested in national unification than in international understanding. The military conflict had provided him with an opportunity to complete the political consolidation of Central Europe which had proved unattainable by diplomatic means. He skillfully utilized the patriotic enthusiasm aroused by the war to secure entry of the states below the Main into the North German Confederation. While hostilities were still in progress, he concluded the agreements establishing the German Empire. He had recognized that the achievement of unity could not be postponed until the return of peace. The end of the struggle against France, he reasoned, would lead to a revival of particularism, just as the end of the struggle against Austria had done. The union of north and south had to be completed while nationalism remained at flood tide. The treaties of unification received legislative approval before the war was over, and on January 18, 1871, William I was proclaimed emperor of a united nation by the princes of Germany gathered in the Hall of Mirrors in Versailles.

The political structure of the empire was designed by Bismarck to provide the appearance of liberal government without its reality. The twenty-five states comprising the federal union retained a substantial measure of self-government with regard to their internal affairs. Yet on fundamental questions of foreign or domestic policy they were under the control of a conservative and militaristic Prussia. The preponderance of the Hohenzollern kingdom, which contained almost two thirds of the area and the population of the nation, was reinforced by the constitutional provision that its ruler was to be the emperor of Germany. To assist him in the performance of his duties, Bismarck created the office of chancellor which he himself assumed. As chief executive officer responsible only to his imperial master, he could exert the same powerful influence over the German government as he exercised in the Prussian government.

In order to encourage the impression that the new order would prove responsive to the will of the people, Bismarck established a legislative assembly or Reichstag elected by equal and direct manhood suffrage. At a time when all the leading states of Europe except France still retained a property qualification for voting, the introduction of an unrestricted franchise in Germany was a bold experiment. Both liberals and conservatives had serious doubts about what they regarded as an irrevocable step toward the democratization of politics. But Bismarck ignored their warnings. He remained convinced that the established order would be able to win the support of the lower classes against the forces of particularism as well as reformism. He insured himself against the danger of popular sovereignty, moreover, by creating a federal council or Bundesrat whose approval was required for the adoption of all laws. Its members were appointed by the state governments, with Prussia entitled to seventeen votes out of a total of fifty-eight. Besides, the parliamentary parties of Central Europe were too weak and inexperienced to oppose effectively the will of those in power. The structure of politics thus rested on a complicated system of checks and balances calculated to maintain a traditional form of authority behind a façade of semiliberal institutions.

Most Germans gladly accepted this contrived empire constructed out of compromises and expedients. Not only did it provide them with the political unity they had sought for such a long time, but it gave them military preponderance and material prosperity as well. The impressive victories over Denmark, Austria, and France won by the Prussian army in the space of only seven years established its reputation throughout Europe as a model of soldierly discipline and efficiency. A nation which had for centuries been a battleground of other powers found it intoxicating to be suddenly respected and feared. The establishment of the empire, moreover, introduced a period of rapid economic expansion in Central Europe. The growth of the factory system, which had slowed down during the wars of unification in the 1860s, quickened once again after the return of peace in the 1870s. The age of Bismarck marked the transition of Germany from an agricultural to an industrial economy. When he had first entered politics around the middle of the century, his countrymen had lived mostly in villages and had derived their livelihood primarily from husbandry. When he retired from public life some forty years later, the nation had become industrialized, commercialized, and urbanized. No other state in Europe experienced such a profound transformation of its way of life in such a brief span of time. The result was a significant improvement in the standard of living of most Germans which encouraged loyalty to the empire despite its political weaknesses and social injustices.

Bismarck had recognized even before he became prime minister of Prussia that all attempts to halt the advance of industrial capitalism in Central Europe were bound to fail. Their only effect would be to alienate from the established order those classes of society whose wealth and intelligence were essential for its survival. He contended therefore that the true task of conservatism was not to antagonize but to conciliate the bourgeoisie. His main objective became the achievement of a compromise between the traditional aristocratic forces in national life and the new business interests which were gaining importance as a result of industrialization. The empire created in Germany by blood and iron was the political manifestation of this compromise. The nobility, which had historically been predominant, continued to occupy a privileged position in the army, the bureaucracy, the court, and the countryside. The middle class, on the other hand, received full freedom to exercise its talents in the world of industry, commerce, and banking. The government opposed parliamentary democracy which would have threatened the inherited rights and prerogatives of the aristocracy, but it also rejected royal absolutism which had traditionally been the ally of conservative agrarian interests. The compromise of 1871 made possible the continuing preponderance in German life of authoritarian and hierarchical values at the expense of the lower classes. For it soon became apparent that national unification was of greater benefit to the nobleman and the businessman than to the peasant or the worker. The civic and material achievements of the empire served to disguise its social inequities and moral shortcomings.

There were those who recognized that beneath the veneer of power and prosperity festered oppression and injustice. The empire was from its beginning the object of disapproval which grew more vehement with time. Criticism of the new order in Central Europe assumed two basic forms, the traditionalistic and the radical. The former represented the attitude of the conservatives, particularists, and clericalists who believed that Bismarck had violated the spirit of the nation. In place of princely rule, decentralized government, and religious equilibrium, he had introduced parliamentary authority, administrative uniformity, and Protestant preponderance. The empire he had built was unhistorical, antitraditional, and godless. Such views were common among aristocrats loyal to the teachings of legitimism, among bureaucrats in the secondary governments resentful of Prussian domination, among peasants clinging to their ancestral way of life, and among Catholics apprehensive of a state in which they formed a minority. Many Germans looked back with nostalgia to the days when life had been harder but simpler. The achievements of their nation in politics and economics failed to reconcile them to a new order in which allegiance was based on expediency and unity was divorced from freedom. Throughout his years as chancellor Bismarck denounced those who were in his opinion unpatriotic. He included among them the millions of his countrymen still faithful to the civic ideals of particularism and clericalism. Not even his great accomplishments had succeeded in uprooting the loyalties of a prenational and preindustrial age.

Yet more dangerous to the new order than the defenders of tradition were the advocates of change. The former yearned for the return of a past which had vanished beyond recall. The latter represented the demands of the future. Their criticism of the new order was not that it was too innovative, but that it was not innovative enough. They maintained that Bismarck had disguised the preservation of authoritarian rule behind a mask of representative institutions. In their opinion, what the nation needed was genuine civic and social democracy, not palliatives, anodynes, and nostrums. Those supporting the opposition on the left were partly bourgeois reformers who favored a system of government resting on popular sovereignty, and partly proletarian radicals who sought the overthrow of the established form of property relations. Though in disagreement regarding important questions of state and society, they shared a basic hostility toward the compromise between nobleman and businessman on which Bismarck had based national unification. They were as yet too weak to challenge the new order successfully, but the process of industrialization was steadily increasing their strength. Sooner or later the inner tensions of the empire were bound to lead to its reform or downfall.

But at first the new order had little to fear from its opponents. Weak and disorganized, they were in no position to offer effective resistance to the will of the government. Bismarck, on the other hand, basking in the sunshine of political success and economic progress, could afford to disregard the carping of his enemies. And yet he sensed that in the long run they represented a serious threat to the interests on which the German Empire rested. He decided therefore to crush his domestic foes by the same strategy of force which had proved so effective against his foreign adversaries. The chancellor declared war first against the forces on the right which continued to oppose the new order for reasons of religious and political traditionalism. A campaign against ultramontane influence, he calculated, would not only stimulate nationalist sentiment, but would attract liberal support as well. He could pose as a latter-day Voltaire leading the armies of freedom and reason against papal obscurantism. Success in this battle would silence clericalism, weaken particularism, and intimidate radicalism. Immediately after the achievement of national unification, Bismarck opened a crusade against the political authority of Catholicism which received the name of *Kulturkampf*, the struggle for culture. But in fact the conflict between church and state raging in Germany during the 1870s had little to do with culture. It was rather an attempt by the new order to consolidate the victory over its enemies abroad with a victory over its enemies at home.

The chancellor soon discovered, however, that it was easier to defeat Danes, Austrians, and Frenchmen than Germans. The Catholics of the empire rallied to the defense of their church, encouraged by the support they found among many conservative and particularistic Protestants. They fought Bismarck with weapons which he himself had forged. Ten years before, while Prussia was still struggling for hegemony in Central Europe, he had decided to build political unity on a foundation of manhood suffrage. His calculation had been that the masses would be swayed by monarchical loyalty to support the government against its opponents on the right as well as the left. It now became clear that he had been mistaken. The enfranchisement of the masses served the interests not of the new order but of its enemies, the clericalists and the socialists. The chancellor had assumed that the politics of the 1870s would resemble those of the 1860s, when liberals and conservatives had vied for the favor of a propertied and educated electorate. He had hoped to use the proletariat to counterbalance the political ambitions of both the aristocracy and the bourgeoisie. But he had failed to foresee that the civic emancipation of the lower classes would lead to the emergence of movements and ideologies fundamentally different from those which had prevailed under a system of elite politics.

The *Kulturkampf* revealed the gravity of his error. The embattled clericalists formed the Center party, which succeeded in winning the support of all classes of the population in the Catholic regions of the empire. Instead of driving a wedge between the hierarchy of the church and its communicants, the government brought them closer together in the defense of their religious interests. What had been expected to be a short victorious campaign against a demoralized foe turned into an exhausting war of attrition. Bismarck declared defiantly that "we shall not go to Canossa, either in the flesh or in the spirit." But he was in fact increasingly willing to settle for a compromise midway between Rome and Berlin. The *Kulturkampf* had become a millstone about his neck. It was dividing the nation, not uniting it. It was alienating the conservatives, who saw in the attack on clericalism the specter of secularism. It was strengthening the liberals, who hoped to use the conflict between church and state as a means of enhancing the influence of parliament. And it was encouraging the radicals, who intensified their agitation among the masses. The chancellor concluded that he must extricate himself from the struggle with Catholicism which he had so rashly initiated.

What made him especially anxious to end the stalemated war on the right was the growing danger on the left. While he had been preoccupied with the struggle against clericalism, radicalism had been winning converts among the workers in the cities. When Bismarck had first become prime minister of Prussia, he had regarded the socialists as impractical but innocuous. He had even contemplated an alliance with them directed against the liberal bourgeoisie, although he eventually decided that they were too weak to help him in the conflict between crown and parliament. His attitude toward them changed, however, after the establishment of the empire. For one thing, he was now the ally rather than the opponent of the middle class. For another, the socialists were shifting from an acceptance of the existing state which Ferdinand Lassalle had preached to the incitement of international revolution which Karl Marx was advocating. But most important, socialism was becoming strong enough to constitute a serious threat to the established system of political and social values. It was no longer a speculative theory of visionaries, but the militant ideology of a mass movement. The chancellor saw in it a danger greater even than clericalism, because its challenge to the new order in Central Europe was more fundamental. Gradually abandoning the *Kulturkampf*, he prepared to grapple with this new adversary. But the configuration of political forces in the 1880s was different from that of the 1870s. In the war against Catholicism, Bismarck had been allied with the liberals. In the war against radicalism, his most reliable supporters were the conservatives. The threat from the left drove the chancellor farther and farther to the right, which had always been his spiritual home.

The tactics he employed in his new campaign were subtler and cleverer. The *Kulturkampf* had taught him that brute strength alone was not enough to crush a determined foe. Bismarck therefore attacked the socialists with a combination of ruthlessness and temperateness designed to divide them. Their right to organize and propagandize was suppressed, although they could continue to run for public office. But the chancellor attached even greater importance to an improvement in the material condition of the urban proletariat. He recognized that the basic source of strength of radicalism was not agitation but privation. Hunger and disease were the most eloquent spokesmen for the left. By the same token, a program of economic reform raising the standard of living of the lower classes might diminish the appeal of socialism. This was the calculation behind the system of social insurance which the government introduced during the 1880s. Germany became the first nation in the world to enact comprehensive legislation protecting the worker against sickness, accident, invalidity, and old age. At a time when the prevailing view among the educated was that only the impersonal laws of economics could determine the condition of labor, Bismarck advanced the principle that society must in its own interest mitigate the struggle for existence. The alternative to an enlightened regulation of the marketplace was a war of all against all. The chancellor's recognition of this truth led to the most enduring achievement of his long career.

The struggle against radicalism, however, was also the source of his bitterest disappointment. He had expected the strategy of the carrot and the stick to appease the urban proletariat. Instead the workers of Germany continued to move to the left in increasing numbers. The longer Bismarck fought, the stronger his foe became. The system of social insurance which he established was too little and too late. The lower classes wanted more than protection against out-and-out starvation. They wanted respect, equality, and freedom. It was not enough for them to be the wards of the state; they wanted to become its masters. The defeat which the chancellor suffered in the campaign against the socialists was all the more galling because he had planned it with such care. He had sought to avoid the mistakes of the *Kulturkampf*. He had not relied on force exclusively, but had tried to win over the moderates in the opposing camp. And yet it had all been in vain. The concessions he had offered proved as ineffectual as the penalties he had imposed. The aging statesman began now to experience a recurrent mood of pessimism. He was increasingly assailed by doubts about the empire he had created. Perhaps he had misjudged the strength of national sentiment among his countrymen. Perhaps he had overestimated the gratitude they would feel for all the things he had done for them. The chancellor wrestled endlessly with gloomy forebodings which were crowding in on him from all sides.

Yet there was consolation in the thought that at least his mastery of foreign affairs appeared unchallengeable. The diplomatic vigor which he had first displayed at the federal diet in Frankfurt am Main remained unimpaired thirty years later in the imperial chancellery in Berlin. Thanks to his skill and resourcefulness, Germany continued to occupy the central position in the constellation of Great Powers. His genius was more suited to the problems his nation encountered abroad than to those it had to face at home. The forces of industrialization which were transforming the social structure of Europe had not yet altered its system of diplomacy. The late nineteenth century was the Indian summer of the balance of power which had for centuries determined relations among the states of the Continent. The issues confronting Bismarck in his dealings with other governments would have been familiar to Metternich or even Richelieu. They were the issues arising out of an attempt to maintain diplomatic stability through the equilibrium of international tension. The chancellor might have been perplexed by the political strains and economic dislocations which his country was experiencing under the impact of industrial capitalism, but he felt completely at home in the world of diplomacy. Here he had to deal with situations for which he was ideally prepared by temperament and training. The considerations motivating the statesmen of the Great Powers in the 1880s were not fundamentally different from those which had motivated them in the 1850s. The international complications confronting the German chancellor were in essence comparable to those which the Prussian prime minister had faced. Talent combined with experience to make Bismarck the last greater defender of the traditional balance of power.

His toil in behalf of Germany manifested his interest in the stability of Europe. He was no cosmopolite, to be sure, no pacifist or internationalist. He regarded the ideal of perpetual peace as unattainable and perhaps even undesirable. Like so many men of his generation, he believed that rivalry among states was an essential condition of progress. Yet Bismarck cannot be dismissed as a narrow-minded nationalist concerned only for the achievement of power. While the main goal of his statecraft was the greatness of his nation, he sought that greatness within a context of international equilibrium and tranquillity. He wanted Berlin to be *primus inter pares* in the diplomatic arena, strong enough to defend its vital interests, but not strong enough to embark on wild adventures. The chancellor had recognized that power could be even more dangerous than powerlessness. He therefore pursued limited objectives in war as well as diplomacy. He sought to defeat those who opposed him, not destroy them. And having defeated them, he saw no point in bearing a grudge. He did not hesitate to invite conflict in order to satisfy what he considered the essential political and diplomatic needs of his nation. Once these had been met, however, he rejected the temptation of boundless conquest. Both Austria and France had been at his mercy, yet he allowed them to remain Great Powers. His moderation arose partly out of fear of intervention by the neutral countries. But it also rested on the conviction that a diplomatic balance maintained through the existence of several major states was essential for the well-being of Europe.

His pursuit of peace after 1871 reflected also an uneasy feeling that the greatest threat to the German Empire lurked not abroad but at home. The Hohenzollern armies had defeated foreign enemies on a dozen battlefields. But could they also defeat domestic enemies who used ideas instead of weapons? The uprising of the Paris Commune, the assassination of Czar Alexander II, the founding of the Second International, they were like flashes of lightning which seemed to foretell the coming of some terrible storm. The chancellor was increasingly alarmed. He sensed that the most dangerous opponents of everything for which he stood were not Frenchmen, Englishmen, or Russians, but those Germans who advocated the reconstruction of state and society in Central Europe. The rising tide of radicalism was bringing with it beliefs which endangered the complex of class relations on which the political and economic system of the Continent rested. An armed conflict among the Great Powers, Bismarck feared, would lead not to the predominance of one over another, but to general exhaustion and revolution. His efforts in behalf of international stability were motivated in part at least by the conviction that all governments had an interest in the preservation of the established social order which transcended their diplomatic differences. The chancellor's determination to maintain peace cannot be separated from his determination to resist radicalism. They were both part of a grand strategy for the defense of a traditional system of authority which was under attack by the forces of reform.

The fact that Bismarck managed to preserve the equilibrium of Europe while preserving the hegemony of Germany has often been ascribed to some secret diplomatic formula which brought him success where others met failure. This view is erroneous. The chancellor was not a discoverer of new methods for dealing with foreign affairs, but a remarkably skillful practitioner of old ones. He relied on the historic balance of power to safeguard the *status quo* which he had helped create by the force of arms. His accomplishments were a result of the familiar virtues of effective diplomacy—flexibility, moderation, resourcefulness, and boldness. Even the keystone of his system of alignments was the old combination of Russia, Austria, and Germany on which the Holy Alliance had rested. The three conservative empires of the East, united by a common devotion to the principle of legitimacy, a common hierarchical structure of society, and a common aristocratic system of landownership, had fought together in defense of autocracy during the age of Metternich. What Bismarck did was to revive this diplomatic configuration as an instrument for the achievement of stability on the Continent.

But since the problem of maintaining peace became more and more difficult, he had to forge new international links of mounting complexity. The informal understanding with Austria was replaced by a hard and fast defensive alliance. The gentleman's agreement with Russia became the precursor of a secret nonaggression pact. Italy established close diplomatic ties with Germany. England was induced to help maintain the *status quo* in the Mediterranean. France received encouragement to seek compensation in Africa and Asia for the losses she had suffered on the Rhine. The web of promises and obligations became so intricate that it began to confuse those who could not perceive its underlying pattern. Even William I was occasionally perplexed by the brilliant dexterity of his chancellor. "I would not be in your shoes," he once told Bismarck. "You seem to me at times to be like a rider who juggles on horseback with five balls, never letting one fall." The peace of Europe rested on the shoulders of the diplomatic wizard in Berlin who bore his burden of responsibility with an inexhaustible patience.

The complexity of the structure of alliances which he erected was, however, a source of weakness as well as strength. It achieved the fundamental objective sought by the chancellor, the maintenance of stability. But it also made that stability depend on a man of genius who was inimitable and irreplaceable. Only Bismarck could pursue the policies which Bismarck had initiated. He more than any other statesman was the architect of the labyrinth of ties and commitments which ultimately led to the outbreak of a world war. To be sure, he had used those ties and commitments to preserve the equilibrium of the Continent. Once he retired from office, however, his successors found themselves bound to a system of diplomacy they could neither control nor abandon. He has therefore been criticized for establishing a pattern of international relations which helped bring on the tragedy of 1914. Yet the charge is not altogether fair. The alliances concluded by the chancellor were a symptom rather than a cause of the underlying tension leading to the political collapse of Europe. The growing conflicts among the Great Powers in the last decades of the nineteenth century reflected civic ideals and social attitudes which equated struggle with progress and bellicosity with patriotism. Bismarck failed to subdue the forces which in time drove the Continent to the holocaust, but he did not create or foster them. Their roots reached deep down to the fundamental beliefs and values of society.

The fact that the stability of Europe as well as the predominance of Germany began to weaken after Bismarck's retirement has encouraged a popular belief in his infallibility. If only he had remained at the helm, his admirers have argued, the world might have escaped the tragedy of war and the fatherland would have been spared the humiliation of defeat. But such a view rests on hero worship rather than sober judgment. Perhaps the old statesman could have gone on casting his spell over the diplomacy of the Continent to the end of his days. Yet if the emperor had not removed him from the office in 1890, death would have done so in 1898. Not even Bismarck was immortal. And after his death the pattern of alliances which he had constructed would have begun to disintegrate as rapidly as it did after his retirement. For the methods he employed in international relations rested on talent rather than principle; their source was skill rather than theory. The system reflected a man, not the man a system. The chancellor, moreover, guarded the secret of his success with jealous vigilance. No subordinate was initiated into the mysteries of his statecraft; no apprentice was taught to carry on the work of the master. Indeed, Bismarck felt a profound distrust of those who had minds of their own. Originality or independence in others appeared to him to be insubordination or disloyalty. He preferred to surround himself with faithful second-raters who never questioned his judgment or challenged his preeminence. By basing the conduct of affairs of state so largely on himself, he ensured that his departure from public life would leave a void which no one could fill. The difficulty experienced by his successors in maintaining the dominant position of the empire was the result not of accident but of design.

Bismarck's hunger for power, his intolerance of dissent, and his resentment of criticism grew with the passage of time. He waged an unremitting struggle against those members of the court who sought to reduce his authority. He worked tirelessly to restrict the role of representative institutions in public life, encouraging dissension among the legislative parties, pitting one political leader against another, supporting sometimes the liberals and sometimes the conservatives, and exploiting the weakness and inexperience of the parliamentary system. He denounced those who dared defy him, like the clericalists or the socialists, as traitors to the nation. And when they refused to bow to his threats, he declared out-and-out war against them. Thanks to his efforts, the prerogative of the crown was placed beyond the reach of popular opinion. Thereby he intended to make impregnable not only the position of the emperor, but that of the chancellor as well. For behind his determination to protect the authority of William I lay hidden his determination to protect the authority of Bismarck.

He was always on his guard against danger from any direction, the right or the left, the bourgeoisie or the aristocracy, the court or the mob. The only civic institution in which he had complete faith was the monarchy, and yet it was the monarchy which ultimately proved to be the cause of his downfall. The one force he had made invincible turned against him and destroyed him. It was not the courtiers or the politicians or the publicists or the radicals who brought about his dismissal from office, but the emperor. The accession of William II in 1888 brought to the throne of Germany a man whose love of power equaled Bismarck's. A clash between two such imperious personalities was as inevitable as its outcome was predictable. The chancellor, by making the crown immune to the pressure of public opinion, had deprived himself of the only source of support which might have saved him. In 1890 the old statesman was brusquely dismissed from the office he had filled with such great distinction for such a long time.

From the galling retirement into which William II had forced him, Bismarck could watch with grim satisfaction as his successors tinkered and fumbled with the system of diplomacy which in his hands had been highly effective. He lived long enough to see the hegemony of Germany challenged by the resurgence of France. The increasing strength of the domestic opponents of the empire, moreover, paralleled the growing boldness of its foreign adversaries. The clumsy blandishments of the emperor proved as ineffectual in dealing with civic discontent as the stern prohibitions of the chancellor had been. The state was entering on a steep descent from predominance to war and revolution. Yet the difference between the Bismarckian and the Wilhelmian age was one of method and procedure rather than faith and allegiance. The chancellor had dealt with international relations in a spirit of moderation, seeking objectives which were essentially limited and peaceful. The emperor transformed his personal neuroticism into a style of statecraft. Under his influence the foreign office began to strut, posture, threaten, and bully. The diplomatic assets which Bismarck had painstakingly accumulated were squandered in reckless adventures and fruitless confrontations. But that merely demonstrated that the system of government rested on men rather than laws, on personalities rather than principles. Boundless authority entrusted to a genius could bring victory and power; in the hands of a mediocrity it led to defeat and chaos.

The fatal weakness of the age of Bismarck was its inability to come to grips with the fundamental social changes which the process of industrialization was effecting in Central Europe. Instead of attempting to satisfy the demand for civic freedom and economic justice which was an inevitable result of the politicization of the masses, it sought to maintain authoritarian attitudes and hierarchical values behind a veneer of parliamentary rule and diplomatic preponderance. The compromise of 1871 between tradition and reform was in the long run bound to fail.

This seemed clear even before the dismissal of the iron chancellor, and under his successors it became a certainty. The German Empire had been founded in the flush of victory over a hated foe. But as the nation returned to the sober realities of everyday life, it began to see the imperfections in the form of government which had been imposed on it in a moment of intoxication. The result was a rising tide of discontent which even a Bismarck could not halt. The collapse in 1918 of the political system created by him resulted in part from a rejection of the ends and means he had advocated. But it was also in part the outcome of beliefs and institutions which he had spent his entire lifetime defending.

I
Crosscurrents of Politics

The late 1850s marked the opening of a period of ferment in Central Europe which did not come to an end until the establishment of the German Empire more than a decade later. After long years of reaction following the failure of the Revolution of 1848, national energies turned once again to the task of political consolidation. There was a growing conviction among men of property and education that the constitutional inadequacies of the German Confederation had to be corrected by a process of liberalization and centralization. But how? Many patriots, especially in the north, maintained that only Prussia could take the lead in the task of civic regeneration. She was strong, efficient, and progressive. Austria, on the other hand, had too many Slavs, Hungarians, and Italians in her population to devote herself single-mindedly to the greatness of Germany. The Prussophile reformers organized the *kleindeutsch* movement seeking to create a new federal union led by the Hohenzollerns which would exclude the heterogeneous Habsburg crownlands. Yet there were other patriots, most of them in the Catholic regions of the south and west, who felt that the separation of Austria from the Germanic commonwealth would do violence to traditions rooted in a thousand years of history. They wanted to gain political consolidation through the *grossdeutsch* movement, hoping that the Habsburgs would agree to become the architects of a new Germany. The struggle of Prussophile and Austrophile dominated the politics of Central Europe until it was finally decided in 1866 on the field of battle.

The international constellation was favorable to political unification east of the Rhine. The Great Powers, which had once regarded the prospect of a united Germany with suspicion, were now prepared to accept national consolidation in Central Europe. Russia, chastened by her defeat in the Crimean War and absorbed in the task of domestic reform, was in no position to interfere in the affairs of her western neighbors. Besides, most diplomats in St. Petersburg were willing to see the aggrandizement of Prussia at the expense of Austria, which they had come to view as the sworn enemy of the Romanov empire. The attitude of England was determined by her fear of France. The government in London regarded Napoleon III as the great threat to peace and stability; he was suspected of seeking to emulate the military glory of his imperious uncle. Had he not intervened in the Balkans, Italy, and Mexico? There was a widespread belief, moreover, that he had designs on Belgium and the Rhineland. A united Germany would serve as a useful check to his overweening ambition. As for the enigmatic emperor of the French, he had his own reasons for looking upon the movement for national unification in Central Europe with cautious approval. The growing hostility between Austria and Prussia might lead to a civil war in the German Confederation which Paris could mediate for a handsome price. It would not be the first time that France had profited from a quarrel among Germans.

There were in fact more opponents of national unification inside Central Europe than outside. Nationalism was a powerful force in the bourgeois world of business, journalism, and learning, but the upper and lower classes were by and large satisfied with the prevailing form of government. Courtiers, bureaucrats, army officers, small farmers, and skilled artisans had little to gain from political consolidation. Their customary way of life might indeed be disrupted by a new federal union built on the ruins of historic traditions and established rights. There was a strong undercurrent of support for the existing system of confederacy, although it was not as vocal and organized as the movement for national unification. Its spokesmen maintained that centralization was incompatible with the Teutonic love of liberty. History had demonstrated that the genius of the German people could flourish only in an atmosphere of diversity and localism. The independence of the princes of Central Europe, moreover, was guaranteed by treaties hallowed through custom. To violate sacred pledges in the name of nationalism, argued the particularists, would undermine the loyalty to royal authority in Central Europe. Once principle was sacrificed to expediency, however idealistic the justification, no crown would be safe and no government secure. The struggle for national unification was thus waged in a society whose aristocracy was traditionalist and whose proletariat was apathetic. The masses of the population, ignorant and impoverished, remained generally indifferent to the war of ideologies which raged about them. Politics in the middle of the nineteenth century was still the preserve of well-to-do minorities.

This was the configuration of ideas and forces in the German Confederation when Bismarck became the prime minister of Prussia. The immediate occasion of his appointment was a struggle between crown and parliament over control of the army. But behind this issue, important in its own right, lay the even more important question of the form and structure of political authority in Central Europe. The new head of the cabinet in Berlin defied easy classification. He was neither a nationalist nor a particularist, neither a liberal nor a conservative, neither an innovator nor a reactionary in the usual sense of those terms. To be sure, he believed that the established institutions of society—throne, nobility, bureaucracy, and army—must retain their dominant influence in a changing world. Yet he also recognized that their preservation depended on their ability to adjust to the needs and demands of an age of industrialism. His conclusion was that the established order must either become the instrument of nationalism or be destroyed by it. It must assume the appearance of parliamentary rule in order to escape its reality. The traditional teachings of legitimism regarding the nature of state and society would therefore have to be modified in accordance with new economic and political developments. In short, Bismarck sought to achieve conservative ends by revolutionary means. The measure of his skill as a statesman was his success in frustrating and defeating the forces of democracy in Central Europe.

1. Prince Hohenlohe Supports National Unification

Prince Chlodwig zu Hohenlohe-Schillingsfürst was not a typical representative of the *kleindeutsch* movement. A Catholic, a Bavarian, and a grand aristocrat, he belonged by background and tradition to those classes of society which felt that national unification under the Hohenzollerns would be a calamity. Yet the weakness of the German Confederation persuaded him that political consolidation had become a necessity and that Prussia rather than Austria was the foreordained instrument of nationalism in Central Europe. Writing in 1862, he explained why he believed that the only choice before his country was whether unity would be achieved through reform or revolution.

AMONG GERMAN statesmen and politicians there are many who declare the dissatisfaction which has recently seized upon the people to be wholly groundless. In their opinion the political condition of Germany, though it no doubt leaves much to be desired, is, on the whole, satisfactory, and only deliberate ill-will could blind any one to the advantages offered by the existing federal constitution. These gentlemen compare the Germany of today with Germany as rearranged by the Imperial Commission of 1803,* and consider the federative organization of the German Confederation as it emerged from the laborious negotiations of the Congress of Vienna infinitely preferable to the disorganization of the old Empire. In this they are no doubt right, for the worst defects of our present military organization are perfection compared with the old system of district contingents, etc., in the days of the German Empire. The most regrettable resolutions of the Diet of the Confederation are miracles of wisdom compared to the deliberations of the Diet of Regensburg and our present division of states looks imposing when placed side by side with the patchwork map of the German Empire at the time of the Peace of Lunéville.

If, nevertheless, the commendable points of our Federal Constitution are not appreciated, and the desire for its reform finds determined expression on all sides, the reason will be found to lie mainly in one cause—among many—which has perhaps not received suffi-

SOURCE: *Memoirs of Prince Chlodwig of Hohenlohe-Schillingsfüerst,* 2 vols. (New York: Macmillan, 1906), vol. I, pp. 109–110, 117–118.

* The *Reichsdeputationshauptschluss* of February 25, 1803, embodied the decisions arrived at by a commission appointed by the Reichstag of the old Empire. It provided (*inter alia*) for the secularization of all the ecclesiastical principalities, etc., mediatized most of the Imperial free cities, and effected a considerable rearrangement of the territories of the smaller states.

cient attention. It is a well-known fact that in no part of Germany does the idea of German unity enjoy greater popularity than in the southwestern states.

While Austria and Prussia treat the question of an improvement in the Federal Constitution either as an unimportant detail or use it as a means of increasing their influence in Germany, or for their own aggrandizement, in southwestern Germany it is regarded as a matter of life and death and is the unceasing object of anxious thought to politicians and eager excitement to the masses.

No one in his senses will attribute this movement to revolutionary agitators. Movements of this kind cannot be artificially produced, their roots lie deep. We believe that the true cause lies in the fact—more or less consciously recognized—that the greater portion of the German nation has no voice in determining its destinies, these destinies in relation to the outside world being settled by Austria and Prussia alone, to the exclusion of the other sixteen millions of Germans. This sense of exclusion weighs more heavily and is more bitter because southwest Germany is the true source of the race, where the strain is purest, whereas in Austria and Prussia the Teutonic element is largely mingled with the Slav. Here, too, in the southwest, lies the cradle of our greatest ruling Houses; from this part of Germany more particularly came the men who have exercised the greatest influence over the intellectual development of the nation; even to the present day the most prominent statesmen in Austria and Prussia were of south German origin. This bitterness is naturally intensified the more the people of these parts become conscious of their intellectual and material superiority, and yet find their political activity restricted to more or less local interests.

It is incontestable that, for the political education and invigoration of a people, they must have a share in these human interests which are called high politics. It is certain that in petty and narrow circumstances the individual citizen's horizon is restricted, and his energy, soundness of judgment and strength of character collapse and give place to a bourgeois sentimentality and an unwholesome spirit of cosmopolitanism. It cannot therefore be denied that the cry for German unity, which now goes up from the German states of the middle and lesser ranks, is even as the struggle of a sick man to obtain the longed-for remedy which he knows will cure his disease, and which alone can save his life.

There are social philosophers who will say in reply, the Germans are a *Kulturvolk*, whose mission is rather to guide the intellectual development and solve the great questions of humanity than to descend into the arena of political strife. We can only hope that those who find comfort in this thought are endowed with the resignation of the Jews, for the Jews, too, were a *Kulturvolk*. But we refuse to believe that the German nation has sunk so low as to find consolation for its political impotence in an empty name. . . .

The German question is at present occupying all statesmen, not only of Germany but of all Europe. And very naturally. Every question of the present day which is seized upon and exploited by the party of revolution must absorb the attention of all thinking men, to a greater or less extent in proportion as the grievances and discontent underlying such "questions" are well founded. What we call "questions" nowadays are widespread movements, oscillations of the whole human race, enigmas which have to be solved. The German question did not spring fully armed from the heads of the demagogues; it arose out of the nature of things, and its spirit permeates every party in Germany. For a whole people whose separate component States are united by the tie of a common language and literature, who are moved by common interests, and who in consequence of increasing travelling facilities come daily into closer connection with one another, will not endure indefinitely a state of disintegration which degrades them to the position of being the plaything of foreign intrigues and the scorn of foreign nations.

Herein lies the great danger, and this is the reason why even the most peaceable and conservative people in Germany have been driven to declare: "We must have union, and since we cannot achieve it by lawful methods, then it must be by revolution."

Thus demagogy enlists decent people on its side and swells to a power which no Government can control. The question is: Can the revolution, which, though not immediate, is unavoidable, be obviated by prompt measures of reform? . . .

The word Pan-German has two meanings. Either it means "one great German Republic," in which the German-Austrian States would be included, or it is an empty phrase coined to work against Prussia and lull the good citizen to sleep. The Pan-German Federative State may be all very well in theory; in practice it is out of the question. It premises the renunciation by the rulers of certain sovereign rights which only the revolution will force them to give up. But if it came to that, if the revolution were such a power as to be able to force the German rulers to obey her behests, she would certainly not be satisfied with a Federative State.

A practical Pan-German program has never existed and never will exist.

The antagonism between Prussia and Austria may be deplored, but cannot be argued away. It is just as impossible that Prussia should be under Austria as Austria under Prussia. The monarchs and diplomatists can do nothing either for or against it. The people themselves will not have it so. All of this talk of the revival of a German Empire under the House of Hapsburg is mere visionary nonsense.

But if we do not want a Pan-German Republic, if we see that a continuance of the present state of affairs must lead to revolution, we must think of some plan which is not outside the bounds of possibility. The logical result is that we come back to Herr von Radowitz's idea: a Federal State under Prussia and an alliance with Austria.

This plan miscarried because in 1849 people were not yet convinced that any other plan was impossible. Thirteen years have passed since then, and the idea has gained ground every day. But the idea of a Federal State also came to grief through the opposition of the Catholic party in Germany, to whom the prospect of putting themselves under a Protestant Emperor was most distasteful. There, I think, the Catholic party is wrong. By clinging to the Pan-German program it only hinders reform without getting any nearer to the realisation of its desires. It works for stagnation and therefore revolution, whereas under a Prussian sovereign it would lose nothing, but would gain greater freedom for the Church. The position of the Catholics in Prussia as compared to their position elsewhere in Germany is a proof of this.

It lies with this party now to decide whether the reform of the German Confederation shall be accomplished by peaceful methods or by revolution. If it takes up the idea of a National Assembly the various Governments will be obliged to yield. A conservative element will thereby be introduced into the movement which will be a guarantee for its remaining purely a movement of reform.

2. Lord Palmerston Favors a Strong Germany

Most European governments were, for reasons of principle or self-interest, ready to accept a greater degree of political centralization in the German Confederation. The British prime minister, Lord Palmerston, for example, although he condemned the war which Prussia and Austria had waged against Denmark in 1864 over the duchies of Schleswig and Holstein, believed that an increase in strength of the Hohenzollern kingdom would reinforce the balance of power on the Continent. In a letter to the foreign secretary, Lord Russell, he expressed support for the establishment of a strong Germany as a counterweight to France and Russia.

IT WAS DISHONEST and unjust to deprive Denmark of Sleswig and Holstein. It is another question how those two Duchies, when separated from Denmark, can be disposed of best for the interests of Europe. I should say that, with that view, it is better that they should go to increase the power of Prussia than that they should form another little state to be added to the cluster of small bodies politic which encumber Germany, and render it of less force than it ought to be in the general balance of power in the world. Prussia is too weak as she now is ever to be honest or independent in her action; and, with a view to the future, it is desirable that Germany, in the aggregate, should be strong, in order to control those two ambitious and aggressive powers, France and Russia, that press upon her west and east. As to France, we know how restless and aggressive she is, and how ready to break loose for Belgium, for the Rhine, for anything she would be likely to get without too great an exertion. As to Russia, she will, in due time, become a power almost as great as the old Roman Empire. She can become mistress of all Asia, except British India, whenever she chooses to take it; and when enlightened arrangements shall have made her revenue proportioned to her territory, and railways shall have abridged distances, her command of men will become enormous, her pecuniary means gigantic, and her power of transporting armies over great distances most formidable. Germany ought to be strong in order to resist Russian aggression, and a strong Prussia is

SOURCE: Evelyn Ashley, *The Life and Correspondence of Henry John Temple, Viscount Palmerston*, 2 vols. (London: R. Bentley & Son, 1879), vol. II, pp. 445–446.

essential to German strength. Therefore, though I heartily condemn the whole of the proceedings of Austria and Prussia about
the Duchies, I own that I should rather see them incorporated with
Prussia than converted into an additional asteroid in the system of
Europe.

3. Onno Klopp Criticizes Prussia

While most of the adherents of particularism and traditionalism in
Central Europe were to be found in the aristocracy and the peasantry,
the old order also had its defenders among intellectuals. Onno Klopp
was a Hanoverian historian who saw in Prussia the embodiment of the
political evils of authoritarianism and centralization. In a pamphlet
published after the Seven Weeks' War, he argued that the spirit of
Germany was rooted in the freedom and diversity which the Hohenzollerns were seeking to destroy.

IT IS AN INJUSTICE and an untruth to say, that there lives in the
German nation, an irresistible impulse towards *Unity*. There exists
on the contrary in Germany a strong and vivid sentiment that all
the members form one family, and the wish to see them united by a
common defensive system against the foreigner, and by common
institutions of civilization and progress in the interior. Yet all this,
not otherwise than on the primary condition of independence of
the several German populations.

As long as Germany exists it has never been one centralized state.
During the very time of her power and greatness, under the Saxon
and Salic emperors, and also in the beginning of the reign of the
Hohenstaufen family, the separation of the different tribes was
more developed and exclusive than ever before or afterwards. The
Empire was a federation of the different national Duchies, each of
them forming a separate state, with a king at their head who as king
of Germany had an acknowledged right to the Roman Imperial
Crown. The people, as such, do not know this history so profoundly, but it lives in their blood. One may know the history of
his forefathers and be able to expound it or not, each single man is
still the produce of the past, and is connected with it as the fruit is
with the root of the tree. The individual may by a decided effort
of his will separate himself partly or entirely from it, and even

SOURCE: Onno Klopp, *Who Is the Real Enemy of Germany?* (London:
John Murray Ltd, 1868), pp. 25–29.

turn in a hostile way against the feelings of the community:—but the totality cannot do it. They follow the road, which is prescribed to them by their national talents and their history.

The ways of the German nation have never led them the road of the so-called Unity. The very idea is foreign to them. It attaches to nothing tangible or solid, to no historical reminiscence, however traditional or obscure it may be, to no configuration of the German soil, nor to a political or historical preponderance of any capital town, not even to an intellectual preponderance of any of the tribes or countries. The German people, taken in their proper and true sense, have, in spite of their want of historical knowledge, through their common sound sense, a far keener appreciation of the said German Unity than the best intentioned National Liberals. This Unity is only made intelligible and tangible to the people through Prussianism, which wants to begin by subjugating, *at first, all of us other Germans;* not by Prussia being absorbed by Germany, but by Prussia absorbing Germany; in other words: by Prussianising Germany.

We repeat it with emphasis:—the real German people, the country people, from the North Sea to the Alps, know nothing of the theory that the German nationality requires a single and united state. They were happy with their separate existence, and their peculiarities. They were, in spite of many special evils, throughout, quite satisfied with their government. For, with the exception of Austria, there was not a German country, which was behind-hand with the state of the Hohenzollerns, neither in well regulated administration, nor in the righteousness and consciousness of the distribution of justice, in the care for schools, nor in any of the real benefits of life in general; on the contrary, there were many of the states, for instance the kingdom of Hanover, which, in all these respects, were in advance of the state of the Hohenzollerns; the burden of the taxes and the imposts for military purposes were less burdensome, and the system of centralization less developed and felt. The old German principle of self-government in the communes was everywhere better preserved, and liberty of conscience and religious freedom far greater than in Prussia.

We must be allowed a few words in explanation of this last sentence.

In all the other states, the governments have since two hundred years renounced the mischievous theory, dating from the Reformation, that the ruler of the country is the chief arbiter of the religion of the inhabitants (*cujus regio, ejus religio*). The Hohenzollerns alone have, down to our own time, in application of their principle of uniformity, and for the development of the same, made use of that theory like a rich booty, although they have in practice employed milder forms. The *"Evangelical Union"* [of Lutherans and Calvinists], which in itself has neither flesh nor bone, and has nothing positive in an ecclesiastical or dogmatic sense, and which, on the contrary, is essentially a negation of religious positivism;— this eminently Prussian state religion, is the work of the Prussian kings, and has been forced upon the Lutheran communion, at one time by force, at another by stratagem.

Is there a German Catholic who really believes that, because the Hohenzollern policy has at one time abstained with well calculated prudence from interfering with his right of conscience, he can always rely with safety that they will do the same in future, and that his religion will be safe and protected? Other German governments will sometimes, as we have seen in our days, momentarily act *unjustly* towards Catholicism; but they can never be so *inimically disposed to it in principle*, as every power must be, which aims at a separate state religion. The Hohenzollern state is therein more circumspect than Russia, because circumstances compel it to act with greater reserve. But the consequences of the principle of the Hohenzollerns who have acquired the country of Prussia proper through felony and sacrilege, tend necessarily and inevitably towards the establishment of *Cæsaropapismus*, the absolute subordination of the Church, of ecclesiastical life, to the state and its organs, and therefore the favoring of all the means tending to the accomplishment of that object. If this tendency is less perceptible (on account of the precaution taken to hide it), with reference to the Catholic Church as such, it shows itself more in the province closely related to it—the school. In no country of Europe has the state monopoly of public instruction been so extensively employed and made use of, for bringing about a spiritual and intellectual uniformity than in the state of Hohenzollern. This state monopoly of instruction is quite incompatible with the principle of free instruction, which the Catholic religion is, more than any other corporation, obliged to defend. The monopoly of instruction which no other state has understood so well to appropriate as that of the Hohenzollerns, is one of the most important levers of its

political life, one of the most effective means of propagating absolutism on the one part, and servility on the other.

We repeat it:—Neither in material well-being, nor as regards the
progress of moral and intellectual culture, was or is any other
German country behind that of the Hohenzollerns; on the contrary, in many respects, some of them, are far more advanced.

The supposition that the truly German people will spontaneously sacrifice these true and great blessings, which each single man
here enjoys but the subjects of the Hohenzollern dynasty, in
exchange for the chimerical project of the so-called German—
meaning Prussian—Unity, is against human nature.

These good people are told that it is a great advantage to belong
to a great state—of course to that great power, Prussia! The honor
and benefit is in the eyes of the present generation exactly worth as
much as in the eyes of their fathers was the glory to belong to the
grande nation of Napoleon I.

4. Count Beust Praises the Old Order

The statesmen of the secondary states looked with suspicion on the
efforts of Vienna as well as Berlin to become the focus of the national
movement in Central Europe. To them the maintenance of the confederal system was the best defense of their political rights and interests. The most talented among them, the Saxon prime minister, Friedrich Ferdinand von Beust, insisted many years later in his memoirs that
the German Confederation was in many respects superior to the
German Empire by which it was superseded. The old order had been
more peaceful, more representative, more innovative, and more con-
siderate.

WAS THE GERMAN CONFEDERATION in reality so objectionable? It
is a fact that during the fifty years of its existence, external peace
was undisturbed, and Germany was not involved in a single war. It
is said . . . that this happy result was owing to the long understanding between Austria and Prussia. Undoubtedly. But this
understanding was created and facilitated by the Confederation as
the connecting link. So long as that understanding lasted, no
German government had any other program than complete union
with those united Powers. Only when Prussia began after 1848 to

SOURCE: *Memoirs of Friedrich Ferdinand, Count von Beust*, 2 vols.
(London: Remington, 1887), vol. I, pp. 283–285, 343–345.

pursue the policy of gradually expelling Austria from Germany, did it become inevitable that some governments should side with Prussia, others with Austria. But we must not forget that not one of the German governments of that time ever took a single step that might have warranted foreign countries in interfering in German affairs. If there were times when excessive deference was shown to Russia, and later on perhaps to France, we must look for the reason elsewhere than in Frankfort. For years the German courts were trained by Vienna and Berlin in the fear of God and of the Czar Nicholas, and they did not give the first example of sub-servience to Napoleon III. But when the moment came for the German Confederate princes to defend themselves and their coun-try, as in 1840 and 1859, they rose nobly and patriotically as one man. And I must add this consideration, which is often overlooked in the present day: It is highly satisfactory and desirable to be always hearing of the German Empire and its allies for the preser-vation of peace. But the more welcome the result of these efforts, the more essential is their necessity. This is a logical and irrefrag-able conclusion. In the days of the German Confederation we heard little of such efforts, because peace was regarded as a matter of course—which it has ceased to be since 1866 and 1870.

The severe judgment passed on the Confederation was extended to the system of federal union, and the restrictions on the indepen-dence of the federal states. But can it be forgotten that the repre-sentative system did not owe its origin and development to the two Great Powers, in whose dominions it was only introduced after having flourished for twenty or thirty years in the German Central States, in spite of the opposition of Vienna and Berlin? Can it be maintained that this system, which has long been identified with progress in Germany, as in France and Italy, only acquired full development and respect in the German Empire? There are still many who advocate the imposition of limits to popular representa-tion; but not one of them will assert that the time will not come when the representative system will be wanted, not as a curb for the higher, but as a safety valve for the lower classes. These times are sure to come, and a grave responsibility will fall on those who are now using their power to bring that system into discredit.

Not only in this sphere of political organization, but also in legislation and administration, it was the smaller and not the great states that took the lead and did much that was beneficial. I will instance the construction of railways. The Nürnberg-Fürth line was the first short railway in Germany, and the Leipzig-Dresden, afterwards continued to Magdeburg, was the first long one. I was secretary of legation at Berlin when the Committee of the Leipzig-Dresden railway was formed. How many times did I hear sneering remarks on "the Saxon wiseacres!" The minister of foreign affairs, who became later on my uncle by marriage, confidentially warned me not to have anything to do with this undertaking. And need I remind my readers how powerfully arts and sciences were promoted by the multiplicity of the German cities where kings held their court? It may be retorted that there is nothing to prevent the minor states from continuing to pursue this beneficial course. But I must point out that there is more than one of the most important branches of legislation and administration in which they are no longer able to have a decisive voice. There is further a lack—from what causes I need not state—of that spirit of mutual emulation among the independent sovereigns which was so powerful in promoting many undertakings. . . .

And how strangely has the idea of the Trias,* which I represented, been distorted! It is worthy of notice that this combination . . . never received any sympathy in foreign countries, least of all in France. The French cabinet perceived plainly what Germany was so blind as to ignore, that the third group could not be tampered with, and that it would be the best bulwark against special alliances with foreign powers, such as that of Prussia with Italy, as it would then side with the power not making the alliance.

As to the argument drawn from the state of Italy before it was united, there was really no analogy between Italy and Germany. In the former country there was no confederation of the various states; each of them depended more or less on foreign powers. Even Piedmont followed the lead of Austria up to 1847; those states which belonged to branches of the House of Austria did so naturally, and Naples oscillated between the influence of Austria and that of France.

Very different was the state of affairs in the various states of the German Confederation. Was there one of them that Gladstone could have held up to public abhorrence as he did the kingdom of

* The scheme for dividing Germany into three groups, composed of Austria, Prussia, and the smaller states.

Naples? I was on a short visit to Saxony after 1870, at the time when Prince Bismarck was first attempting to make the railways of the various states an imperial monopoly. This measure excited bitter opposition, which a National Liberal paper deplored with the words: "This narrow, local spirit reminds us of the worst times of Beust." "Nay, it explains the worst times of Beust," said I to a friend. In those times the Saxon had not yet the gratification of having conquered Alsace, but the Alsatian manufactories were not competing with the Saxon; nor had the Saxon the gratification of possessing a navy ready equipped for war; but the products of his industry were being sent across the sea far more frequently than now. He had not the satisfaction of being a member of the greatest military power in Europe; but he enjoyed the harmless pleasure of hearing Saxony raise her voice in the Confederation, and seeing her minister become a member of a European Conference. He paid for this less dearly than now, when he is obliged to contribute sixty thousand men to the imperial army—three times the number that was then considered sufficient to preserve the peace and security of the country. And finally, he did not possess the satisfaction of knowing that if he were ill-treated at Buenos Aires, a man-of-war would be sent to punish his tormentors. Such a disaster, however, rarely happened, while he was often in a position to want help and support in Paris, London, and St Petersburg, in which case he used to receive from the Saxon ministers at those places every possible assistance, as they had both time and means to devote to him. Now, on the other hand, the German embassy throws him into the common pot, where little remains for each individual, considering the multitude of applicants.

5. Bismarck Condemns the German Confederation

Bismarck's civic ideas and ideals had originally been those of the Junker class into which he had been born. He had believed in the maintenance of the German Confederation and in collaboration with the Austrian Empire. But during his years as Prussian representative at the federal diet his view of politics in Central Europe underwent a drastic change. In a long memorial which he submitted to his government early in 1858, he advocated a policy of opposition to the con-

SOURCE: Moritz Busch, *Our Chancellor: Sketches for a Historical Picture*, 2 vols. (New York: Charles Scribner's Sons, 1884), vol. I, pp. 344–347, 348–350.

federal system in defiance of the diplomats in Vienna and Frankfurt am Main. He was now ready to sacrifice the principles of legitimism to the dictates of *Realpolitik*.

OPINIONS MAY DIFFER as to whether or not a close alliance with Austria be desirable. But experience permits no doubt that pliancy and assurances of friendship are not the means by which Prussia can succeed in living upon endurable, not to mention secure, terms with Austria. Gratitude for favors received, patriotic sympathies— in a word, *feelings* of any description do not guide the policy of Austria. Her interests constrain her to fight against and detract from Prussia's prestige and influence in Germany to the best of her ability, but in case of war or any of the multifarious dangers by which Austria is surrounded becoming imminent, she desires to be able to count upon the fullest support on the part of Prussia's armed forces. In this twin necessity lies Prussia's only possibility of coming to a clear and satisfactory arrangement with the southern German Great Power; she must give Vienna plainly to understand that her support, at a moment of peril to the Empire, will be languid and even doubtful, unless Austria shall observe greater moderation in her German policy, and make terms with Prussia. . . . Hitherto, Prussia's attempts to lead up to better relations with Vienna have only resulted in her being denounced to the Central States as aiming at Dualism. As long as Prussia shall shrink from such denunciations and lay the flattering unction to her soul that she is capable of competing against Austria for the favor of the German Central State governments, so long will she lack a solid basis whereupon to found an understanding with Austria. As matters stand Prussia's only prospect is—as soon as her eyes shall be fully opened to the inutility of her friendly pliancy towards the Bund and to the fact that she is being tricked and fooled in every direction—to make up her mind to a rupture, perhaps at a moment extremely unfavourable to her.

Very different would be the mutual relations of the German Great Powers should Prussia resolve to emancipate them from the conventional formula of disingenuous expressions of good will and reestablish them upon the firm basis of respective interests; which would be done were Prussia to inform Austria that for the future she would limit her adhesion to the Bund (as long as its present constitution and actual political tendencies of its members should endure) to a strict fulfilment of her incontestable duties; that she would decline to cooperate with the Bund beyond that limit, and to make any concession to the presidency or majority; that she distinctly refused to enter into any Customs' Union with Austria: that, so long as others should also observe the treaties with equal exactitude, she would march to Austria's assistance with the federal contingent whenever the *German frontiers* should be attacked; but that any further concession would depend upon Austria's behavior towards Prussia, and upon the degree of community characterising their political aims. Only by such language as this and by acting up to it can Prussia secure honorable and tenable relations with Austria—possibly even a firm alliance with her; and in this manner moreover, the German Confederation may be saved from the danger of total dissolution with which it is at present threatened by the extravagance of the anti-Prussian federal policy.

Proportionately to the decisiveness with which the Prussian government shall give Austria to understand that Prussia does not regard the federal diet as the exclusive organ of German interests, that she is resolved not to merge herself in the majority of the federal assembly, and that she will have nothing to do with the Bund beyond fulfilling her treaty obligations, her outlines will reveal themselves to the eye of Germany in their natural grandeur and importance.

The leading position occupied by Prussia before 1848 was not due to the favor of the Central States and Federal Assembly, but to the fact that she had gone ahead in every branch of state development—that everything specifically Prussian was recognised by the remaining federal states as a model, and imitated by them as such. The overthrow of this state of affairs by the Revolution, and the mistrust thereby awakened in the German governments necessarily resulted in a violent reaction against Prussian influence—which reaction, as well as the novelty of Austria's appearance in the federal field as her competitor, render it extremely difficult just now for Prussia to recover her lost ground. Nevertheless, that is the only way to achieve the position which is requisite to her for the fulfilment of her mission as a great state; and in this direction she possesses great advantages over Austria and other German realms. . . .

If Prussia takes up a position independent of the Confederation, she will become, by virtue of her intrinsic force, the natural center of crystallization for those connections of which her neighbors stand in as urgent need as herself. In such connections she will be backed up by the weight of her greatness and speciality as a purely German state, as well as by the similarity of her requirements and developments to those of the German people at large. The neighboring federal states will endeavor to come to an understanding with her for these reasons, as soon as they shall be firmly convinced that Prussia will not agree to any of the more favorable conditions they had theretofore expected to obtain from her through the agency of the Confederation. They will be all the more conciliatory and easy to manage when they shall have recognized that Prussia is resolved to bear, in every respect, with the inconveniences of an isolated position, rather than allow them to dictate laws to her for the regulation of her own behavior and interests. Those inconveniences, for most of them—particularly for Saxony, Brunswick, both Hesses and Nassau, by reason of their smallness, land-bound situation and frontier conditions—are much harder to endure *à la longue*, than for Prussia, whether they concern customs' uniformity, railway projects, common exchange and trade laws, postal arrangements, paper currency, banking business or any of the other subjects which the Austrian presidency and the majority states propose to submit to the federal legislature. Hanover alone, thanks to her seaboard and position between Prussia's eastern and western provinces, may advance some claim to consider herself independent of Prussia, compared with the other German states. . . . Being in accord with Hanover, Prussia may carry out any project she may entertain with respect to the territories above mentioned, without any considerable inconvenience to herself; Hanover, therefore, is the only German central state upon which Prussia's German policy must be brought to bear, energetically and dexterously, unhindered by difficulties or partial failures, so as to gain her good-will and allay her mistrust.

But, even if Prussia should not succeed in this enterprise, she has much more to hope from the independent exertion of her own strength than from protracted tolerance of her adversaries' federal policy. In no part of Germany, and in very few foreign states, is the popular feeling of contentment with the government and of willingness to meet it half way, trustfully and self-sacrificially, so dependent as in Prussia upon the conviction that an independent and dignified position is assured to the country at home and abroad; and the consciousness that Prussia is outweighed in Germany by Austria—that Bavarian, Saxon, Hessian and Wuertemberg majorities can claim to exercise any influence whatsoever upon Prussia against her will—would, even in this epoch of materialism, more certainly stimulate the Prussian people to angry discontent than would the majority of its real or alleged internal grievances; whereas, on the contrary, we know that any gratification of his *amour propre* with regard to foreign nations renders the typical Prussian readily oblivious of his home grievances.

6. He Advocates Opposition to Austria

A year later, after his transfer from the federal diet in Frankfurt am Main to the Prussian legation in St. Petersburg, Bismarck elaborated on his political views in a letter to his chief, Foreign Minister Alexander von Schleinitz. Here he spoke even more forcefully about the need to oppose the Austrian government in the German question and to challenge the policies of the secondary states. He still advocated diplomatic means of enhancing the role which Berlin played in the affairs of Central Europe. Yet he also clearly suggested that military force might be required to achieve the objectives he espoused.

I HAVE BROUGHT AWAY, as the result of my experience, from the eight years of my official life at Frankfort, the conviction that the present arrangements of the Bund form for Prussia an oppressive and, in critical times, a perilous tie, without affording us in exchange the same equivalents which Austria derives from them, while she retains at the same time a much greater freedom of separate action. The two powers are not measured by the princes and governments of the smaller states with the same measure; the interpretation of the objects and laws of the Bund are modified according to the requirements of the Austrian policy. In face of your Excellency's intimate knowledge of the question, I may refrain from demonstrating this by going into the details of the history of the policy of the Bund since the year 1850, and I confine myself to naming the items of the reorganization of the Diet, the question of the German navy, the differences in the matter of the Zollverein, the legislation respecting trade, the press, the constitution, the

SOURCE: *Prince Bismarck's Letters to His Wife, His Sister, and Others, from 1844 to 1870* (London: Chapman & Hall, 1878), pp. 107–114, 116.

fortresses of the Bund at Rastatt and Mainz, and the questions of Neufchâtel and the Eastern question. *Invariably we found ourselves confronted by the same compact majority, the same demand on Prussia's compliance.* In the Eastern question, Austria's specific weight proved itself so superior to ours that even the unison of the wishes and inclinations of the allied governments, with the endeavors of Prussia, could only oppose to her a temporarily resisting dam. Almost without exception, our allies gave us then to understand, or even openly declared, that they were powerless to uphold the Bund with us, if Austria meant to go her own way, although it is indubitable that the laws of the Bund and true German interests were on the side of our peaceful policy; this was, at any rate at that time, the opinion of almost all the allied princes. Would these ever in a similar manner sacrifice their own inclinations and interests to the needs or even to the security of Prussia? Certainly not, since their attachment to Austria rests predominantly on false interests, which dictate to both sides an united front against Prussia, the repression of all progressive development of Prussia's power and influence as a lasting basis of their common policy. The completion of the present formation of the Bund, by placing Austria at its head, is the natural aim of the policy of the German princes and their ministers. This can only be achieved in their sense at the expense of Prussia, and is necessarily directed against her alone, as long as Prussia will not limit herself to the useful task of insuring her allies, who have an equal interest and duty in the matter as herself, against too great a preponderance on the part of Austria, and to bear, with never-failing complacency and devotion to the wishes of the majority, the disproportion of her duties to her rights in the Bund. This tendency of the policy of the middle States will reappear with the constancy of the magnet after every transitory oscillation, because it represents no arbitrary product of single circumstances or persons, but forms for the smaller states a natural and necessary result of the conditions of the Bund. We have no means of coming to a satisfactory and reliable arrangement with her within the circle of the present Diet treaties.

Since the time our allies in the Bund, nine years ago, commenced, under Austria's leadership, to bring to the light of day, from the hitherto disregarded arsenal of the fundamental laws of the Bund, such principles as can promote their system; and since the time the resolutions, which could only have significance in the sense of their originators, so far as they were supported by the agreement of Prussia and Austria, were attempted to be worked with the object of keeping Prussian policy in a state of tutelage, we have had to experience uninterruptedly the pressure of the situation in which we have been placed by the conditions of the Bund and its eventual historical development. We had to tell ourselves, however, that in quiet and regular times we might indeed with able management, weaken the evil in its consequences, though we could do nothing to effect a cure; while, in dangerous times like the present, it is only too natural that the other side, which finds itself in possession of all the advantages of the arrangements, willingly admits that such irregularity has occurred, but declares, "in the general interest," the present moment utterly unsuited to bring bygone matters and "internal" disputes into discussion. For us, however, an opportunity, if we leave the present one unused, will perhaps not turn up again so soon and we must afterwards once more resignedly confine ourselves to the fact that in more orderly times the matter admits of no alteration.

His Royal Highness the Prince Regent [of Prussia] has taken up a position which has the undivided applause of all those who are capable of entertaining any judgment concerning Prussian policy, and who do not allow their view of it to be dimmed by party passions. With respect to this position, a part of our allies of the Bund seek by inconsiderate and fanatical endeavors to lead us astray. If the states of [the secondary governments] are so wantonly ready to follow the first impulse of the war cry of the indiscriminating and changeable opinion of the hour, they do so perhaps not without the secret thought of the facility with which a small state can, in case of need, change its colors. But when they want, at the same time, to avail themselves of the arrangements of the Bund to send a power like Prussia under fire, if we are expected to stake our lives and property for the political wisdom and thirst for action of governments to whose existence our protection is indispensable; if these states want to give us the directing impulse, and if, as a means to this end, they contemplate *theories of the rights of the Bund, the recognition of which would put an end to all independence of Prussian policy;* then, in my judgment, if we do not want to surrender altogether, it will be time to remember that the leaders who expect us to follow them, serve other interests than those of Prussia, and that they so understand the cause of Germany, which they are always talking about, that it cannot, at the same time, be the cause of Prussia.

I am going, perhaps, too far in expressing the view that we ought to seize upon every legitimate occasion which our allies offer us, to attain that revision of our mutual relations which Prussia needs that she may be able to live permanently in orderly relations with the smaller German states. I think we should readily take up the gauntlet, and should look upon it as no misfortune, but as an improving step of the crisis toward convalescence, were a majority in Frankfort to arrive at a resolution in which we perceive an overstepping of its competency, an arbitrary alteration of the object for which the Bund exists, and a breach of the treaties in connection with the Bund. *The more unequivocally such a violation comes to light the better.* In Austria, France, Russia, we shall not easily find the conditions again so favorable for allowing us an improvement of our position in Germany, and our allies of the Bund are on the best road to afford us a perfectly just occasion for it, and without even our aiding their arrogance. . . .

I see in our relation with the Bund an error of Prussia's, which, sooner or later, we shall have to repair ferro et igni, unless we take advantage betimes of a favorable season to employ a healing remedy against it. If the Bund were simply abolished today, without putting anything in its stead, I believe that by virtue of this negative acquisition better and more natural relations than heretofore would be formed between Prussia and her German neighbors.

7. He Rejects the Principle of Legitimacy

The conviction that Prussia must take the lead in the political consolidation of Germany forced Bismarck to break with the teachings of legitimism. In a letter to his friend Alexander von Below-Hohendorf, which he wrote a year before becoming prime minister, he criticized the program of the Conservative party of Prussia for respecting the rights of the secondary states of Central Europe. He urged instead the aggrandizement of the Hohenzollerns at the expense of the other dynasties. To achieve this goal he was even prepared to support the

SOURCE: *Prince Bismarck's Letters to His Wife, His Sister, and Others, from 1844 to 1870* (London: Chapman & Hall, 1878), pp. 165–167.

creation of a national parliament which Berlin might use to increase its political influence in the German Confederation.

THIS SYSTEM of the solidarity of the conservative interests of all countries is a dangerous fiction, as long as there does not prevail the fullest and most honest reciprocity in all countries under the sun. If Prussia, isolated, carries this out, it becomes a quixotism which will but weaken our king and his government for the accomplishment of their own proper task, which is to exercise the power which God has granted to the crown of Prussia for *Prussia's* protection against wrong from without or within. We shall arrive at last at making the perfectly unhistorical, godless, and lawless humbug of the sovereignty of the German princes, who use the circumstances of our Bund as a pedestal from the height of which they play at European power—the bantling of the conservative party in Prussia. Our *Government* is, as it is, in Prussia liberal and abroad legitimist; we protect the rights of foreign crowns with more obstinacy than our own, and become so enthusiastic for the sovereign rights of the small states, which Napoleon created and Metternich endorsed, as to be blind to all the dangers with which the independence of Prussia and Germany is threatened in the future, as long as the absurdity of the present constitution of the Bund exists, which is nothing else than a hothouse and conservatory of the dangerous and revolutionary efforts of particularism. I should have wished that, instead of the vague thrust at the German republic, it had been openly stated in the program what we desire to have altered and established in Germany, be it through an effort legally to bring about changes in the constitution of the Bund, or in the way of associations formed after the analogy of the Zollverein and the Coburg military convention, which might after due notice be dissolved. We have the double task to bear witness that the existing constitution of the Bund is *not* our ideal, but that we are openly striving for the necessary alterations by legal means, and do not want to go *beyond* the measure requisite for the safety and prosperity of all. We want a closer consolidation of the German force of defence as much as we require our daily bread; we want a new and plastic arrangement in the department of the customs; and a number of institutions in common, to protect our material interests against the drawbacks which arise from the unnatural configuration of the interior boundaries of Germany. That it is our intention straightforwardly and earnestly to demand these things ought to be placed beyond all doubt. Moreover I do not comprehend why we *so gingerly start back from the idea of a representation of the people, be it in the Bund or in a Customs and Union Parliament.* An institution which has legitimate worth in every German state, which we conservatives would not like to be without, even in Prussia, we can certainly not combat as revolutionary. National aspirations would, up to the present moment, be easily met by very moderate concessions, which would still be recognised as valuable. A very conservative national representation might be obtained, and yet the thanks of the liberals earned thereby.

8. He Voices His Belief in Dynastic Loyalty

By the time Bismarck became head of the Prussian government in September 1862, he was a hard-bitten revolutionary of the right. Rejecting the theories of princely solidarity and confederal government which most conservatives embraced, he was ready to violate solemn treaties, promote national aspirations, and even collaborate with liberal politicians in order to reach his political goal. Yet the underlying purpose of his statecraft remained the defense of crown and nobility against the assaults of democracy. Many years later in his memoirs he expressed his belief that dynastic loyalty was the basic force in the civic life of Central Europe.

NEVER, not even at Frankfort, did I doubt that the key to German politics was to be found in princes and dynasties, not in publicists, whether in parliament and the press, or on the barricades. The opinion of the cultivated public as uttered in parliament and the press might promote and sustain the determination of the dynasties, but perhaps provoked their resistance more frequently than it urged them forward in the direction of national unity. The weaker dynasties leant for shelter upon the national cause, rulers and houses that felt themselves more capable of resistance mistrusted the movement, because with the promotion of German unity there was a prospect of the diminution of their independence in favor of the central authority or the popular representative body. The Prussian dynasty might anticipate that the hegemony in the future

SOURCE: *Bismarck: The Man and the Statesman*, 2 vols. (New York and London: Harper & Row, 1899), vol. I, pp. 318–324.

German Empire would eventually fall to it, with an increase of consideration and power. It could foresee its own advantage, so far as it were not absorbed by a national parliament, in the lowering of status so much dreaded by the other dynasties. From the time that the idea of the dual entity, Austria-Prussia, under the influence of which I had come to the Frankfort federal diet, had given place to the sense of the necessity of defending our position against attacks and stratagems on the part of the president, when once I had received the impression that the mutual support of Austria and Prussia was a youthful dream, resulting from the aftereffects of the war of liberation and the notions of schools, and had convinced myself that the Austria with which I had until then reckoned did not exist for Prussia, I acquired the conviction that on the basis of the authority of the federal diet it would not be possible even to recover for Prussia that position which she had held in the *Bund* before the events of March, to say nothing of such a reform of the federal constitution as might have afforded the German people a prospect of the realisation of their pretension to a position recognised by international law as one of the great European nations.

I remember a crisis in my views which occurred in Frankfort when Prince Schwarzenberg's dispatch of December 7, 1850, till then unknown to me, first came under my eyes. In this he represents the results of Olmütz as if it had depended upon him to "humiliate" Prussia or magnanimously to pardon her. The Mecklenburg envoy, Herr von Oertzen, my honorable Conservative confidant and colleague in dualist policy, with whom I discussed the dispatch, attempted to salve my wounded Prussian feelings. Notwithstanding the poor show, so humiliating to those feelings, which we had made at Olmütz and Dresden, I had come to Frankfort well-disposed towards Austria. The insight into Schwartzenberg's policy of *avilir puis démolir*, which I there obtained by documentary evidence, dispelled my youthful illusions. The Gordian knot of German circumstance was not to be untied by the gentle methods of dual policy, could only be cut by the sword: it came to this, that the king of Prussia, conscious or unconscious, and with him the Prussian army, must be gained for the national cause, whether from the "Borussian" point of view one regarded the hegemony of Prussia or from the national point of view the unification of Germany as the main object: both aims were coextensive. So much was clear to me, and I hinted at it when in the budget committee (September 30, 1862) I made the much misrepresented deliverance concerning iron and blood.

Prussia was nominally a Great Power, at any rate the fifth. The transcendent genius of Frederick the Great had given her this position, and it had been reestablished by the mighty achievements of the people in 1813. But for the chivalrous attitude observed under the influence of Stein, or at any rate under German influence, by the Emperor Alexander I from 1812 to the Congress of Vienna, it would have remained a question whether the diplomatic methods of the Humboldts and Hardenbergs of that day, and the timidity of Frederick William III, would have sufficed to turn the national enthusiasm of four million Prussians—the population was no larger at the peace of Tilsit—and of perhaps an equal number of sympathizers in Old Prussian or German lands, to such practical account as to effect even the remodeling of the Prussian state as it took place in 1815. Prussia's material weight did not then correspond to her moral significance and her achievement in the war of liberation.

In order that German patriotism should be active and effective, it needs as a rule to hang on the peg of dependence upon a dynasty; independent of dynasty it rarely comes to the rising point, though in theory it daily does so, in parliament, in the press, in public meeting; in practice the German needs either attachment to a dynasty or the goad of anger, hurrying him into action: the latter phenomenon, however, by its own nature is not permanent. It is as a Prussian, a Hanoverian, a Wurtemberger, a Bavarian, or a Hessian, rather than as a German, that he is disposed to give unequivocal proof of patriotism; and in the lower orders and the parliamentary groups it will be long before it is otherwise. We cannot say that the Hanoverian, Hessian, and other dynasties were at any special pains to win the affections of their subjects; but nevertheless the German patriotism of their subjects is essentially conditioned by their attachment to the dynasty after which they call themselves. It is not differences of stock, but dynastic relations upon which in their origin the centrifugal elements repose. It is not attachment to Swabian, Lower Saxon, Thuringian, or other particular stock that counts for most, but the dynastic incorporation with the people of some severed portion of a ruling princely family, as in the instances of Brunswick, Brabant, and Wittelsbach dynasties. The cohesion of the kingdom of Bavaria does not rest merely on the Bavarian stock as it is found in South Bavaria and in Austria: the Swabian of Augsburg, the Alleman of the Palatinate, the Frank of the Main, though of widely different blood, call themselves Bavarians with as much satisfaction as does the Old Bavarian at Munich or Landshut, and for no other reason than that they have been connected with the latter for three generations through the common dynasty. It is to dynastic influences that those stocks which present the most marked characteristics, as the Low German, the *Platt-Deutsch*, the Saxon, owe their greater depth and distinctness of differentiation. The German's love of Fatherland has need of a prince on whom it can concentrate its attachment. Suppose that all the German dynasties were suddenly deposed; there would then be no likelihood that the German national senti-ment would suffice to hold all Germans together from the point of view of international law amid the friction of European politics, even in the form of federated Hanse towns and imperial village communes. The Germans would fall a prey to more closely welded nations if they once lost the tie which resides in the princes' sense of community of rank.

History shows that in Germany the Prussian stock is that of which the individual character is most strongly stamped, and yet no one could decisively answer the question whether, supposing the Hohenzollern dynasty and all its rightful successors to have passed away, the political cohesion of Prussia would survive. Is it quite certain that the eastern and the western divisions, that Pomer-anians and Hanoverians, natives of Holstein and Silesia, of Aachen and Königsberg, would then continue as they now are, bound together in the indisruptible unity of the Prussian state? Or Bavaria —if the Wittelsbach dynasty were to vanish and leave not a trace behind, would Bavaria continue to hold together in isolated unity? Some dynasties have many memories which are not exactly of the kind to inspire attachment in the heterogeneous fragments out of which their states have, as a matter of history, been formed. Schleswig-Holstein has absolutely no dynastic memories, least of all any opposed to the House of Gottorp, and yet the prospect of the possible formation there of a small, independent, brand new little court with ministers, court-marshals, and orders, in which the life of a petty state should be sustained at the cost of what Austria and Prussia would manage in the *Bund*, called forth very strong particularist movements in the Elbe duchies. The Grand Duchy of

Baden has hardly a dynastic memory since the time of the Margrave Ludwig before Belgrade; the rapid growth of this little principality under French protection in the confederation of the Rhine, the court life of the last princes of the old line, the matrimonial alliance with the Beauharnais house, the Caspar Hauser story, the revolutionary proceedings of 1832, the banishment of the Grand Duke Leopold, the citizens' patron, the banishment of the reigning house in 1849, have not been able to break the power which subservience to dynasty has in that country, and Baden in 1866 fought against Prussia and the German idea because constrained thereto by the dynastic interests of the reigning house.

The other nations of Europe have need of no such go-between for their patriotism and national sentiment. Poles, Hungarians, Italians, Spaniards, Frenchmen would under any or without any dynasty preserve their homogeneous national unity. The Teutonic stocks of the north, the Swedes and the Danes, have shown themselves pretty free from dynastic sentiment; and in England, though external respect for the Crown is demanded by good society, and the formal maintenance of monarchy is held expedient by all parties that have hitherto had any share in government, I do not anticipate the disruption of the nation, or that such sentiments as were common in the time of the Jacobites would attain to any practical form, if in the course of its historical development the British people should come to deem a change of dynasty or the transition to a republican form of government necessary or expedient. The preponderance of dynastic attachment, and the use of a dynasty as the indispensable cement to hold together a definite portion of the nation calling itself by the name of the dynasty is a specific peculiarity of the German Empire. The particular nationalities, which among us have shaped themselves on the bases of dynastic family and possession, include in most cases heterogeneous elements, whose cohesion rests neither on identity of stock nor on similarity of historical development, but exclusively on the fact of some (in most cases questionable) acquisition by the dynasty whether by the right of the strong, or hereditary succession by affinity or compact of inheritance, or by some reversionary grant obtained from the imperial court as the price of a vote.

II
The Overthrow of the Confederation

The most important task facing Bismarck during his first four years as prime minister was the termination of the constitutional conflict in Prussia. Parliament, determined to show that it was more than a rubber stamp for the wishes of the government, refused to approve the budget until its demands regarding the reorganization of the army had been met. The crown, afraid that the politicians were seeking to gain control over the armed forces, would not yield. The impasse was complete, each side vowing not to retreat from what it believed to be its constitutional rights. In the meantime the cabinet continued to incur and pay public expenditures without legislative authorization. The lawmakers did not feel strong enough to oppose the ministry by a call to revolution, but neither did the ministry feel strong enough to execute a *coup d'état* by abolishing parliament. The result was a war of attrition without prospect of compromise.

Bismarck, looking for a way out of the deadlock before it exhausted both combatants, briefly contemplated the possibility of forming an alliance with the lower classes which might help him defeat bourgeois liberalism in return for an ambitious program of social reform. But the thought of tampering with the rights of property made him uncomfortable. He preferred to pursue a policy of political integration in Central Europe on the assumption that success in foreign affairs would enable him to resolve the domestic conflict. His calculation was that the opposition would subordinate liberal principles to national goals.

The opportunity to test this assumption came late in 1863 with the recrudescence of the Schleswig-Holstein question, which had been troubling the international relations of Europe intermittently for more than fifteen years. The two northern duchies, though inhabited largely by a German population, were bound by a personal union to Denmark. When the government in Copenhagen attempted to bring Schleswig under its direct control, the nationalists in the German Confederation loudly protested against what they considered an act of illegal encroachment. To Bismarck the situation offered the possibility of military victory and territorial expansion. He persuaded Austria to join Prussia in a brief war against the Danes which led to the surrender of Schleswig-Holstein to the joint control of Berlin and Vienna. This arrangement became the prelude to further diplomatic wrangles which had a direct bearing on the issues of nationalism and liberalism in Central Europe. Bismarck would probably have been willing to continue to collaborate with Austria on the condition that he receive a free hand to establish Prussian hegemony over northern Germany. This was a concession, however, which Emperor Francis Joseph refused to make. The Habsburgs had interests in the region above the Main River which they were reluctant to sacrifice to Hohenzollern ambition. Their unwillingness to agree to a division of the German Confederation into spheres of influence led to a test of armed strength between the two leading powers of Central Europe.

The Seven Weeks' War ended the Austro-Prussian dualism which had shaped the history of Germany for more than a hundred years. The military conflict was the result not of ideals and enthusiasms but of calculating self-interest. Long afterward Helmuth von Moltke, the chief of staff of the Hohenzollern armies, admitted:

> The war of 1866 did not arise from self-defense against a threat to our own existence, nor was it called forth by public opinion and the voice of the people. It was a struggle recognized in council as necessary, aimed at for a very long time, and prepared with calmness. It was a struggle not for the acquisition of land, the expansion of territory, or material gain, but for an ideal good, for a position of power.

Yet never had a war for such a great political objective been waged with so little popular support. The conservatives, nurtured on ideals of particularism, looked upon national unification with suspicion. The liberals believed that the recourse to arms was only the last mad gamble of a prime minister who had come to the end of his rope. The princes, though most of them backed Austria, wanted to avoid a conflict in which they had nothing to gain and everything to lose. And the masses regarded with apathy a war for goals they did not understand and for gains they would not share. Only the statesmen in Berlin and Vienna willingly accepted a struggle which they had come to consider inevitable.

The issue was decided on the battlefield of Sadowa. The Gordian knot which diplomats and legislators had been vainly trying to untie for so many years was cut by the Prussian sword in less than a month. The war was over before those who witnessed it could fully grasp all the implications of the struggle. The triumph of the Hohenzollerns led to a political reorganization of Central Europe which profoundly altered institutions and allegiances rooted in ancient tradition. First of all, the important role Austria had played in the history of the Teutonic peoples for an entire millenium came to an end with her forcible separation from Germany. Second, the tendency toward localism and multiformity, dominant in Central Europe since the late Middle Ages, was reversed with the establishment of the North German Confederation. Third, the rise to eminence of the Hohenzollerns, which had begun two centuries before with the Great Elector, now reached its culmination with the attainment by William I of the position of the leading monarch in Central Europe. Finally, Bismarck's success in achieving national unification through war dealt a heavy blow to the forces of liberalism which had opposed him. When the prime minister extended the olive branch to his foes by offering them political influence in return for their legitimation of his unconstitutional rule, most of them accepted. Their surrender of principle to expediency was to have far-reaching consequences for the future of Germany.

1. Queen Victoria Appeals to William I to Preserve Peace

Most monarchs and statesmen of Europe felt alarm during the spring of 1866 at the prospect of civil war in the German Confederation. The outbreak of hostilities between Prussia and Austria might upset the international equilibrium and involve the other Great Powers. Queen Victoria of England wrote to William I tearfully imploring him to avert a calamity for which he would be held responsible. To her the real author of the threat to peace was not the king but that evil man in Berlin, Bismarck.

AT THIS FEARFUL MOMENT I cannot be silent, without raising my voice, earnestly, and in the name of all that is most holy and sacred, against the threatened probability of war. It is in your power to avert the calamities of a war, the results of which are too fearful to be even thought of, and in which thousands of innocent lives will be lost, and brother will be arrayed against brother.

War is ever fearful, but when it is begun for mere objects of ambition, for imaginary affronts and wrongs, it is still more fearful. You are deceived, you are made to believe that you are to be attacked, and I, your true friend and sister, hear your honored name attacked and abused for the faults and recklessness of others —or, rather more, of *one* man!

As you value the life of thousands, as you value the sacred trust, which as a sovereign you have in your keeping, of maintaining the peace of the world and of promoting the happiness of your own country and of the rest of Germany, and if you have any regard for the memory of him who was your friend (my beloved husband), and for my affection and friendship—pause before you permit so fearful an act as the commencement of a war, the responsibility of which will rest on *you alone*, to be committed.

I have ever had confidence in your spirit of justice, and in your Christian humanity, and I cannot, will not, think that I shall have appealed to your heart in vain!

SOURCE: George Earle Buckle, ed., *The Letters of Queen Victoria: Second Series*, 3 vols. (London and New York: John Murray Ltd, 1926–28), vol. I, pp. 317–318. Reprinted by permission of the publisher.

2. Karl von Bodelschwingh Pleads for the Avoidance of Civil War in Germany

The Prussian conservatives had regarded Bismarck as one of their own, but the prospect of a war against Austria filled them with foreboding. They found it hard to reject the theories of particularism and confederacy for the sake of dynastic self-interest. Karl von Bodelschwingh, who served as minister of finance in the cabinet in Berlin, could not force himself to disregard the teachings of legitimism which he had unquestioningly accepted all his life. In a letter to the prime minister he pleaded for the avoidance of a civil war in Central Europe.

THE MATTER is so urgent that I will not keep back for the other documents the decision I arrived at today as the result of yesterday's deliberation of the ministry of state on the issue of exchequer bills. Kindly permit me, however, to disburden my heart in the following lines.

You could not deny me the testimony that it has always been my endeavor to keep our finances intact, and at least not to impair their old, good reputation. And now I find myself confronted with demands from the minister for war which I know no *sure* way of meeting—after I have offered no firm opposition to the retarded summoning of the Landtag and the dissolution of the same, but have finally coincided with the view of *all* my colleagues, for which I reproach myself bitterly. It is true I knew at the time of that debate only of moderate warlike preparations, and did not in the slightest anticipate that they would gradually develop into the mobilization of the whole army. I cannot alter the situation, however, and I have too slight a grasp of it in many points to form a definite opinion as to its further development. You know well enough that I have always wished for a peaceable settlement, and have expressed myself in that sense.

As Roon [the minister of war] recently characterized the mobilization of the whole army as a possible means of maintaining peace, and as you informed us in general terms yesterday, in reply to questions, that negotiations were still pending with Austria, I . . . cannot relinquish the hope that with the help of God your

SOURCE: *The Correspondence of William I and Bismarck*, 2 vols. (New York: F. A. Stokes Company, 1903), vol. I, pp. 72–74.

circumspect efforts may result in preserving us from the incalculable horrors of war.

The Almighty God, whose hand recently* protected you so wondrously, thereby, I think, clearly manifested that He intends you to work for peace—and I have no fear of being misunderstood when I entreat you, from the bottom of my heart, so to conduct and hasten the negotiations with Austria, that they will soon arrive at a conclusion honorable to both sides. If, dearest friend, you are animated with thoughts of peace and wishes for peace, I have firm trust that God will succor you and give you wisdom, and also that our dear, loved king will certainly most joyfully and most efficiently strengthen you in the work of peace, for which Germany and the Fatherland will laud the king and you.

I cannot get rid of the conviction, which oppresses me, and most grievously torments me, that the war once enkindled can and will, even if it ends favorably, yield no benefit in any way proportionate to the sacrifices of men and well-being, and the derangement of our finances it will entail, and which in all probability will compel us to make concessions to France which threaten to tear in pieces the glorious pages of our history on which the wars for freedom and the successes attained in them are inscribed.

And then the *possibility* of an unsuccessful war? I shudder when I recall to my mind the events of my earliest youth!

The crises caused already by the mobilization are appallingly great. From all sides come appeals for help—and we are deprived of the possibility of granting it; and how will the appeals and our impossibility to render help increase if—what God in His mercy forbid—war really breaks out.

Impute to Austria, I entreat and implore you most earnestly, with her equal rights to Schleswig-Holstein, only what is fair, and not offensive to her honor—and endeavor to secure us an honorable peace—and *then* solve the German question in such a manner that both Prussia and Austria will gain internal power and strength. I have such great trust in your circumspection and energy that I am confident God will in His mercy bless your work of peace.

You must and will not misunderstand me when I disburden my overcharged heart with these candid words; I know to whom they

* Refers to the attempt on Bismarck's life, made by Cohen-Blind on May 7, 1866.

are addressed, and feel assured of their friendly reception. If you scold me for not having expressed myself thus in our previous deliberations, I willingly submit to this reproach, and venture only to put forward as my excuse that I was afraid I should not be able to express myself in quite the right manner, and with the necessary calm, and might thus have been provocative.

3. The Liberals Oppose the Approaching Conflict

The liberals were as opposed to a war between Prussia and Austria as the conservatives. They hoped to achieve national unification not through arms, but through the popular will expressed in the constitution which the Frankfurt Parliament had adopted almost twenty years before. On the eve of hostilities a meeting of middle-of-the-road politicians from all parts of Germany condemned the approaching conflict for serving only the selfish interests of princes and for inviting the intervention of foreign states.

THE VICTORY of our arms [over Denmark] has restored our northern boundaries to us. Such a victory would have elevated the national spirit in every well-ordered state. But in Prussia, through the disrespect shown for the rights of the reconquered provinces, through the effort of the Prussian government to annex them by force, and through the fatal jealousy of the two great powers, it has led to a conflict that reaches far beyond the original object of the dispute.

We condemn the imminent war as a cabinet enterprise, serving merely dynastic ends. It is unworthy of a civilized nation, threatens all achievements of fifty years of peace, and adds fuel to the greed of foreign countries.

Princes and ministers who will be responsible for this unnatural war, or who increase its dangers for the sake of special interests, will be guilty of a grave crime against the nation.

The curse, and the punishment for high treason, shall strike those who will give up German territory in their negotiations with foreign powers.

If it should not be possible to prevent this war, in the eleventh hour, through the expression of the unanimous will of the people,

SOURCE: *Bebel's Reminiscences* (New York: Socialist Literature Company, 1911), pp. 151–153.

we should at least strive to prevent that Germany be divided into two great camps by limiting this war to the smallest space.

This seems to us the most effective means of hastening the reestablishment of peace, keeping off the intervention of foreign powers, protecting the frontiers by the armed forces of the neutral states and, in case that this war should assume a European character, meeting the enemy outside with fresh forces.

These states, then, are in duty bound, so long as their position is respected, not to plunge without necessity into the war between the two Great Powers. Particularly the states of the southwestern group should keep their forces unweakened, in order to stand up in case of need for the integrity of the German territory.

It shall be the duty of the state legislatures, when deciding on demands for military purposes, to ask such guarantees from their governments as will insure the employment of such grants in the above-mentioned direction, and in the true interest of the fatherland. Only in this way can the danger be averted, of making way for a new era of general reaction in Germany under the present complicated circumstances.

Just as a German parliament is the only authority that can decide on the German interests in Slesvig-Holstein, so the settlement of the German constitutional question by a freely elected German representation of the people will alone be able to prevent the return of such fatal conditions effectively. Consequently, all state legislatures, and the entire nation, should demand the immediate calling of a parliament, elected according to the national election law of April 14, 1849.

4. The Austrian Manifesto of War

On June 17, 1866, Emperor Francis Joseph of Austria issued a manifesto of war seeking to justify to public opinion at home and abroad the armed conflict which was about to begin. He spoke of his vain efforts to preserve peace, of his firm determination to resist aggression, and of his unshakable devotion to the cause of freedom. He called on Providence and history to vindicate the purity of his motives. The blame for the forthcoming bloodshed would rest squarely on the other side.

SOURCE: Edward Hertslet, *The Map of Europe by Treaty*, 4 vols. (London: Butterworths, 1875–91), vol. III, pp. 1690–1692.

THE MOST PERNICIOUS of wars, a war of Germans against Germans, has become inevitable, and I now summon before the tribunal of history—before the tribunal of an eternal and all-powerful God, those persons who have brought it about, and make them responsible for the misfortunes which may fall on individuals, families, districts, and countries.

I decide upon fighting, confident in the goodness of my cause and upheld by the feeling of the inherent power of a great Empire, and in which the prince and the people are united in one and the same idea, in one and the same hope, those of defending the rights of Austria.

At the sight of my valiant armies, so ready for the fight, which form the bulwark, the rampart against which the forces of the enemy will dash themselves to pieces, I feel my courage and my confidence redoubled, and I can but feel a good hope when I meet the gaze of my faithful peoples, united and determined, and their ready devotion for every sacrifice.

The pure flame of patriotic enthusiasm strives with the same intensity throughout my empire. At the first call, the soldiers on furlough immediately joined their standards; volunteers enroll themselves in special regiments; the whole population able to bear arms in the threatened provinces fly to arms, and with the noblest self-denial they all strive to lessen the evils of war, and to provide for the wants of the army.

But one feeling animates the inhabitants of my kingdoms and provinces: they feel the ties which unite them, the strength which comes from union.

At this serious, but at the same time such an edifying moment, I doubly regret that the understanding on the constitutional questions are not sufficiently advanced to admit of my assembling the Representatives of all my kingdoms around my throne; actually deprived of that prop, my duty as a Sovereign is only the clearer, and my resolution to secure for ever the constitutional rights of my empire can but be strengthened.

We shall not be alone in the struggle which is about to take place. The princes and peoples of Germany know that their liberty and independence are menaced by a power which listens but to the dictates of egotism and is under the influence of an ungovernable craving after aggrandizement; and they also know that in Austria they have an upholder of the freedom, power, and integrity of the whole of the German Fatherland. We and our German brethren have taken up arms in defence of the most precious rights of nations. We have been forced so to do, and we neither can nor will disarm until the internal development of my empire and of the German states which are allied with it has been secured, and also their power and influence in Europe.

My hopes are not based on unity of purpose or power alone. I confide in an Almighty and just God, whom my house from its very foundation has faithfully served, a God who never forsakes those who righteously put their trust in Him. To Him I pray for assistance and success, and I call on my peoples to join me in that prayer.

5. The Prussian Manifesto of War

A day later, on June 18, 1866, King William I of Prussia issued his manifesto of war. The style and rhetoric were the same as in the Austrian manifesto; only the roles of hero and villain were reversed. It was Berlin, not Vienna, which sought to maintain peace, defend its frontiers, and preserve its independence. Since the cause of the Hohenzollerns was manifestly more just than that of the Habsburgs, God would surely grant victory to the heirs of Scharnhorst, Blücher, and Frederick the Great.

AT THE MOMENT of the departure of the Prussian army for a decisive struggle, I feel called upon to speak to my people, to the sons and grandsons of the brave fathers to whom, a century ago, my father, who rests in God, addressed these memorable words:

"The country is in danger!"

Only a few years since, of my free will, and ignoring all previous injuries, I gave the emperor of Austria a friendly hand, when there was an intention of delivering up a German country to foreign dominion.

From blood shed in common, I was in hopes that an alliance based upon mutual esteem and furthering the prosperity and power of Germany would issue from the Austrian and Prussian brotherhood in arms. I have been deceived. Austria will not forget that her princes formerly reigned over Germany; and will not consider Prussia as her natural ally, but as a hostile rival.

SOURCE: Edward Hertslet, *The Map of Europe by Treaty*, 4 vols. (London: Butterworths, 1875–91), vol. III, pp. 1693–1694.

In her opinion, Prussia must be opposed in all its tendencies, because that which is beneficial to Prussia is objectionable to Austria.

The old and fatal jealousy has been revived: Prussia must be weakened, destroyed, dishonored; Treaties have no longer any value. Not only are the princes of the Germanic Confederation called upon, but they are drawn into a breach of the Confederation. Wherever we cast our eyes in Germany, we are surrounded by enemies whose war cry is the humiliation of Prussia. But the spirit of 1813 lives in the Prussian people.

Who shall wrest from us an inch of Prussian territory if we are firmly resolved to keep the conquests of our fathers—if the king and the people, united more firmly than ever by the dangers of the country, consider as their first and most sacred duty to give their possessions and their blood to preserve her honor?

In the foresight, full of solicitude of what has just happened, I was obliged for years past, as the first duty of my royal functions, to prepare the civil portion of the Prussian people for a great development of power.

Like myself, every Prussian will confidently cast his eyes upon the armed force which defends our frontiers.

With their king at their head, the Prussian nation will truly feel itself a people in arms.

Our opponents deceive themselves if they imagine Prussia to be paralyzed by dissensions at home. Before the enemy these disappear, and all hitherto opposed to one another stand henceforth united in triumph or misfortune.

I have done everything to save Prussia from the expenses and sacrifices of a war; my people know it; God also knows it, He who searches our hearts.

Up to the last moment I have striven, in conjunction with France, Great Britain, and Russia, to come to an amicable arrangement.

Austria refused, and other German states have openly sided with her.

Let it then be so!

It is not my fault if my people are forced to maintain a difficult struggle, and perhaps to bear hard trials; but no other choice was left.

We are compelled to fight for existence. We must go forth to battle for life or death against those who wish to humiliate the Prussia of the great Elector, of the great Frederic, of the Prussia such as she has come out of the War of Independence, from the position to which the spirit of her princes, the bravery, devotedness, and morality of her people have raised her.

Let us implore the Almighty, He who rules the destinies of peoples and battles, that He may bless our arms.

If God give us the victory, we shall be strong enough to reunite more firmly and more prosperously those loosened ties of Germany which they who fear the right and the power of the national spirit have torn asunder.

6. The Preliminary Peace of Nikolsburg

On July 26, 1866, the preliminary peace of Nikolsburg concluded the war between Austria and Prussia which had begun the previous month. The result of the brief conflict was a revolution in Central Europe. Under the terms of the treaty the German Confederation was dissolved, and the Habsburg lands were expelled from the Teutonic commonwealth of which they had been a part for more than a thousand years. The Hohenzollerns were now free to establish their domination over the rest of Germany.

Art. I. With the exception of the Lombardo-Venetian kingdom,* the territory of the Austrian monarchy remains intact. His Majesty the King of Prussia engages to withdraw his troops from the Austrian territories occupied by them as soon as the peace shall be concluded, under reservation of the arrangements to be made upon the definite conclusion of the peace for guaranteeing the payment of the war indemnity.

Art. II. His Majesty the Emperor of Austria recognises the dissolution of the Germanic Confederation as it has existed hitherto, and consents to a new organization of Germany without the participation of the Empire of Austria. His Majesty likewise promises to recognise the closer union which will be founded by His Majesty the King of Prussia, to the north of the line of the Main,

SOURCE: Edward Hertslet, *The Map of Europe by Treaty*, 4 vols. (London: Butterworths, 1875–91), vol. III, pp. 1698–1701.

* The Lombardo-Venetian kingdom was ceded by Austria to Italy by the Treaty of Prague of 23d August, 1866.

and he declares that he consents to the German states south of that line entering into a union, the national relations of which, with the North German Confederation, are to be the subject of an ulterior agreement between the two parties.

Art. III. His Majesty the Emperor of Austria transfers to His Majesty the King of Prussia all the rights which the treaty of Vienna of 30th October, 1864, recognized as belonging to him over the Duchies of Schleswig and Holstein, with this reservation, that the people of the northern districts of Schleswig shall be again united to Denmark if they express a desire to be so by a vote freely given.

Art. IV. His Majesty the Emperor of Austria undertakes to pay His Majesty the King of Prussia the sum of 40,000,000 thalers to cover a part of the expenses which Prussia has been put to by the war. But from this sum may be deducted the amount of the indemnity for the costs of war which His Majesty the Emperor of Austria still has the right of exacting from the Duchies of Schleswig and Holstein, by virtue of Article XII of the Treaty of Peace of 30th October, 1864 before cited, say 15,000,000 thalers, with 5,000,000 in addition, as the equivalent of the cost of providing for the Prussian army, maintained by the Austrian countries occupied by that army until the time of the conclusion of the peace.

Art. V. In conformity with the wish expressed by His Majesty the Emperor of Austria, His Majesty the King of Prussia declares his willingness to let the territorial state of the kingdom of Saxony continue in its present extent, when the modifications are made which are to take place in Germany; reserving to himself, however, to regulate in detail, by a special peace with His Majesty the King of Saxony, the questions as to Saxony's part in the expenses of the war, as well as the future position of the kingdom of Saxony in the North German Confederation.

On the other hand, His Majesty the Emperor of Austria promises to recognise the new organization which the King of Prussia will establish in the north of Germany, including the territorial modifications consequent thereon.

Art. VI. His Majesty the King of Prussia undertakes to prevail upon His Majesty the King of Italy, his ally, to give his approval to the preliminaries of peace and to the armistice based on those preliminaries, so soon as the Venetian kingdom shall have been put at the disposal of His Majesty the King of Italy by a declaration of His Majesty the Emperor of the French.

Art. VII. The ratifications of the present convention shall be exchanged at Nikolsburg in the space of two days at the latest.

Art. VIII. Immediately after the ratification of the present convention shall have been effected and exchanged, their Majesties the Emperor of Austria and the King of Prussia will appoint plenipotentiaries, who will meet at a place to be hereafter named, to conclude the peace upon the basis of the present preliminary treaty, and to agree upon the details of the conditions.

Art. IX. For that purpose the contracting states, after having decided upon these preliminaries, will conclude an armistice for the Austrian and Saxon armies on the one part, and for the Prussian army on the other part, of which the detailed conditions, from the military point of view, are to be immediately determined. That armistice shall date from the 2d of August, the day to which the present suspension of arms shall be prolonged.

The armistice shall, at the same time, be concluded with Bavaria, and General the Baron von Manteuffel will be instructed to conclude with the kingdom of Wurtemberg and the grand duchies of Baden and Hesse-Darmstadt, as soon as those states shall propose it, an armistice beginning on the 2d August, and founded on the state of military possession at the time.

7. An English Diplomat Criticizes the North German Confederation

John Ward was a member of the British foreign service with more than twenty-five years of experience in Central Europe. His memoirs, which appeared early in the 1870s, spoke critically of the constitution of the North German Confederation. Not only was it too conservative for his taste, but it represented the triumph of self-interest over principle. What would happen to the community of nations if expediency became the sole guide of diplomatic conduct? The thought was disturbing.

SUBJECT TO THE MODIFICATIONS made in consequence of the accession of the southern states, at the close of 1870, the constitution thus introduced has remained in force. It consolidated the military

SOURCE: John Ward, *Experiences of a Diplomatist, 1840–1870* (London: Macmillan and Co., 1872), pp. 247–248.

power of Prussia as the head of the union, and established national unity in a number of matters affecting the social intercourse of the people, and their material well-being. But it did little or nothing for securing the liberty of the subject in Germany; it did not guarantee either a free press, or the right of public meetings; it did not proclaim the equality of all classes of society before the law; in short, it made no mention of those important constitutional principles which were enunciated in the "fundamental rights" (*Grundrechte*) of the German people, adopted by the Frankfort national assembly, and published by the Archduke John as *Reichsverweser*, on the 27th of December, 1848. The new constitution permitted the continuance of the local legislatures, or diets, of all the separate states; and it also permitted the separate governments to send and receive diplomatic agents at their discretion. The centralization, therefore, which was aimed at by patriotic men in 1848 and 1849, was very far from being completed, and the North German union was regarded by the liberal party rather as a *basis* capable of further extension, than as an actual realization of the long-cherished wants and wishes of the German nation.

The party of Austria and the secondary states, mortified and indignant at their defeat, exclaimed against the violation by Prussia of international law and federal engagements, and denounced Count Bismarck's policy as altogether revolutionary and unjustifiable. Among the many treatises and pamphlets on this subject, which issued from the press, Bishop Keteler's work on Germany since the war of 1866 excited much attention. The bishop pointed out the great evils which must result to society from the utter disregard of the principles of justice and morality by the Prussian government. Its partisans, said he, sought to vindicate all sorts of wickedness, because such acts were alleged to be in the future interest of Germany. To defend them, we ought to be prepared to defend likewise the crimes of the first French revolution, and of all the other revolutions which have since disturbed the peace of society, and retarded its progress in virtue and happiness.

It will be the office of future historians to pass judgment on Count Bismarck's public acts, and to decide whether the circumstances in which his country were placed were such as to justify the apparent violations of public morality with which he is chargeable. It may be true that Prussia found herself cramped and inconvenienced by being subject to the laws of the old Germanic confederation; but she voluntarily entered into that confederation in 1815, and renewed her engagements after the Dresden conferences of 1851. The motives which influenced the Berlin cabinet were specifically Prussian, and its policy was directed to the exclusion of the Austrian hegemony from the Germanic body. This was forcibly accomplished, and the power of Prussia immeasurably raised, by her victorious campaign of 1866. Still the moral question has not been satisfactorily solved. Is a state at liberty to withdraw from international treaties, when such treaties are found inconvenient to her own ambition? The same question has recently been raised by Russia, in a case of less importance certainly, but calculated to excite alarm in the minds of those who had been accustomed to regard treaties as sacred and inviolable compacts between civilized states. Are we approaching a time when might will be generally acknowledged to go before right, and when mankind will be content to secure their peace by the same means as the creatures of flood and field alluded to by the poet?

> For why? because the good old rule
> Sufficeth them, the simple plan,
> That they should take who have the power,
> And they should keep who can.*

8. The British Minister Resident in Frankfurt am Main Describes the Ordeal of the City

The triumph of Prussia over Austria meant the end of the independence which the secondary states of Central Europe had enjoyed under the German Confederation. The victors showed little consideration for the vanquished, trampling on the rights and liberties of those who had dared oppose them. In a dispatch of July 20, 1866, Great Britain's minister resident in Frankfurt am Main, Robert Morier, described to the foreign secretary the ordeal which the city had been forced to endure under the Prussian occupation.

I HAVE THE HONOR to report to Your Lordship that the Prussian army under the command of General von Falckenstein occupied Francfort on the evening of the 16th instant. As far as I was able to judge of the temper of the population during the few days which intervened after the departure of the federal troops, the Francfort

SOURCE: Veit Valentin, *Bismarcks Reichsgründung im Urteil englischer Diplomaten* (Amsterdam: Elsevier, 1937), pp. 526–528.
* William Wordsworth, "Rob Roy's Grave."

citizens, though traditionally partisans of Austria, were more favorably disposed toward Prussia just now than they had been at any previous time during the progress of the events which have led to the present catastrophe. Here as elsewhere the unitarian party, though probably less numerous in Francfort than in any other town north of the Main, had been gathering strength in exact proportion to the successes of the Prussian arms. The logic of theory had suddenly found itself reinforced by the logic of facts, and the theorists were not slow to improve the occasion. Moreover a conviction of the uselessness of prolonging the conflict, disgust at the utter helplessness exhibited by the federal army, the horror produced by the sounds and sights of actual war so near to the precincts of the peaceful city, and impatience at the restrictions placed on free intercourse and communication, all combined to make the population ready to hail as a benefactor anyone strong enough to set order in this confusion and to restore to its normal condition the shaken framework of society.

I am profoundly convinced from the impression produced upon my mind by frequent conversations with persons of different classes in the course of Sunday and Monday and by the general appearance of the crowds which flocked to witness the entry of the Prussian troops and whose air betokens anything rather than the fears of a people about to fall a prey to a conquering army, that the advent of the Prussian troops exactly coincided with that kind of crisis in men's minds which would have enabled Prussian statesmanship with a little management to effect the moral conquest of this important center and attach it firmly to the cause of Prussian ascendency. I deeply regret to have to place on record that not only has this not been done by Prussia but that by an evidently preconcerted system of extreme harshness, and by a carefully prepared *mise en scène* of military rigor a revulsion of feeling has been produced which commencing with a flush of anger has rapidly changed, as blow has followed blow upon the devoted city, into a passion of agonizing fear. I myself witnessed the entry of the troops, and as the first squadron of Huzzars galloped into the town they were greeted with repeated cheers, as these however were followed by battalion upon battalion of men who marched past with the arrogant and defiant looks of conquerors, the cheers died out and I overheard many whispered remarks which proved to me that the conviction was already then settling on men's minds of an evil time to come.

The experiences of the first night's billeting and the steps taken the next morning confirmed this conviction, and it was easy on the morrow to read in the faces of the civilian population how deeply the iron had entered into their soul.

Knowing how apt people are to exaggerate in cases of this kind I have been careful in sifting the evidence adduced in individual cases, and I regret to have to state upon the evidence thus sifted that the mode of billeting the soldiers on the inhabitants has been carried on with a vindictive barbarity directed against individuals supposed to be Austrian in their sympathies which testifies to a preconcerted plan as mean in the motive which originally dictated it, as it has been thorough and efficacious in the method of its execution. The first act of General von Falckenstein was to seize and throw into the common jail two of the leading senators of the city Messrs. Speltz and Bernus, the former of whom had rendered himself obnoxious as police minister by petty acts of annoyance towards Prussian subjects, but against the latter of whom nothing else can be urged but his having been very active in his hospitality upon the occasion of the Emperor of Austria's Congress of Princes in 1863, for which he received from His Imperial Majesty the title of a Baron of the Empire. Together with these two gentlemen, who I should mention have since been liberated by an order from Berlin, all the editors of journals hostile to Prussia were committed to the cells of common vagabonds in the city lockup. The next step of General von Falckenstein was to levy a contribution of 6,000,000 (six millions) of florins and of 300 saddle horses of a superior kind for which every gentleman's stable was ransacked. He then dissolved the senate and dismissed the burgomasters from their functions, naming two senators, Messrs. Müller and Fellner, as civil commissaries to execute his orders. These gentlemen one of whom is the late burgomaster and other the late representative of the city of Francfort at the Diet have submitted to this painful task in the hope of thereby diminishing the rigor of the treatment inflicted on the town. These were the acts of General von Falckenstein, an officer noted throughout the Prussian army for his rare knowledge of the most obsolete usages of war, and for the practical skill which he was known to possess in applying this knowledge. He had established his reputation in Jutland. When it was yesterday noised abroad that he had been suddenly called elsewhere and he was to be succeeded by General v. Manteuffel, a universal feeling of relief became manifest. It was generally believed that he had overstepped his instructions, that the worst was over, and that his successor would endeavour to efface the evil impression produced. General v. Manteuffel took the command today and at twelve o'clock sent a communication to Messrs. Müller and Fellner, the civil commissaries, consisting of four lines only, to the following effect: "The town of Francfort has to pay within 24 hours the sum of twenty five million florins in silver as war contribution." Upon these gentlemen remonstrating with His Excellency and representing to him that this sum in silver could not be collected within the town of Francfort in the time specified, General Manteuffel desired them to inform the citizens that if not paid up the town would be given up to pillage. Upon this the commissaries summoned a meeting of twenty of the leading citizens of Francfort, the result of whose deliberations is not yet known to me, but I believe that the utmost they hope to obtain is some slight respite upon giving their personal security that the sum required will be paid.

9. Queen Victoria's Daughter Condemns the Prussian Occupation of Hesse-Darmstadt

There were complaints from many sources about the conduct of the Prussians in the territories they occupied during the conflict with Austria. Princess Alice, a daughter of Queen Victoria, had married the heir to the throne of Hesse-Darmstadt, which sided with Vienna in the Seven Weeks' War. The Hohenzollern armies seized the grand duchy in the course of the hostilities, and in a letter to her mother of July 21, 1866, the princess spoke bitterly of the harsh treatment her adopted country had to suffer.

THOUGH NO TRAINS go or come, consequently neither letters nor newspapers since we are conquered, we mean to make an attempt of sending this letter by diligence. The Prussians marched in this morning, their bands playing and making as great a demonstration as they could. My parents-in-law were with me at the moment, and my father-in-law walked up and down the room in despair and

SOURCE: George Earle Buckle, ed., *The Letters of Queen Victoria: Second Series,* 3 vols. (London and New York: John Murray Ltd, 1926–28), vol. I, pp. 358–359. Reprinted by permission of the publisher.

indignation, in feeling that his home and his country were no more his own; as the Prussians pay for nothing and demand everything, the place will soon be ruined, the inhabitants here had done so much for their own troops and wounded already. Amongst the Prussians chiefly, and amongst the other troops, there is but one voice, how beautifully our Hessians fought, with such personal bravery, officers and men; some Prussian officers said here, *Es ist eine Ehre mit ihren Landsleuten zu kämpfen, sic fechten wie die Löwen.* I would like this to be known in England, for through all ages the Hessians have had the reputation for bravery; we only lost 500 in all, and five officers killed, the others were slightly wounded, but a few badly.

I do not know where dear Louis [her husband] is now. Please God he is safe, but the anxiety is fearful. I am well, baby too; the wish to get well keeps me up, as I wish to get about again.

We must get the gracious permission of the Prussians for anything we want, we smuggle people with our things with difficulty out of the town, if we wish anything, but the Prussians watch so well, to prevent our communicating with our troops or with anywhere outside, that we are the most complete prisoners. This goes so far, we have difficulty in getting any decent meat, or the common luxuries of life, for the Prussians devour everything, and we can get nothing even from Frankfort. We hope and pray daily that this dreadful existence may soon change, for it is past all bearing, and we are ready to give up everything for the sake of peace, after having suffered so much; and the longer it lasts, the worse it gets. My mother-in-law is exemplary as always, looks out for the wounded and never thinks of herself. From our army we hear the greatest praise of dear Louis, of whom all are so fond and proud. Now good-bye, dearest Mama, please let brothers and sisters see the letter, if it ever reaches you.

10. The King of Hanover Protests the Loss of His Kingdom

Nowhere in Central Europe was opposition to the domination of Prussia greater than in Hanover. Even after the conclusion of peace, many inhabitants of the Guelph kingdom refused to transfer their

SOURCE: Edward Hertslet, *The Map of Europe by Treaty*, 4 vols. (London: Butterworths, 1875–91), vol. III, pp. 1746–1748.

allegiance to the Hohenzollerns. The deposed ruler George V continued to denounce the new order from his exile in Austria, and to exhort his former subjects to remain faithful to him and his dynasty. In a declaration of September 23, 1866, he solemnly protested against the incorporation of his state into the Prussian monarchy.

WE HAVE ENDEAVORED to secure the preservation of our kingdom by every means in our power. With that intention we were even disposed to abdicate our royal rights in favor of our well-beloved son and heir to our crown, the Prince Royal Ernest Augustus, on condition that Prussia should place him in immediate possession of the crown and kingdom of Hanover. On the other side our faithful subjects, courageously defying the rigorous, arbitrary, and despotic regimen imposed upon them by Prussian administration, lost no opportunity of manifesting their ardent desire to remain under a dynasty which is dear to them, which for the last 1,000 years has shared the destinies of the country, and has made every effort to secure its prosperity and to consolidate its well-being.

Useless efforts!

His Majesty the King of Prussia, after having occupied our kingdom in a surreptitious manner, has thought that he could take definitive possession of it, and declared it annexed to his States, on the 20th September of this year.

The only motive alleged by the Prussian government to justify this arbitrary act, unheard of in the records of German history, is that which he pretends to find in the right of conquest.

Now, the right of conquest supposes a war made in conformity with the principles of the law of nations. But there has never been between us and the King of Prussia a war of such a nature. Moreover, as we have already stated above, it could not take place according to the fundamental laws of the Germanic Confederation, and it ought to have been morally impossible from one of our near relatives, of a friendly sovereign, of a German prince!

We consequently found ourselves, purely and simply, in the position of legitimate self-defence, in the face of an aggression which nothing could justify, and which we had not provoked.

With the facts above described in view, we loudly and solemnly protest:

Against the unjustifiable invasion of our territory, which detachments of the army of the King of Prussia presumed to make on the 15th June, 1866, and following days;

Against the occupation of our kingdom by the same army detachments;

Against the usurpation of our rights and prerogatives committed by the agents of Prussia, and against any which they may still commit;

Against the losses which we and our royal House have suffered, or which we may be made to suffer, on the part of Prussia, in respect of our property, revenues, or estates, of whatever nature they may be;

Against the spoliations suffered by the public treasury of Hanover under Prussian administration, and against those which it may have to bear in future;

Against the prosecutions, losses, and injuries to which our faithful subjects may have been exposed, in consequence of the unjust and illegal acts of the administration of the King of Prussia, or to which they may be subject in future;

Against the obstacles which the said administration brutally put to the manifestation of our well-beloved subjects in favor of the preservation of our dynasty and the dynasty of Hanover, whilst it has provoked, and favored by most disloyal means, manifestations in a contrary sense;

Against the ill-will of the King of Prussia, who has repelled the steps which we have taken, or which we have ordered to be taken with him, or with his government, in order to reestablish peace between us;

Finally, we specially protest, in the face of the universe against the taking possession of our kingdom, and against its incorporation with Prussia, announced as definitive on the 20th September of this year, as well as against all consequences of that act, declaring that that incorporation or annexation is an infamous usurpation, a culpable and odious spoliation, a flagrant violation of European treaties, of all the principles of the law of nations, and of the inviolability of states and thrones;

This solemn declaration, which we also make in the name of our legitimate successors, has principally for its object to place beyond prejudice the rights of sovereignty which belong to us by order of succession, and which have been sanctioned and guaranteed by the European powers.

We claim the support of all the powers which have recognized our sovereignty and the independence of our kingdom, convinced as we are, that they will never admit that *la force prime le droit*, since such a principle, now applied by Prussia, might hereafter threaten the existence of all the monarchies and of all the legitimate states of the world.

We finally declare that we shall never renounce our rights of sovereignty over our states; and that we shall always consider as illegal, null and void, all the acts which the Prussian government or its agents have committed, or may commit, in consequence of that usurpation, all responsibility for which we cast upon him who is their author.

Let all those who are interested therein consider themselves as warned.

We will look to future events full of confidence in the justice of our cause, and animated by the firm hope that Divine Providence will not delay in putting a stop to the machinations, iniquities, and violence to which so many states and so many peoples are now victims as well as ourselves and our brave Hanoverians.

11. Another of Queen Victoria's Daughters Rejoices at the Prussian Successes

The protests of the vanquished were drowned by the jubilation of the victors. While Queen Victoria's daughter Alice was among the losers, her daughter Victoria, wife of the crown prince of Prussia, was on the side of the winners. Though a woman of liberal sympathies, the princess did not remain immune to the intoxication of victory. In a letter to her mother written after the termination of hostilities, she expressed her feelings at the moment of reunion with her husband who had come back from the war.

THE DAY AFTER I wrote to you darling Fritz arrived. I drove into a wood with the children and met him there. We were much overcome and our feelings were of a most mingled nature, as you can easily understand.

He is looking well, only thinner and perhaps a little older, at least his beard and his serious expression made him appear so. He has gone through a *great* deal, but is as humble and modest about

SOURCE: George Earle Buckle, ed., *The Letters of Queen Victoria: Second Series*, 3 vols. (London and New York: John Murray Ltd, 1926–28), vol. I, pp. 365–367. Reprinted by permission of the publisher.

all he has done as possible, which all really good and right-minded men must be. . . .

At this sad time one *must separate* one's *feelings* for one's relations quite from one's *judgment* of *political necessities,* or one would be swayed to and fro on *all sides* by the hopes, wishes, and desires expressed by those one would be sorry to grieve; it is one of the consequences resulting from this war. Nothing will or can ever shake Fritz's principles of sound liberalism and justice, but you know by experience that one must proceed in the direction given by the political events which have come to pass.

Those who are now in such precarious positions might have *quite well* foreseen what danger they were running into; *they were told beforehand what they would have to expect;* they *chose* to go with Austria and they now share the sad fate she confers on her allies. Those who have taken our side or remained neutral are quite unharmed, for example Uncle Ernest, the Duke of Anhalt, the Grand Dukes of Mecklenburg, etc. . . . [Those who fought against us] believed the *untrue* statement of Austria about the strength of her own forces, and would not see that Prussia was likely to be victorious, and so the poor things have broken their own necks. Oh, how cruel it is to have one's heart and one's head thus set at right angles!

A *liberal German-feeling* reasonable Prussian government would have prevented it all! But as it was not to be decided *à l'amiable,* as rivers of blood had flowed, and the *sword* decided this contest, the victor *must* make his own terms and they *must* be hard ones for many!

I cannot and will not forget that I am a Prussian, but as such I know it is very difficult to make you, or any other non-German, see how our case lies. We have made *enormous* sacrifices, and the nation expects them not to be in vain.

12. William I Addresses the Legislature in Berlin after the Victory over Austria

Prussia's victory on the field of battle prepared the way for a reconciliation between crown and parliament. On August 5, 1866, King William opened the new session of the legislature with a speech which urged the adoption of a bill of indemnity granting retroactive approval

SOURCE: *British and Foreign State Papers,* 56 (1865–66): 1032–1034.

to the ministry for its conduct of affairs of state during the previous four years in defiance of established constitutional procedure. He was in effect offering a compromise by which the theory of liberal government would be sacrificed for the reality of national unification.

ON SEEING the representatives of the country gathered around me, my feelings impel me before all else to give expression from this place to my own and my people's thanks for God's grace which has aided Prussia, at the cost of heavy but productive sacrifices, not only to avert the dangers of a hostile attack from our frontiers, but also by the rapid victories of our army, to add new laurels to the hereditary renown of the nation, and to pave the way for the national development of Germany.

Under the evident blessing of God all who could bear arms answered with enthusiasm the call to the combat for the independence of the Fatherland; and our heroic army, supported by few but faithful allies, proceeded from success to success, from victory to victory, in the east as well as in the west. Much precious blood has flowed; the Fatherland bewails many a brave one, who, rejoicing in victory, died the hero's death, till our banners waved in one line from the Carpathians to the Rhine.

By their united endeavours the government and the representatives of the people will have to bring to maturity the fruits that must proceed from the bloody seed, if it is not to have been sown in vain.

Dear Gentlemen of both Houses of the Landtag!

My Government can look with satisfaction on the financial condition of the state. Careful foresight and conscientious economy have placed it in a position to overcome the great financial difficulties which are the natural result of the present situation of affairs.

Although in late years considerable sacrifices have been imposed on the treasury through the war with Denmark, it has been possible to defray the expenses of the war up to the present time out of the revenues of the state and other available resources, without further burthen to the country than the legal supplies in kind demanded for warlike purposes. I the more confidently hope that the supplies necessary for the successful termination of the war, and for the payment of the supplies in kind, while still maintaining order and security in the finances, will be readily granted by you.

It has not been possible in late years to come to an agreement with the representatives of the country on the settlement of the estimates. The state disbursements which have been made during that period, therefore, have not the legal basis which, as I again acknowledge, can only be given to the estimates according to Article XCIX of the constitution, by a law which is to be agreed upon every year between my government and both Houses of the Landtag. If my government has nevertheless for several years carried on the financial department of the state without this legal basis, it has been after careful consideration, and with the conscientious conviction that the continuation of a regular administration, the fulfilment of the legal obligations towards the creditors and the functionaries of the state, the maintenance of the army and of the state institutions, were vital questions, and that therefore such a proceeding was one of those unavoidable necessities from which no government that studies the interests of the country can or ought to withdraw. I feel confident that late events will aid in so far attaining the indispensable understanding, that the indemnity which is to be solicited of the national representatives will be readily granted to my government for the administration conducted without the budget law, and that thus the conflict that has been going on may be the more surely terminated for ever, as it may be hoped that the political situation of the Fatherland will allow an extension of the frontiers of the state and the establishment of an united federal army under the command of Prussia, the charges of which will be equally borne by all the members of the Confederation. The proposals which are requisite in this respect for a convocation of the national representatives of the federal states will be immediately laid before the Landtag.

Gentlemen, you feel with me, the whole Fatherland feels, the great importance of the moment which brings me back to my home. May Providence bless Prussia's future as graciously as the time just past has been visibly blessed. God grant it.

13. Heinrich von Sybel Describes the Reconciliation between Crown and Parliament in Prussia

Heinrich von Sybel was a prominent historian who as a member of the Prussian legislature during the constitutional conflict had opposed Bismarck. But the events of the Seven Weeks' War converted him. In the semiofficial history of national unification which he published some twenty-five years later, he described the decision of most liberals to accept a reconciliation with the government as an act of statesmanlike moderation. Like so many of his countrymen, he bowed down before the idol of success.

THE GOVERNMENT had already, on the 14th of August, sent to the House the draft of an indemnity bill, containing the motion to grant to the ministry of state indemnity for the expenses incurred during the years 1862–1865, a general outline of which was appended; while for the year 1866, since the state of things was no longer adapted to the establishment of a regular budget, the government desired a loan of 154 million thalers. In the budget committee, to whose consideration the matter was referred, it was very soon evident that a large majority favored the acceptance of the bill.

The only determined opposition came from the members of the Party of Progress, who were not able to find in the draft of the bill the necessary security for the reestablishment of constitutional rights. These, therefore, approved the loan for 1866, but wished to decline for the present the proposal about the indemnity and to leave it with the government to make the request again after the budget for 1867 should have been fixed upon.

To this the reply was made that if the present promise of the Government to adopt the budget for 1867 were not to be trusted, then the passage and adoption of this latter could not be looked upon as a sure guaranty for the acceptance of a regular budget for 1868. The main thing, it was asserted, was the serious intention of the government to return to the basis of the constitution; and this determination was believed to be sufficiently indicated in the bill. The whole dispute arose, it was said, from a difference of opinion

SOURCE: Heinrich von Sybel, *The Founding of the German Empire by William I*, 7 vols. (New York: T. Y. Crowell, 1890–98), vol. V, pp. 487–490.

about the new organization of the army, and who could at this late day think of undertaking any essential changes in the same? For, indeed, it was very probable that if it had been possible to foresee the last war and its consequences, the House would not have thought of refusing its approval to the new military constitution. The matter of the organization of the army must be settled anew, it was argued, by a definite law; but such a law would not under the existing state of things have to be passed by the Prussian Lower House but by the North German Parliament. The report revised by the deputy Twesten in accordance with these sentiments was adopted by the committee by a vote of twenty-five to eight.

In the House the discussion was, as ever, more lively, and the views more sharply opposed to one another. The whole Party of Progress set themselves determinedly against the bill. Waldeck considered that nothing whatever had been offered that justified any expectation of more constitutional conduct on the part of the government. Schultze-Delitzsch declared that the whole war had been carried on not only without the consent, but even against the will, of the Prussian people; and he was *naïve* enough to refer to those melancholy addresses of peace of May and June as a brilliant proof of Prussia's careful prudence compared with the tumult of war which prevailed then at Vienna.

Virchow explained that he and his friends had known of a better way leading to German unity than Bismarck's, namely, the way of freedom. But as things now stood, he said, they were willing to sacrifice their wishes to Bismarck, and were willing to support his foreign policy, but must so much the more energetically defend constitutional rights. As if Benedek in June would have allowed himself to be deterred from marching upon Berlin by the fiery enthusiasm of the Party of Progress for freedom! or as if there could have been at this time any worse foe to Bismarck's German policy conceivable than the continuance of the internal quarrel! The professor of Catholic theology, Michelis, supplemented these remarks by the brilliant observation that Tetzel in 1517 was accused unjustly for having sold indulgences for future sins, but that this bill did indeed involve a pardon for all the future sins of the ministry.

The Conservative party, delighted at the favorable sentiments, declared with great ardor that it would vote for the indemnity bill in accordance with the wishes of the government, although strictly speaking, something entirely different would be more properly in order, namely, a hearty vote of thanks to the government for not having taken account of the foolish behavior of the House. The mediatory position held by Bismarck and Von der Heydt also received eloquent support from the parties of the Center. Lasker and Georg Vincke, at other times seldom to be found on the same side, and also, at the close of the discussion, Twesten, who had made the report, demonstrated with convincing force the importance of the present situation, the consequence of a continued quarrel with the government, and the power of public opinion which demanded unity of action.

The final vote on the report resulted in 230 in favor and 75 against, the latter including the Party of Progress, some few members of the Left Center, and the Catholic fraction. The Upper House followed this example on the 8th of September, after Herr von Kleist-Retzow had given vent to his regrets at the injurious compliance on the part of the government. The vote of the Upper House resulted in the unanimous acceptance of the bill as drawn up by the House of Deputies.

Internal peace was thus secured and the four years' contest over the constitution was ended. With good practical sense, that question which lay at the very bottom of the quarrel, namely, what was to happen if again sometime the budget should not be passed, was left to future decision; and it was considered sufficient to heal the present wound by mutually trusting to the royal word: "It will not happen again."

14. Ferdinand Freiligrath Mourns the Tragedy of Fratricidal Conflict

While countless Germans were rejoicing at the triumph of nationalism in the Seven Weeks' War, the democratic poet Ferdinand Freiligrath felt only the tragedy of a conflict between brothers. In his exile in London he composed a poem, "Westphalian Summer Song," which expressed sorrow over the civil war in Central Europe. It voiced the feelings of the mute millions to whom the price of unification was too high for its value.

SOURCE: Ferdinand Freiligrath, *Poems*, 2d ed. (Leipzig: B. Tauchnitz, 1871), pp. 236–237.

In lightning and in summer's rain,
  In noon-sun hot and glowing,
Full gaily, oh Westphalia's grain,
  Art shooting up and growing!
Old Hellweg's rye, so lithe and strong,
Seven feet and more thy stems are long,
  How gloriously dost ripen!

I grow and ripen fast and strong,
  The year with gifts is mellow,
To satisfy both old and young
  I ripen rich and yellow;
But dost thou not, oh wand'rer, know
That he who joyfully did sow,
  Can never cut and reap me?

Forth through my swaying ears he went,
  In rank and order starting,
With clenched fist and tearful eye
  From house and home departing;
Loud summoned by the drum and horn,
He goes to crush his brother's corn
  In brother-war unhallowed.

Who then for this year's harvest-home
  Will fetch the girls to foot it?
Alas! Who'll wave the harvest wreath,
  Upon the barn who'll put it?
The reaper's name is Death, I wot,
He mows this year with grape and shot;
  Well know I who has hired him.

A little bird sings on the Haar:
  'Where Elbe and Maine are hieing,
There he, who was a plough-boy here,
  All stiff and stark is lying;
His homestead's pride, forth did he go,
A brother's bullet laid him low!——'
  I rustle to the breezes.

III
War with France

The outcome of the battle of Sadowa was a blow to Paris almost as much as to Vienna. The government of Napoleon III had encouraged civil strife in Central Europe in the hope that a dispute among the Germans would be of advantage to the French. Instead it found itself facing a powerful new state east of the Rhine which represented a potential threat to the Second Empire. Domestic difficulties in France, moreover, encouraged the involvement of the regime in foreign adventures. As the imperial system came under growing criticism for political shortsightedness, its supporters began to feel that only some great diplomatic or military success could silence the opposition. War, in other words, might be the sole alternative to revolution. On the other side of the frontier in Germany the prospect of an armed conflict also appeared increasingly attractive. Bismarck had at first hoped that the political consolidation of the north would lead to union with the south. In this expectation, however, he was soon disappointed. Fear of Prussia actually increased below the Main in the years after Sadowa. Berlin sought to reach its objective indirectly by establishing a Zollverein parliament in which representatives from the northern and southern states would sit side by side to deliberate on questions of trade and customs. From a discussion of commercial problems it would be only a short step to a discussion of economic problems in general, and from economics it would again be only a short step to politics. But in the elections of the southern delegates to the Zollverein parliament the particularists won an impressive victory. It became clear to Bismarck that only a common patriotic struggle against foreign aggression could reverse the ebbing tide of nationalism.

Under the circumstances a conflict between France and Germany was bound to come. Its immediate occasion, though not its ultimate cause, was the candidacy of Prince Leopold, a member of the Hohenzollern family, for the throne of Spain. The French foreign minister Antoine Alfred Agénor de Gramont resolved to avert the threat to his nation's security even at the risk of war. His initial diplomatic moves met with success when the prince withdrew from consideration by the authorities in Madrid. To Bismarck this conciliatory step was a source of bitter disappointment. But then the French overplayed their hand by deciding to ask William I for an assurance that the candidacy of Leopold would not be renewed at any time in the future. When the imperial ambassador Vincent Benedetti presented this demand to the king vacationing in Bad Ems, he received a polite yet firm refusal. A telegram describing the incident was sent to Berlin by Heinrich Abeken, an official of the foreign ministry who was in the royal retinue. Bismarck, after editing the text to create the impression that there had been a quarrel between the king and the ambassador, released it to the press. The result was an outburst of indignation in France as well as Germany, each side convinced that its national honor had been offended. Paris took the initiative by declaring war, thereby alienating public opinion in the neutral countries and driving the south German states into the arms of Prussia. Yet Bismarck had not been more peaceable than Gramont, only more deft and clever.

The course of hostilities soon revealed that the victories of the Prussian army over Denmark and Austria had been no accident. Its organization and training were of the highest order, and in Moltke it had the most brilliant strategist since Napoleon I. France, which had won the reputation of the leading military power on the Continent by virtue of successful campaigns in the Crimea and northern Italy, now met more than her match. The Germans won one important battle after another in the border region, and then on September 2 they forced a large French army headed by the emperor himself to surrender at Sedan. The war seemed to be over, for what further resistance could Paris offer? Yet, in fact, the struggle was to continue for another five months. In 1870 as in 1792 defeat on the battlefield led to the overthrow of the monarchy and the establishment of a republic in France. The new government announced that it was ready to negotiate a peace of reconciliation, but that it would not yield "an inch of our territory or a stone of our fortresses." When the victors refused to abandon their demands for territorial gain, hostilities continued. The most important military operation in the renewed struggle was the siege of Paris. The republic displayed impressive energy in raising new armies and providing them with supplies. But the bravery of raw recruits was no substitute for training and experience. It gradually became apparent that Gambetta and Favre could not emulate the accomplishments of Robespierre and Carnot. The French capital surrendered on January 28, 1871, and soon thereafter peace negotiations began.

The war was officially concluded by the preliminary treaty of February 26 signed at German headquarters in Versailles and by the definitive treaty of Frankfurt am Main on May 10. The harshness of the terms aggravated the hostility between Frenchmen and Germans which had originated centuries before in the age of Richelieu and Mazarin. Even the neutral countries, although they had at first regarded the outcome of the war as a just retribution for Napoleonic presumptuousness, were shocked by the severity of the victors. France had to pay within three years an indemnity of five billion francs, an exorbitant sum in those times, and she had to support an army of occupation until the obligation had been fully discharged. But worse of all, she had to cede Alsace and part of Lorraine. This was the provision which aroused the greatest bitterness. That the population of the two provinces did not want to submit to German rule was beyond dispute. The right of conquest, however, prevailed over the principle of self-determination. The cruel treaty which Germany imposed on France avenged the humiliating peace which Napoleon I had forced Prussia to accept some sixty years before. More than that, it marked the rise of a new military power whose ruthlessness aroused fear throughout the Continent. A nation of poets and philosophers had suddenly become a nation of warriors and conquerors. The transformation was to have fateful consequences not only for Germany, but for all of Europe.

1. Prince Napoleon Expresses Fear of the North German Confederation

The establishment of the North German Confederation aroused alarm among French politicians of every political opinion. Most of them, regardless of party or ideology, expressed concern for the future security of their nation. On a visit to Berlin in 1868 Prince Napoleon, cousin of the emperor of France, confided his fears to Lord Augustus Loftus, the British ambassador. The latter left a detailed account of the conversation which reflected the widespread anxiety aroused west of the Rhine by the achievement of national unification in Central Europe. To the prince even war was not too high a price to pay for ending the German menace.

I HAD A LONG CONVERSATION with His Imperial Highness on the day after his arrival. It then appeared to me that his attention was mostly, if not entirely, occupied with the present and future of Germany. He disclaimed any identification with the present ministry or policy of France, and frankly said that he was in opposition to the government, and that, consequently, his opinions were purely private and personal. He spoke of the reconstruction of Germany, saying that what had been done was now a *fait accompli*, and recognized by France. He did not seem to entertain any hopes, or even a wish, that what had been so far effected could be altered. He even said that the absorption of the smaller northern states was of no importance to France. "But," observed His Imperial Highness, "the unification of Germany under Prussia is still in progress. The Zollverein parliament is a step further to the absorption of southern Germany. Where is this to end? What limit is to be placed to the Germany of the future—or, rather, to Prussia? France has accepted the boundary of Northern Germany to the Main, as laid down by the Treaty of [Nikolsburg]. The entry of the southern states is inevitable—it is only a work of time. Can France—can Europe—look quietly on and witness passively this absorbing process without requiring some guarantee as to the limits which shall constitute Germany? What would Europe say if France were to enter into a similar Zollverein treaty with Belgium, and if Belgian representatives should sit in a parliament assembled at Paris? Why, the Powers would instantly raise their voices

SOURCE: *The Diplomatic Reminiscences of Lord Augustus Loftus, 1862–1879*, 2 vols. (London, Paris, and Melbourne: Cassell & Co., 1894), vol. I, pp. 216–220.

against the absorption of Belgium and the obliteration of her existence as an independent state!

"Then, again," said His Imperial Highness, "if the principle of nationality is carried out—the only legitimate grounds for such a policy—what will become of the eight millions of Austro-Germans? Will their turn come next? And how will it be possible for them to avoid being drawn into the same vortex?

"It may be very well to say that Germany is not an aggressive Power, but who can say when she may not become so? and that she may not some day reclaim Alsace and Lorraine, or seek to unite within her boundaries the Russo-German provinces of the Baltic?

"The Germany of today under Prussia has united thirty millions. When the southern states shall join, she will have an additional eight millions; and if the Austro-German provinces should later fall within her grasp, Germany will form a vast national amalgamation of nearly fifty millions of people.

"I have no objection," His Imperial Highness went on, "to the limits laid down by the Treaty of [Nikolsburg]. They are a *fait accompli*; and France has, wisely or not, accepted them. But I want to know—is that arrangement to be looked upon as *final*? If southern Germany is still to follow in the wake, I again say, Let it be so. But what concessions will Germany and Prussia be prepared to make in return for this aggrandisement? If the principle of absorption is to be thus passively permitted by Europe, who should not others absorb likewise?

"You English have chosen to withdraw yourselves from the political arena of Europe, and this abstention of England from active participation in European politics is a great misfortune for Europe, and will later prove to be a great misfortune for herself. You pretend to abstain from interfering in European affairs except on questions which directly affect your interests; but is not this question of Germany one which affects the well-being and peace of Europe? and must it not consequently concern the interests of your country?

"Look at past history! Europe is now suffering from the wrongs committed in Poland.

"There are two points on which England keeps a watchful and jealous eye—namely, Belgium and Constantinople. If an idea is ever mooted which could menace the independence of Belgium, England will immediately raise her voice. If Russia discloses any secret design on Constantinople, there again you raise a cry of alarm. But as regards the change brought about and in operation in Germany you are apparently apathetic, and foresee no danger likely to affect your interests.

"The present state of things is intolerable, and cannot last, for there is no basis of international law. Treaties are no sooner signed than they are violated. Old landmarks have been torn down, and no fixed ones have taken their place. There is consequently nothing but confusion and insecurity, and the result must necessarily be some great catastrophe, which, if the statesmen of Europe had foresight and courage, might be averted. If they continue in their present apathy, they will be awakened some morning by a *coup de tonnerre*.

"Let a Germany be constituted, but let its limits be fixed and final, so that it may not be led to aspire to future aggrandizement; and let the arrangement concluded be placed under an European guarantee.

"If you English," continued the Prince, "remain in your present state of abstention from European affairs, you will some day see that Russia will profit by the moment when we shall be otherwise engaged to seize Constantinople, and, having obtained her prize, will leave Prussia in the lurch. To us, in such a moment, the Eastern question will be of secondary consequence in comparison with our interests nearer home.

"How would you be able, single-handed, to oppose Russia in the East? You will have to submit to a *fait accompli*, which will seriously affect your prestige, if not your interests, in the East. If in a war with Prussia we should be victorious, we can make peace by compensating ourselves. We shall not expend our blood and treasure for nothing."

2. The Effect of the Ems Telegram

Since a victorious war would serve the interests of Paris as well as Berlin, there were statesmen on each side of the Rhine who were willing to engage in a test of strength between France and Germany. The occasion for an outbreak of hostilities came in July 1870 in connection with the candidacy of Prince Leopold of Hohenzollern-

Source: *Bismarck: The Man and the Statesman*, 2 vols. (New York and London: Harper & Row, 1899), vol. II, pp. 96–98, 100–102.

Sigmaringen for the throne of Spain. By exerting diplomatic pressure on William I, the French cabinet won a significant initial success with the withdrawal of the prince from further negotiations with Madrid. But when the imperial government tried to obtain additional concessions from the king of Prussia, it gave Bismarck the opportunity to provoke an armed conflict which both parties had invited.

HAVING DECIDED to resign [after the abandonment of the Hohenzollern candidacy], I invited [Roon] and Moltke to dine with me alone on the 13th, and communicated to them at table my views and projects for doing so. Both were greatly depressed, and reproached me indirectly with selfishly availing myself of my greater facility for withdrawing from service. I maintained the position that I could not offer up my sense of honor to politics, that both of them, being professional soldiers and consequently without freedom of choice, need not take the same point of view as a responsible foreign minister. During our conversation I was informed that a telegram from Ems, in cipher, if I recollect rightly, of about 200 "groups," was being deciphered. When the copy was handed to me it showed that Abeken had drawn up and signed the telegram at his Majesty's command, and I read it out to my guests,* whose dejection was so great that they turned away from food and drink. On a repeated examination of the document I lingered upon the authorization of his Majesty, which included a command, immediately to

---

* The telegram handed in at Ems on July 13, 1870, at 3:50 p.m. and received in Berlin at 6:09, ran as deciphered:

"His Majesty writes to me: 'Count Benedetti spoke to me on the promenade, in order to demand from me, finally in a very importunate manner, that I should authorize him to telegraph at once that I bound myself for all future time never again to give my consent if the Hohenzollerns should renew their candidature. I refused at last somewhat sternly, as it is neither right nor possible to undertake engagements of this kind à tout jamais. Naturally I told him that I had as yet received no news, and as he was earlier informed about Paris and Madrid than myself, he could clearly see that my government once more had no hand in the matter.' His Majesty has since received a letter from the Prince. His Majesty having told Count Benedetti that he was awaiting news from the Prince, has decided, with reference to the above demand, upon the representation of Count Eulenburg and myself, not to receive Count Benedetti again, but only to let him be informed through an aide-de-camp: That his Majesty had now received from the Prince confirmation of the news which Benedetti had already received from Paris, and had nothing further to say to the ambassador. His Majesty leaves it to your Excellency whether Benedetti's fresh demand and its rejection should not be at once communicated both to our ambassadors and to the press."

communicate Benedetti's fresh demand and its rejection both to our ambassadors and to the press. I put a few questions to Moltke as to the extent of his confidence in the state of our preparations, especially as to the time they would still require in order to meet this sudden risk of war. He answered that if there was to be war he expected no advantage to us by deferring its outbreak; and even if we should not be strong enough at first to protect all the territories on the left bank of the Rhine against French invasion, our preparations would nevertheless soon overtake those of the French, while at a later period this advantage would be diminished; he regarded a rapid outbreak as, on the whole, more favorable to us than delay. . . .

[Various] considerations, conscious and unconscious, strengthened my opinion that war could be avoided only at the cost of the honor of Prussia and of the national confidence in it. Under this conviction I made use of the royal authorization communicated to me through Abeken, to publish the contents of the telegram; and in the presence of my two guests I reduced the telegram by striking out words, but without adding or altering, to the following form: "After the news of the renunciation of the hereditary Prince of Hohenzollern had been officially communicated to the imperial government of France by the royal government of Spain, the French ambassador at Ems further demanded of his Majesty the King that he would authorize him to telegraph to Paris that his Majesty the King bound himself for all future time never again to give his consent if the Hohenzollerns should renew their candidature. His Majesty the King thereupon decided not to receive the French ambassador again, and sent to tell him through the aide-de-camp on duty that his Majesty had nothing further to communicate to the ambassador." The difference in the effect of the abbreviated text of the Ems telegram as compared with that produced by the original was not the result of stronger words but of the form, which made this announcement appear decisive, while Abeken's version would only have been regarded as a fragment of a negotiation still pending, and to be continued at Berlin.

After I had read out the concentrated edition to my two guests, Moltke remarked: "Now it has a different ring; it sounded before like a parley; now it is like a flourish in answer to a challenge." I went on to explain: "If in execution of his Majesty's order I at once communicate this text, which contains no alteration in or addition to the telegram, not only to the newspapers, but also by telegraph to all our embassies, it will be known in Paris before midnight, and not only on account of its contents, but also on account of the manner of its distribution, will have the effect of a red rag upon the Gallic bull. Fight we must if we do not want to act the part of the vanquished without a battle. Success, however, essentially depends upon the impression which the origination of the war makes upon us and others; it is important that we should be the party attacked, and this Gallic overweening and touchiness will make us if we announce in the face of Europe, so far as we can without the speaking-tube of the Reichstag, that we fearlessly meet the public threats of France."

This explanation brought about in the two generals a revulsion to a more joyous mood, the liveliness of which surprised me. They had suddenly recovered their pleasure in eating and drinking and spoke in a more cheerful vein. Roon said: "Our God of old lives still and will not let us perish in disgrace." Moltke so far relinquished his passive equanimity that, glancing up joyously towards the ceiling and abandoning his usual punctiliousness of speech, he smote his hand upon his breast and said: "If I may but live to lead our armies in such a war, then the devil may come directly afterwards and fetch away the 'old carcass.'" He was less robust at that time than afterwards, and doubted whether he would survive the hardships of the campaign.

3. Ferdinand Freiligrath Overflows with Patriotism

Although Central Europe had watched the coming of the Seven Weeks' War with fear and foreboding, the Franco-Prussian War aroused wild patriotic enthusiasm. The new conflict was not a deadly quarrel among brothers, but a justified struggle against an insolent foreign aggressor. Even many of those who had been critical of the North German Confederation could not remain indifferent to the possibility of its overthrow at the hands of Napoleonic Caesarism. Ferdinand Freiligrath, overcoming his scruples about Bismarck, wrote a poem, "Hurrah, Germania!" which voiced the mood of the nation as it marched into battle against the hated French.

SOURCE: Ferdinand Freiligrath, *Poems*, 2d ed. (Leipzig: B. Tauchnitz, 1871), pp. 247–250.

Hurrah! thou lady proud and fair,
  Hurrah! Germania mine!
What fire is in thine eye as there
  Thou bendest o'er the Rhine!
How in July's full blaze dost thou
  Flash forth thy sword, and go,
With heart elate and knitted brow,
  To strike the invader low!
    Hurrah! Hurrah! Hurrah!
    Hurrah! Germania!

No thought hadst thou, so calm and light,
  Of war or battle plain,
But on thy broad fields, waving bright,
  Didst mow the golden grain,
With clashing sickles, wreaths of corn
  Thy sheaves didst garner in,
When, hark! across the Rhine War's horn
  Breaks through the merry din!
    Hurrah! Hurrah! Hurrah!
    Hurrah! Germania!

Down sickle then and wreath of wheat
  Amidst the corn were cast,
And, starting fiercely to thy feet,
  Thy heart beat loud and fast;
Then with a shout I heard thee call,
  "Well, since you will, you may!
Up, up, my children, one and all,
  On to the Rhine! Away!"
    Hurrah! Hurrah! Hurrah!
    Hurrah! Germania!

From port to port the summons flew,
  Rang o'er our German wave,
The Oder on her harness drew,
  The Elbe girt on her glaive;
Neckar and Weser swell the tide,
  Main flashes to the sun,
Old feuds, old hates are dash'd aside,
  All German men are one!
    Hurrah! Hurrah! Hurrah!
    Hurrah! Germania!

Swabian and Prussian, hand in hand,
  North, South, one host, one vow!
"What is the German's Fatherland?"
  Who asks that question now?
One soul, one arm, one close-knit frame,

One will are we to-day;
Hurrah, Germania! thou proud dame,
Oh, glorious time, hurrah!
Hurrah! Hurrah! Hurrah!
Hurrah! Germania!

Germania now, let come what may,
Will stand unshook through all;
This is our country's festal day;
Now woe betide thee, Gaul!
Woe worth the hour a robber thrust
Thy sword into thy hand!
A curse upon him that we must
Unsheathe our German brand!
Hurrah! Hurrah! Hurrah!
Hurrah! Germania!

For home and hearth, for wife and child,
For all loved things that we
Are bound to keep all undefiled
From foreign ruffianry!
For German right, for German speech,
For German household ways,
For German homesteads, all and each,
Strike home through battle's blaze!
Hurrah! Hurrah! Hurrah!
Hurrah! Germania!

Up, Germans, up, with God! The die
Clicks loud,—we wait the throw!
Oh, who may think without a sigh,
What blood is doom'd to flow?
Yet, look thou up, with fearless heart!
Thou must, thou shalt prevail!
Great, glorious, free as ne'er thou wert,
All hail, Germania, hail!
Hurrah! Victoria!
Hurrah! Germania!

4. The Bavarian Legislature Decides to Support Prussia

The outburst of national sentiment engendered by the struggle against France overcame the forces of particularism in southern Germany. Although Bavaria had concluded an alliance with Prussia after the Seven Weeks' War, public opinion in the Wittelsbach kingdom had

SOURCE: *Memoirs of Prince von Bülow*, 4 vols. (Boston: Little, Brown and Company, 1931–32), vol. IV, pp. 163–165.

continued to regard Berlin as a center of authoritarianism, expansionism, and militarism. The events of the summer of 1870 produced a drastic change in attitude below the Main. In his memoirs the statesman Bernhard von Bülow left a vivid though partisan account of the crucial debate of the legislature in Munich regarding entry into the war on the side of the Hohenzollerns.

PRINCE CHLODWIG HOHENLOHE, my chief in the Paris embassy and predecessor in the chancellorship, has more than once given me a graphic description of the proceedings in the decisive session of the Bavarian Second Chamber. He had been present in the imperial councillors' gallery. The Special Committee had decided, by seven votes against three, to refuse the government's proposal of a special credit of 5.6 million guilders for the mobilization of the Bavarian army, and by six votes against three declared for armed neutrality. This resolution was presented by the deputy Jörg, the leader of the "Patriots" and publisher of the *Historisch-Politische Blätter*.

At the very beginning of his speech Jörg had the audacity to persist in declaring that the quarrel between Prussia and France lay outside the realm of German integrity and honor. The whole of the present complication had, he said, originated in the policy of the Prussian ruling house. On the front bench of the Liberals sat the Imperial Baron von Stauffenberg, who was then scarcely thirty-three years old. He came of a family that had formerly belonged to the mediatized nobility in Franconia and Swabia, and one which had been invested with the office of Hereditary Cup Bearer by the Dukes of Alemania. But he was noble in spirit and not merely by birth.

Von Stauffenberg got up, spat, threatened to beat his unpatriotic colleague with his fist, and called him a knave. Unconcerned, and apparently not very sensitive in matters of honor, Jörg went on to say that Prussia might not be able to afford Bavaria any protection in the event of a French invasion, even if she wished to do so. But she did not, he said, wish to protect Bavaria. Many people believed that Prussia deliberately wished to render Bavaria absolutely helpless, so as to be able to swallow her at her leisure. On the other hand, he continued, the Duc de Gramont had solemnly declared that noble France did not intend to acquire one single square foot of German territory, but was ready to give Bavaria a special guarantee that she should possess the Palatinate. After Jörg, in a loud voice, had again expressed the opinion that Bavaria would be badly treated in the event of a victory of Prussia, but never by France, for that would indeed be a blow against French interests, Baron von Stauffenberg, his cheeks blazing with anger, rose to his feet again. He seized a chair which was standing near him, and with a powerful throw, hurled it at the wretched Jörg. The people in the packed public gallery broke into tumultuous cheers. Jörg, whose courage apparently did not stand on a level with his infamous mind, lost the thread of his discourse, and closed with the mumbled rather than spoken declaration that as he was a man who had concerned himself with politics and with the study of public affairs all his life, his opinion was valuable and significant. The war of 1870, he said, was only the logical consequence of 1866, and did not concern Bavaria in the least.

Full of dignity, calmly and firmly, Count Bray, the premier, replied to the "Patriot" Jörg: "The matter before us is one of keeping or breaking the treaty. We must declare our attitude toward Germany." The unrestrained applause of the Liberals and government benches resounded when these words were spoken. The premier concluded: "I have not lived until now merely to renounce my principles, revoke my signature." After him the minister of war, the good Baron von Prankh, stood up to speak. Like the premier before him, he spoke not as a politician, not as a jurist, but only as a soldier, a true Bavarian, an old Bavarian, but also a German. In a manly speech he made a last appeal to the Chamber. "Let us stand by Germany," he said. "Otherwise we are dishonored and lost." In vain the "Patriots" Dr. Ruhland and Dr. Westermayer, prelate and priest of St. Peter's, Munich, tried to help Jörg, the party chief. In their ecclesiastical capacity they were agitators rather than priests. The former protested against thrusting the sons of Bavaria into a sanguinary war with an enemy who had never given personal offence to the Bavarians themselves. Dr. Westermayer held the sanctimonious opinion that there was a standpoint in morals where care for the hearth and home took precedence over the duty of helping a menaced neighbour. When he uttered this sentence, Westermayer was interrupted by a storm of indignation and shouts of "Shame!" from the Left and the gallery. When he hinted that the Bavarian Palatinate had an urgent interest in Bavarian neutrality in the Franco-German war, the Palatine deputies who were present, protested and cried out that the Palatinate recognized the threatening danger, but wished to be on the side of its German brothers. When the gallery cheered the Palatine deputies, who were patriots in the true sense of the word, the Speaker of the Chamber, Weiss, who was also a "Patriot," threatened to have the gallery cleared, but finally did not dare to carry out his intention.

The Liberal deputies, Fischer, Völk, Edel, Marquardsen, and Barth, drawing attention to the cheers for the Fatherland that could be heard inside the House and came from the crowds outside the Chamber, appealed in fiery words to German patriotism and German honor. The Speaker, Weiss, made a last weak attempt to adjourn the debate because "pressure" was being brought to bear upon the discussion, but after some irresolution, finally allowed the vote to be taken. Jörg's motion in Committee was defeated by 89 votes to 58, and the government's proposal accepted by 101 votes to 47.

When the deputies left the Chamber, they and the ministers and imperial counsellors were greeted with joy and acclamation by the crowd. As Hohenlohe could observe, Jörg and his close friends did not at first dare to go out into the streets, but chose to wait until the excitement in the town had died down, and then crept home. The Bavarian First Chamber, which had unanimously and without debate voted the credit demanded by the government, gave a fine example of patriotic sentiment and political insight that made a great impression both in Germany and abroad.

5. The Surrender of Napoleon III at Sedan

The first phase of the Franco-Prussian War was a series of important though costly German successes in fighting along the frontier which culminated on September 2, 1870, in the capitulation at Sedan of Napoleon III and a large French army. The enigmatic emperor whose schemes and ambitions had once been the subject of fearful speculation in all the capitals of Europe proved in the end to be only a sick, prematurely old man reflecting sadly on his vanished glory. In a letter to William I, Bismarck described the surrender of the defeated ruler and the end of the Napoleonic legend.

AFTER I CAME HERE yesterday evening, by your Royal Majesty's command, to take part in the negotiations on the capitulation, these

SOURCE: *The Correspondence of William I and Bismarck*, 2 vols. (New York: F. A. Stokes Company, 1903), vol. I, pp. 124–128.

were interrupted until 1 o'clock in the night, by time for consideration, which General Wimpffen solicited, being granted, after
General von Moltke had definitely stated that no other terms will
be granted than the laying down of arms, and that the bombard-
ment would recommence at 9 o'clock in the morning if the capitulation were not concluded by that time. At about 6 o'clock this
morning General Reille was announced, who informed me that the
Emperor wished to see me, and was already on his way here from
Sedan. The General returned at once to report to his Majesty that I
was following, and shortly afterwards I met the Emperor near
Fresnois, about half way between this place and Sedan. His Majesty was driving in an open carriage with three officers of high
rank, and was escorted by three others on horseback. Of these
officers I knew personally Generals Castelnau, Reille, Moskowa,
who seemed to be wounded in the foot, and Vaubert. As soon as I
reached the carriage I dismounted, walked to the Emperor's side at
the carriage door, and asked for His Majesty's orders. The Emperor at first expressed the wish to see Your Imperial Majesty,
evidently in the belief that Your Majesty was also at Donchery.
When I replied that at present Your Majesty's headquarters were
at Vendresse, 13 miles away, the Emperor inquired whether Your
Majesty had decided where he should go, and what my opinion on
the subject was. I replied that, as it was quite dark when I arrived
here, I knew nothing of the district, and offered to place at his
disposal at once the house in which I was staying at Donchery. The
Emperor accepted this offer, and drove off at a walking pace in the
direction of Donchery; about a hundred yards from the Maas
bridge, which leads into the town, he stopped in front of a lonely,
workman's cottage, and asked me if he could not stay there. I had
the house examined by councillor of legation Count Bismarck-
Bohlen, who in the meantime had followed me; when it was reported that the interior arrangements were very poor and
inadequate, but that there were no wounded men in the house, the
Emperor alighted, and invited me to accompany him inside. Here,
in a very small room containing a table and two chairs, I had about
an hour's conversation with the Emperor. His Majesty emphasized
especially the wish to obtain more favorable conditions of capitulation for the army. I declined from the outset to treat this question
with His Majesty, as this was a purely military question, to be
settled between General von Moltke and General von Wimpffen.

On the other hand, I asked if His Majesty were inclined to peace negotiations. The Emperor replied that, as a prisoner, he was not now in a position to do so, and to my further inquiry by whom, in his opinion, the executive power was at present represented in France, His Majesty referred me to the government in Paris. When this point, which was indistinct in the Emperor's letter to Your Majesty yesterday, was cleared up, I recognized, and did not conceal the fact from the Emperor, that the situation today, as yesterday, was still a purely military one, and emphasized the necessity arising from it for us to obtain by the capitulation of Sedan above all things a material pledge for the security of the military results we had attained. I had already weighed from all sides with General von Moltke yesterday evening, the question whether it would be possible, without detriment to the German interests, to offer to the military feelings of honor of an army which had fought well more favorable terms than those already laid down. After due and careful consideration we both came to the conclusion that this could not be done. When, therefore, General von Moltke, who in the meantime had arrived from the town, went to Your Majesty to submit the Emperor's wishes, he did not do so, as Your Majesty is well aware, with the intention of advocating them.

The Emperor then went out into the open air, and invited me to sit beside him just outside the door of the cottage. His Majesty asked whether it would not be practicable to allow the French army to cross into Belgium, to be disarmed and detained there. I had discussed also this eventuality with General v. Voltke on the previous evening, and adduced the motive already given for not entering into the question of this course of procedure. With respect to the political situation, I myself took no initiative, and the Emperor went no further than to deplore the ill-fortune of the war, stating that he himself had not wished for war, but was driven into it by the pressure of public opinion in France. I did not regard it as my office to point out at that moment that what the Emperor characterized as public opinion was only the artificial product of certain ambitious coteries of the French press, with a very narrow political horizon. I merely replied that nobody in Germany wished for the war, especially not Your Majesty, and that no German government would have considered the Spanish question of so much interest as to be worth a war. I continued that Your Majesty's attitude toward the Spanish succession question was finally determined by the misgiving whether it was right, for personal and dynastic considerations, to mar the endeavor of the Spanish nation to reestablish, by this selection of a king, their internal organization on a permanent basis; that Your Majesty, in view of the good relations existing for so many years between the princes of the Hohenzollern House and the Emperor, had never entertained any doubt but that the hereditary prince would succeed in arriving at a satisfactory understanding with His Majesty the Emperor respecting the acceptance of the Spanish election, that, however, Your Majesty had regarded this, not as a German or a Prussian, but as a Spanish affair.

In the meantime, between 9 and 10 o'clock, inquiries in the town, and especially *reconnaissances* on the part of the officers of the general staff had revealed the fact that the castle of Bellevue, near Fresnois, was suited for the accommodation of the Emperor, and was not yet occupied by the wounded. I reported this to His Majesty by designating Fresnois as the place I should propose to Your Majesty for the meeting, and therefore referred it to the Emperor whether His Majesty would proceed there at once, as a longer stay in the little workman's cottage would be uncomfortable, and the Emperor would perhaps need some rest. His Majesty readily assented, and I accompanied the Emperor, who was preceded by an escort of honor from Your Majesty's own Cuirassier Regiment, to the castle of Bellevue, where in the meantime the rest of the Emperor's suite and his carriages, whose coming had, it appears, been considered doubtful, had arrived from Sedan. General Wimpffen had also arrived, and with him, in anticipation of the return of General von Moltke, the discussion of the capitulation negotiations, which were broken off yesterday, was resumed by General v. Podbielski in the presence of Lieut. Col. von Verdy and the chief of General v. Wimpffen's staff, these two officers acting as secretaries. I took part only in the commencement of the same by setting forth the political and judicial situation in accordance with the information furnished me by the Emperor himself, as it was thereupon reported to me by Major Count von Nostitz, by direction of General von Moltke, that Your Majesty wished to see the Emperor only after the capitulation of the army had been concluded—on the receipt of which announcement the hope cherished by the opposite party of securing other terms than those decided on was given up. I then rode off in the direction of Chehery with the intention of reporting the situation to Your Majesty, met General v. Moltke on the way, bringing the text of the capitulation approved by Your Majesty, and this, when we arrived with it at Fresnois, was accepted and signed without opposition. The demeanor of General v. Wimpffen, as also that of the other French generals, during the previous night was very dignified, and this brave officer could not forbear expressing to me how deeply he was pained that he should have been called upon, forty-eight hours after his arrival from Africa, and half a day after he had assumed command, to set his name to a capitulation so fatal to the French arms, that, however, lack of provisions and ammunition, and the absolute impossibility of any further defence imposed upon him, as a general, the duty of suppressing his personal feelings, as further bloodshed could in no way alter the situation. The permission for the officers to be released on parole was received with great thankfulness, as an expression of Your Majesty's intention not to hurt the feelings of an army, which had fought bravely, beyond the point demanded by the necessity of our political interests. General v. Wimpffen also subsequently gave expression to this feeling in a letter in which he thanks General v. Moltke for the consideration he showed in conducting the negotiations.

6. Jules Favre Vows Never to Cede French Territory

The defeat of Napoleon III at Sedan led to the proclamation of a republic in France. The new government hoped to repeat the miracle of 1792 by enlisting the forces of patriotism and democracy in the defense of the nation. On September 6, 1870, Jules Favre, now the foreign minister in Paris, dispatched a manifesto to the French diplomatic representatives abroad who were to submit it in turn to the governments to which they had been accredited. It expressed the desire of the republic for an honorable peace but vowed that under no circumstances would territorial cessions be made to the German invaders.

THE EVENTS which have just taken place in Paris explain themselves so well by the inexorable logic of facts that it is useless to insist at length on their meaning and bearing. In ceding to an irresistible impulse which had been but too long restrained, the

SOURCE: *The Annual Register* (1870), pt. I, pp. 174–176.

population of Paris has obeyed a necessity superior to that of its own safety; it did not wish to perish with the criminal government which was leading France to her ruin; it has not pronounced the deposition of Napoleon III. and of his dynasty; it has registered it in the name of right, justice, and public safety, and the sentence was so well ratified beforehand by the conscience of all that no one, even among the most noisy defenders of the power that was falling, raised his voice to uphold it. It collapsed of itself under the weight of its faults, and amid the acclamations of an immense people, without a single drop of blood being shed, without any one individual being deprived of his personal liberty, and we have been able to see—a thing unheard of in history—the citizens, upon whom the popular voice conferred the perilous mandate to fight and conquer, not thinking for a moment of their political adversaries who, but the day before, threatened them with execution. It is by refusing to their adversaries the honor of being subject to any sort of repression that they have shown them their blindness and their impotence. Order has not been disturbed for a single moment. Our confidence in the wisdom and patriotism of the national guard and of the whole population permits us to affirm that it will not be disturbed. Rescued from the shame and the danger of a government which has proved itself a traitor to all its duties, each one now comprehends that the first act of the national sovereignty, at last reconquered, must be one of self-control—the seeking for strength in respect for right. Moreover, time must not be lost; the enemies are at our gates; we have but one thought—namely, their expulsion from our territory. But this obligation, which we resolutely accept, we did not impose upon France. She would not be in her present position if our voice had been listened to. We have energetically defended, even at the cost of our popularity, the policy of peace. We still maintain the same opinion with increasing conviction. Our heart breaks at the sight of these human massacres, wherein it sacrifices the flower of two nations, that a little good sense and a great deal of liberty would have preserved from such frightful catastrophes. We cannot find any expression capable of rendering our admiration for our heroic army, sacrificed by the incapacity of the supreme commander, but showing itself greater in its defeats than in the most brilliant victory; for, in spite of the knowledge of faults which compromised its safety, the army has immolated itself with sublime heroism in the face of certain death, redeeming thus the honor of France from the stain cast upon her by her government. All honor to the army! The nation looks towards it with open arms. The imperial power wished to divide them. Misfortune and duty join them in a solemn embrace, sealed by patriotism and liberty. This alliance renders us invincible. Ready for every emergency, we look with calmness on the position of affairs, made what it is, not by us but by others. This position I will explain in a few words, and I submit it to the judgment of my country and of Europe. We loudly condemned the war, and, while protesting our respect for the rights of peoples, we asked that Germany should be left mistress of her own destinies. We wished that liberty should be at the same time our common tie and our common shield. We were convinced that these moral forces would for ever insure peace, but as a sanction we claimed an arm for every citizen, a civil organization, and the election of leaders. Then we should have remained invincible on our own soil. The government of the Emperor, which had long since separated its interests from those of the country, opposed that policy.

We take it up with the hope that, taught by experience, France will have the wisdom to put it into practice. On his side, the King of Prussia declared that he made war, not against France, but against the imperial dynasty. The dynasty has fallen to the ground. France raises herself free. Does the King of Prussia wish to continue an impious struggle, which will be at least as fatal to him as to us? Does he wish to give to the world of the nineteenth century the cruel spectacle of two nations destroying one another, and in forgetfulness of humanity, reason, and science, heaping corpse upon corpse and ruin upon ruin? He is free to assume this responsibility in the face of the world and of history. If it is a challenge we accept it. We will not cede either an inch of our territory or a stone of our fortresses. A shameful peace would mean a war of extermination at an early date. We will only treat for a durable peace. In this our interest is that of the whole of Europe, and we have reason to hope that, freed from all dynastic considerations, the question will thus present itself before the cabinets of Europe. But should we be alone we shall not yield. We have a resolute army, well-provisioned forts, a well-established enceinte, and, above all, the breasts of 300,000 combatants determined to hold out to the last. When they piously lay crowns at the feet of the statue of Strasburg [this city was undergoing its siege], they do not obey merely an enthusiastic sentiment of admiration, they adopt their heroic *mot d'ordre*, they swear to be worthy of their brethren of Alsace, and to die as they have done. After the forts we have the ramparts; after the ramparts we have the barricades. Paris can hold out for three months and conquer. If she succumbs, France will start up at her appeal and avenge her. France would continue the struggle, and the aggressor would perish.

Such is, sir, what Europe must know. We have not accepted power with any other object; we will not keep it a moment if we should not find the population of Paris and the whole of France decided to share our resolutions. I sum up these resolves briefly in presence of God who hears me, in the face of posterity, which shall judge us. We wish only for peace, but if this disastrous war, which we have condemned, is continued against us, we shall do our duty to the last, and I have the firm confidence that our cause, which is that of right and justice, will triumph in the end. It is in this manner that I invite you to explain the situation to the minister of the court to which you are accredited, and in whose hands you will place a copy of this document.

7. Johann Jacoby Opposes the Annexation of Alsace-Lorraine

The appeal of the French republic for a peace without annexations was rejected by most Germans. They found it hard to practice the virtues of charity and forgiveness at a moment of triumph on the field of battle. Only here and there a voice warned against a policy of aggrandizement based on the right of conquest. Johann Jacoby was a lifelong democrat who had consistently opposed the forces of authoritarianism and militarism in Germany. In the fall of 1870 he spoke out at a public meeting against the acquisition of Alsace-Lorraine, and was promptly jailed for his temerity.

THE CHIEF QUESTION, the decision of which alone has any importance for us, is this: Has Prussia or Germany the right to appropriate Alsace and Lorraine? They tell us Alsace and Lorraine belonged formerly to the German empire. France possessed herself of these lands by craft and by force. Now that we have beaten the French, it is no more than what is right and proper that we should recover from them the spoil, and demand back the property stolen

SOURCE: *The Annual Register* (1870), pt. I, pp. 234–235.

from us. Gentlemen, do not let yourselves be led away by well-sounding words, and, though they offer you the empire of the world, be not tempted to worship the idols of power. Test this well-sounding phrase, and you will find that it is nothing but a disguise for the old and barbarous right of force. Alsace and Lorraine, they say, were formerly German property, and must again become German. How so, we inquire? have, then, Alsace and Lorraine no inhabitants? Or are, perchance, the inhabitants of these provinces to be regarded as having no volition, as a thing that one may at once take possession of, and dispose of just as one likes? Have they lost all their rights through the war, have they become slaves, whose fate is at the arbitrary disposal of the conqueror? Even the most ardent and insatiate partisan of annexation allows that the inhabitants of Alsace and Lorraine are in heart and soul French, and wish to remain French. And however much they might have offended us, it would be contrary to all human justice should we try to Germanize them compulsorily, and incorporate them against their will either with Prussia or any other German state. Gentlemen, there is an old German proverb, which has been raised to a universal moral law on account of its being so true—"Do not unto others what you would not they should do unto you." How should we and our "national Liberals" feel if at some future time a victorious Pole should demand back and seek to annex the provinces of Posen and West Russia? And yet the same grounds might be urged for this that are now brought forward to support an annexation of Alsace and Lorraine. No, gentlemen! It is our duty to oppose such tendencies of national egotism. Let us hold fast to the principles of justice as much in public life as in private life! Let us openly declare it to be our deep and inmost conviction that every incorporation of foreign territory against the wishes of the inhabitants is a violation of the right of self-constitution common to all people, and therefore as objectionable as it is pernicious. Let us, without being led astray by the intoxication of victory, raise a protest against every violence offered to the inhabitants of Alsace and Lorraine. Only he who respects the liberty of others is himself worthy of liberty.

8. The Crown Prince of Prussia Broods on the
Effects of Blood and Iron

The refusal of the Prussian government to abandon its annexationist plans meant that the war would continue to the bitter end. The brilliant successes of the summer campaign were followed by a long and exhausting siege of Paris. Public opinion in the neutral countries, which had at first blamed France for starting the conflict, now began to regard Germany as the aggressor. As the year 1870 drew to a close, the crown prince of Prussia brooded at headquarters in Versailles on the evil consequences of a statecraft of blood and iron. He confided to his diary a profound distrust of Bismarck.

THE LONGER this struggle lasts, the better for the enemy and the worse for us. The public opinion of Europe has not remained unaffected by the spectacle. We are no longer looked upon as the innocent sufferers of wrong, but rather as the arrogant victors, no longer content with the conquest of the foe, but fain to bring about his utter ruin. No more do the French appear in the eyes of neutrals as a mendacious, contemptible nation, but as the heroic-hearted people that against overwhelming odds is defending its dearest possessions in honourable fight. Nay, in their sympathy with France men go so far as to hate Germany. In this nation of thinkers and philosophers, poets and artists, idealists and enthusiasts, the world will recognize nothing but a people of conquerors and destroyers, to which no pledged word, no treaty concluded, is sacred, which speaks with rude insolence of others that had done it no hurt and scornfully makes mock even of the gifts offered it as tokens of sympathy and good will. Utterly false as these views are, we cannot, unfortunately, deny their existence and are bound to own that they are indeed well fitted to tarnish the brightness of the good name we have hitherto enjoyed. True, we are indisputably the foremost people of the world in civilization, yet at the moment it must seem as though we are neither loved nor respected, but only feared. We are deemed capable of every wickedness and the distrust felt for us grows ever more and more pronounced. Nor is this

SOURCE: From the book *Emperor Frederick II: The War Diary of the Emperor Frederick II*, translated by Alfred Richmond Allison (Frederick A. Stokes and Company, 1926), pp. 240–242. Reprinted by courtesy of J. B. Lippincott Company.

the consequence of this war only—so far has the theory, initiated by Bismarck and for years holding the stage, of "Blood and Iron" brought us! What good to us is all power, all martial glory and renown, if hatred and mistrust meet us at every turn, if every step we advance in our development is a subject for suspicion and grudging? Bismarck has made us great and powerful, but he has robbed us of our friends, the sympathies of the world, and—our conscience. I still hold fast today to the conviction that Germany, without blood and iron, simply by the justice of her cause, could make "moral conquests" and, united, become free and powerful. A preponderance of quite another kind than that gained by mere force of arms was within our reach, for German culture, German science and German genius must have won us respect, love and—honor. The insolent, brutal "Junker" willed it otherwise. . . .

The future holds for us the noble, but infinitely difficult task of freeing the beloved German Fatherland from the baseless suspicion with which the world today regards her. We must prove that the power acquired is not to beget dangers, but to bring with it a blessing, the blessing of peace and civilization. But how hard it will be to combat the worship of brute force and mere outward success, to enlighten men's minds, to direct ambition and emulation once more to worthy and healthy objects! God grant it may soon be possible to find the means to bring about an honorable peace and put an end to useless bloodshed, before it has cost us too excessive sacrifices! Even now the Bavarians, Saxons, and Württembergers have suffered terribly, and the ranks of our officers are sadly dwindled, without any prospect of speedily filling the gaps. But at home the lofty spirit of holy, patriotic enthusiasm such as was shown in those unforgettable days of July, has materially declined and given place to a feeling of discouragement. Yet our gallant army bears all privations and sufferings with unparalleled courage; to our soldiers and Fatherland we owe it to be steadfast in patience and confidence and to face the future with a strong heart and undaunted eyes. As the beginning of the mighty war was fortunate beyond all hope and expectation, so must we in thankfulness and confidence trust that, in spite of all changes and chances that may still befall, the end will correspond with the beginning.

9. Heinrich Abeken Exults at the Conclusion
of the War with France

The siege of Paris became a grueling test of endurance which proved
that the Germans could hold out longer than the French. The beleaguered city, on the verge of starvation, finally surrendered, and on
February 26, 1871, a preliminary treaty was signed concluding the war.
It imposed a Carthaginian peace on the exhausted republic. While the
losers saw in it a boundless lust for conquest, the winners exulted at the
fulfillment of a glorious destiny. Heinrich Abeken, a counselor of the
foreign office who was in the entourage of William I, described in
letters to his wife the negotiations which brought hostilities to an
end.

THAT A PEACE was concluded such as has not been known in
Germany for a thousand years, a peace before which that of 1815
is as nothing, may indeed, be a cause of pride to you. And it has
been gained by German power only, without any foreign help, and
indeed, in spite of the envy, and in opposition to the sympathies of
foreign nations which have not dared to meddle with it. It is a
peace which gives back to Germany two strong fortresses, and a
most beautiful province, a province that will be grateful to us for
having kept it with our blood from decay, and from falling into the
hands of the devil of foreigners.

It is indeed a great day, and the King and Crown Prince, and also
Bismarck and the rest of us, feel it deeply! . . .

I think the peace will delight you. Metz is secured! I had no end
of anxiety about it, and dreaded lest those who wished to relinquish
it might prevail. To give up Belfort which is entirely French and of
importance to France in a defensive war, but not in a war of attack
against Germany, is, to my idea, quite without danger; it is a sort
of compensation for Metz. Five billions of francs or fifteen hundred million thalers, are such a fabulous sum that no one can grasp
it. . . .

The peace was signed shortly after I despatched my last letter.
We are busy winding up affairs, so there is scarcely time to send
the letters off. The contracting parties were in the minister's little
room upstairs; those on the German side, were Bismarck, Count

SOURCE: *Bismarck's Pen: The Life of Heinrich Abeken* (London:
George Allen & Unwin, 1911), pp. 350–352, 354.

Bray, the Bavarian minister, Freiherr von Wächter, the minister for Würtemberg, and Herr Jolly, for Baden. On the French side, were Thiers and Jules Favre, he who said: *"Pas un pouce de notre territoire, pas une pierre de nos fortresses."* At last all was written and had to be sent up stairs, again to be read and agreed upon, and the gentlemen did this themselves, without having an official to do it for them. At a quarter to five the minister sent for me, and said to me in Latin: *"Mandate Regi quod signatum,"* inform the King that it has been signed, and I at once drove off in a carriage. The groom of the chamber said: "His Majesty has been expecting you." Then the aide-de-camp announced me, and I walked in without despatches this time, made the short announcement and congratulated the King. He was greatly moved and shook hands with me repeatedly, saying what a great and glorious achievement it was, what a mighty deed in the history of Germany. Much of course remains to be done, and a great work lies before us, but the foundation is laid, and God will help in the building of it. The King commanded me to give the minister his warm approval, and say how he regretted not to see and thank him himself today for all the loyalty and wisdom with which he had carried out, under great mental and bodily exertion, his difficult work. And true it was, for these last days were trying ones for the minister, and he would scarcely desire to live them over again. That would be too much for any one man. When I returned, I again had to go to the King with the signed document. I read it to him and he examined the signatures with great care.

I found the party at table on my return, the Frenchmen having left for Paris, wishing to go to Bordeaux this evening. I hear the train at this moment puffing and rolling past. It is probably the one which is taking them to Bordeaux. We sat at table for a long time, the minister in high good humor. He had been obliged to be excused from dining with His Majesty who was giving a dinner party to the king of Würtemberg. I went to the Crown Prince for the minister after dinner, to announce the news and to hand him the document, though he had, of course, heard everything from his father. . . .

To my great delight I find every one satisfied with the preliminaries for peace. More was not expected, and it is surprising that so much has been obtained. It is something enormous, beyond anything the German people have experienced, nor has anything like it been known in the history of the world. The surrendered territory is not large compared with the rest of France or Germany, but the moral significance, the winning back of the lost, and the way it has been won, sets a seal upon the character of the work. I am glad this is generally recognized.

10. Jacob Burckhardt Worries about the Triumph of Armed Might

The Germans may have rejoiced at the magnitude of their victory over an ancient foe, but observers in the neutral countries were disturbed by the effects of the Franco-Prussian War. Jacob Burckhardt, a Swiss cultural historian with patrician aesthetic tastes and conservative political sympathies, looked with dismay at the bitter struggle between his country's two powerful neighbors. Writing to a friend during and after the hostilities, he expressed the fear that a new age of militarism and industrialism would undermine the spiritual values on which his lifework as a scholar had been built.

WHAT HAS NOT HAPPENED in the last three months! Who could have believed that the struggle would have lasted far into a horrible winter, and would still show no sign of ending on the last day of the year? I shall remember the end of this year my whole life long! And not as regards my own, private, fate. The two great intellectual peoples of the Continent are in the process of completely sloughing their culture, and a quite enormous amount of all that delighted and interested a man before 1870 will hardly touch the man of 1871—but what a tremendous spectacle, if the new world is born in great suffering.

The change in the German spirit will be as great as in the French; at first the clergy of both confessions will look upon themselves as the heirs of the spiritual disintegration, but something quite different will soon make itself felt, to one side. The shares of the "Philosopher" will rise sharply, whereas Hegel, after this year's jubilee publications, may very possibly make his definitive jubilee retirement.

The worst of all this is not the present war, but the era of wars

SOURCE: Alexander Dru, ed., *The Letters of Jacob Burckhardt* (New York: Pantheon Books, Inc., 1955), pp. 145, 151–152. Reprinted by permission of Pantheon Books and Routledge & Kegan Paul Ltd, London, England.

upon which we have entered, and to this the new mentality will have to adapt itself. O, how much the cultured will have to throw overboard as a spiritual luxury that they have come to love! And how very different from us the coming generation will be. It may well be that, to the young, we shall appear very much as the French *émigrés*, intent on a life of pleasure, appeared to those to whom they fled.

Just think how much of all that has been written up to now is going to die out! What novels and dramas are people going to look at? Are the authors, loved by publisher and public alike, because they met and flattered the needs of the century, indeed, of the year and the month, going to survive? Anything that is to live on must contain a goodly portion of the eternal. And if anything lasting is to be created, it can only be through an overwhelmingly powerful effort of real poetry. . . .

Bismarck has only taken into his own hands what would have happened in due course without him and in opposition to him. He saw the growing wave of social democracy would somehow or other bring about a state of naked power, whether through the democrats themselves, or through the governments, and said: *Ipse faciam*, and embarked on three wars, 1864, 1866, 1870.

But we are only at the beginning. Don't you feel that everything we do now seems more or less amateurish, capricious, and becomes increasingly ridiculous by contrast with the high purposefulness of the military machine worked out to the last details? The latter is bound to become the model of existence. It will be most interesting for you, my dear Sir, to observe how the machinery of state and administration is transformed and militarized; for me—how schools and education are put through the cure, etc. Of all classes, the workers are going to have the strangest time; I have a suspicion that, for the time being, sounds completely mad, and yet I cannot rid myself of it: that the military state will have to turn "industrialist." The accumulations of beings, the mounds of men in the yards and factories cannot be left for all eternity in their need and thirst for riches; a planned and controlled degree of poverty, with promotion and uniforms, starting and ending daily to the roll of drums, that is what ought to come logically. (I know enough history, of course, to know that things do not always work out logically.) Of course, what is done will have to be well done—and then no mercy, whether for those above or those below. In the paper yesterday or the day before the program of the carpenters' union in Berlin was given, which you will easily find in the Berlin papers. *Lisez et réflechissez!*

The development of a clever and lasting sovereign power is still in swaddling clothes; it may perhaps wear its *toga virilis* for the first time in Germany. There are still vast uncharted seas to be discovered in this sphere. The Prussian dynasty is so placed that it and its staff can never again be powerful enough. There can be no question of stopping on this path; the salvation of Germany itself is in forging ahead.

IV
The Founding of an Empire

The consummation of national unification in Central Europe was a direct result of the war against France which began in the summer of 1870. Prior to the outbreak of hostilities the prospect of a union between north and south had been receding into the distant future. Public opinion below the Main remained distrustful of Prussian designs and ambitions. Bismarck himself had concluded in a mood of resignation that "if Germany were still to attain her national goal in the nineteenth century, that would seem to me to be something great. And if it were to be in ten or actually five years, that would be something extraordinary, an unexpected gift by the grace of God." Yet the blunders of the French government in the dispute over the Hohenzollern candidacy for the Spanish throne made possible in a few months what the blandishments of Berlin had failed to accomplish in the years since Sadowa. The coming of war led to a revival of national sentiment in Central Europe which had been gradually waning. In the Bavarian legislature a particularist deputy declared enthusiastically that he was now in favor of support for the Prussians: "Yesterday we could still use the pretext that the Spanish question is nothing to us. But already today the desire for war is awaking more and more, and not only in the younger generation. Men with gray hair also feel themselves carried along by the national movement." The common struggle against a foreign enemy created the opportunity to complete the work of national unification which had remained unfinished after the Seven Weeks' War. Bismarck's objectives thus became to use the military struggle against France for the attainment of the political consolidation of Germany.

Most nationalists recognized that the union of north and south would have to be achieved before the war came to an end. For once hostilities were over, the old jealousies and suspicions would promptly reassert themselves. Patriotic sentiments had for the time being gained the upper hand over particularism, but they had not destroyed it. Eduard Lasker, one of the leading liberal politicians in Prussia, emphasized this point a few weeks after the outbreak of the conflict with France:

> It is a task of especially outstanding importance for us that the war unfailingly bring about the transformation of the North German Confederation into the German [Empire]. The line of the Main must fall now and a united Germany must be established. Otherwise our people would be deprived of the prize of struggle and victory. This great task must not be subordinated to either military success or to the moral authority which the war will bring us in any event or to the reacquisition of German lands. . . . There exists the danger that the right moment will be allowed to slip away.

Bismarck, however, had no intention of letting the right moment slip away. Even before the battle of Sedan he began to plan for the entry of the southern states into the North German Confederation. Despite his declaration that negotiations would be conducted "without the exercise of coercion or pressure from any direction," he did not hesitate to use threats as well as concessions in dealing with the governments below the Main. During the autumn months the leaders of the states at war with France concluded treaties providing for the political integration of north and south. Only parliamentary approval was now needed to complete the achievement of national unification.

The particularists tried to make a last stand against the ratification of the treaties in the legislatures of the signatory governments. But the combination of patriotic fervor, military success, and political pressure proved too much for them. They were defeated in one state after another. Many of those who accepted the victory of nationalism, however, were acting out of expediency rather than conviction. Ludwig II, for example, the king of Bavaria, came out in favor of the bestowal of the imperial dignity on the Hohenzollerns. Yet while his avowed motive was love for the Fatherland, in his private correspondence he mentioned other considerations: "If Bavaria could stand alone free from the confederation, then it would make no difference. But since this would be a sheer political impossibility, for the people and the army would oppose it and the crown would therefore lose all support, it is, however frightful and shocking it may be, an act of political wisdom [to accept the inevitable]. It is lamentable that it turned out this way, but it can no longer be changed." The Reichstag of the North German Confederation and the legislatures of the southern states promptly approved the treaties of unification. Only in Munich did particularism put up serious resistance, but there too the nationalists triumphed by the substantial margin of 102 votes to 48. The last obstacle to the establishment of the German Empire had now been removed.

On January 18, 1871, the anniversary of the day a hundred and seventy years before when the Hohenzollerns first assumed the royal title, William I of Prussia received the even more exalted imperial dignity. In the presence of the sovereign rulers of Central Europe and the victorious commanders of the Teutonic armies, the aged monarch was proclaimed German emperor in the Hall of Mirrors in Versailles. The magnificent palace from which the kings of France had once launched their dread campaigns against the Holy Roman Empire now became the scene of the greatest political achievement of their ancient foes. The symbolism of the ceremony which marked the establishment of the new state was not a result of chance. The architects of the German Empire were announcing to the world that the time when rapacious invaders could batten on the spoils of Central Europe was over. Yet the events of that momentous day had still another significance which the participants failed to understand. In a speech before the Reichstag Ludwig Windthorst, a brilliant spokesman for particularism, warned that "Versailles is also the place of the shorn hedges. Gentlemen, I fear that many of those who have guided the shears in this enterprise or who think they have guided them could discover to their surprise that they are the ones who have been shorn." More than that, Versailles was "the birthplace of the military absolutism which Louis XIV brought to its flowering. I of course do not assert, gentlemen, that [this absolutism] is also already here. But I know that the birthplace exerts an important influence on a growing human being. And so I am afraid that this birthplace and the godparents, the cannon before Saint-Denis etc., have nevertheless left some impression on this child."

Here was a point of crucial importance. The unification of Germany had been achieved under the auspices of militarism and authoritarianism. It had become an instrument of those forces in the civic life of Central Europe which sought to maintain the dominant position of crown, army, and aristocracy. The vigor of middle-class liberalism was sapped by victory in battle as much as by defeat in parliament. It would take another century and two world wars before democratic institutions could become firmly rooted in German soil. The form which political consolidation assumed, moreover, had an important effect on foreign as well as domestic affairs. A new military power had suddenly appeared on the European scene combining material might with civic immaturity. The result was bound to be a disturbance of the equilibrium in the international relations of the Continent. The founders of the German Empire, to be sure, were determined to use the great strength of their nation with moderation and restraint. Bismarck was no wild-eyed jingoist bent on conquest. But could anyone feel confident that his successors would be equally cautious? That was the question troubling the capitals of Europe. During the Franco-Prussian War the historian Georg Gottfried Gervinus had spoken of "the peculiar double nature" of the German nation, "which throughout its entire history has so often oscillated between one-sided Teutonism and hazy universalism, self-idolatry and xenophilism, nationalism and humanism, between the warlike mission of a people in arms and the peaceful mission of a people of culture." The founding of the German Empire represented the triumph of the mailed fist over the libertarian principle in the life of Central Europe.

1. Onno Klopp Argues That Germany Has Not Been Unified but Subjugated

The establishment of the North German Confederation failed to convince all Germans that Prussia was the chosen instrument of national consolidation in Central Europe. On the contrary, many of them continued to argue that all Berlin sought was the advantage of the Hohenzollern dynasty without regard for the interests of the nation as a whole. Especially in the south suspicion of Prussian designs remained a powerful force in political life. Onno Klopp, the Hanoverian particularist who had gone into exile when his state lost its independence, insisted that the outcome of the Seven Weeks' War was not the unification but the subjugation of Germany.

THE SUCCESS with which the Prussian expedition against Austria, in 1866, has been crowned, and the subsequent impunity of the unheard of spoliation committed, by the chief of the House of Hohenzollern, upon sovereign German princes, his near relatives and faithful allies, has, as is often the case in this world, where actions are generally measured by the standard of success, induced the general opinion of Europe to pass a milder judgment upon the policy of Bismarck and his king than would otherwise have been the case. In Germany especially, but chiefly in the northern parts of it, the rallying cry of German unity, raised by the wily minister and his pliant tools, took the desired effect, and made the easily swayed multitude look upon a stern and despotic king, who could by no means boast of the love of his people, as a sort of hero, who would regenerate the Fatherland, and with whose reign a new era would begin for united Germany; whilst the most unpopular and hated minister, whom, like Dionisius of Syracus, patriots considered it a virtue to extirpate, became, as with a turn of the enchanted wand, the most popular man throughout the land—a second Brutus who, for the love of his country, had dissimulated his real character for years. The masses, however, were always easily imposed upon by appearances; history shows it, in its fullest extent. Oppression and tyranny were invariably forgiven to the conquering hero by his subjects, and even posterity often looks with an admiring eye upon such men, as Napoleon I, the Czar Peter, Frederick II of Prussia, Charles XII of Sweden, and others.

In the latter part of the nineteenth century, however, when hero

SOURCE: Onno Klopp, *Who Is the Real Enemy of Germany?* (London: John Murray Ltd, 1868), pp. iii–vii.

note problem of alternative

worship has been given up, when even in bigotted Spain the saints
have been taken out of their niches and placed in a heap in a
corner, and political and religious liberty begin to spread their
beneficial wings over the country, it is time for the peoples of
Europe closer to scrutinize the acts and proceedings of their governments and to judge them by a different standard as heretofore,
viz: the interest of the reigning families and their followers.

Thousands of German lives have been sacrificed in the late war
between Prussia and Austria, and what was the object? what the
cause and the effect? According to Count Bismarck, the object of
it was German unity. What mockery! The object of the war was
the aggrandizement of Prussia. The cause of the war was, according to that truth-loving minister, Austrian arrogance. Poor Austria,
beaten by France, threatened by Italy, bullied by Prussia, where
could her arrogance come from?

Now let us come to the effect or result of the war, which was
undertaken by Prussia for the sake of German unity. The victor
invariably dictates the law; the chief article of the treaty of [Nik-
olsburg], dictated by Prussia, is the exclusion of Austria forever
from Germany. Let us well note this fact:—Thirteen million
Germans are for ever excluded from Germany by the dictates of
Prussia. This is certainly a curious way to begin the unification of
Germany by excluding one-fourth part of its inhabitants from the
Fatherland, by forbidding them from calling themselves Germans.
It is clear from this, that the result for Germany, as a whole, was
the loss of one-fourth of the country. Nor was there the slightest
gain for any of the integral parts of Germany. Neither the kingdom of Bavaria, nor the kingdoms of Würtemberg or Saxony, or
any of the smaller states, have gained anything by it; on the contrary, they have lost by the treaties of August 1866, part of their
rights as sovereign and independent States, whilst Hanover, Elec-
toral Hesse, etc., etc., have entirely lost their independence. Who
then gained by the war? Nobody but Prussia; by Prussia is here
meant not the Prussian people, who have only gained an augmenta-
tion of taxes, a deficit in the budget, a further restriction of the
freedom of the press, and of personal liberties. By Prussia is meant
only the dynasty of the Hohenzollerns and their followers; just as
Count Bismark means by German unity, the subjugation of the
best part of Germany by Prussia.

The danger threatens not only Germany alone, but the whole of civilized Europe. The House of Hohenzollern stands not alone with its projects of aggrandizement and dominion; there is another reigning family, (equally unscrupulous and even more powerful, always ready to seize an occasion of extending its dominions, and willing to assist Prussia in her nefarious projects,) which has but lately ordered an increase of its army of the small amount of 240,000 men in times of peace. The Hohenzollern and Romanow Houses are an ever threatening danger to the peace and civilization of Europe. To unmask part of the designs of the Hohenzollern dynasty, to show that they are the real enemies of Germany and of European tranquility, [these] pages have been written. . . . Military and despotic monarchies governed by daring and unscrupulous men have been and may again become scourges of the world, and when ruling over warlike races, the words of the poet may again become true, when he said:—

> *Quidquid delirant reges plectuntur Achivi.*

2. Émile Ollivier Maintains That Bismarck Provoked the Franco-Prussian War in Order to Absorb South Germany

The resistance of the states below the Main to Bismarck's blandishments after 1866 meant that only a powerful new stimulus to national sentiment in Central Europe could bring about the union of north and south. The outbreak of hostilities between France and Germany, for example, might consummate the process of political consolidation which had remained incomplete after Sadowa. That was why Émile Ollivier, who had been prime minister in Paris when the Franco-Prussian War began, maintained long afterward that the conflict had been the result of a clever plot by Bismarck to use patriotic enthusiasm as the means of attaining his political ends. The charge was exaggerated but not entirely unjustified.

IN 1866, on the field of Sadowa, Austria not only lost her former preponderance in the Germanic Confederation, but was excluded therefrom. The intervention of France prevented the victory of Prussia from being complete: she was allowed to annex certain territory, but the states of the south were set outside of her Confederation, and the Main became the artificial boundary between

SOURCE: Émile Ollivier, *The Franco-Prussian War and Its Hidden Causes* (Boston: Little, Brown and Company, 1912), pp. 13, 400–404.

the two sections of Germany. Thenceforth Bismarck's policy had but one object: to destroy that boundary and to throw bridges across the Main whereby the two sections of Germany might be united. With keen and intelligent foresight, he saw that there could be no drawing together of the states of the north and those of the south so long as the gory memories of 1866 stood between them. A campaign made by them in common against France seemed to him the only means of wiping out all trace of these internal dissensions.

For some time he hoped that France would seek such a rencounter, and would try to recover the preponderance of which the victory of Sadowa had deprived her; but France perorated, sulked, and did not stir. . . .

The cause of the conflict between Germany and France was only one of those "artificial fatalities," born of the false conceptions or unhealthy ambitions of statesmen, which with lapse of time become worn out, transformed, and often extinguished. If France had but resolutely made up her mind not to meddle in the affairs of Germany, not to regard German unity as a menace or as a lessening of her own importance, it would have seemed perfectly natural to her that a nation so powerful in every way—in intelligence, imagination, poetry, science, and arms—should shape herself as she chose, with full liberty of spontaneous action.

On the other hand, if the German professors, content with the memories of 1814 and of Waterloo, could but have made up their minds to forget the Palatinate and Jena, on the instant this alleged fatality of war would have vanished, and the only relation between the two nations, established by mutual consent, would have been one of friendly cooperation in the common task of spreading light and of emancipation from real fatalities. That was the hope to which I devoted my conduct in international matters, and which, as minister, I would have brought to fruition had my power endured.

But there was a man to whom it was important that that artificial fatality should exist and should end in war. It was that powerful genius, who, not choosing to abandon to time the glory of achieving slowly the work of unity, whose hour of triumph was inevitable, determined to hasten the evolution, to force upon the present what the future would have accomplished freely, and to retain for himself alone the glory which his successors would otherwise have shared. With him out of the way, war between France and Germany would have ceased to be predestined, and the son of Napoleon III would have escaped it as well as his father.

Napoleon III wanted peace, but with a vacillating will; Bismarck wanted war, with an inflexible will: the inflexible will overcame the vacillating will. A fresh proof, as that profound thinker Gustave Le Bon so forcibly says, that "the faith that raises mountains is named the will. It is the true creator of things."

So that it is a pitiful thing to read these labored dissertations of our trumpery historians, searching for what they call responsibilities, and struggling to incriminate, some the statesmen of the opposition, others those of the government. Unquestionably the opposition were so short-sighted as to keep alive an irritable agitation in men's minds; unquestionably the Emperor should not have reopened, by a fruitless demand of guaranties, a question already closed by a triumphant solution. But neither the declamations of the opposition, nor the mistake of Napoleon III, were the decisive cause of the war. No Frenchman was responsible for it. The only man who will have the glory or the shame of it, whichever posterity may adjudge it to be, is the man of iron, whose indomitable and heroic will controlled events and made them serve his ambition.

Demosthenes said to the Athenians: "Let an orator rise and say to you: 'It is Diopithus who causes all your ills; it is Chares, or Aristophone,' or any other that it pleases him to name, and instantly you applaud and exclaim loudly, 'Oh! how truly he speaks!' But let a plain-spoken man say to you: 'O Athenians! the sole author of your ills is Philip'—that truth angers you; it is even as an arrow that wounds you." And I say to our Athenians: "The war was let loose upon us neither by Diopithus, nor by Chares, nor by Aristophon, but by Philip, and in 1870 Philip's name was Bismarck."

One of Bismarck's panegyrists, Johannes, Scherr, has described most excellently the character that should be attributed to the creator of German unity.

> After producing so many giants of thought, Germany was destined to produce, at last, a hero of deeds. In the age of the Reformation, and later, we had had an abundance of idealists, but not a politician. We lacked the practical genius, the genius unhampered by schedules. Yes, just that, in very truth! For reflecting and experienced men must needs leave where it deserves to be,

that is to say, in the child's primer, the worn-out commonplace which declares that "the most honest politician is the best." There has never been such a thing as an honest politician, in the ordinary sense of the phrase, and there ought never to be. The creative statesman should perform his allotted task without taking pains to find out whether his adversaries consider it "dishonest," or whether it is unpleasant or harmful to them. It is not the ethereal arguments of a subjective idealism, but stern realities, super-prosaic material interests, as well as commonplace and exalted passions, which in combination make the science of statecraft.

Thus would Bismarck have liked to be praised—in such terms it is fitting to speak of that extraordinary man, the craftiest of foxes, the boldest of lions, who had the art of fascinating and of terrifying, of making of truth itself an instrument of falsehood; to whom gratitude, forgiveness of injuries, and respect for the vanquished were as entirely unknown as all other noble sentiments save that of devotion to his country's ambition; who deemed legitimate everything that contributes to success and who, by his contempt for the importunities of morality, dazzled the imagination of mankind.

After the affair of the duchies, as our ambassador, Talleyrand, was seeking some roundabout phrase by which to express a certain degree of disapproval, "Don't put yourself out," said Bismarck, "nobody but my king thinks that I acted honorably."

Esthetically, I like him thus. So long as he denies the evidence, plays the virtuous, the guileless man, outdoes himself in tartufferie, he lowers himself to the point of making himself contemptible. As soon as he reveals his true self and boasts of his audacious knaveries which raised his Germany, until then divided and impotent, to the first rank among the nations, then he is as great as Satan—a Satan beautiful to look upon. Bismarck hatching in the dark the Hohenzollern candidacy, without a suspicion that war will inevitably be the result, would be a zany to be hooted at; Bismarck devising that same plot because it is the sole means of causing the outbreak of the war which he must have in order to achieve the unity of his Fatherland, is a mighty statesman, of sinister but impressive grandeur. He will not thereby have opened for himself the gates of any paradise; he will have won forever one of the most exalted places in the German pantheon of terrestrial apotheoses.

3. William I Speaks before the Reichstag at the Outbreak
of Hostilities

The advent of a military conflict in which the Hohenzollerns appeared to be victims of the aggressive designs of Napoleon III had the effect of reviving the feeling of nationalism in Central Europe. In the address with which William I opened a special session of the Reichstag of the North German Confederation on July 19, 1870, the monarch touched on those themes which were most likely to encourage a *rapprochement* between north and south. He spoke of the peaceful intentions of his government, of the unreasonable demands of the French cabinet, and of the unshakable determination of all Germans on both sides of the Main to resist foreign presumptuousness. The words were designed to strengthen the sense of unity which the coming of the war had engendered.

ON WELCOMING YOU, in the name of the confederate governments on your last assembling in this place, I was in a position to declare, with joyful thankfulness, that my sincere efforts to meet the wishes of the people and the requirements of civilization by preventing any breach of the peace, had, by God's help, not been unsuccessful.

If, notwithstanding this, the menace and danger of war have imposed on the confederate governments the duty of summoning you to an extraordinary session, you as well as ourselves will have the lively convictions that the North German Confederation were endeavoring to develop the national strength of the German people not to endanger but to become a strong support of the general peace; and that if we call upon these popular energies now to defend our independence, we are only following the dictates of honor and duty.

The candidature of a German prince to the Spanish throne, whose proposal and withdrawal of whom the Confederation governments were equally strangers, and was only so far of interest to the North German Confederation, that the government of that friendly nation seemed to build upon it the hope of finding therein the guarantee for the orderly and peaceful government of a country which had undergone many trials, has afforded a pretext to the

SOURCE: Edward Hertslet, *The Map of Europe by Treaty*, 4 vols. (London: Butterworths, 1875–91), vol. III, pp. 1881–1882.

government of the Emperor of the French to put forward the *casus belli* in a manner long unknown in diplomatic intercourse, and in spite of the removal of this pretext, to adhere to it with that disregard of the rights of the people to the blessings of peace, or which history furnishes analogous examples in the case of former rulers of France.

If Germany in past centuries has silently borne with such outrages upon her rights and honor, she did so because in her disunion she knew not how strong she was. Today, when the bands of intellectual and just unity, which the wars of freedom began to draw together, binds the German races indeed closer, and therefore more intimately: today, when the armaments of Germany no longer leave an opening to the enemy, Germany possesses in herself the will and the power to repulse renewed acts of French violence.

This language is dictated by no boasting spirit, the confederate governments and myself act in the full assurance that victory and defeat rest with the Ruler of Battles. We have weighed with a steadfast gaze the responsibility which awaits, before the judgment seat of God and of men, him who forces two great and peace-loving peoples in the heart of Europe into a devastating war. The German, as well as the French people, both of them equally enjoying and desiring the blessings of Christian civilization and increasing prosperity, should be destined to a more holy contest than the bloody one of arms. Yet the governing power of France have known how to work on the well-balanced but susceptible feelings of our great neighboring people by calculated misrepresentation for personal interests and passions.

The more confederated governments have felt that they have done all which honor and dignity permit to maintain for Europe the blessings of peace; and the clearer it appears to all eyes that the sword has been forced into our hand, with greater confidence we turn, supported by the unanimous will of the German government of the south, as well as of the north, to the love of the Fatherland and willingness for sacrifice of the German people to the summons to protect her honor and independence.

We will, after the examples of our father, do battle for our freedom and our right against the violence of a foreign conqueror; and in this struggle, in which we have no good but the attainment of lasting peace for Europe, God will be with us as He was with our fathers.

4. The Crown Princess of Prussia Is Delighted at the
Defeat of France

The national enthusiasm aroused by the coming of the war was soon
intensified by the brilliant victories won through the common effort of
soldiers from all parts of Germany. The comradeship of arms established on the field of battle prepared the way for the political union of
north and south. A few days after Sedan the crown princess of Prussia
wrote to her mother, Queen Victoria of England, that the downfall of
Napoleon III was a just retribution for Gallic frivolity and irresponsi-
bility. Yet more than that, the triumph of the German armies must
lead to the annexation of Alsace-Lorraine and the consummation of
national unity. Although the princess had been a bitter opponent of
Bismarck, patriotic exultation transformed her for the time being into
a supporter of his policy.

WHAT ASTOUNDING NEWS! Really I could hardly believe my ears,
when I heard it. Here the excitement and delight of the people
know no bounds. Poor Emperor! his career has ended, and he
brought his fall upon himself, and one cannot but pity him—especially for having been the unhappy cause of so much bloodshed
and so much woe, which never, never can be cured! So many
hearths made dismal, so many happy homes miserable, so many
hearts broken, and above all, so many unfortunate men groaning in
untold suffering! Unhappy Emperor! he has all this to answer for,
and yet he is a kind-hearted and feeling man! He has done the best
thing he could for himself under the circumstances, he is *sure* of
the most chivalrous and generous treatment at the hands of the
King, and he has of his own free will surrendered to his equal,
which is not so humiliating as being driven from throne and
country by an infuriated populace. Such a downfall is a melancholy thing, but it is meant to teach deep lessons; may we all learn
what frivolity, conceit, and immorality lead to! The French people
have trusted in their own excellence, have completely deceived
themselves; where is their army, where are their statesmen? They
despised and hated the Germans whom they considered it quite
lawful to insult; how they have been punished!
    Whether the war be at an end or no, we do not know, having

SOURCE: George Earle Buckle, ed., *The Letters of Queen Victoria:
Second Series*, 3 vols. (London and New York: John Murray Ltd,
1926–28), vol. II, pp. 58–61. Reprinted by permission of the publisher.

had no letters or details since these last events; but as there is no French army left, I do not see with whom we are to fight? The march to Paris is continued and what difficulties our army will have to encounter there I do not the least know. It would be grievous for art's sake were that beautiful capital to suffer; I trust it will not come to that. Whether the republic will be inclined to make peace, who can tell? I fear not. What has become of the Empress and Prince Imperial we have not heard; poor things, I hope they are in safety; they will most likely never see their lovely Paris again! When I think of '48 and '55, and even of last December, when I last saw the Emperor and Empress, it seems like a dream. But even then everyone felt that the Empire was standing, as it were, on a barrel of gunpowder and that the least spark would set fire to the whole thing, and no wonder that with such triflers as the Duc de Gramont and MM. Ollivier and Benedetti the conflagration soon began. Had the Emperor been his former self and held the reins of government tightly, it would perhaps not have happened; but his health and energy are gone; he was grown apathetic and incapable of directing matters himself, and, *as despotism always falls*, his reign has ended—more like the bursting of a soap bubble, than the fall of a mighty monument, which buries all beneath its ruins. What a retribution it seems for the bloody drama of Mexico and for the treatment of the Orleans!

Voices are loud *everywhere* in all classes in defense of Germany regaining her old provinces of Elsass and Lothringen. I cannot say I think it is a good thing; but I do not see how the government are to resist the resolute determination of the German nation to wrest them back at all hazards! I have been to Frankfort today over the hospitals and seeing different notabilities; everybody is most patriotic.

We have now no less than 120,000 French prisoners in Germany! is it not marvellous? Add to that more than fifty generals and the sovereign himself. And even *now*, the French *will not* believe that they have been really and fairly defeated; they attribute it all to chance and accident and deny each of our victories. . . .

All this misery draws hearts closer together and brings together those who in happy and quiet days would have passed one another without taking any notice. The feeling of belonging to *one great* nation for the first time obliterates all feelings of north, south, high and low, all particularism; this I must say is very delicious to experience; simplifies all things and gives a new impulse to all exer-

tions. Poor Germany! she has dearly bought her unity and
independence with the blood of her sons. It is a great satisfaction to
me to see how Prussian *Wesen*, discipline, habits, etc. etc., is now
appreciated and seen in its true light; its superiority acknowledged
with pleasure and pride, instead of jealousy, fear, scorn and hatred.
We owe to Frederick the Great and his father, to Scharnhorst,
Stein, and Hardenberg, what we are, and we said it with gratitude
and not in vainglory or conceit. We are worthy of England's
sympathy and approbation, and feel sure that it will not long be
withheld from us. Fritz [the crown prince] writes that he has seen
many letters which have been seized from one French officer to
another, giving the most awful description of the French army, as
regards honesty and morality. The stealing and plundering that
goes on is incredible, *not only* among the Turcos. . . .

When I think of the Emperor and Empress in the zenith of their
glory, in '55 and at the time of the exhibition when all the sovereigns in Europe paid them their court, and they were so amiable
and courteous to all, it seems a *curious* contrast! Gay and charming
Paris! *What* mischief that very court, and still more that very
attractive Paris, has done to English society, to the stage and to
literature! *What harm* to the young and brilliant aristocracy of
London! It would be well if they would pause and think that
immoderate frivolity and luxury depraves and ruins and ultimately
leads to a national misfortune. Our poverty, our dull towns, our
plodding, hardworking *serious life*, has made us strong and determined; is wholesome for us. I should grieve were we to imitate
Paris and be so taken up with pleasure that no time was left for self-
examination and serious thought! Ancient history teaches the same
lesson as modern history—a hard and stern one for those who have
to learn it by sad experience; the poor Emperor has leisure now to
study it!

5. Prince Hohenlohe in the Bavarian Legislature Advocates Union with the North

Bismarck had recognized from the outset that the war with France
offered a unique opportunity to defeat the forces of particularism in
the south and complete the work of national unification. Negotiations

Source: *Memoirs of Prince Chlodwig of Hohenlohe-Schillingsfuerst*, 2
vols. (New York: Macmillan, 1906), vol. II, pp. 34–38.

between Berlin and the governments below the Main began in earnest after the defeat of Napoleon III. In the course of the fall, agreements were reached regarding the terms under which the southern states would join the North German Confederation. Prince Hohenlohe, the Bavarian statesman who had long been an advocate of collaboration with Prussia, argued in the upper house of the legislature in Munich that the Wittelsbach kingdom should sacrifice its independence for the sake of national unity.

I INTEND to vote for the acceptance of the convention, and if I venture to justify my action by a few words, it is not with the intention of proving to you that these conventions do not infringe the independence of Bavaria. I agree with the previous speaker that the independence of Bavaria, or, in better words, the isolated position of Bavaria in Germany is more permanently shaken by this convention than it has been by any constitutional or international federation in which Bavaria has been involved since the conclusion of the Peace of Westphalia. But, my lords, it seems to me that the question is not whether Bavarian independence is endangered by this convention and whether we must therefore reject it, but that the question should be formulated as follows: Shall we accept this convention notwithstanding the limitations upon our independence which it involves? This question I must answer with a decided affirmative. I base my arguments, not upon the reasons which the proposer has adduced in favor of acceptance, but upon the facts before us. But I beg of you not to misunderstand me. I am no blind worshipper of success. I think that my political past is evidence of the fact. If I, therefore, speak of the deciding power of historical facts, I refer, not merely to the great events of this year, but to the whole course of German development. It seems to me that two facts, above all others, have tended to guide German policy into new paths, to modify the position of Bavaria, as it has developed during recent centuries, and to unite the country more closely to Germany.

One of these facts is the awakened spirit of nationalism throughout the German people, and the other is the changed position of the German Great Powers. When Bavaria became a kingdom in 1806 she reached the highest point of that policy which I have styled isolation, and which found its explanation, if not its justification, in the general condition of the German Empire and the absence of any national feeling. The German Federation had been tottering since the Peace of Westphalia, and it finally collapsed entirely. Bavaria had, formally at least, attained full sovereignty. Yet a few years afterwards the kingdom surrendered important rights in favor of the German Federation, and the deciding motive in this case was respect for the growing sense of nationality throughout the German people. When the war of liberation had begun, it was impossible to continue the policy of the Rhine Federation. In the year 1866, after the dissolution of the German Federation, when Bavaria for the second time secured a doubtful freedom to determine her own course, the kingdom immediately hastened to sacrifice the independence she had secured in the convention of August 22, apparently guided by the idea that German nationalism would make the pursuit of any other policy impossible except that which was expressed in the convention. You also, my lords, were witnesses of a similar turning point in Bavarian history in the autumn of 1867, when the renewal of the customs union and the acceptance or refusal of the conventions therewith connected came before you for discussion.

The majority of you at that time could not decide to secure that economic isolation of Bavaria which would necessarily have resulted in political isolation. After serious doubts, you made your determination and voted as you did, because a non-German policy was no longer possible in a German state. When in the summer of this year the decisive moment approached and it seemed possible for the last time to enter upon a course which would have replaced Bavaria in the position of 1806, you resisted the temptations which one party placed before the Bavarian people and which are rightly termed unpatriotic. You rejected that neutrality which would have led to an alliance with France, and unanimously resolved to embark upon that course which was not only the course of honor for ourselves, but has become the path of honor and of imperishable glory for our army. At that time a political opponent cried to me: "Now the German Empire is complete." The prophecy has been fulfilled, not, as a previous speaker has observed, because military alliance necessarily implies subordination to the power of the stronger ally; it has been fulfilled because German nationalism has become a power in this war and a force to which the preference for long-standing institutions must give way, and before which the antipathetic tendencies of the German races have disappeared.

This consciousness of nationality is no mere abstraction; it has

found a practical basis in the rising power of the House of Hohenzollern. As the position of Bavaria within the German Empire resulted from the decay of the imperial power, so was the position of
Bavaria in the German alliance the result of the dualism; in the
rivalry of the two great German powers lay the reason and principle of Bavarian independence during the last fifty years. Then, in
1866, the success of the Prussian armies broke the tie and excluded
Austria from Germany, and the predominance of Prussia in Germany was no longer doubtful. Since that date Bavaria was confronted with the choice either of joining the efforts of those who
wished to destroy the results of 1866 by a renewed struggle or of
facing the facts as they were and attempting to secure the most
favorable position for Bavarian independence.

You know, my lords, that I am of the latter opinion, and you
know the efforts which the Bavarian government has made during
my tenure of office to secure this object. If these efforts have remained unsuccessful, I cannot entirely acquit my political opponents at home and abroad of all blame. The small sacrifice at the
price of which union with North Germany was to be attained
seemed to my political opponents at home to imply an undue
limitation of our independence; my foreign opponents who were
able to make their influence felt regarded this sacrifice as an
infringement of the Peace of [Nikolsburg].

The phrase which solved the problem at that time was the
maintenance of the *status quo*, which was uttered not without
some secret hope of the restoration of the *status quo ante*, that is to
say, of the restoration of a condition similar to the old German
Federation, and implying the overthrow of Prussia. These plans
and hopes were defeated by the power of the Prussian people and
army, which our opponents underestimated, by the national spirit
of southern Germany, and finally and especially by the noble resolve made by our king in July of this year; those hopes have now
been buried in the battles of the German war and in the conventions of Versailles. These conventions, however, are not the result
of north German treachery or of south German weakness; they
are, and I think I have demonstrated the fact, the natural result of
an historical development in which neither the individual nor states
of the size of Bavaria can possibly interfere.

As regards the several articles of the convention, I do not propose a detailed consideration, the less so as I have no intention of

proposing any changes in the measure or of supporting such changes if they should be brought forward. I am ready openly to admit that the value of many of those rights reserved for Bavaria herself in the convention seems to me more than doubtful. I could have wished that less stress had been laid upon securing particularism, upon maintaining special institutions and fragments of legislation for the Bavarian government as such; I should have preferred to see more stress laid upon the participation of Bavaria as a federal member of the German community in the administration of the affairs of the Federation.

As I have said, I do not wish to criticize; on the contrary, I hasten to express my belief that the men who have brought this convention forward under great difficulties have performed a most meritorious service; for the details of the convention are overshadowed by the great achievement implied in the new foundation of the German Empire. The foundation has now been laid on which Germany may rise to a great future, and the generous initiative of our king, together with the unqualified assent of the German princes, is a guarantee that the new German Empire will become a real and vital force. Our votes today are to secure that this empire will be based upon a strong central government and a free representative assembly; from henceforward the fruitless agitations of particularism will be replaced by a German policy in which we can loyally and honorably cooperate. As His Royal Highness* has justly observed, a firmly established German Empire will be able to open those permanent friendly relations with the neighboring Empire of Austria-Hungary which are the sole guarantee for the peace of Europe; henceforward every German may pride himself in every quarter of the globe upon the fact that he is a citizen of the German Empire, an empire protecting his person and working in his interest. If these objects are attained, then, my lords, we can truly say that by voting for this convention we have helped to the accomplishment of a great object, and that the blood and tears which this war has caused have not been shed in vain.

* A reference to the speech of Prince Ludwig of Bavaria, who spoke before the prince rose.

6. The Crown Prince of Prussia Describes the Proclamation of the German Empire

The complicated negotiations among the allies in the war against France ended at last with the union of north and south to form the German Empire. On January 18, 1871, while the cannon boomed around beleaguered Paris, the princes of Central Europe gathered in the Hall of Mirrors in Versailles to proclaim William I ruler of the new state. In his diary the heir to the Prussian throne described the events of that momentous day marking the triumph of a national movement which had begun within the lifetime of some of those present at the ceremony. A major political power was making its first appearance on the European stage.

THE CEREMONY may in the strictest sense of the word be called unique, and I am truly rejoiced to have lived to see it. Only in the course of time shall we realize its full importance, what it means to have witnessed in the stately *Salle des Glaces* of Louis XIV's Palace at Versailles the reestablishment of the German Empire achieved on the French battlefields and the proclamation of the chosen, hereditary emperor.

There were present at Versailles today, besides the King and myself, and with us Prince Karl and Prince Adalbert: the Grand Dukes of Baden, Saxe-Weimar and Oldenburg, the Dukes of Saxe-Coburg, Saxe-Meiningen and Saxe-Altenburg, the Princes of Schaumburg-Lippe and Schwartzburg-Rudolstadt, the Crown Prince and Prince Georg of Saxony, the Princes Otto, Luitpold and Leopold of Bavaria, the Princes Wilhelm and August and the Dukes Eugen, father and son, of Württemberg, the Landgrave Friedrich zu Hesse, the Hereditary Grand Dukes of Saxe-Weimar, Mecklenburg-Schwerin, Mecklenburg-Strelitz and Oldenburg, the Hereditary Princes of Hohenzollern, Anhalt, Saxe-Meiningen and the Duke Friedrich zu Schleswig-Holstein. Absent were: Prince Friedrich Karl, as also the Princes Albrecht, father and son, who are still in the field against the enemy, and besides these the Prince zu Hohenzollern, whose invalid state prevents his taking part in the

SOURCE: From the book *Emperor Frederick II: The War Diary of the Emperor Frederick II*, translated by Alfred Richmond Allison (Frederick A. Stokes and Company, 1926), pp. 270–273. Reprinted by courtesy of J. B. Lippincott Company.

war and in this great day, which sees the fulfilment of his ardent
desires also. All the above-named assembled in the *appartements de
la Reine*, which the company reached by the stairway famous
under the name of the *escalier de marbre*, occupied by doubled
guards posted at successive stages, to wait the King's arrival in the
Salle du sacre de Napoleon I. Fires burned everywhere in the open
grates, but diffused only a moderate degree of warmth. While we
were waiting for His Majesty, Prince Karl communicated to me a
note sent him by the King, in which the latter notified that, as he
was today assuming with the designation of "Emperor" only the
outward form of that dignity, as a major sometimes takes brevet
rank as lieutenant-colonel, this title had no wide signification, and
therefore would make no alteration whatever either in the designation of the royal family or in my own! Typical of the difference
between the formal recognition and the real significance of today's
ceremony is the wording of the official notification from the court
chamberlain, which ran: "The ceremony of installation will be
held in the Hall of Mirrors at the Palace of Versailles at midday
twelve o'clock, a short prayer and after that the proclamation,"
etc. The whole of our domestic household had earnestly begged to
be allowed to attend the ceremony, a request I gladly granted. The
mounted military gendarmes asked expressly to be allowed to ride
before my carriage, a privilege I also accorded to my dragoon
escort; so it was with a highly imposing cavalcade I made a formal
entry into the *Cour Royale*. I had given leave to all men of the
garrison not on duty to promenade as they chose between the
préfecture and the palace, so as to be able to see the King; thus we
arrived at the latter between a regular lane of soldiers. Cannon
salvoes, however, I could not sanction because of the numbers of
wounded men lying here. The dress ordered for the occasion was
tunic, helmet, sash, and decorations; but I had not laid aside my
high boots even for today, but retained this service equipment,
nevertheless wearing the English garter at the knee in honor of my
wife and as an omen of an intimate union of the Empire with
England. The guard of honor in the *Cour Royale* and to escort the
colors was supplied by the gallant Royal Grenadier regiment. The
King appeared in the uniform of the 1st Guards regiment, with the
ribbon of the Order of the Black Eagle, which, considering its
special connection with the war, implies a good deal; besides this,
he wore today many German orders, stars and crosses, but along

with these the insignia of the Russian Order of St. George. To begin with, he addressed the German princes in some words of thanks for their share in adding importance to the ceremony in hand; after which we followed him to the *Salle des Glaces.*

In the salons and the *Chambre à coucher de la Reine* was stationed the guard of the King's staff as guard of honor. In the *Salle des Glaces*, to the left if one came in from the *Salon de la Paix*, and with backs to the window, stood the Prussian and Bavarian non-commissioned officers and men appearing as deputations, and over against them the officers—all decorated with the Iron Cross. As, over and above these, all officers and officials who were not on duty and could be got at in cantonments had permission to be here today, the gigantic hall was so full that the *Salon de la Paix* had also to be used. The platform was at the opposite end in front of the *Salon de la Guerre*. In the central window stood a field altar, before which the King took his stand, surrounded in a half-circle by all the princes, and where Chaplain Rogge from Potsdam was to read the abridged liturgy and offer a simple prayer. As the order to the men, "Off helmets for prayer," had been forgotten, I was obliged myself to give it out loud, on which the choir of singers, made up of musicians from the different regiments here, accompanied by the band of military music, struck up the hymn *Sei Lob und Ehr* with fine effect in these great rooms. But the "simple prayer" consisted of a criticism of Louis XIV, with a rather tactless and tedious historical-religious dissertation on the significance of the 18th January for Prussia; the conclusion, which dwelt upon the German question and its solution as affected by today's event, struck another note by its fervent and effective language. During this part of the ceremony I let my eyes wander over the assembly and turn to the ceiling where Louis XIV's self-glorifications, expressed in allegories and explanatory boastful inscriptions, have for special contrast the disruption of Germany, and asked myself more than once if it was really true that we were at Versailles to witness there the reestablishment of the German Empire—so like a dream did the whole thing seem to me.

Then, after the Te Deum had been sung, the King proceeded, followed by us all, to the platform erected before the *Salon de la Guerre*, on which the noncommissioned officers with the flags and standards were already posted, and summoned the ensign with the shot-riddled colors of the 1st battalion of the Foot Guards regiment, as well as the three of his Grenadier regiment, one of whom carried another no less torn, to come right up to him, so that they stood close behind His Majesty and elbow to elbow with me. To right and left of these specially conspicuous central groups the German reigning princes and hereditary princes took their place, behind whom again the flags and standards were lined up.

After His Majesty had read aloud in the familiar fashion a short address to the German sovereigns, Count Bismarck came forward, looking in the grimmest of humors, and read out in an expressionless, businesslike way and without any trace of warmth or feeling for the occasion, the address "to the German people." At the words "Enlarger of the Empire," I noticed a quiver stir the whole assemblage, which otherwise stood there without a word.

Then the Grand Duke of Baden came forward with the unaffected, quiet dignity that is so peculiarly his, and, with uplifted right hand, cried in a loud voice: "Long live His Imperial Majesty the Emperor William!" A thundering hurrah, at the least six times repeated, shook the room, while the flags and standards waved above the head of the new Emperor of Germany and *Heil dir im Siegerkranz* rang out. The moment was extraordinarily affecting, indeed overwhelming, and was in every way wonderfully fine. I bent a knee before the Emperor and kissed his hand, whereupon he raised me and embraced me with deep emotion. My feelings I cannot describe, all quite understood them; even among the flag bearers I remarked unmistakable signs of emotion.

Then the princes, one after the other, offered their congratulations, which the King accepted with a friendly handshake, a sort of defile past being formed, though never really marshalled properly because of the unavoidable crush. Next the King went along the line of flags and their bearers; then he stepped down from the platform and, making his way down the hall, spoke a few words in passing to the officers and men standing on either side. I had sent orders to the band, directly the Emperor was on the point of leaving the hall, to play the Hohenfriedberg march, so that His Majesty parted from the assemblage to the strains of that noble air, and finally left the palace amid the cheers of the staff guard of honor.

7. Henrik Ibsen Is Afraid of German Militarism

There were some people in Germany and many more outside who considered it a bad omen that national unification had been achieved in Central Europe as the fruit of military success and under the aegis of authoritarian rule. They saw the danger that a powerful new nation born on the field of battle might use its great strength for irresponsible and aggressive purposes. The famous Norwegian dramatist Henrik Ibsen shared this concern. In a poem written during the Franco-Prussian War he expressed his fear of German militarism. Behind the brilliance of Bismarck's successes and Moltke's victories he beheld the specter of future armed conflict on the Continent.

> *Then think of our own day's heroes,*
> *of these Blumenthals and Fritzes,*
> *of the Herren Generale*
> *number this and number that!*
> *Under Prussia's ghastly colours—*
> *sorrow's clout of black and white—*
> *ne'er burst forth achievement's larvae*
> *as the butterfly of song.*
> *They perhaps their silk may spin*
> *for a time, but die therein.*
>
> *Just in victory lies defeat;*
> *Prussia's sword proves Prussia's scourge.*
> *Ne'er poetic inspiration*
> *springs from problems that they solve.*
> *Deeds win no response in song,*
> *if a people noble, free,*
> *beauty-loving, are transformed*
> *into staff-machinery,—*
> *bristling with the dirks of cunning*
> *from the time that Herr von Moltke*
> *murdered battle's poesy.*
>
> *So demonic is the power*
> *that received our world to rule:*
> *and the Sphinx, her wisdom guarding,*
> *when her riddle's solved, is slain.*
>
> *Cipher-victories are doomed.*
> *Soon the moment's blast will veer;*
> *like a storm on desert-plain*
> *it will fell the false gods' race.*

SOURCE: Henrik Isben, "Balloon Letter," *English Review*, 18 (1914): 511–512.

> Bismarck and the other old ones
> will, like Memnon's column-stumps,
> stiff on saga-chair be sitting
> songless to the morning sun.

8. William I Defines the Mission of the New State

The architects of national unification in Central Europe, however, regarded the establishment of the empire as the beginning of an era of political stability and material progress. After the conclusion of hostilities, William I opened the first meeting of the Reichstag of a united Germany with a speech emphasizing the peaceful mission of the new state. The victories of the future, he suggested, would have to be won on the battlefields of diplomacy, industry, and scholarship. Those who heard the aged monarch's words were moved by the vision of a powerful but magnanimous nation confidently facing its destiny. In fact this assessment of the fate awaiting the German Empire proved overoptimistic.

IN SEEING assembled around me for the first time the German Reichstag, after the glorious but severe struggle which Germany has victoriously maintained in the cause of her independence, I feel myself bound, first of all, to express my humble thanks to God for the world-renowned success with which he has blessed the faithful unity of the German allies, the heroism and discipline of our army and the willing sacrifices of the German people.

We have accomplished what has been since the time of our fathers the ambition of Germany: unity and organization, security of our frontier, independence of our national development.

The consciousness of her unity had always lived, though concealed, in the German people; it burst forth in the enthusiasm with which the whole nation rose to defend the threatened Fatherland, and on the battlefields of France registered in indelible characters its will to become and to remain one people.

The spirit which governs the German people and pervades their culture and civilization, not less than the constitution of the empire and its military establishments, preserves Germany amidst its victories from all attempts to abuse the power which it has won by its unity. The respect which Germany claims for its own independence it is ready to accord to the independence of all other states and peoples, be they weak or strong. New Germany, as she has come out

SOURCE: *British and Foreign State Papers*, 62 (1871–72): 1239–1241.

of the fiery ordeal of the present war, will be a sure guarantee of the peace of Europe, inasmuch as she is strong and self-conscious enough to testify that the administration of her own affairs is her exclusive as well as ample and satisfying inheritance. . . .

The honorable duty of the first German Reichstag will, first of all, be to heal, as far as possible, the wounds inflicted by the war, and to give substantial proof of the Fatherland's gratitude towards those who purchased the victory with their blood and their lives. You will, at the same time, Gentlemen, begin the labors, in which the representatives of the German Empire will cooperate in the completion of the task assigned to you by the constitution, viz., the defense of the existing laws of Germany and the care of the well-being of the German people.

The preparatory labors for the regular legislation have unfortunately suffered delays and interruptions on account of the war; the proposals which will be laid before you, therefore, spring directly from the new organization of Germany.

The isolated constitutional regulations contained in the several treaties of November last will find their regular place and proper expression in a new framing of the constitution of the Empire. The share of each confederate state in the expenses of the Empire requires a legal decision. Your assistance will be required for the introduction proposed by the Bavarian government of North German laws into Bavaria. The dispositions concerning the war indemnity to be paid by France will be made with your consent, the necessities of the Empire and the just claims of its members being taken into consideration, and the accounts of the expenses incurred in the war will be laid before you as soon as circumstances will permit.

The position of the regained German territory will require a series of regulations, the bases of which must be determined by the Imperial Legislature. A law concerning the pensions of officers and soldiers, and concerning the support of those they have left behind will regulate equally for the whole German army the claims of those who have by their devotion to the Fatherland equally deserved the thanks of the nation.

Gentlemen, may the restoration of the German Empire be the omen of new greatness for Germany; may the war of the German Empire, which we have so gloriously carried on be followed by a no less glorious peace, and may the task of the German people ever remain to prove themselves the victors in the struggle for the blessings of peace.

May God grant this!

9. Bismarck Declares That His Nation Has Now Achieved Its Legitimate Objectives

Bismarck believed that victory in the war against France had given the German Empire all the territorial gains it could reasonably demand. It was now a satisfied state which had succeeded in realizing its legitimate aspirations. Henceforth the task facing Berlin would be the preservation of what had been achieved. This was the theme on which the chancellor dwelt after the return of peace in a conversation with the British ambassador, Odo Russell. He even went so far as to say that he considered the English system of administration superior to the German, although that was no doubt a polite compliment rather than a heartfelt conviction.

In the first instance he wished to solicit my cooperation in contradicting calumny. It had been reported to him that the queen of Holland who, for incomprehensible reasons of her own was a bitter enemy of Prussia and of German unity, had succeeded during her frequent visits to England in propagating the idea that Prussia sought to annex the Netherlands with a view to acquiring colonies and a fleet for Germany, and Her Majesty had even persuaded Monsieur Rouher* to commit himself to the statement that Germany wanted the Zuider Sea. This idea was utterly unfounded. No German government could ever desire, nor would public opinion ever consent to the annexation of the Netherlands to the German Empire. Germany had long struggled for national unity and now that it was happily established, he thought forty millions of united Germans were sufficient to maintain the national independence they had acquired without having to resort to the conquest of peaceful industrious and friendly neighbors like the Dutch.

He neither desired colonies or fleets for Germany. Colonies in

Source: Paul Knaplund, ed., *Letters from the Berlin Embassy, 1871–1874, 1880–1885* (Washington, D.C.: USGPO, 1944), pp. 87–89.

* Eugene Rouher (1814–1884), close friend of Napoleon III and sometimes called the vice emperor; under the Republic he returned to France and led the Bonapartist party in the chamber of deputies, in which he sat (1872–1881).

his opinion would only be a cause of weakness, because colonies could only be defended by powerful fleets, and Germany's geographical position did not necessitate her development into a first class maritime power. A fleet was sufficient for Germany that could cope with fleets like those of Austria, Egypt, Holland, and perhaps Italy, scarcely with that of Russia, but it could not be a German interest so long as she had no colonies to rivalize with maritime powers like England, America, or France. Many colonies had been offered to him, he had rejected them and wished only for coaling stations acquired by treaty from other nations.

Germany was now large enough and strong enough in his opinion, and even the Emperor William's insatiable desire for more territory had not led him to covet the possession of the Netherlands.

He had had trouble & vexation enough to combat the Emperor's desire to annex the German provinces of Austria, the population of which certainly desired to form part of the great German family, but that desire he would oppose so long as he was in power, because he preferred the alliance and friendship of Austria to the annexation of provinces that would add nothing to the strength and security of Germany and the loss of which would lessen the value of Austria as an ally.

The Swiss, for instance, were a German-speaking nation, but Switzerland was of greater value as an independent friendly neighbor to Germany than as a province of the German Empire.

After the Danish War the Emperor had not spoken to him for a week so displeased was His Majesty with him for not having annexed a larger portion of Denmark. In his opinion Germany had too many Danish-speaking subjects and he would willingly pay out of his own pocket to rid Germany of them, but public opinion would not yet allow a German minister to give up any portion of territory so recently acquired. In like manner he held that Germany had too many Polish subjects, but how to deal with them was a question which must depend on the success of the measures now under discussion for the neutralization of the antinational Roman Catholic element in the new Empire. It was now evident that the strength of Germany was in the Protestant north, her weakness in the Catholic south.

Prince Bismarck paused and puffed away the smoke from his long meerschaum pipe for some time in silence, and then he added in measured terms: "Our honor may compell us to deal differently with the south of Germany than we originally wished or intended." He then rang his bell, called for a bottle of beer and another pipe and went on to . . . repeat his grievance against his imperial master for resisting the introduction of a system of administration under a responsible premier as in England which he (Prince Bismarck) considered the best method of developing the political education of the Germans and teaching them the art of self-government. If, however, he should have the misfortune of outliving the Emperor William, he foresaw no difficulty in persuading the Crown Prince to follow the good example of England, which His Imperial Highness understood and appreciated as the best for Germany.

After indulging in severe criticism of General Roon and Count Itzenplitz for administrative incapacity under the present difficult circumstances, a degree of incapacity which ought to convince the Emperor William of the necessity of a change of ministers if he was not a slave to habit and "routine," Prince Bismarck indulged in self-congratulation of having resigned the Prussian premiership and left his former colleagues to fight their battles with His Majesty without him, and on being solely responsible to himself and unhampered by colleagues in the management of imperial affairs as German chancellor.

V
Critics of the New Order

The establishment of the German Empire marked the end of a period of armed conflict and political readjustment in Europe which extended from the outbreak of the Crimean War in 1853 to the conclusion of the Franco-Prussian War in 1871. During those two decades the Great Powers succeeded in dealing by military means with a number of international problems which had proved to be insoluble by diplomatic methods. The situation in the Balkans had been stabilized, the political consolidation of the Italian peninsula had been effected, and the Austro-Prussian dualism in Central Europe had been ended with the achievement of national unification under the Hohenzollerns. Thereafter the Continent entered an era of tranquillity which remained undisturbed by major conflicts until the coming of a world war in the summer of 1914. Yet the years of peace following the treaty of Frankfurt am Main were not years of security. The balance of power which had prevailed in Europe for more than half a century had been suddenly disturbed by the emergence of a strong and ambitious Germany whose military success aroused a feeling of apprehension among other nations. The result was the steady growth of diplomatic alliances and armed forces, an unfavorable omen for the future peace of the Continent. To some observers of the international scene the triumph of Prussia appeared to be the starting signal for an armaments race whose outcome could prove tragic for the entire world. They saw in Bismarck not the unifier of Germany but the gravedigger of Europe.

The Iron Chancellor encountered criticism, moreover, among those groups in society whose position he had sought to protect. The diplomatic methods he employed and the political institutions he created in order to achieve national unification were designed to maintain the preponderance of crown and aristocracy in Central Europe. Yet there were those at court and among the nobility who remained dissatisfied with the form of government established by the German Empire. Some of them felt that Bismarck had made too many concessions to liberalism and nationalism. He had preserved representative institutions, when he should have destroyed them. He had introduced equal manhood suffrage, when he should have disfranchised the uneducated and the propertyless. He had subordinated the states to the empire, when he should have exalted Prussia at the expense of Germany. The opposition of highborn conservatives was reinforced by the opposition of influential courtiers and members of the imperial family. Many of those close to the throne believed that the chancellor was too inflexible and authoritarian. By resisting the forces of reform which had prevailed in Western Europe he was preparing the way for a political crisis in Central Europe. Besides, he was ambitious, imperious, devious. He had become powerful enough to thwart the will of the emperor himself. Such a servant was a danger to his master. Bismarck knew what was being whispered behind his back. Yet he fumed and raged against his blue-blooded enemies without being able to silence them. The political system which he himself had created protected those who were seeking to overthrow him.

Intrigue in aristocratic circles, however, was in the long run less dangerous for the chancellor than dissatisfaction among the masses of the population. Although national unification had been accepted by most Germans with varying degrees of enthusiasm, there was a substantial minority which refused to become reconciled to the new order. It included first of all those who remained faithful to the traditions of particularism and heterogeneity in Central Europe. There were Hanoverians, Bavarians, and Saxons who mourned the loss of their peculiar identity and separate independence. There were Poles, Danes, and Alsatians who resisted all efforts by the government to transform them into Germans. But most important, there were Catholics who felt isolated in an empire in which they constituted a minority subject to a political system whose religious loyalty was predominantly Protestant. Bismarck hoped to strike a blow at this traditionalist opposition by declaring war against clericalism and ultramontanism. Throughout the 1870s he was engaged in the *Kulturkampf*, a bitter struggle with the Catholic church by which he sought to restrict the authority of the hierarchy regarding questions of priestly education, clerical discipline, and government policy. The outcome was the first serious defeat of his public career. Not only did the clergy adopt a strategy of passive resistance which frustrated the civil authorities, but out of the conflict emerged the Center party which skillfully defended the interests of Catholicism in parliament. The chancellor was gradually forced to seek a graceful retreat out of a hopeless impasse.

The new order in Central Europe was criticized by radicals as well as traditionalists. Bismarck's success in achieving national unification through blood and iron failed to convince all liberals that a sham parliamentarianism could provide answers to the pressing problems of state and society. There were many believers in democracy who felt that the German Empire was indifferent to the will of the people. But sooner or later it would have to bow before the advance of popular sovereignty and would then be replaced by a reign of freedom and justice. The democrats opposed the new order because it was too much like the old order. Only the complete triumph of civic liberty, they argued, could meet the needs of the nation. Yet even this position was not militant enough for the socialists, who were beginning to make their appearance in the political life of Central Europe. To them the democratization of the government would be futile without the transformation of the economy. They maintained that the difference between the propertied and the propertyless would have to disappear and the domination of the exploited by the exploiters would have to end before a just form of society could be established. The opponents of the new order were as yet too weak and divided to constitute a serious threat to the existing system of authority in the German Empire. But they gained strength steadily, and half a century later they succeeded in overthrowing the political edifice which Bismarck had worked so hard to erect.

1. Vincent Benedetti Charges Bismarck
with Duplicity

The establishment of the German Empire produced a feeling of uneasiness among all the Great Powers. But none regarded the new order in Central Europe with greater distrust than France. The attitude of the Third Republic was determined by memories of the past as much as by fears for the future. Vincent Benedetti, who had been French ambassador to Prussia in 1870 and who had been a participant in the unfortunate interview in Bad Ems which led to the outbreak of war, never forgave Bismarck for what he considered a bottomless duplicity. In a book published more than twenty years after that fateful summer, he attacked the German chancellor for his dishonesty and the German government for its aggressiveness.

THE GERMANS of our times have taken us back to the early days of their ancestors, who were always under arms, ever ready to invade territory bordering on their possessions. It pleased King William I of Prussia to increase his military power, whilst . . . Bismarck chose to advise his master, who lent a willing ear, to embark in war; and the peaceful condition in which Europe lived until their time, has been so thoroughly upset that there remains no trace of it. After having rearranged the map of Europe to their fancy and advantage, they returned victorious and loaded with laurels to Berlin; but did they take repose and prosperity back to Germany? The Swabian and, even more so, the Pomeranian peasants emigrate to escape the benefits of Prince Bismarck's policy. The heavy taxes, the necessity of concluding alliances, of remaining under arms, either on the western or northern frontier, show, on the contrary, that the adviser, of one mind with the sovereign, has inaugurated a period of heavy burdens and protracted anxiety; that together they have cast the country on the road to ruin or gigantic struggles; unless, as we have already said, the menace of another scourge, social warfare, constrains the various governments to arrive at an understanding guaranteeing a new period of appeasement and concord to the people.

Is there any necessity to mention the disastrous calamities that another war would inflict on Europe? We all foresee them with feelings of horror. Armies of several millions of men are not de-

SOURCE: Vincent Benedetti, *Studies in Diplomacy* (New York: Macmillan, 1896), pp. xliv–xlviii, lxvii–lxix, 260–262.

stroyed in one campaign; a great number of fortresses dotting all
the lines of defense, and provided with every technical improvement of modern times, are not reduced so easily. The struggle
would, therefore, be long, sanguinary, devastating for all the
countries that become the theater of it, on the Rhine, the Alps, the
Vistula. The conviction of this is so painful that sovereigns and
statesmen, all speaking with equal fervor, advocate the preservation
of peace, and, by professions of faith reiterated without end,
repudiate all aggressive intention, and bear witness to their ardent
desire to maintain it. But do they conform to this program by
employing their time and efforts in the preparation of war, by
persevering in a state of things that must necessarily produce it?
One would search history in vain for a precedent authorizing one
to think so. You do not arm for peace, you arm for war, particularly when you do so to excess; when you display such a passion
for arming, there is always a time when you come to blows. . . .
Bismarck well knew this when he assisted King William in developing the Prussian army by battling with the representatives of the
country, by governing without a budget, by devoting, without
credits regularly voted, all the available resources to the military
forces of the kingdom during the first and hardest period of his
long ministry. . . .

Come, Prince von Bismarck, edify us by an honest effort; make a
final avowal, let one sincere word fall from your lips, and this time
again there will be an end to all doubt. Instead of speaking of
France with unseemly disdain, instead of calling the attention of
the deputations who present you their homage, to the copybooks
of our elementary schools, to our folly for conquests, instead of
advising them to close the ranks and keep shoulder to shoulder,
instead of feeding and exalting the hatred of two neighboring
peoples by such language, examine your own conscience. Who was
it, if not Prussia, who in our times pursued and realized vast conquests? You made three wars in six years, sprinkled the bones of
several hundreds of thousands of men from the Baltic to the banks
of the Danube, from the Danube to the banks of the Loire; you
issued triumphant from this triple struggle, loaded with titles,
honors, rewards of every kind. History, assuredly, will not relate
that you deserved well of humanity; but you will none the less
remain the prodigious man of our time. Your prestige was not

seriously affected by your first revelations, and you have been able to tell Europe, without prejudice for the regard in which you are held, what use you could make of your pencil to convey to a communication from your sovereign a feature and a bearing it did not possess. At each of your anniversaries Germany acclaims you with renewed fervor. Why should you not take the noble resolve to set matters straight in regard to those conversations into which you introduced the words Luxembourg, Belgium, and even the canton of Geneva—that French enclave, as you termed it. It will cost you less than to have assumed the responsibility of the last war, as your overtures produced no result.

On a recent occasion, replying to a group of notabilities from Leipzig, you freely expressed the opinion that Germany should continue closely united to Austria, "but that she is nevertheless bound to cultivate friendly intercourse with her eastern neighbor Russia," as that is necessary to her security. But this intercourse existed; it was cordial, intimate, family-like: it was you who upset it at the Berlin Congress; it was you who stripped Russia of all the advantages she had acquired by the treaty of San Stefano after a glorious war sustained at the cost of the greatest sacrifices; it was you, again, who tried to give Austria the influence she exercised in the Lower Danube by assigning to that power Bosnia and Herzegovina which you had snatched from Turkey whose defender you had made yourself. If, on that occasion, you had joined your efforts to those of the plenipotentiaries of the Emperor Alexander II, that faithful prince who gave you his most generous cooperation, no one could have compelled him to renounce the concessions the sultan had made to his conqueror. Russia would have been grateful, and her relations with Germany would have been strengthened and consolidated for long. But you had contracted a debt with her that it displeased you to discharge, as it displeased you, in 1866, to remember the assurances you had lavished on France, and accord her the compensations you had promised her. Those two powers have not forgotten this, and you cannot now fail to see that Germany is reaping at the present day the fruits of your ingratitude. How could so powerful a mind as yours, gifted with such lucid foresight, fall into so grave an error, and voluntarily break those precious bonds which, after having facilitated such vast conquests to Germany, would have guaranteed her the peaceful possession of them? That is for you to say. For my part, I limit myself to conjuring you to go the whole length, and display your frankness even in regard to the Belgium affair.

Consider, Prince Bismarck, that truth, though it come sometimes late, like justice, always succeeds in piercing the obscurity devised to hide it. The force of circumstances sometimes constrains even those who have the least appreciated its value to assist in divulging it. It is thus that, in your speeches, in your circulars, you have never ceased affirming that the war of 1870 was imposed on Germany by a violent aggression of France. In September of that same year, in a first conference with M. Jules Favre, did you not hold this language to him: "I only want peace. It was not Germany who troubled it. You declared war on us without a motive, with the sole design of taking a portion of our territory . . ."? That was reversing the parts—acknowledge it. The following day, at the Château de Ferrières, did you not renew to him the same assurances? "I have no serious reason," you added, "to love Napoleon III. If he had liked, we could have been two sincere allies, and together we would have disposed of Europe, but I would not fight him; I proved that in 1867, on the occasion of the Luxemburg affair. All those about the king were for war; I was the only one to reject it. . . . I merely tell you these things to show you that war was not to my taste: *I would certainly never have waged it had it not been declared against us,* and even when it was declared I could not believe it would occur. . . ."

But there came a time when it pleased you to remind your . . . emperor that he owed you his imperial crown, and, discarding the language you had invariably held for twenty years, you took upon yourself to inform your contemporaries that the reconstruction of the German Empire was your personal work, being the result of a war of which you were the principal author, and which would not have broken out without your intervention. . . .

You will permit me . . . Prince Bismarck, to point out to you that your policy has engendered militarism; that it has placed Europe in the necessity of arming, of arming unceasingly and beyond all measure, that nations live in terror of immense, of frightful catastrophes which some fortuitous event may suddenly cause to explode notwithstanding the prudence of the various governments. To maintain this sad state of things the people stagger beneath the burden of taxation which is out of all proportion with the economic resources of each country. This situation has favored the development of socialistic doctrines, and you know whether they constitute a grave peril for social order. You are the generator of this double evolution; posterity will hold you responsible and call you to account for it. Cease then . . . to excite human passions, to irritate feelings of self-esteem. Apply yourself, on the contrary, to attenuating your errors, either by confessing them, or by appealing to the necessities that compelled you to have recourse to them.

By abstaining to do so you will not free yourself from the responsibility you have incurred in the eyes of public morality. However modest, however feeble my own personal efforts may be, I feel confident they will not pass unperceived. Others will come, persons more competent, supplied with fresh documents, who will make truth evident. New voices will issue from silence to acclaim it. Future historians of our times will have that task to perform, and it will not be a difficult one for them to accomplish. If you then be still of this world, you will regret having failed to provide for this contingency yourself in the nightfall of your existence. If it be too late, you will turn in your grave at a contradiction that would have wounded your feelings. Speak, speak then, whilst it is still time!

"Prince Bismarck," you have said . . . "cannot disappear as a lamp that flares up and goes out. He must go down like a planet." To do this, he must, first of all, pay homage to truth.

2. Empress Augusta Charges Bismarck with Insubordination

Not all of Bismarck's adversaries were abroad. Some of the most formidable ones occupied high positions in Berlin. The Empress Augusta, for example, had long opposed the influence which the chancellor exercised over her husband. Not only did she disapprove of the autocratic tendencies of the government, but she felt that the power of the monarch was being undermined by the ambition of the minister. From the British embassy in the German capital, Odo Russell sent reports to London in 1872 describing the bitterness with which Bismarck regarded the efforts by members of the imperial family to restrict his authority.

SOURCE: Paul Knaplund, ed., *Letters from the Berlin Embassy, 1871–1874, 1880–1885* (Washington, D.C.: USGPO, 1944), pp. 58–59, 66–68.

BANCROFT asked me to dinner [late in April] to meet his nephew Bancroft Davies fresh from Geneva, and Bismarck. Talking to the latter about the empress's journey to England he became excited and said to me: "I wish you would keep the empress forever in England and never let her come back to Berlin for she is interfering in public affairs in a manner that will kill my old king who wants rest and quiet!"

This outburst of temper led me to further inquiries, and I found that the situation at court is as follows:—Bismarck having committed himself publicly to the popular declaration of war against the Church of Rome wants the emperor's sanction to various anti-clerical measures, which the empress who has strong French and Roman sympathies is exerting her influence with His Majesty to counteract. She represents Bismarck as usurping powers that do not belong to him and implores the emperor not to abdicate his independence without reflection. She reminds His Majesty that he never sanctioned Bismarck's anti-Roman policy and that the thousands of congratulatory addresses to Bismarck from all parts of Germany never even alluded to the existence of the king but virtually addressed the chancellor as the sovereign of Germany. If he does not resist these encroachments, Bismarck will become even more powerful than he is and the cause of royalty will be in danger, etc., etc., etc.

The emperor is partly worried partly impressed by the empress's persistent but powerful eloquence and withholds his sanction to Bismarck's proposed policy.

Bismarck, whose nervous system is shattered by overwork and nocturnal beer and pipe orgies, and who can no longer stand contradiction without getting into a passion, frets and fumes at what he calls the ingratitude of a sovereign who owes him everything—political power, military glory and an invincible empire, and whose confidence ought therefore to be boundless.

The old king, who is a pious man, and who is suffering from the moral and physical fatigue of his last campaign thinks he has not long to live and the less so since he has passed the average age of the Hohenzollerns his forefathers, and he ardently desires to die at peace with all the world. The prospect of a conflict with his Catholic subjects grieves him to the Soul, besides which the unexpected so-called revenge policy of Monsieur Thiers fills him with sorrow because he apprehends that his duties to Germany may compel him to undertake another campaign against France which he may not have time to fight out before he dies. His generals tell him that it would be safer to fight France before she is ready than after. Then again comes Bismarck who scorns the generals and tells him he can fight France morally much better through Rome by destroying the unholy alliance of the Church with the enemies of German unity in Europe. Then comes the empress encouraging his peace proclivities by surrounding him with the pleasantest representatives of the Franco Catholic party in Berlin and giving every encouragement to the Gontauts, the Sagans, the Dinos, the Talleyrands, the Castellans, the Radziwills, the Polignacs, the La Ferronages, the Ratibors, etc. etc. . . . Even Cardinal Hohenlohe has been brought from Rome on a visit to his brothers and dying nephew at Berlin.

Bismarck would like to blow them all up, so furious is he at their growing influence at court.—The courtiers are divided among themselves, parties are forming and the situation seems fraught with danger. In all probability when the empress is away Bismarck will get the better of the emperor as he has done before and have his own way, for he is intellectually and politically too strong for them all and has ten thousand strings to his bow in Europe and no rival in Germany. Except perhaps the empress whose popularity as "erste Deutsche Frau and Kaiserin," granddaughter of Karl August etc., etc. defies opposition. For the crown princess the difficulties to contend with will, I fear, be greater coming after the first German empress. . . .

[In September] Bismarck returned from the country to Berlin for two days and called on us late on Saturday night. On taking leave . . . he said he wished to speak to me and so we retired to another room.

Assuming his most cordial, intimate, and confidential manner, he said he wished to apologize for his long absences from Berlin, which were partly owing to bad health and partly to causes which could scarcely have escaped me. The Emperor William was perfectly happy and content reviewing his soldiers and showing them to his imperial guests, or receiving complimentary addresses by post or by telegraph from his subjects, whilst he totally neglected the less agreeable but more necessary duties of government. In fact His Majesty had become unable to take a decided course, and things were consequently at a standstill. His, Bismarck's, influence was neutralized by the never ceasing interference, not to say intrigues, of the Empress Augusta who had more of the statesman in her than the emperor, and whose ultramontane and conservative sympathies stood in the way of national legislation. A modification of the cabinet had become absolutely necessary. Most of the present ministers, his colleagues, were invalids in body and mind and unfit to deal with a new order of things which required new, young, and vigorous intellects. He had appealed in vain to the emperor for a change of ministry, but His Majesty could not make up his mind to part with old friends, and thus legislation had come to a standstill, and government would have to meet parliament under very unfavorable circumstances. His own position between parliament and the crown had become intolerable. Parliament attacked him as a responsible constitutional minister, whilst the emperor, who had never yet realized the meaning of national representation or ministerial responsibility, still expected him to act and obey as the chief clerk of an absolute sovereign.

He was too loyal a subject and too devoted a servant of his old master (mein alter Herr) not to do his utmost to reconcile the conflicting duties imposed upon him, but it often made him feel a hypocrite before his king and his country.

At present, however, he had become useless, while the empress was governing her husband and the country, and he would retire from the stage and let things take their course until parliament met, by which time the sovereign might possibly require his presence. During his absence Balan would carry on the F. O. I would find him an improvement on Thile, who was past work and did wisely to retire. Germany, at present, required working men and not only amiable veterans. . . .

The freedom of Bismarck's language about everything makes it often difficult to report him officially. He is a powerful hater and makes no secret of it. Much as he hates the empress, he hates the crown princess even more, I regret to say. I never allude to Her Imp. Highness in his presence, so as to avoid a quarrel. With the crown prince, Bismarck has made up all his differences, since the war.

From all I gradually hear and observe I fear that the crown princess on ascending the throne of Germany will meet with a more difficult task than is generally known. I hope I may be mistaken! Amen!

3. The Crown Princess Charges Bismarck
with Tyranny

The crown princess was as critical of Bismarck as the empress. Both
she and the crown prince believed that the political system of Germany should follow the example set by England. Yet her hope for the
growth of liberal institutions in Central Europe was constantly frustrated by the policies which the imperial government pursued. In
letters written during the years from 1887 to 1889, a period in which
she herself was empress for a few months, the unhappy woman described her attitude toward the chancellor. She admired his great gifts
as administrator and diplomat, but she regarded him as the evil genius
of her adopted country.

WHAT WE HAVE SUFFERED under this régime!!! How utterly cor-
rupting has his influence been on his school—his employés, on the
political life of Germany! It has made Berlin almost intolerable to
live in, if one is not his abject slave!! His party, his followers and
admirers are fifty times worse than he is! One feels as if one would
like to send up one great cry for deliverance and that if it were
answered, one great deep sigh of relief would be given. Alas, all the
mischief wrought would take years to repair!! Of course those that
only look at the outside aspect of things see Germany strong, great
and united, with a tremendous army (in time of war near three
millions of men!), a minister who can dictate to the world, a sovereign whose head is crowned with laurels, a trade that is making an
effort to outdo all others, the German element making itself
remarked everywhere in the world (even if not loved or trusted).
They cannot think we have any reason to complain, but only to be
thankful. If they did but know at what price all this is bought! . . .

   What a fuss has been made about the . . . anniversary of
Prince Bismarck coming into office! More than one sad and bitter
thought fills our mind when one thinks of the means he has used to
achieve great things and of the havoc he has made of much that
was precious, of good and useful men's lives and reputations, etc.,
and of the evil seeds he has sown, of which we shall some day reap
the fruits.

SOURCE: Frederick Ponsonby, ed., *Letters of the Empress Frederick*
   (New York: Macmillan, 1930), pp. 220, 246–247, 272, 332–333, 368.
   Reprinted by permission of Macmillan, London and Basingstoke.

It is perhaps not his fault, he is *un homme du moyen âge*—with the opinion and principles of those dark days when *la raison du plus fort était toujours la meilleure* and what was humane, moral, progressive and civilized was considered silly and ridiculous, and a Christian and liberal spirit absurd and *unpraktisch*. The young generation see his prestige and his success and are proud of it and like basking in the sunshine of his fame and celebrity. He has done very grand things and has unequalled power and unrivalled strength at this moment! Oh, if they were but used for the good cause, always one would be ready to admire and to bless him! He has made Germany great, but neither loved, free, happy, nor has he developed her immense resources for good! Despotism is the essence of his being; it cannot be right or good in the long run! . . .

What a blessed thing it would be if this regime of Bismarck's omnipotence were not to last forever, if other motives and sentiments and another spirit were to pervade the German government. B. is very great, a man of genius and power, does his best and has done great things for his country. One must be just and grateful, but as you cannot gather grapes of thorns or figs from thistles, so can you not expect from him that which modern Germany lacks and which it thirsts for, and that is peace among its classes, races, religions and parties, good and friendly relations with its neighbors, liberty and the respect of right instead of force, and the protection of the weak against the oppression of the strong. . . .

Prince Bismarck's dodge is always to make the Germans think they are going to be attacked, wronged, insulted, and their interests betrayed if he were not there to protect them. There are many who are silly and ignorant and shortsighted enough to believe all this trash, and who would sacrifice their rights and liberties and their prosperity if only Prince Bismarck would stay and protect them!!! From what? Against what? I really do not think they know!! . . .

Some think when Bismarck is no more that all this party will be scattered to the winds; for as he has no principles he cannot build up. The party have a leader, but no program. They will follow him everywhere and are in constant admiration, but with no firm institutions and principles a party cannot hold together when the leader is gone. Still the mischief will not be over when he disappears, as he has thoroughly corrupted all moral sense in the young men who will come after him. Where is the hand and the

mind to take up Bismarck's position and work on the lines of
honesty and moderate rational progress for the development of
true freedom? I see none.

4. The Particularists Are Opposed to Domination
by Prussia

The opposition to Bismarck at the imperial court was overshadowed
by the opposition in the nation at large. The former arose out of
differences over policies and personalities; the latter out of differences
over allegiances and principles. Particularism, for instance, was too
deeply rooted in the history of Central Europe to be completely destroyed by the victorious statecraft of blood and iron. Sir Henry
Howard, Great Britain's envoy in Munich, reported at the end of 1866
that resistance to national unification remained widespread in Germany
despite the outcome of the Seven Weeks' War. He expressed concern,
moreover, regarding the international consequences of the Prussian
policy of expansion.

THE PRUSSIAN ANNEXATIONS have no doubt considerably advanced
the unification of Germany, but the process of consolidation will
be a slow one, because they were effected by conquest and contrary to the will of the population of the annexed countries, and
the general state of Germany after the war is anything but settled
or satisfactory. In Prussia, the triumphs of the army and a common
feeling amongst all classes in favor of aggrandizement, have divided
the opposition in the chamber of Deputies and have procured for
the government parliamentary successes hardly less remarkable
than those they gained in the field. But nevertheless the internal
conflict in Prussia, though suspended in order not to frustrate
Count Bismarck's external policy, the results of which meet with
such general approbation from all parties in the country, is not
altogether terminated and may break out again any time, the anti-
liberal system of internal government and the political prosecutions
still continuing as before the war. In Hanover, the people by no
means view the incorporation of their country in the light in which
it is represented by some political writers, either ignorant of the
real state of the case, or regardless of the truth, namely in that of
blessing. On the contrary the Hanoverians, a people as highly

SOURCE: Veit Valentin, *Bismarcks Reichsgründung im Urteil englischer
Diplomaten* (Amsterdam: Elsevier, 1937), pp. 528–532.

educated as the Prussians, who would have been ready to make sacrifices in order to promote the public good and to strengthen the common action of Germany, are unable to reconcile themselves to the expulsion of their dynasty, to the total extinction of their separate existence and independence, and to the loss of their own institutions, more liberal than the Prussian and in many respects superior to the latter. The Prussians, as I am credibly informed, meet with ill will and opposition from all classes of the population, with the exception of a portion of that in the towns and in the provinces annexed to Hanover in 1815. On their part, therefore, it will require much delicate handling, patience and time before they can succeed in molding the Hanoverians to their shape and system, and however intelligent and able they may be, they notoriously do not possess the talent of making themselves easily beloved. In Hesse-Cassel, where the people had much ground of complaint against their sovereign and government, and in Nassau, where the government were not popular, the case is no doubt different, but still there has been in both those states much more unwillingness to accept the new order of things than had been anticipated. The Free City Frankfort does not cease to bewail the loss of its independence and of those liberal institutions which it knew how to assert in opposition even to the two most powerful members of the former Confederation, Austria and Prussia, and sees the elements of its prosperity menaced with ruin. As regards the duchy of Holstein, it appears to me that, once separated by treaty from Denmark, under whose rule, notwithstanding certain drawbacks, it enjoyed a prosperity which it has not since known, its lot, as annexed to Prussia, will be a happier one than were it to be erected, as was in contemplation, into a mere vassal state. The same may be said of the duchy of Schleswig, provided Prussia does not evade, as there is every appearance she intends to do, the stipulations of the Treaty of [Nikolsburg], according to which its northern districts are to be reannexed to Denmark, should they desire it.

So much for the annexed states. Of those which are to form with Prussia the Northern Confederation, the only important one is the kingdom of Saxony, and the recent proceedings of the Saxon Chambers show how much more good will Prussia would have caused, and how much easier she would find the task of assimilation, had she evinced more generosity and imposed less severe conditions upon the vanquished. Of the other German states, Hesse-

Darmstadt, with one foot in the Northern Confederation and the other out of it, can hardly be taken into account. Of the independent states, Baden leans entirely to Prussia, and is desirous to accede to the Northern Confederation, but cannot gain admittance, because Prussia has not yet digested her conquests, and is afraid of bringing on a rupture with France by interfering, for the present, with the states south of the Main. In Württemberg, on the contrary, I am told that an anti-Prussian feeling and a wish to see the independence of the country maintained, coupled with an understanding with the other south German states, have at the present decidedly the upper hand.

In Bavaria, the Austrian alliance is entirely abandoned, and public opinion points to the necessity of an alliance with Prussia, more particularly against French aggression, but at the same time the predominant feeling of the country seems at present opposed to such a sacrifice of its independence as would be entailed by an accession to the Northern Confederation as contemplated by Prussia. Had Prussia really intended the formation of a federal state on an equitable basis, Bavaria and the remaining independent states would, there is every probability, have been ready to join it. But in the first place, for the reasons I have alleged, Prussia declines at present to receive them into a confederation with her, and in the second place her object evidently is to create what the Germans call a unity state—in other words not a great German, but an exclusively Prussian one—repugnant to the feelings of the majority of the south Germans. She therefore, it seems, prefers in the first instance consolidating her power in the north of Germany, to seeking the ultimate attainment of her end, on an enlarged scale, through the medium of a confederation comprising the whole of Germany, trusting no doubt to circumstances occurring sooner or later which may enable her to impose her own terms on the south German states. Should Austria hereafter seek to recover her lost position by an alliance with France—a contingency by no means improbable—the position of Bavaria will be a very difficult one, and the interest of Prussia will certainly be . . . to conciliate her as much as possible and not to drive her, as well as the other south German states, into a Franco-Austrian alliance. Of Austria it is no longer permitted to talk as a German power, but it is to be remembered that she has several millions of German subjects, who, to judge by the language lately held in the Diets of the German provinces, are unwilling to accept their exclusion from Germany as a definitive arrangement. Thus a German question arises in Austria and adds another embarrassment to the other almost overwhelming difficulties which beset her path:—whether Austria did not, in part at least, bring on her own misfortunes by numerous political mistakes, and by none greater than that which she committed in endeavoring, without sufficient means, to uphold her position both in Italy and in Germany, is a question which it would now be superfluous to discuss. Suffice it to say, that her present enfeeblement cannot but be a subject of regret, and that her existence as a great power is unquestionably a European interest. Without entering into the question whether the late territorial changes in Germany be ultimately for good or evil, it is unquestionable that the immediate state of things which they have produced is far from satisfactory. Instead of a general disarmament following the peace, the pecuniary and personal burdens of the people are being increased by large additions to the war estimates and to the numerical strength of the armies of the several countries, and science seems to be chiefly valued as the means of inventing new instruments of human destruction. Even Prussia, whose successes have been so brilliant, and whose military organization has proved itself so efficient, is augmenting her army budget and adding largely to her own cavalry force, whilst she is straining the resources of her newly acquired territories for military purposes and requiring her new ally, or rather vassal, the king of Saxony to double his Army.

In those states of Germany, where the general obligation to serve in the army did not previously exist, it is being introduced, and the whole of Germany, like Prussia, will soon be converted into one vast camp. This state of things has indubitably been brought about by the ambition of one power Prussia, who has turned the great superiority of intelligence which she possesses to the cultivating of the art of war rather than of those of peace. It remains to be remarked that the feeling of uneasiness in Germany is augmented by the impression that, when the Paris Exhibition of next year shall have passed over, and when France shall have completed her military preparations, she will seek a war with Germany so as to obtain those compensations for the aggrandizement of Prussia, which she has sketched out, but which she has already learnt, will only be yielded to superior force. Whether the fears thus entertained in regard to the eventual course of France and to the alliances to which it may give rise will be realized or not, some seventeen or eighteen months hence, their existence produces a feeling of uncertainty as to the future and furnishes a motive for military preparation on the part of Germany. In conclusion, I may perhaps be permitted to repeat an opinion, which I have formerly taken the liberty of expressing, that, although, abstractedly speaking, it is in the interest of Great Britain that there should be a strong Prussia to serve as a barrier against France, yet that her aggrandizement, under the present circumstances, cannot be looked upon with unmixed satisfaction from a British point of view. From a defensive, Prussia has become an aggressive power. Her tendencies are Russian. If she has not concluded, as I believe she has not, any treaty of alliance with Russia, she has an understanding with her—equivalent to an alliance in these days, when the fact of engagements being written does not appear to add to their force. The question which has principally drawn Russia closer to Prussia at the present moment and made her overlook the subversion by Prussia of thrones established by treaties to which Russia was a party, is, I understand, that of Poland. The emperor of Russia is jealous of the concessions which Austria is making to her Polish subjects, and which he fears will disturb the tranquillity of his own Polish dominions, whereas he finds in Prussia an ally ready to cooperate in preventing or suppressing any Polish movements. But, although the Polish question may for the present be the principal subject of an understanding between the two powers, have we any security that, should the Oriental question be again brought forward, Prussia, in exchange for the consent of Russia to her further aggrandizement in Germany, will not assist Russia towards her object, in the midst of the general subversion of other treaties, to cancel those which were imposed upon her after the Crimean War, and which have already been infringed by the success of the Prussian maneuver in placing the Prince of Hohenzollern on the throne of the Danubian principalities and to extend her power in the East? The part which Prussia played in that war is not calculated to inspire confidence in this respect. If the alliance of the two great northern powers were to have such a result, which is certainly within the range of possibilities, British interests would undoubtedly be affected. But it would be wearying your Lordship were I further to prosecute the theme of the alliances and complications which may arise out of the present state of things. Suffice it to say, that I trust that my fears, lest the results of the late war should have sown the seeds of fresh and perhaps more extended wars, may not be realized.

5. Pius IX Urges Abandonment of the Kulturkampf

Closely allied with the particularists were the Catholics of Germany who rallied to the defense of their church in its struggle against the state. They charged the new order with the sins of secularism, materialism, centralism, and authoritarianism. The imperial government responded with a bitter condemnation of its opponents whom it considered guilty of disloyalty and subversion. On August 7, 1873, after Berlin had introduced harsh laws against those opposing its religious policy, Pope Pius IX wrote to William I urging him to adopt a more conciliatory course. The war against the Church, he warned, would weaken the monarchical principle itself.

THE MEASURES which have been adopted by your Majesty's government for some time past all aim more and more at the destruction of Catholicism. When I seriously ponder over the causes which may have led to these very hard measures, I confess that I am unable to discover any reasons for such a course. On the other hand, I am informed that Your Majesty does not countenance the proceedings of your government, and does not approve the harshness of the measures adopted against the Catholic religion. If, then, it be true that Your Majesty does not approve thereof—and the letters which Your August Majesty has addressed to me formerly might sufficiently demonstrate that you cannot approve that which is now occurring—if, I say, Your Majesty does not approve of your government continuing in the path it has chosen of further extending its rigorous measures against the religion of Jesus Christ, whereby the latter is most injuriously affected—will Your Majesty, then, not become convinced that these measures have no other effect than that of undermining Your Majesty's own throne? I speak with frankness, for my banner is truth; I speak in order to fulfil one of my duties, which consists in telling the truth to all, even to those who are not Catholics—for everyone who has been baptized belongs in some way or other, which to define more precisely would be here out of place—belongs, I say, to the Pope. I cherish the conviction that Your Majesty will receive my observations with your usual goodness, and will adopt the measures necessary in the present case. While offering to Your most gracious

SOURCE: *The Annual Register* (1873), pt. I, p. 194.

Majesty the expression of my devotion and esteem, I pray to God that He may enfold Your Majesty and myself in one and the same bond of mercy.

6. William I Defends the Policy of his Government

A month after the pope's statement, on September 3, 1873, William I replied to Pius IX. He declared that he agreed completely with the policy pursued by his government in regard to the Catholic church. He blamed the conflict on insubordinate priests and ambitious prelates who refused to render unto Caesar the things which are Caesar's. Finally, he rejected indignantly the papal claim that all Christians, whatever their creed or denomination, were spiritually bound to Rome. The exchange of letters between pope and emperor, despite their avowals of friendship, did nothing to allay the religious struggle in the German Empire.

I AM GLAD that Your Holiness has, as in former times, done me the honor to write to me. I rejoice the more at this since an opportunity is thereby afforded me of correcting errors which, as appears from the contents of the letter of Your Holiness of the 7th of August, must have occurred in the communications you have received relative to German affairs. If the reports which are made to Your Holiness respecting German questions only stated the truth, it would not be possible for Your Holiness to entertain the supposition that my government enters upon a path which I do not approve. According to the constitution of my states such a case cannot happen, since the laws and government measures in Prussia require my consent as sovereign. To my deep sorrow, a portion of my Catholic subjects have organized for the past two years a political party which endeavors to disturb, by intrigues hostile to the state, the religious peace which has existed in Prussia for centuries. Leading Catholic priests have unfortunately not only approved this movement, but joined in it to the extent of open revolt against existing laws. It will not have escaped the observation of Your Holiness that similar indications manifest themselves at the present time in several European and some transatlantic states. It is not my mission to investigate the causes by which the clergy and the faithful of one of the Christian denominations can be induced actively to assist the enemies of all law; but it certainly is my mission to protect internal peace and preserve the authority of the laws in the

SOURCE: *The Annual Register* (1873), pt. I, pp. 194–195.

states whose government has been entrusted to me by God. I am conscious that I owe hereafter an account of the accomplishment of this my kingly duty. I shall maintain order and law in my states against all attacks as long as God gives me the power; I am in duty bound to do it as a Christian monarch, even when to my sorrow I have to fulfill this royal duty against servants of a Church which I suppose acknowledges no less than the Evangelical Church that the commandment of obedience to secular authority is an emanation of the revealed will of God. Many of the priests in Prussia subject to Your Holiness disown, to my regret, the Christian doctrine in this respect, and place my government under the necessity, supported by the great majority of my loyal Catholic and Evangelical subjects, of extorting obedience to the law by worldly means. I willingly entertain the hope that Your Holiness, upon being informed of the true position of affairs, will use your authority to put an end to the agitation carried on amid deplorable distortion of the truth and abuse of priestly authority. The religion of Jesus Christ has, as I attest to Your Holiness before God, nothing to do with these intrigues, any more than has truth, to whose banner invoked by Your Holiness I unreservedly subscribe. There is one more expression in the letter of Your Holiness which I cannot pass over without contradiction, although it is not based upon the previous information, but upon the belief of Your Holiness—namely, the expression that every one that has received baptism belongs to the pope. The Evangelical creed, which, as must be known to Your Holiness, I, like my ancestors and the majority of my subjects, profess, does not permit us to accept in our relations to God any other mediator than our Lord Jesus Christ. The difference of belief does not prevent me living in peace with those who do not share mine, and offering Your Holiness the expression of my personal devotion and esteem.

7. *The British Ambassador Describes Bismarck's Defeat in the* Kulturkampf

Odo Russell, whose diplomatic services earned him a peerage and the title of Lord Ampthill, kept the government of Great Britain well-informed regarding political developments in Central Europe. His

SOURCE: Paul Knaplund, ed., *Letters from the Berlin Embassy, 1871–1874, 1880–1885* (Washington, D.C.: USGPO, 1944), pp. 296–297, 301.

letters for the year 1883 describe the gradual abandonment of the *Kulturkampf* by Bismarck in response to other more pressing problems. It had become clear to the chancellor that he was not only unable to defeat the Catholics, but that he needed their support in parliament for the execution of his policies. The English ambassador had felt all along that it was a mistake to employ political coercion against religious dissent.

NOTWITHSTANDING a general impression to the contrary [Ampthill wrote in April], I cannot but think that the Military Pensions Bill and the increasing demands for the army will meet with more serious opposition in the Reichstag than heretofore. The first attempt to pass the bill has already led to the resignation of two ministers and several under-secretaries. To avoid a future conflict between parliament and the crown, either the emperor or the opposition must give way, and I see no inclination on either side to do so. A conflict would necessarily lead to dissolution, and an appeal to the country would lead to an increase of the numbers of the opposition. It will be interesting to watch the devices Bismarck's fertile brain will generate in dealing with a difficulty, which might in course of time assume the shape of a question before the country as to whom the army & navy are subject in Germany, to parliament or to the crown.

If Bismarck secured the Catholic vote of the Central party by large concessions to the Vatican, he might get a majority, but he shrinks before the humiliation, as he says himself, "of going to Canossa."

The power of the pope is curiously illustrated by the fact that he virtually stands at this moment between the emperor and his parliament in regard to the administration of the German army. . . .

The moral of it all is [concluded the ambassador in October], that even the all-powerful Bismarck, whose *Kulturkampf* is backed by twenty-seven millions of Free-thinkers, cannot root up, out of the soil of enlightened Germany, the errors of popery, notwithstanding old Catholicism, Luther festivals and German philosophy. After waging war for ten years on the pope, Dr. Falk who led the attack in May 1873 has been sent in disgrace to Ham in Hanover as *Oberappelationsgerichts* president to reflect over his defeat, while Prince Bismarck has renewed diplomatic relations with the Vatican to offer large concessions and beg of the pope in return to allow the Catholic opposition majority in the German parliament to pass his social measures and tobacco monopoly for the benefit of the German Fatherland. Politically he is on the high road to Canossa.

In 1873, I ventured, in reply to a query of Prince Bismarck's, to say that after fourteen years residence under the shadow of the Vatican I had convinced myself that the most powerful weapon the state could employ against the errors of popery was religious and political freedom such as we enjoyed in Great Britain, a proposition he energetically and absolutely rejected at the time.

Since then I have heard him assert with equal energy and conviction that Falk was a fool and that he had always thought so.

8. William II Criticizes Bismarck for Initiating the War against Catholicism

The *Kulturkampf,* far from crushing clericalism in the German Empire, politicized the Catholic minority of the nation. The Center party, which had been formed during the struggle to defend the church against the state, remained suspicious of the government long after the conflict itself had come to an end. This was the charge which Emperor William II, writing many years later in his memoirs, directed against Bismarck. The monarch shared the minister's distrust of the political aims of Catholicism. But he maintained that the use of force rather than diplomacy in the war against the ultramontanists had only served to martyrize and popularize them.

IT WAS IN THE DAYS of my youth that that unhappy conflict ran its course which is usually summarized in the catchword *Kulturkampf.* There can no longer be any possible doubt today that this struggle was a crushing disaster for the spiritual unity of Germany, above all in its aftereffects in the strengthening of the Center party. For the Center party, which originally arose from a clerical and particularist opposition to the establishment of the empire, united in itself on the basis of this tendency elements so diverse politically, socially, and denominationally—such as, for example, the Poles, the Alsatians and the Protestant Guelphs—that no one would have predicted for it a lengthy career. It was only the *Kulturkampf* that welded it firmly together. As the representative of the clerical "martyrs" in the struggle against Bismarck's "Diocletian-like perse-

SOURCE: William II, *My Early Life* (London: Menthuen & Co. Ltd, 1926), pp. 204–205. Reprinted by permission of the publisher.

cution of the Christians," it gained its dominating influence over the masses of the Catholic electorate, and remained in being, to the detriment of our country, when the cessation of the *Kulturkampf* had removed the justification for its existence. Unique in Europe as a denominational faction in a political assembly, the party became, as it were, an end in itself. Being spiritually dependent on a foreign power, the papacy, the leaders of the Center party could not deny their inherent antipathy to the Protestant dynasty, or rise to an unreservedly cheerful acceptance of the idea of Empire. In the absence of any consistent program of national policy, the attitude of this denominational party on any fundamental question of politics, any of the essentials of national life, speedily assumed a character of unabashed opportunism and expediency, and has retained it to the present day.

Nothing is farther from my mind than any wish to deny the patriotism of the millions of German supporters of the Center party. I have, nevertheless, as the result of many melancholy experiences, acquired the conviction that the sincere Catholic idealism animating these masses of voters is abused by leaders whose political activities in no way correspond to the real wishes of their followers. That this was, and still is, a possibility can be explained, however, by the disastrous impression left by the *Kulturkampf* in the minds of German Catholics. On that memory the Center party lives to this day; this is even now the source of its power. And thus generations yet to be must suffer because the state of the Bismarck era once pitted itself against the papacy.

9. The Democrats Reject the Outcome of the Seven Weeks' War

While some opponents of the new order criticized it for violating tradition, others attacked it for resisting innovation. Those who wanted to see the development of a democratic form of state and society in Central Europe argued that national unification had merely perpetuated the old system of authority within a new structure of government. Soon after the conclusion of the Seven Weeks' War, a group of radical reformers meeting in Chemnitz founded the Saxon People's party on a platform demanding popular sovereignty. The

SOURCE: *Bebel's Reminiscences* (New York: Socialist Literature Company, 1911), pp. 168–169.

Germany they hoped to create would be based on political democracy, social emancipation, and economic justice.

DEMANDS OF THE DEMOCRACY

1. Unlimited autonomy of the people. Universal, equal and direct suffrage, with secret ballots in all fields of political life (parliament, the legislatures of individual states, the municipalities, etc.). Popular armament, instead of a standing army. A parliament equipped with the greatest possible authority, which shall have to decide particularly about peace and war.

2. Unification of Germany in a democratic form of the state. No hereditary central power. No small Germany under Prussian leadership, no greater Germany under Austrian leadership. No Triad. Such dynastic and particularist aims and others like them, which lead to loss of liberty, disunion and the rule of a foreign power, must be energetically combatted by the democratic party.

3. Abolition of privileges of estate, birth and confession.

4. Improvement of the physical, intellectual and moral culture of the people. Separation of the school from the church and of the state from the church, amelioration of the teachers' institutes, and a dignified position of the teachers, establishment of the public school as a state institution, with free tuition, maintained by state funds. Creation of funds and foundation of institutes for the higher education of those who have graduated from public school.

5. Promotion of the general welfare and emancipation of labor and of the laborers from every oppression and every handicap. Improvement of the condition of the working class, freedom of migration, freedom of occupation, universal German citizenship, promotion and support of cooperatives, especially of cooperatives of production, in order that the antagonism between capital and labor be abolished.

6. Autonomy of the communes.

7. Uplift of the popular consciousness of rights, by the independence of the courts, juries, particularly in political and press cases; public and oral court procedure.

8. Promotion of the political and social culture of the people by means of a free press, free right of assembly and association, right of coalition.

10. Wilhelm Liebknecht Denounces the New Order in Central Europe

The socialists were even more bitter in their denunciation of the new order than the democrats. They believed that nothing less than a complete transformation of political institutions and economic relationships could meet the needs of a modern industrial society. In speeches held on the eve of the Franco-Prussian War, Wilhelm Liebknecht, one of the founders of the Social Democratic Workingmen's party, criticized the form which national unification had assumed in Central Europe. Constitutional government, parliamentary prerogative, and manhood suffrage, he insisted, were only a façade disguising the harsh reality of class rule. The entire existing system of authority and property would have to be altered before the will of the people could prevail.

THE NEW SOCIETY is in irreconcilable contradiction with the ancient state. This new society cannot develop in the feudal state, in the police state, in the military state. Any one desiring the new society must aim above all things at the destruction of the ancient state.

This is a sufficient indication of the attitude of the social democracy on the "rebirth of Germany." The "great deed" of the year 1866 is for German history what the *coup d'état* of December 2, 1851, is for French history. Bismarck's *coup d'état*, like that of Louis Bonaparte, was aimed against democracy. These *coups d'état* are not reprehensible in our eyes because of their use of force—for the ultimate resort of nations, like that of kings, is force—but because of the fact that in the case of France, the *coup d'état* was practiced to the advantage of a host of disreputable adventurers, and in the case of Germany to the advantage of a class no longer having any right to exist, namely, the class of the junkers.

The so-called Prussian constitutional struggle was an attempt on the part of the people, particularly of the bourgeoisie, to attain the state power by means of parliamentary methods. The year 1866 lowered the parliamentary struggle to the status of a feat of stage prestidigitation, and transferred the true theater of war to another field. The North German Reichstag has absolutely no power in

SOURCE: Wilhelm Liebknecht, *Speeches* (New York: International Publishers, 1928), pp. 11–15, 16–18, 28–29. Reprinted by permission of International Publishers Co., Inc. Copyright © 1928.

spite of the universal suffrage; it has not a decisive vote, only an advisory vote; and, being powerless, it cannot be used by the democracy as a battlefield for the attainment of power.

As, in the case of France, the French democracy opposed the emperor with every means at its disposal, so, in the case of Germany, the German democracy has opposed the North German alliance, with all its appurtenances, in a negative and hostile manner. If we should leave this purely negative position, we should not only be relinquishing our principle and the very essence of democracy, but we should also be violating the most fundamental rule of practice. . . .

Very few persons are to be found in the present-day police state, in the state of mental and military regimentation, who are spiritually and mentally independent. The peasant population alone, which in our country is obliged to obey every whim of the authorities without a will of their own, constitutes fully two-thirds of the whole population of the country.

Count Bismarck was well aware of this fact, and his calculations were not in error. By means of the universal suffrage, he set aside the opposition of the well-to-do classes and created a willing majority in the Reichstag, such as he could never have obtained by means of the three-class election system.

In other words, the universal suffrage was not granted the population as a lever of democracy, but as a weapon in the hands of reaction.

This universal suffrage is completely under the control of the government—even more in our country than in France, where the population has more political training, where it has already passed through three revolutions and is now facing the fourth. It may be asserted with safety that no delegate can be elected in Prussia to the Reichstag if the government is seriously opposed to his candidacy.

Let us assume that a candidate comes up for election and that the government is absolutely opposed to having him in the Reichstag. The government will confiscate the newspapers that advocate his election—it will do so legally; it will confiscate his election handbills—also legally; or it will give permits for meetings of electors and then dissolve them—again legally; it will arrest the candidate's campaign managers—quite legally; it will arrest the candidate himself—also legally. . . .

The present-day state is the expression of class rule; it represents the power of capital and is therefore obliged to oppose all those aspirations which aim at the elimination of class rule and the rule of capitalism. It must oppose such efforts, for in opposing them it is defending its own existence. It will never be possible to secure an abolition of the wage labor system by means of strikes and other nonpolitical instruments of agitation. Only after the entire present-day state has fallen will it be possible to install a new system of production. We must therefore take possession of the state and create a new state which shall not know class rule, which shall tolerate neither masters nor slaves, and shall organize society on a cooperative basis. It is not only the content of the state, but also its form, which has essential importance for us; neither can be separated from the other.

Now, though we may be international, we should yet be committing a grave error if we should entirely lose sight of national affairs. Our watchword must be *hic Rhodus, hic salta!* Germany is the place; it is here we must fight! . . .

The suffrage right granted in the North German Confederation is merely a bait for the thoughtless. The Berlin Reichstag is only a sham parliament. . . .

What universal suffrage really amounts to in a state that is not free has been shown sufficiently by the elections to the Reichstag.

In northern Germany, the Reichstag is elected on the basis of universal suffrage, but who will dare maintain that the Reichstag serves as an expression for the opinion of the people?

The Reichstag does not make history but is merely playing a comedy; the members say and act in accordance with the prompter's instructions: and sometimes you can hear him shouting out loud. And is it to this Reichstag that we are to transfer the center of gravity of our struggle? No man can wish such a condition unless our whole struggle is a mere farce in his eyes. "Yes, indeed," we are told, "the Reichstag is at present of course very badly constructed, but perhaps the next Reichstag will be a better one. Let us see to it that good 'delegates' are elected." This would all be very well if the Reichstag were not completely impotent and if the government did not hold the elections altogether in its own hands. . . . Yet, for practical and tactical reasons, I am quite in favor of our participation in the Reichstag elections. It would result in injury to us if we should leave the field entirely to our enemies. Elections, after all, do produce a certain commotion, which it should be our duty to utilize for purposes of agitation. Yet we must not elect our delegates in order that they may take part in this farce-comedy, but for the purpose of permitting them to protest against it, of having them protest again absolutism, which conceals itself behind the forms of parliamentarism, and for the purpose of enabling them to denounce to the people those persons who permit themselves to be used in this comedy. Our delegates must not speak to the Reichstag, but their words must pass over the heads of the members of the Reichstag and reach the people themselves. . . .

I now come to the question of what we are to do during the elections with regard to the other parties participating. Is it possible for us to establish an alliance with other parties? Of course, no other parties could be considered in this connection except the [democratic parties]; but, after what I have just said, I cannot answer this question in any other way than in the negative. . . . The question of republic or monarchy is, in part at least, a question of form only. The principle we are concerned with in the first place is the principle of equality, and this principle may be violated under a republic as well as under a monarchy. A republic based on class rule is a violation of the principle of equality that expresses itself in the person of every capitalist and every proletarian, and vindicates the principle of equality only in its elimination of one individual: namely, the monarch. To be a social democrat means far more than to be a republican without desiring to eliminate class rule, but all those who aim at the elimination of class rule are, of course, republicans also.

Enough has been said. Our path in the coming elections has been indicated to us: we can inflict only harm on ourselves by means of alliances with other parties; such alliances would oblige us to relinquish our place at least in part; and our very strength is in the fact that our attitude is perfectly clear to ourselves and to others, since we make no effort to conceal our goals. Our strength is in our principles. Half-way measures will destroy us. Therefore let us boldly unfurl our flags so that we may be seen by friend and foe; then we shall march surely to liberty!

VI
The Emergence of an Industrial Society

For the bulk of the population of the German Empire the most important development in the age of Bismarck was not military predominance or political consolidation but the industrialization of the economy. The second half of the nineteenth century witnessed the breakthrough of capitalistic entrepreneurship in Central Europe, and the result was a revolution in a way of life which had endured for centuries. Within a single lifetime a nation of farmers and artisans became transformed into a nation of mill hands and factory owners. In the decades following the achievement of national unification, Germany, which had lagged behind England and France in the volume of industrial production, began to advance swiftly in all areas of manufacture and mining. Not only did the usual indices of economic growth like coal, iron, and steel register rapid growth, but technical skill and ingenuity soon established the primacy of Central Europe in such specialized fields as chemicals, pharmaceuticals, optical goods, and electrical equipment. Before long German manufacturers were invading markets in Latin America, the Ottoman Empire, and the Far East which had long been the preserve of Great Britain, while German shippers were building a merchant marine which revived the proud mercantile tradition of the Hanseatic cities. The characteristic form of banking also changed from a family business or small partnership whose funds were invested in government bonds and commercial ventures to a giant joint-stock company which channeled the savings of hundreds of thousands of stockholders to industrial enterprises. Manufacture, mining, trade, transportation, and finance came to constitute an irresistible material force altering the life of Central Europe.

A change in the pattern of society was the inevitable result of a change in the structure of the economy. The rise of industrial capitalism led to the emergence of new classes in the community whose livelihood was derived from new modes of production, distribution, or finance. There was first of all the urban bourgeoisie which controlled an increasing share of the national wealth by virtue of its domination of manufacture, trade, and banking. The political creed which it embraced tended to be cautiously liberal, opposed to the hereditary privileges of the landed aristocracy, but also hostile to socialist egalitarianism or democratic reformism. A counterweight to the new middle class was the new proletariat composed of those who toiled in factories, shops, and mines. Most of the recruits for the industrial labor force were displaced villagers who had been driven from the land by overpopulation and impoverishment. Uprooted, alienated, and brutalized, they were slowly beginning to grope toward an awareness of their strength and their destiny. At the same time the process of industrialization had the effect of weakening the economic position of the class which had traditionally been dominant in German society, the landed aristocracy. As the importance of agriculture declined, noblemen were increasingly forced to maintain their privileged status by exerting a powerful influence over court, army, and bureaucracy. Finally, there were the peasant masses, exploited and oppressed, which sought to escape rural impoverishment through mass migration to the city or to the fertile fields of the New World.

The effect of industrial capitalism on the way of life in the German Empire was profound. It led to a rapid expansion of the population which increased from less than forty million in 1860 to about fifty million in 1890. Although neither birth rate nor death rate changed substantially during those years, the fact that the former remained consistently higher than the latter resulted in demographic growth. Steady employment provided by a prosperous economy encouraged marriage and fecundity, while medical progress checked disease and mortality. The consequence was a swift rise in the number of inhabitants of Central Europe. The change in the distribution of population, moreover, was as significant as the change in its size. The proliferation of factories and mines had the effect of drawing surplus labor from the country to the city. Especially the young and ambitious found life in the village oppressive and stultifying. Their hope was that the urban community would provide them with a greater opportunity for economic advancement than could be found on farms and pastures. The great centers of manufacture and trade like Berlin, Hamburg,

Breslau, Leipzig, and Frankfurt am Main became a magnet attract-
ing countless rustics in search of a better life. For most of them,
however, work in the mills proved as unrewarding as labor in the
fields. Industrialization created a new economic aristocracy of
businessmen and financiers dominating the wealth of the nation.
But to factory workers or independent handicraftsmen it offered
little more than toil, drudgery, and a bare subsistence. The steady
flow across the Atlantic of emigrants from Central Europe was
evidence of the bitter struggle for existence which the masses had
to endure during the age of Bismarck.

Social tension was the inevitable result of a basic alteration in
the economic structure which benefited the urban bourgeoisie
more than the urban proletariat. To many reformers the destruction of the traditional way of life in Central Europe presaged the
intensification of class conflict and the danger of political revolution. Yet there seemed to be no easy solution to the problems
created by industrialization. There were those who argued that
only the complete overthrow of the system of private ownership
could end the exploitation of the workingman. Others advocated
remedies which were less drastic. The state, for example, might use
its authority to check the most destructive consequences of unrestrained competition in the labor market. Yet the prevailing opinion among the propertied classes of Central Europe was that the
laws of economics like the laws of nature were hard but ineluc-
table. To regulate industrial conditions in order to meet human
needs must lead to the decline of initiative and the erosion of self-
reliance. The way to escape poverty was through hard work, good
character, and a clean life. The gospel of rugged individualism,
however, won more converts among businessmen than among
workers. Unable to satisfy its fundamental demands within the
existing state, the urban proletariat began to seek the solution to its
economic problems outside the established order of society.

1. The Poverty of the Urban Working Class

The way of life of the worker in the cities of Germany was similar to that of the worker in the cities of England, France, or America. Wages were low, hours long, and conditions hard. A British government commission reporting on the position of labor in Central Europe provided valuable statistical data regarding the economic situation of millers, bakers, and confectioners in the late nineteenth century. But the picture of bitter impoverishment which it presented could have been drawn for most other occupations as well. The struggle for existence in shops and factories was pitiless.

THE STATISTICS published with the help of the German Millers' Union . . . show that this industry is still very low down in the scale of organization. The average annual earnings in 1889 were 609 marks, in 1890 only 596 marks. In some districts the yearly income was as low as 397 marks in 1889, and 361 marks in 1890, whilst in one of the seventeen sections distinguished under the Accident Insurance Law for this industry, it rose to 754 marks in 1889 and 784 marks in 1890. Five of the sections showed a rise of from 2 to 30 marks during this period, but on the other hand wages fell in twelve sections by amounts varying from 5 to 49 marks. Some millers pay their assistants no fixed wages at all, but allow them to be mainly dependent upon the gratuities of customers. Throughout the industry it is usual to give board and lodging in lieu of wages, or with a very small pecuniary addition, and the board and lodging provided are frequently of the most wretched description. The length of the working day is often excessive. Only 12 percent of the mills sending in returns limited the hours of work to twelve in addition to overtime, 14 percent worked 14 hours, 11½ percent from 15 to 16, 45 percent from 17 to 18, 8 percent from 19 to 20, and in 7 percent it was not unusual for 36 hours to be worked at a stretch. Only about one mill in nine ceased work on Sundays, two-thirds worked as long on Sundays as on weekdays, and in the remainder work was carried on for periods varying from 6 to 12 hours. The factory inspector for East and West Prussia reports that, when questioning members of the trade as to the hours of work, he was told that "it would be a poor miller who needed more than four hours' sleep." Similar reports were received from the inspector for Posen. The Millers' Union demand

SOURCE: Royal Commission on Labour, *Foreign Reports: Germany* (London, 1893), pp. 62–63.

a 12 hours' working day, Sunday rest, the abolition of payment in kind, or where that is not attainable a reform in the quality of the board and lodging provided, the inspection of mills, prohibition of night work for apprentices, and a restriction in the number of apprentices to a certain proportion of the adult workmen employed. Their organization is as yet too weak to enforce its demands, and in the kingdom of Saxony it has been denied the right of legal personality. . . .

Very complete statistics with regard to the working hours of bakers and confectioners were collected . . . by the Imperial Office of Statistics in consequence of the attention aroused by the publication . . . of the results of a private inquiry conducted by Herr Bebel. This inquiry had elicited the following statistics for regular daily work:

WEEK DAYS

Number of Establishments	Number of Hours	Percentage of Total Number Investigated
7	9	
20	10	
38	11	23.2
89	12	
89	13	
141	14	48.5
91	15	
76	16	
62	17	
30	18	28.7
16	19	
4	20	

Overtime is not included in these figures, nor, as a rule, the time employed in getting the work ready, which would, as a rule, increase the hours by at least one. The largest cities are especially remarkable for the length of the working hours in bakeries. In Berlin, Herr Bebel stated that 86.6 percent of the establishments worked over 14 hours a day; in Frankfurt am Main, the percentage was 85.3; in Offenburg, 84.6; in Altona, 68; in Dresden, 59; in Leipzig, 58.7; and in Hamburg, 52.2. The official inquiry . . . took in the smaller towns and country districts to a much greater extent than had been done by Herr Bebel, and pursued its investigations with great minuteness. . . .

According to these statistics, work in 42.6 percent of the ordinary bakeries begins before midnight; if the large towns are taken

SUNDAYS

Number of Establishments	Number of Hours	Percentage of Total Number Investigated
18	None	2.8
4	4	
4	5	
5	6	
5	7	15.3
22	8	
21	9	
40	10	
41	11	
93	12	34.3
94	13	
101	14	27.9
72	15	
54	16	
46	17	
22	18	20.6
10	19	
8	20	

alone, the percentage rises to 77.9. South Germany includes the largest number of cases, and mid-Germany the fewest; the respective percentages are 53.2 percent and 18.6 percent. In rather more than half the establishments working at night the daily hours, including intervals, do not exceed 12; the employers give the percentage as 59.4, and the employed as 47. The conditions are most unfavorable in this respect in north-west Germany, and most favorable in mid-Germany. The percentage of establishments working long hours appears to rise in proportion to the size of the towns, and it is stated that the larger establishments work longer than those employing only one or two hands. Regular overtime is worked in about 30 percent of all the ordinary bakeries on one or two days in the week for two hours or more, and before festivals and on similar occasions 78 percent work overtime. Thirty-five percent of the bakeries professing to work by day only begin before 5:30 A.M., and thus encroach upon the hours included under night work by the industrial code. The daily hours do not exceed 12 in 76 percent of these bakeries; according to the employed the percentage should be 72.1, and according to the employers, 81.8. Northeastern and southern Germany return the shortest hours, mid-Germany the longest. Regular overtime is worked in 36.4 percent of the day bakeries, and overtime on special occasions in 66.7 percent. Sunday work is only reported in 22.4

percent, whilst in ordinary night bakeries the percentage is 93.7. The hours in confectioners' bakeries are very similar to those of day bakeries; in 65.3 percent they do not exceed 12. In mid- and south Germany the average working day is shorter than in north Germany; Sunday is the day upon which there is the greatest demand for confectioners' wares, and 89.7 percent of their bakeries are busy on Sunday.

2. Housing Conditions in the Big City

The average worker in the German Empire led a life of unremitting want. Earnings covered by and large the cost of only the barest necessities. The diet was monotonous, consisting mostly of bread and potatoes, with no meat as a rule except on Sunday. Housing conditions were deplorable, many proletarian families occupying damp cellars or drafty attics. No wonder that disease was rampant in the urban slums. Yet the steady migration of population from the countryside to the city kept rents at a high level which often amounted to 25 percent of the income of a lower-class family.

THE WEAVER'S BUDGET given by Dr. von Schulze-Gaevernitz is as follows:

WEEKLY BUDGET OF NORTH GERMAN WEAVER WITH WIFE AND FOUR CHILDREN

Income		Expenditure	
	M		M
Wages of father	15	42 lbs. rye bread (second	
Amount paid by children for		quality)	5.60
board and lodging	7	30 pints potatoes	1.80
Total	22	2 lbs. rolls	2.0
		2 lbs. meal (second quality)	0.40
		¾ lbs. meat (Sunday) ⎫	
		½ suet ⎬	0.45
		vegetables	3.40
		coffee	0.20
		2½ lbs. butter	3.40
		6 pints skimmed milk	0.60
		rent	3.20
		sick and old age	
		insurance	0.65
		school money	0.15
		Total	21.85

SOURCE: Royal Commission on Labour, *Foreign Reports: Germany* (London, 1893), pp. 104–105.

The great lack of suitable dwellings for the working classes in the large towns of Germany, the degree of overcrowding that exists, and the heavy rents, which must be paid, have been illustrated by a series of tables compiled by Herr Trüdinger, of the Tübingen University.

CHARACTER OF DWELLINGS IN SIX OF THE LARGE CITIES OF GERMANY

City	Year	Number of Dwellings	Proportion per 1,000 with the Possibility of Heating				Proportion per 1,000 Situated in			
			No rooms	One room	Two rooms	More than two rooms	Cellars	Ground floor	Attics	Other floors
Berlin	1880	255,929	13	498	265	224	91	146	163	589
Hamburg	"	88,826	10	393	284	300	65	204	55	546
Breslau	"	60,615	6	590	217	187	41	132	122	688
Dresden	"	49,833	2	593	204	241	29	148	170	604
Leipzig	"	28,510	1	285	272	442	20	157	135	682
Frankfurt am Main	"	27,763	1	236	222	541	1	174	43	715

PROPORTION OF THE POPULATION LIVING UNDER THE ABOVE CONDITIONS

City	Year	Proportion per 1,000 Inhabitants Living in Dwellings Situated in				Proportion per 1,000 Dwellings		Average number of Inhabitants in Dwellings, with Possibility of Heating		
		Cellars	Ground floor	Attics	Other floors	Small	Of these very over-crowded	No rooms	One rooms	Two rooms
Berlin	1880	92	148	155	587	776	115	3.1	3.7	4.5
Hamburg	"	61	194	54	402	687	107	3.5	3.7	4.5
Breslau	"	38	128	111	698	813	144	3.5	3.8	4.4
Dresden	"	27	147	168	578	756	125	2.2	3.6	4.4
Leipzig	"	17	151	145	673	558	—	2.4	3.8	5.1
Frankfurt am Main	"	1	167	36	692	459	27	2.4	3.5	4.3

In Berlin the conditions are specially bad, and the average number of persons inhabiting one tenement (*Grundstück*) has risen from 60.7 in 1880 to 66.0 in 1885. Subletting was shown by the census of 1880 to be exceedingly frequent, 7.1 percent of the population took in persons who boarded and lodged with them, and 15.3 percent took in persons to sleep (*Schlafleute*). One instance is given of a household taking 34 such night lodgers, in another case there were eleven, including two women. Thirty-eight percent of the families taking night lodgers lived in a single room; one instance is mentioned in which a man and his wife with a family shared their one room with seven men and one woman. Though the worst kind of night shelters, known as "Pennen," have now been suppressed by the police, it is still "the opinion of experienced observers . . . that the evils existing in the large towns of England are less crying than in Germany."

According to a table constructed by Herr Trüdinger the proportion borne by house rent to income in five of the chief towns of Germany was as follows:

Income M	Percentage of House Rent to Income in						
	Berlin 1876 (6,170 cases)	Hamburg			Breslau 1880 (34,897 cases)	Leipzig 1875 (4,021 cases)	Dresden 1880 (30,825 cases)
		1868 (13,059 cases)	1874 (14,691 .cases)	1882 (17,289 cases)			
Under 600	—	22.3	24.2	26.5	28.7	29.9	26.8
601–1,200	24.7	18.8	20.9	23.5	21.0	21.2	18.4
1,201–1,800	21.8	19.9	21.1	18.9	20.8	19.7	16.3
1,800–2,400	21.6	20.3	20.9	19.5	19.1	20.4	15.9
2,401–3,000	18.6	19.5	19.2	18.8	19.7	18.3	15.4
3,001–3,600	21.3	19.6	19.0	17.9	19.8	16.9	15.3
3,601–4,800	18.6	19.1	17.8	17.8	18.3	15.5	15.4
4,801–6,000	17.9	18.6	17.4	18.3	18.3	15.4	14.6
6,001–12,000	15.0	16.0	15.5	16.7	13.7	13.1	13.0
12,001–30,000	11.7	11.5	10.8	12.2	8.9	8.4	9.9
30,000–60,000	8.8	6.7	7.4	8.1	3.6	5.5	7.1
Over 60,000	3.6	3.7	3.8	3.9	3.4	1.9	3.9

The poorest classes therefore must pay a house rent equal to about a quarter of their income.

3. The Employment of Women and Children

Poverty and hopelessness led to crime and immorality, especially among those whose earnings were the lowest. Women were often forced into prostitution and children into thievery as the only means of sustaining themselves. While church and school in imperial Germany extolled the virtues of honesty, sobriety, and continence, vice flourished in the slums of the city. Many observers commented with concern on the social and moral consequences of industrialization, but

SOURCE: Royal Commission on Labour, *Foreign Reports: Germany* (London, 1893), pp. 42–43.

the solutions they offered differed widely, ranging from improved religious instruction to the abolition of private property. The problems created by the growth of the factory system in Central Europe were as difficult as they were serious.

TAKING WAGES above 24 marks a week as high, those between 15 marks and 24 marks as medium, and those below 15 marks as low, it will be found that the proportion of men, women, and of both together in these three classes is as follows:

	Low Wages	Medium Wages	High Wages
	Percent	Percent	Percent
Men and women together	29.8	49.8	20.4
Men alone	20.9	56.2	22.9
Women alone	99.2	0.7	0.1

Almost all the women, therefore, are in receipt of low wages, and of the 99.2 percent, only 19.76 percent receive more than 10 marks a week. More than 70 percent receive less than 10 marks, or according to Dr. Wörishoffer, "a miserable pittance"; and as many as 54.05 percent, or more than half, earn less even than 8 marks.

When it is remembered that the cost of board and lodging for a single woman amounts in Mannheim, at any rate, to about five marks a week, it is clear that a weekly wage of from six to eight marks leaves little margin for clothes, or for sickness and unforeseen expenses. The temptations to which girls with such narrow means are exposed, are strongly insisted upon by Herr Bebel and the socialist writers generally, and used as an argument to prove the false basis upon which in their opinion society and the institution of the family rest. Without entirely accepting the very strong statements made as to the general level of morality amongst factory women in Germany by writers of a pronounced socialist tendency such as Frau Minna Wettstein-Adelt, it must be admitted that the evidence of the factory inspectors, and especially of so careful a writer as Herr Wörishoffer, indicates a deplorable state of things. The want of proper separation of the sexes whilst at work, the inadequacy of accommodation in factories, and the overcrowding in the workmen's dwellings, which makes it possible for working girls to lodge with a family inhabiting one or two rooms only and taking other lodgers of both sexes, have all contributed to produce the want of self-respect which characterizes large sections of the women factory workers in Germany. Though the girls in the town factories present the roughest exterior, the moral level is said to be lowest amongst those working in country factories in the neighborhood of large towns. Comparatively few women of the working classes belong to the Social Democratic party; according to Frau Minna Wettstein-Adelt, such as there are are drawn from amongst the married women. Efforts are being made, however, by women of the upper and middle classes to disseminate the more advanced views of the socialists with regard to the position of women amongst the factory workers. According to these views, which find their fullest expression in Herr Bebel's "Women and Socialism" (*Die Frau und der Sozialismus*) the existence of a society based upon competition and recognizing only one form of legitimate marriage, drives women with diminishing earnings to support themselves by immorality, whilst, on the other hand, it postpones the period at which a man can undertake the support of a wife and family to an age far later than is dictated by nature. "Prostitution is, therefore, an inevitable consequence of the *bourgeois* constitution of society. . . ."

The employment of child labor in Germany shows a considerable proportionate decrease as compared with the middle of the century, but at the same time a decided increase during the last few years. In 1853 the number of children employed in Prussian factories was 32,000; 8,000 were between 9 and 12 years of age, and 24,000 between 12 and 14. In 1888 and 1890 no children under 12 were to be found in Prussian factories, and the numbers of those between 12 and 14 were only 6,225 and 6,636. The abuses attendant upon the employment of children in the middle of the century have been described by Professor Thun, who states that in the textile industries of Gladbach and Aix-la-Chapelle it was not unusual to find children employed at only five or six years of age, and that the profits to be drawn from child labor of this kind were an encouragement to early marriages. In 1875, when an inquiry was made by the Federal Council into the question of the labor of women and children, the number of children employed throughout the German empire was 88,000, 24 percent of whom were between 12 and 14, and 76 percent between 14 and 16. The proportion of child to adult labor was about 1 to 10. The weekly wages of children between 12 and 14 varied from 1 mark to 9 marks, those of children between 14 and 16 from 1½ marks to 13½ marks; the average wage of the first class was 3 marks and that of the second 5 marks. No complete or continuous statistics of child labor in Germany are available, but its fluctuations can be traced in various districts. In Berlin, for instance, the number of children employed between 12 and 16 years of age increased from 1,998 in 1874 to 2,579 in 1879; the percentage of child labor to the total labor employed was 3.1 in the first year, and 4.6 in the last.

4. The Position of the Rural Proletariat

The economic and social conditions of the agricultural laborer were as harsh as those of the industrial worker. The farm hand had no more to eat than the mill hand, and a crowded peasant cottage was no larger than an average dwelling in the slums of the city. The rural proletariat was therefore abandoning the countryside in search for a better way of life. What drove it from its ancestral fields and villages was not only the hard toil of husbandry, but a growing dissatisfaction with the drudgery and hopelessness of existence on a small farm or aristocratic estate.

THE AGRARIAN QUESTION, as at present understood in Germany, is to a great extent the outcome of the last twenty years, and is by no means coincident with the period of lowest wages and least amount of material prosperity for the agricultural laborer. Indeed, as Dr. Kaerger has expressed it, the agrarian question exists rather from the standpoint of the employer than from that of the employed, and springs from the scarcity of agricultural labor more than from any necessity for improvement in the condition of the laborer. Since the beginning of the present century agriculture in Germany has passed through three main stages. Up to 1830 the destruction caused by the Napoleonic wars was still severely felt; 80 percent of the great estates in Prussia came into the market, and the price of land fell to half of its taxable value. The ruin of so many of the landed aristocracy was the opportunity of the merchant classes, who became purchasers of land on a very extensive scale. The rising price of corn and the capital at the disposal of the new landowners brought about an era of prosperity which continued until 1870. The great landowners, both on account of their superior knowledge and the comparative ease with which they could

SOURCE: Royal Commission on Labour, *Foreign Reports: Germany* (London, 1893), p. 52.

obtain the necessary credit, took the lead in introducing improved methods of cultivation. Many of the smaller holdings (*Bauerhöfe*) were bought up, and the small farmers as well as the better class of agricultural laborers emigrated in consequence to America. Shortly after 1870 came the reaction. Prices fell, agricultural labor became scarce, the influence of the higher wages obtainable in the building and factory industries began to make itself felt, and the present agrarian difficulty first made its appearance. For a time the Agrarian, or Conservative Socialist party, to which the great landowners belonged, was wholly in favor of reactionary measures, such as the limitation of the right of free migration, higher protective duties upon foreign produce, and more stringent legislation against breach of contract on the part of domestic servants and farm laborers. Both the older and newer schools of Academic Socialists, however, who have made a study of the land question, lay greater stress upon its social aspects and point out that if the agricultural laborer is to be attached to the soil it must be by providing him with some means of satisfying his demand for a fuller recognition of his independence, and a more favorable prospect of realizing his social aspirations. They support their view by showing that, except in a few isolated cases, the general consensus of opinion in the country as a whole indicates a very great change for the better in the economic condition of the laborer during the last ten or twenty years. He is better fed and better clothed, better educated and better able to procure the means of recreation; nevertheless the migration statistics . . . indicate a continuous movement of the population from the agricultural east to the industrial west. Except in a few southern districts, such as Bavaria, where peculiar conditions prevail, the agrarian question proper, interpreted in Germany to mean the difficulty of procuring a sufficient supply of labor, scarcely exists in the west. With regard to the east, on the contrary, Dr. Weber points out . . . that unless some means can be adopted for checking the outflow of the German population, there is every reason to fear that their places will be supplied by an inroad of Slavs, and that thus an element of disintegration already existing will be increased. . . . The inquiry instituted . . . by the Economic Club (*Verein für Sozialpolitik*) has brought out clearly the predominant influence of the social over the economic factors in agrarian discontent. The gulf which separates the employer from the employed in the east, and the lack of opportunity for acquiring land are, in the opinion of the members of the Economic Club reporting on the subject, mainly responsible for its depopulation. Up to the present time it has appeared almost impossible to supply the remedy, though the great landowners are sufficiently ready to divide much of their land into small holdings, if this or any other measure would secure them a permanent supply of suitable labor.

5. The Causes and Effects of Emigration from Germany

For many inhabitants of Central Europe the only escape from poverty and exploitation was emigration. During the years between Bismarck's appointment as prime minister of Prussia in 1862 and his dismissal as chancellor of Germany in 1890 almost three million people left the empire to seek a better way of life in the New World. Most of them were land-hungry peasants driven overseas by rural hardship, but there were also mill hands, artisans, and shopkeepers hoping to make a new start on the other side of the Atlantic. The report of a British government commission analyzed the causes and effects of emigration from the German Empire.

SOME INDICATIONS have already been given of the causes which are at work in this vast migratory movement of the German population. The difficulty of distinguishing between the various factors, social, political, and economic, which combine to produce such a result, can scarcely be overestimated; but the immense preponderance of natives of the agricultural districts amongst the emigrants point to the defective conditions of agriculture as the main source of the discontent with home surroundings, which must always precede any migration of population. Putting for a moment this important factor on one side, due weight must be allowed to the social and political causes which combine to produce the result. Amongst these may be enumerated the attitude of the German government prior to 1890 towards the great body of German Socialists, and the discontent felt, at any rate in time of peace, with the German military system. The desire for a fuller life, and for the advantages offered by the towns, have drawn a vast number of the best and most intelligent of the laboring classes from the east of

SOURCE: Royal Commission on Labour, *Foreign Reports: Germany* (London, 1893), pp. 98–99.

Germany to the west. "It is not so much the desire to obtain more money," says the last report of the East Prussian Association (*Ostpreusslicher Centralverein*), "which impels, at any rate, the unmarried people to emigrate. . . . It is much more the wish for an independent life, and for pleasures and amusements which here, in the east, we cannot offer to the country folk." But, as Dr. Max Sering says, the cause lies even deeper, and must be sought in "the ideals of freedom and human dignity," which have produced "a striving after a higher social status," even independently of material advantage or of intellectual gain. The growth of education, and the enlightenment which the term of military service brings to the agricultural laborer, have helped to foster these social aspirations, and it is rare to find the children, even in Mecklenburg, where the conditions of labor are specially favorable, content to follow the calling of their fathers. This attraction attaching to the conditions of town life is exercised even more strongly by those of the United States, and it is fostered by the ceaseless efforts of rival steamship companies and their agents to present those attractions in glowing terms, and to minimize the cost and difficulties of transport. Further, the letters and remittances of friends and relations, who have already emigrated, produce a very great effect upon those remaining at home; and perhaps this has contributed as much as anything else to the increased migration. Nevertheless, as has been well pointed out by Herr Lindig, neither the efforts of unscrupulous agents, nor the representations of friends and relations, would have sufficed to induce such an immense number of persons to forsake their homes, if the economic condition of the German laborer had been satisfactory. Low wages, lack of employment, the decay of the lesser industries, and the too rapid influx of would-be factory-workers into the towns, combine to produce a state of things compared with which the United States appear to have everything to offer. As Professor von Philippovich has said, the tide of emigration can only be stemmed in states which seek "to make home home-like to the wanderers by raising their economic and social conditions." On the other hand, the economic and political conditions of the countries to which the emigrants go may in the future be expected to exercise a still greater influence; and it is not improbable that the attitude now adopted by the United States toward immigration, combined with the increasing difficulty of obtaining land, may have a deterrent effect upon German emigration. For, in the main, this emigration is an agricultural emigration, and all writers on the subject are agreed that the dearest wish of the agricultural laborer in Germany is to become a landowner, on however small a scale. It is this desire, uniting as it does the economic, social, and political factors already distinguished, which is mainly responsible for the migration of population in Germany. Statistics have shown that there are two main districts from which the emigrants go—the south-west and the north-east. In the one case, the population has outgrown both the land supply and the supply of supplementary employment; in the other, the conditions of labor on the great estates render it more and more difficult for the laborer to emancipate himself from his state of servitude. . . . Even apart from the difficulty of securing a small plot of ground in a country of great estates, the agricultural laborer cannot, under existing conditions, acquire the purchase money even by years of saving; so that, as Dr. Lindig has said,

> the agricultural question is first and foremost a question of wages. . . . The small receipts, and the impossibility of saving anything which can help him to rise in the social scale, causes the laborer to seek conditions which afford a better prospect. These he finds in factory labor at home, or in emigration to America, where wages are high and the price of land proportionately small; there he may hope to attain the goal of his ambition and to become independent, whereas here it is hard, indeed, even for the most skilled and most diligent, to save enough for the purchase money of a piece of land.

At the same time, it must be pointed out to those who regard small holdings as the universal and unfailing remedy, that of late a large number of small German proprietors have found themselves forced, by the continued depression of prices, to give up their holdings, and to emigrate. This is due largely to the poverty of the land which the great landowners had given for settlement, but it is a fact worthy of notice by the advocates of rural colonization.

To ascertain the exact economic effect of the migration of labor is, if possible, still more difficult than to determine its causes. On the one hand, the mother country gains by the settlement of lands which afford fresh markets for her products, and by the employment even over the seas of her surplus population. On the other hand, emigration beyond certain reasonable limits involves a drain upon the productive and military force of the country, and the relief afforded to the labor market may easily be neutralized by the presence of an excessive number of old men and children. . . .

On the whole, it seems clear that though the eastern provinces suffer greatly from the drain upon agricultural labor, the inhabitants of more thickly peopled districts, and the representatives of the decaying small industries, would be in an even worse condition than at present were it not for the facilities afforded for migration.

6. The Political Immaturity of the Masses

The growth of class consciousness among the laboring masses of Germany was slow. The nation continued to be dominated by the attitudes and loyalties of an agrarian society, although the process of industrialization was rapidly changing the role which the village had traditionally played in the life of Central Europe. In his memoirs August Bebel, a leader of the Social Democratic Workingmen's party, described the political immaturity of the lower classes in the 1860s. The urban proletariat had not yet developed a sense of its needs and interests as a distinct economic group in the national community.

WHILE THE industrial development of Germany had made considerable headway at that time, nevertheless this country was still overwhelmingly a land of small business men and small farmers. Three-fourths of the industrial laborers were artisans. With the exception of work in the heavy industries, such as mining, iron construction and machine building, factory labor was despised by the artisan journeymen. The products of factories were considered cheap as well as nasty, a stigma which the representative of Germany at the world's exposition at Philadelphia, Privy Counselor Reuleaux, still impressed upon German factory labor sixteen years later. In the eyes of the artisan, the factory laborer was an inferior, and to be called a laborer instead of a journeyman or an apprentice, was considered an insult by many. Moreover, the vast majority of the journeyman and apprentices still harbored the delusion that they would be masters some day, particularly when professional liberty was proclaimed in Saxony and other states in the beginning of the sixties. The political intelligence of these workers was low. In the fifties, during the period of blackest reaction, in which all political life was dead, they had been raised and had not been given

SOURCE: *Bebel's Reminiscences* (New York: Socialist Literature Company, 1911), pp. 56–57.

any opportunity to educate themselves politically. Workingmen's clubs or artisans' clubs were exceptions and served every other purpose but political enlightenment. Workingmen's clubs of a political nature were not even tolerated in most German states or were even prohibited by a decision of the federal diet in 1856, for in the opinion of this parliament in Frankfurt am Main, a workingmen's club was identical with the spreading of socialism and communism. And to us of the younger generation, socialism and communism were at that time utterly strange conceptions. It is true that here and there, for instance in Leipsic, a few individuals, like Fritzsche, Vahlteich, the tailor Schilling, existed, who had heard of Weitling's communism, and had read his writings, but these men were exceptions. Never did I hear at that time of any laborer who knew anything of the *Communist Manifesto*, or of the activity of Marx and Engels during the years of the revolution in the Rhineland.

All this shows that the working class at that time occupied a position in which it had neither a class interest of its own, nor knew anything of the existence of a social question.

7. *Johann Jacoby Appeals for Social Harmony*

The social effects of the industrialization of the economy of Central Europe aroused concern among well-intentioned reformers who were appalled by the impoverishment and brutalization of the urban proletariat. Most of them sought to bring about a reconciliation between the interests of capital and labor which would avert the horrors of class war. Johann Jacoby's profound faith in democracy led him to the espousal of popular sovereignty in politics and mass welfare in economics. A speech which he gave early in 1870 appealed for the establishment of social harmony through the sacrifice of private advantage to the common good.

WITH REGARD to the workman himself, it is needful, above all, that he should have a clear idea of his position, and that he should learn to know and to respect the nobler side of human nature that is within him.

We have already said that, in general, the wages of the laborer suffice only for the miserable support of himself and of his family. If any one doubts this pitiful condition of wages, we would refer

SOURCE: Johann Jacoby, *The Social Question* (London, 1870), pp. 6–9.

him to the testimony rendered some time back by a Commission of the Customs to Parliament, in a report upon the estimate of the wages of workmen; it is written in striking terms.

> We cannot allow the assertion that there is a sensible difference between the wages of the workman and the means necessary for his bare maintenance to pass unnoticed. The amount of wages is precisely the point around which the whole of the social question practically moves. Workmen affirm the insufficiency of wages, the employers do not contest this in principle, but they declare the amount of wages to be a fixed link in the chain of economic phenomena, and that under the control of the market in which they find themselves, they cannot arbitrarily change it without breaking the whole chain. As long as this contest is not decided, and we fear that it may be eternal . . . we must rest ourselves as being the sole point of any real solid foundation upon the opinion that the two terms, "wages" and "means of indispensable existence," generally compensate each other.

"The indestructible chain of economic phenomena!" Really one could scarcely find a more striking expression! Doubtless, the lords of capital and the dispensers of labor will not be impeded in the accumulation of capital upon capital; but very heavily does this "chain of economic phenomena" weigh upon the working classes. And yet here again the saying of the poet confirms itself—

There dwells a spirit of good even in that which is evil!

The dominant industrial system whilst necessitating the assemblage of large masses of laborers in the same locality, furnishes at the same time the first step for doing away with the evil it engenders. As man learns from a glass the knowledge of the features of his own face, so the salaried workman attains to a complete acquaintance of his situation only by perceiving his own condition reflected in the common misery of his companions in suffering. In common with his equally ill-favored and equally oppressed companions, by constant intercourse and exchange of ideas with his equals, by the mutual cooperation of reciprocal assistance and of defense against the common danger, there is developed by degrees among the workmen a bond of brotherhood, which supports individuals, educates them, and urges the whole body to struggle for their social rights. It is a singular occurrence that it should be production by capital that itself assembles and disciplines the forces destined to put an end to the domination of capital and of the classes which represent it.

It is from these great industrial agglomerations that the working-men's movement has arisen, which for this last ten years has spread itself from England to France, to Belgium, to Germany, to Switzerland, and has acquired by the foundation of the International Association a precise form and a positive power. On all sides we find societies taking root, whose object is the amelioration of the material condition of the working classes; societies of artisans and of laborers, associations for instruction, for assistance, for consumption, for advances, and for credit, unions for manufacture and production. It is to be foreseen, that under the pressure of prevailing financial and economical relationships, all these institutions proceeding from the workman alone, and founded upon the principle of "self-help," will prove insufficient in the face of the common wants. But their services will have been considerable in aiding the intellectual and moral development of the working class and in starting a serious reform in the condition of labor. The true meaning of the inappreciable value of these associations consists in that, irrespectively of their specific end, they form a school for the members of the Association, and render them capable of managing their own affairs as well as of cooperating efficaciously with others. By education, by progress in the knowledge of affairs, and by the development of a friendly lien among the workmen, they prepare them insensibly to pass from the wage system now in vigor to the system of production by association, which is that of the future.

It was the spirit of association which elevated the laborious citizen class, in the middle ages, to such a high degree of civilization, of well-being, of power, and of importance. The awakening of this spirit of association, will lead us in our own days, to results, similar, yet more fruitful, not for a single state, but for the entire human society.

The labor question, as we understand it, is not a question of mere bread and money; it is a question of justice, of civilization, and of humanity. Our pretended saviors of the state and society, "the glorious conquests of politics by blood and iron," will long, like a superannuated legend, have fallen into the profoundest oblivion, when it will be accorded as a merit to our time to have awakened and fostered the spirit of association, the germ of human virtue and greatness. By this means, our epoch will have laid the foundations of a new social life founded upon the principles of equality and fraternity. The creation of the most insignificant workingman's association, will be to the future historian of civilization of more importance than the sanguinary day of Sadowa! . . .

What ought the manufacturer, the enterprising possessor of capital, to do?

All we ask of him is simply to consider in each workman, "the man"; we ask of him to recognize, and to treat the hired man he employs as a being who has exactly the same rights as himself—in one word, as his equal.

Every medal, it is said, has two sides; in this saying there is a good deal of popular good sense; the most difficult problems of science and of life find therein a satisfactory solution. Just as the medal, man also has two sides: the one peculiar to him as an individual; the other general, stamping him as a member of a great community. In fact, these two sides are inseparable and without a defined limit, for it is but in their entirety, and in their unity that they constitute man; but it is nevertheless possible that one of these two sides, temporarily or lastingly, may manifest itself in excess, and thus exercise a decisive influence upon our thoughts and upon our actions.

Let us suppose, for example, that it is the more particular or individual side, which allows itself to be felt and becomes preponderate in the conscience of a man. First of all, there will result a more exaggerated appreciation of personality, a deeper sentiment of his personal value and a greater confidence in self. "Aid yourself! Man is his own architect." This is one man's motto, the rule of his thought and his actions. If he preserves at the same time his sentiment on the other side, that is on the general side of his existence, if he does not lose sight of the entirety, which binds him to his equals, he will say, that his own isolated forces will not suffice to procure for himself a life worthy of a man; that man can only live and prosper in the society of his fellow creatures, and that a fraternal cooperation with others is his interest if well understood.

Reverence for others, the sentiment of community and the spirit of fraternity, will constitute the necessary counterpoise to his egotism and self-confidence. But the case is quite different when this personal egotism develops itself to excess. Even then he will doubtless not overlook the insufficiency of his isolated individual power, for the consciousness of the general and universal side can never be completely stifled, but it is the consequences which he therefrom deduces, which are quite different; he will consider other men not as beings who are his equals, not as members of a great whole to which he himself belongs, and in which they have all equal rights with himself, but as members subordinated to his individual self, as simple instruments, destined to the satisfaction of his own wants and desires. It is thus that the personal feeling, so laudable in itself, degenerates into egotism—confidence in self into arrogance. Cupidity, pride, ambition, will decide him to make of his neighbor a servant of his will, and of that which he deemd his own interest.

What we have just said of each man in particular is true also of man in the abstract; the same forces which act upon the mind of the individual, act also upon the life of peoples, and upon the history of the human race.

Domination of man over man, right of the stronger, exploitation of the weaker, these are the characteristic features, which distinguished alike the history of antiquity and that of the middle ages. Is it otherwise at the present time?

Does not social order even today, notwithstanding our boasted progress, repose upon the same principle of human servitude?

8. He Advances a Program of Economic Reform

The social program with which bourgeois reformers in the age of Bismarck hoped to prevent class conflict will seem quite moderate to those living a hundred years later. They called on the authorities to shorten the working day, prohibit child labor, introduce a progressive income tax, and encourage the establishment of workers' associations. In their view such measures would reconcile the proletariat to the state and would allay strife between the propertied and the propertyless. This was the objective which Johann Jacoby sought to attain by his eloquent appeal for humanitarian reform. Philanthropic idealism was for him the only alternative to violent revolution.

FOR THE WORKING CLASSES in particular, and . . . having in view the general interest, we ask—

Reduction of the hours of labor, and a fixation of the day's work.

SOURCE: Johann Jacoby, *The Social Question* (London, 1870), pp. 15–16.

The paid laborer (or receiver of wages) must also have time and the leisure to form his mind and watch the affairs of the state. The congress of the English Workingmen's Association, which was held in the month of August last year, at Birmingham, advises a period of eight hours as a common measure for all trades, and expresses the conviction that by this means, will be fortified the physical and intellectual energy of the workman, and we shall thereby further morals, and diminish the number of the unemployed.

Prohibition of the employment of children in manufacturies, and an equal rate of wages, both for women as well as for men, are necessary steps to prevent the diminution of wages, and to the decline of the rising generation.

Furthermore, we desire the abolition of indirect contributions, and the establishment of a tax progressive and proportional to the fortune of the individual.

Every tax upon consumption, is a tax upon the strength of the laborer, and consequently, an impediment to the production of wealth, and a prejudice to the well-being of the people.

Finally, reform of the system of credit, and the furtherance of associations, both industrial and agricultural, by the means of the institution of credit, or by the protection of the state.

It is necessary to lay open the road to credit to the workman. What the state has done hitherto, and to such an extent directly and indirectly for the support and protection of capital, it must now effect, and that in its own interest, for the advancement of the working classes and workingmen's association.

Nothing is so advantageous to the community as justice in all things.

These are the first conditions of the reform of labor. Workmen have been advised, perhaps with good intentions, to keep themselves aloof from all politics, and to concentrate all their attention on their economic interest, as if we could separate economic and political interests, as we cleave wood with a hatchet. Whoever has followed the course of our considerations will not doubt, I hope, that it is just the working classes whose interest it most imports to modify public relationships on the side of libérty! The assistance of the state, no less than that of the individual, is necessary to secure to each workman the complete and intact product of his labor, that is to say, the possibility of an existence worthy of a human being.

The state alone can come to the workman's aid, and the free state alone will do it! . . .

The wage system answers now as little to the exigencies of justice and humanity, as slavery and serfdom in former times.

Just as it was with slavery and serfdom, the wage system was formerly a progress by which society has derived incontestable advantages.

The social question of our times consists therefore in the abolition of the wage system, without prejudice to the advantages resulting from the common labor of great collective industry.

There is for this but one means, the system of free labor by association—the cooperative system. The present time is a transition period from the wage system (system of production by means of capital) to the system of labor by association.

In order that this transition may be effected in a peaceful manner, it is requisite that the workmen, employers, and the state act in common.

It is the duty of workmen to unite, in order to resist the oppression of capital and to raise themselves by education to moral and material independence.

It is the duty of the employer to engage himself in the cause of the workman's well-being in a philanthropic spirit, and especially to accord to him a share of the profits of labor.

Finally, the state, by the protection of association, by fixing the hours of labor, and by giving gratuitous instruction, ought to further the efforts of workmen towards civilization. Upon the state devolves, at the same time, the duty of protecting the system of production by association on a large scale, of a reform in the system of banks of credit, and of the institution of state credit.

As such help can only be expected from a free state, it is clear that the workmen and their friends must, before all, procure for themselves political liberty.

Political liberty, social liberty, liberty of the citizen, without sacrificing the majority of mankind as wage laborers—this is the problem of our era.

The conquests of the *blood and iron* policy, the din of arms, which has reverberated in our day, the struggles and the combats which occur for the sake of dominion and power, for fortune and for advancement—these are but ripples on the surface of the stream of time; in the hidden depths, slowly but steadily advances the science of nature and of mind, and with this science, the consciousness of the independence of man—the world-moving idea of the liberty, equality, and fraternity of all. Years and years may pass away, and still that saying of the Scripture will be fulfilled—that joyful message which the electric wire brought as a first greeting from free America to Europe encumbered with arms: "Peace on earth and good will toward men."

9. Heinrich von Treitschke Defends the Inequality of Classes

Most people of means and education, however, regarded programs of economic reform and social reconciliation as visionary. They believed that distinctions in wealth and position were eternal and immutable. The historian Heinrich von Treitschke preached in his lectures that the culture of the few was made possible only by the labor of the many. Any attempt to alter the distribution of property or to broaden the accessibility of learning must lead to the decline of society. It was reassuring to the well-to-do classes of Central Europe to hear that their domination of the economy was the result not of greed or exploitation but of the fundamental laws of progress.

WHEN WE EXAMINE more closely the whole fabric of these conditions of mutual interdependence which we call society we find that under all its forms it tends naturally towards aristocracy. The Social Democrats imply in their very title the absurdity of their aspirations. Just as the state presupposes an irremovable distinction between those in whom authority is vested and those who must submit to it, so also does the nature of society imply differences of social standing and economic condition amongst its members. In short, all social life is built upon class organization. Wise legislation may prevent it from being oppressive and make the transition from class to class as easy as possible, but no power on earth will ever be able to substitute a new and artificial organization of society for the distinctions between its groups which have arisen naturally and automatically.

It is a fundamental rule of human nature that the largest portion of the energy of the human race must be consumed in supplying the primary necessities of existence. The chief aim of a savage's life is to make that life secure, and mankind is by nature so frail and

SOURCE: Heinrich von Treitschke, *Politics*, 2 vols. (New York: Macmillan, 1916), vol. I, pp. 41–45.

needy that the immense majority of men, even on the higher levels of culture must always and everywhere devote themselves to breadwinning and the material cares of life. To put it simply: the masses must for ever remain the masses. There would be no culture without kitchenmaids.

Obviously education could never thrive if there was nobody to do the rough work. Millions must plough and forge and dig in order that a few thousands may write and paint and study.

It sounds harsh, but it is true for all time, and whining and complaining can never alter it. Moreover the outcry against it does not spring from love of humanity but from the materialism and modern conceit of education. It is profoundly untrue to regard education as the essential factor in history, or as the rock on which human happiness is founded. Would it not be monstrous to maintain that women are less happy than men? Does the superior learning of the savant place him on a higher plane than the laborer? Personally I am not imbued with this arrogance of learning, and truly great natures have never been tainted with it. I have always felt a deep respect for the homely virtues of the poor. Happiness is not to be sought in intellectual attainments, but in the hidden treasures of the heart, in the strength of love and of an easy conscience, which are accessible to the humble as well as to the great. Goethe has often proclaimed that it is the moral forces which distinguish human beings from other creatures:

> *Edel sei der Mensch,*
> *Hülfreich und gut,*
> *Denn das allein*
> *Unterscheidet ihn*
> *Von allen Wesen,*
> *Die wir kennen.*

A man must be noble, kind and good at need, for that alone raises him above all other beings that we know of.

Again he says, "High thinking is not vital."

It is precisely in the differentiation of classes that the moral wealth of mankind is exhibited. The virtues of wealth stand side by side with those of poverty, with which we neither could nor should dispense, and which by their vigor and sincerity put to shame the jaded victim of over-culture. There is a hearty joy in living which can only flourish under simple conditions of life. Herein we find a remarkable equalization of the apparently cruel classifications of society. Want is a relative conception. It is the task of government to reduce and mitigate distress, but its abolition is neither possible nor desirable. The economy of Nature has here set definite limits upon human endeavor, and on the other hand man's pleasure in life is so overwhelming that a healthy race will increase and spread wherever there is space for them.

We are told indeed that the innumerable inventions of a highly developed commercial community will make the supply of the primary necessities of life increasingly easier, but this is a delusion, for needs and desires lie so near the root of human nature that every material want which is satisfied generates another in endless succession. When the first railway was built it was generally assumed that a great number of horses would in future be superfluous, since the mail coaches would cease to run upon the highroads. Exactly the contrary has happened, because more horses are now used on the byroads which lead to the railways than were formerly required in the whole of Germany.

So it will remain true that the great mass of humanity is always laboring for the elementary requirements of the race. Nor can any one seriously wish that everybody should receive a highly intellectual education. We have already overstepped the limits of prudence in this direction and it would be a disaster if still more Germans wished to matriculate. The modern Greeks have squandered away their future by developing two characteristics with an appalling one-sidedness: firstly by cultivating an appetite for information which has raised the number of students in Athens to more than 3000, whose highest ideal is that of the schoolmaster, and secondly by neglecting their army. They cannot strike, and therefore it has become doubtful whether they will ever possess Constantinople, however much it is to be desired that they should. There are then nations who, to their great detriment, are over-cultured, and there is still truth in the old saying about the hallowed soil of manual work.

Let us hear no clap-trap about the disinherited. No doubt there have been times when those in possession have grossly abused their power, but as a rule the social balance is kept.

There must be give and take between the higher and the lower grades of society, and in fact there is. The artisan can only pursue his craft by means of the upper classes, and it is the wholesale contractors who virtually direct labor.

10. Helmuth von Moltke Opposes the Forces of Revolution

Those who believed that the existing system of property relations should remain unchanged and unchallenged were ready to use repression in its defense. When in 1878 the government introduced in the Reichstag a bill designed to crush the socialist movement, Helmuth von Moltke rose to speak in support of an attack against radicalism. The military hero of the wars of national unification warned against the forces of subversion which had provoked civil strife in France in the days of the Paris Commune and which were now threatening Germany with revolution and chaos. According to him, only force could save the Fatherland.

I SINCERELY HOPE that the Honorable Members, who yesterday and today have opposed the government measures, may not, all too soon, be placed in the position of having to demand of the government the introduction either of this very law, or of one similar to it, but imposing, possibly, even greater restrictions. It is quite possible that the measure requires improvement in several points, and that many paragraphs will have to be altered; it appears to me, however, that the conviction has everywhere gained ground that we are in need of some better protection against the dangers which, by the progressive organization of social democracy, threaten the state in its innermost constitution. I fear that the leaders of this organization are already now pressed back to within measurable distance of that line beyond which they will be required to make their promises and pledges good.

These gentlemen will be the first to understand what difficulties this will involve. They cannot gainsay the fact that the first distribution of property must be followed by a hundred more; that where all are equally rich, all are equally poor; that want, misery and privation are inseparable conditions of human existence; that no form of government, no legislation and, generally, no human disposition, will ever banish misery and want from the world. What would become of the development of the human race if these cogent elements had no place in God's creation! No, the future will not be without its cares and its toil; but a man who is hungry and cold considers little what the future may have in store;

SOURCE: Helmuth von Moltke, *Essays, Speeches, and Memoirs*, 2 vols. (New York: Harper & Row, 1893), vol. II, pp. 76–78.

he snatches eagerly at the means which the present offers him. Passions long restrained, blighted hopes, will incite him to deeds of violence which his leaders are utterly unable to prevent; for revolution has hitherto devoured its leaders first of all.

What, then, is the position of the government? Gentlemen, we should cease to look upon the government as, in a certain sense, a hostile power which is to be held in check, and hampered as much as possible. Let us invest the government with that fullness of power which is indispensable to the safeguarding of all interests! The history of the Commune in Paris attests the consequences that follow when a government allows the reins of authority to slip out of its hands, and when the direction of affairs is controlled by the masses. The opportunity was then offered to democracy to carry out its ideas, under circumstances when, at least for a time, it could set up its own ideal form of government. Nothing, however, was gained, gentlemen; much, on the contrary, was destroyed. The official French reports of this sad episode in the history of France allow us to peer into an abyss of depravity; they depict circumstances and events of the nineteenth century which one would have deemed impossible if they had not occurred under our very eyes—before the astonished gaze of our armies of occupation, which would have made short work of the whole thing had they not been obliged to look impassively on, with "ordered arms."

Gentlemen, our laboring classes, even the most misguided amongst them, do not contemplate such consequences as these, but, on the downward road, it is always the better elements which are carried along by the worse. Behind the moderate liberal comes the man who is prepared to go much further than he. That is the mistake which so many make; they believe that they can, without danger, bring things down to their own level, and there stop, just as if they could abruptly arrest the rush of a train going at full speed—without peril to the necks of the passengers. Gentlemen, from behind the honest revolutionist those dark shapes may be descried emerging, the . . . apparitions of 1848, the *professeurs des barricades* and the *pétroleuses* of the Commune of 1871.

Gentlemen, you may today throw out this bill in the well-grounded expectation that the government will be strong enough to deal with any violent excesses and, if necessary, to put them down by armed force; but, gentlemen, that is but a sorry shift—it averts the danger of the moment, but it does not remedy the evil from which the danger springs. If now we have here a way pointed out to us, by which it may be possible to avoid the employment of such pitiable means by adopting preventive measures, by a sensible temporary restriction of misused liberty, then, I say, we should lend a helping hand in the interest of all social and national order, in the interest especially of the suffering classes among our fellow-citizens, who can never be benefited by any sudden overturning, but only by the slower processes of legislation, moral education, and individual labor. For my part I intend to vote in favor of the motion.

VII
The Growth of Radicalism

One of the most important effects of the industrial revolution in Central Europe was the development of class consciousness among those who labored in mines, shops, and factories. At first the workers, most of them uprooted villagers still bewildered by the new way of life in the city, were interested in little beyond the problems of their meager everyday existence. But after the mid-century more and more of them began to be aware of their needs and interests as a distinct group in society, and the way was thus opened for the formation of a political movement seeking to satisfy those needs and interests. The founder of the first Socialist party in Germany was Ferdinand Lassalle, a brilliant publicist who turned his attention to the economic and social problems of the urban masses. A doer rather than a thinker, he lacked patience for the slow process of educating the working class to the importance of organization. What he wanted was immediate success on such a grand scale as to destroy the opposition once and for all. Since the proletariat was still too backward to fight for its own liberation, Lassalle proposed to enlist the aid of the state in the war against capitalism. Why could not the government of Prussia be persuaded that the future of the kingdom depended on its willingness to assist the lower classes by establishing workers' cooperatives capable of competing with private enterprise? The introduction of direct manhood suffrage would give the proletariat the political strength to force princes and ministers into the struggle against the capitalistic system. This was the program on which Lassalle in 1863 founded the General German Workingmen's Society.

The party grew slowly, too slowly for its fiery leader who had hoped to take Central Europe by storm with his words and ideas. By the time of his death in the summer of 1864, he had attracted only about 4,600 followers. Yet this was a promising beginning in view of the political immaturity of the urban proletariat. Before long, moreover, the General German Workingmen's Society was challenged by another socialist movement which sought the same end by different means. The disciples of Marx differed from those of Lassalle in their rejection of the established state, their scorn for parliamentary methods, and their emphasis on the international character of the class struggle. After the Seven Weeks' War they formed an alliance with the petty bourgeois democrats in the secondary states of Germany. But as they gained strength and confidence, their leaders Wilhelm Liebknecht and August Bebel decided to organize a political party of their own. In 1868 a convention in Nürnberg of labor associations which had originally accepted the ideals of liberal reform voted to become affiliated with the First International. A year later came the final break between middle-class and lower-class radicalism with the formation at Eisenach of the Social Democratic Workingmen's party on a program derived primarily from the teachings of Marx. There were now two socialist parties in Central Europe, divided by sharp disagreements regarding organization and strategy, but united in a common hostility toward the capitalistic system.

The political and economic policies of the new order established through national unification led to a gradual *rapprochement* between Lassalleans and Marxians. The former, who had assumed that the state could be compelled by direct manhood suffrage to support the proletariat in the battle against the bourgeoisie, discovered that Bismarck had concluded an alliance with the middle-of-the-road parties victorious in the elections to the Reichstag of the North German Confederation. The latter, who had hoped that the verdict of Sadowa would be reversed by mass opposition to the hegemony of Prussia, were forced to the conclusion that a federal union of small, autonomous, democratic states in Central Europe was only a pipe dream. The differences between the two wings of socialism diminished further as a result of the Franco-Prussian War. Both of them opposed the continuation of hostilities after Sedan, both condemned the annexation of Alsace-Lorraine, both criticized the treaties by which the south joined the North German Confederation, both disapproved the assumption of the imperial crown by the king of Prussia. Their boldest gesture of defiance toward the new order, however, was their support of the Paris Commune. While the propertied classes looked with horror on the radical regime established in the capital of France, the socialists came out unequivocally in favor of the Communards. It was a dangerous position to take in a country, still marveling at the triumph of nationalism, which had been suddenly frightened by the red specter on the Seine.

As the gulf separating socialism from the new order in Central Europe widened, the Lassalleans and the Marxians were forced into collaboration against the common enemy. The doctrinal differences between them, which had seemed insuperable a few years before, lost their importance in the light of the concrete political experience of the German Empire. What did it matter whether the Prussian state was theoretically capable of becoming an instrument of reform or whether it was inherently a tool of despotism? The important point was that under existing conditions it was the protector of the propertied classes. What did it matter whether the struggle against capitalism should in principle be waged on a national or an international basis? For the time being the proletariat of each country would have to fight its own battle against oppression and exploitation. The socialists incurred serious risks by scorning the spoils of victory over France and rejecting the fruits of national unification. Yet in the Reichstag election of 1871 they received more than 100,000 votes, and in the Reichstag election of 1874 the figure rose to about 350,000 votes. These were impressive achievements reflecting the steady growth of class consciousness among the masses during the decade which had elapsed since the time when the General German Workingmen's Society could not even attract 5,000 members. The advantages to be gained from a union of the two wings of the labor movement were now great enough to overcome the last doctrinal scruples. In 1875 a convention held in Gotha joined Lassalleans and Marxians in the Socialist Workingmen's party of Germany. The urban proletariat had at last found an effective weapon for the defense of its vital economic interests.

1. Ferdinand Lassalle Maintains That the State Must Protect the Proletariat

To Ferdinand Lassalle the state was not simply a political instrument of the dominant class in society, but an independent moral force standing above parties and interests. He believed therefore that the emancipation of the proletariat could be achieved with the aid of the existing government, once the latter became convinced that the welfare of the nation depended on the establishment of a new social system. This was the point of a speech which he held before an audience of factory workers in Berlin in the spring of 1862.

THE MORAL IDEA of the capitalist is this—that nothing whatsoever is to be guaranteed to any individual but the unimpeded exercise of his faculties.

If we were all equally strong, equally wise, equally educated, and equally rich, this idea might be regarded as a sufficient and a moral one; but since we are not so, and cannot be so, this thought is not sufficient, and therefore, in its consequences, leads necessarily to a serious immorality; for its result is that the stronger, abler, richer man exploits the weaker and becomes his master.

The moral idea of the working class, on the other hand, is that the unimpeded and free exercise of individual faculties by the individual is not sufficient, but that in a morally adjusted community there must be added to it solidarity of interests, mutual consideration, and mutual helpfulness in development.

In contrast to such a condition the capitalist class has this conception of the moral purposes of the state—that it consists exclusively and entirely in protecting the personal liberty of the individual and his property.

This is a policeman's idea, gentlemen—a policeman's idea because the state can think of itself only in the guise of a policeman whose whole office consists in preventing robbery and burglary. Unfortunately this conception is to be found, in consequence of imperfect thinking, not only among acknowledged liberals, but, often enough, even among many supposed to be democrats. If the capitalist class were to carry their thought to its logical extreme

SOURCE: Ferdinand Lassalle, "The Workingmen's Program," in *The German Classics of the Nineteenth and Twentieth Centuries*, ed. Kuno Francke, 20 vols. (Albany and New York: German Publication Society, 1913–14), vol. X, pp. 428–431.

they would have to admit that, according to their idea, if there were no thieves or robbers the state would be entirely unnecessary.

The [working] class conceives of the purpose of the state in a quite different manner, and its conception of it is the true one.

History is a struggle with nature—that is, with misery, with ignorance, with poverty, with weakness, and, accordingly, with restrictions of all kinds to which we were subject when the human race appeared in the beginning of history. A constantly advancing victory over this weakness—that is the development of liberty which history portrays.

In this struggle we should never have taken a step forward, nor should we ever take another, if we had carried it on, or tried to carry it on, as individuals, each for himself alone.

It is the state which has the office of perfecting this development of freedom, and of the human race to freedom. The state is this unity of individuals in a moral composite—a unity which increases a millionfold the powers of all individuals who are included in this union, which multiplies a millionfold the powers which are at the command of them all as individuals.

The purpose of the state, then, is not to protect merely the personal liberty of the individual and the property which, according to the idea of the capitalist, he must have before he can participate in the state; the purpose of the state is, rather, through this union to put individuals in a position to attain objects, to reach a condition of existence which they could never reach as individuals, to empower them to attain a standard of education, power, and liberty which would be utterly impossible for them, one and all, merely as individuals. The object of the state is, accordingly, to bring the human being to positive and progressive development— in a word, to shape human destiny, i.e., the culture of which mankind is capable, into actual existence. It is the training and development of the human race for freedom.

Such is the real moral nature of the state—its true and higher task. This is so truly the case that for all time it has been carried out through the force of circumstances, by the state, even without its will, even without its knowledge, even against the will of its leaders.

But the working class, the lower classes of society in general, have, on account of the helpless position in which their members find themselves as individuals, the sure instinct that just this must be the function of the state—the aiding of the individual, by the union of all, to such a development as would be unobtainable by him merely as an individual.

The state then, brought under the control of the idea of the working class, would no longer be driven on, as all states have been up to this time, unconsciously and often reluctantly, by the nature of things and the force of circumstances; but it would make this moral nature of the state its task, with the greatest clearness and complete consciousness. It would accomplish with ready willingness and the most complete consistency that which, up to this time, has been forced only in the dimmest outlines from the opposing will, and just for this reason it would necessarily promote a flourishing of intellect, a development of happiness, education, prosperity, and liberty, such as would stand without example in the world's history, in comparison with which the most lauded conditions in earlier times would drop into a pale shadow. . . .

Nothing is more effective in impressing upon a class a dignified and deeply moral stamp than the consciousness that it is destined to be the ruling class; that it is called upon to elevate the principle of its class to the principle of the whole historical period; to make its idea the leading truth of the whole of society, and so, in turn, to shape society into a reflection of its own character. The lofty historical honor of this destiny must lay hold upon all your thoughts. It is no longer becoming to you to indulge in the vices of the oppressed, or the idle distractions of the thoughtless, or even the harmless frivolity of the insignificant. You are the rock upon which the church of the present is to be built.

The lofty moral earnestness of this thought should entirely fill your mind, should fill your hearts and shape your whole life to be worthy of it and conformable to it. The moral earnestness of this thought, without ever leaving you, must stand for better thoughts in your shop during your work, in your leisure hours, your walks, your meetings; and, even when you lie down to rest on your hard couch, it is this thought which must fill and occupy your soul until it passes into the realm of dreams. The more exclusively you fill your minds with this moral earnestness, the more undividedly you are influenced by its warmth—of this you may be assured—the more you will hasten the time in which our present historical period has to accomplish its task, the sooner you will bring about the fulfillment of this work.

2. He Explains the Iron Law of Wages

The Lassallean theories of social reform attracted the attention of a committee of workers in Leipzig which was planning early in 1863 to convoke a labor congress representing the urban proletariat of all of Germany. In reply to the committee's request for advice, Lassalle elaborated on his views regarding the injustice of the capitalistic system and the nature of economic exploitation. He maintained that the masses could not achieve emancipation by their own unaided efforts, for an inexorable law of wages inherent in private ownership kept them permanently subservient to the bourgeoisie.

THE WORKING CLASS must establish itself as an independent political party, and must make the universal, equal, and direct franchise the banner and watchword of this party. Representation of the working class in the legislative bodies of Germany—nothing else can satisfy its legitimate interests from a political point of view. To begin a peaceful and law-abiding agitation for this by all lawful means is and must be, from a political point of view, the program of the workingmen's party. . . .

But you propose to establish institutions for savings, funds for retiring pensions, insurance against accidents and sickness? I am willing to recognize the relative usefulness of these institutions, although it is a subordinate one and hardly worth notice.

But let us make a complete distinction between two questions which have absolutely nothing to do with each other.

Is it your object to make the misery of individual workingmen more endurable; to counteract the effects of thoughtlessness, sickness, old age, accidents of all kinds, through which by chance or necessity individual workingmen are forced even below the normal condition of the working class? For such objects all these institutions are entirely appropriate means. Only it would not be worthwhile in that case to begin a movement for such a purpose throughout all Germany, to stir up a general agitation in the whole working class of the nation. You must not bring mountains into

SOURCE: Ferdinand Lassalle, "Open Letter to the Central Committee for the Summoning of a General German Workingmen's Congress at Leipzig," in *The German Classics of the Nineteenth and Twentieth Centuries,* ed. Kuno Francke, 20 vols. (Albany and New York: German Publication Society, 1913–14), vol. X, pp. 494–496, 501–503.

labor in order that a ridiculous mouse appear. This so extremely limited and subordinate purpose can better be left to local unions and local organizations, which can always handle it far better.

Or is this your object: To improve the normal condition of the whole working class and elevate it above its present level? In truth this is and must be your purpose, but this sharp line of distinction is necessary, which I have drawn between these two objects, which must not be confused with each other, in order to show you, better than I could through a long exposition, how utterly powerless these institutions are to attain this second object, and therefore how utterly outside the scope of the present workingmen's movement. . . .

The relentless economic law which, under present conditions, fixes the wages by the law of demand and supply of labor is this: The average wage always remains at the lowest point which will maintain existence and propagate the race at the standard of living accepted by the people. This is the point about which the actual wage always oscillates like a pendulum, without ever rising above or falling below it for any length of time. It cannot permanently rise above this average, for then, through the easier situation of the workingman, an increase of the working population and therefore of the supply of hands would ensue, which would bring the wage again to a point below its former scale.

Neither can the wage fall permanently far below what is necessary to support life, for then arise emigration, celibacy, and avoidance of childbearing, and, finally, a reduction of the number of laborers, which then diminishes still more the supply of hands, and therefore brings the wage back to its former position again.

The real average wage, therefore, is fixed by a constant movement about this point of equilibrium, to which it must constantly return, sometimes rising a little above it (period of prosperity in some or all industries), sometimes falling a little below it (period of more or less general distress and industrial crises).

The limitation of the average wage to the amount necessary to exist and propagate the race under the accepted standard of living in a community—that, I repeat, is the inexorable and cruel law which determines the wage under present conditions.

This law can be denied by no one. I could cite as many authorities for it as there are great and famous names in economic science, and even from the liberal school itself, for it is just the liberal school of political economy which has discovered this law and proved it. This inexorable and cruel law, gentlemen, you must above all things fix deeply in your minds and base upon it all your thinking.

In this connection I can give you and the whole working class an infallible means of escaping once for all the many attempts to deceive and mislead you. To everyone who talks to you about the improvement of the situation of the working class, you must first put the question: Does he acknowledge the existence of this law, or not? If he does not, you must say to yourself at the start that this man is either trying to deceive you, or has the most pitiable ignorance in the science of political economy; for, as I said, there is not a single economist of the liberal school worthy of mention who denies it—Adam Smith as well as Say, Ricardo as well as Malthus, Bastiat as well as John Stuart Mill, are unanimous in recognizing it. There is an agreement on this point among all men of science. And if he who talks to you about the condition of workingmen has recognized this law, then ask further: How does he expect to abolish this law? And, if he can give no answer to this, then coolly turn your back upon him. He is an idle prattler, who is trying to deceive you or himself, or dazzle you with empty talk.

Let us consider for a moment the effect and the nature of this law. It is stated in other words as follows: From the product of industry there is first withdrawn and divided among the workingmen the amount which is required to maintain their existence (wage). The whole remainder of the product (profit) goes to the employer. It is therefore a consequence of this inexorable and cruel law that you (and for this reason in my pamphlet on the working class to which you refer in your letter I have called you the class of the disinherited) are forever necessarily excluded from the productiveness which increases in amount through the progress of civilization, i.e., from the increased product of industry, from the increased earning power of your own work! For you there remain forever the bare necessities of life, for the employer everything produced by labor beyond this amount.

3. He Stresses the Importance of Direct Manhood Suffrage

Since under capitalism the working class lived in perpetual poverty, reasoned Lassalle, the only way to end the exploitation of labor was through the establishment by the state of industrial enterprises which the workers themselves would own and operate. But how could the rulers of Central Europe be persuaded to become the gravediggers of the bourgeoisie? The answer which Lassalle preached to the masses was that the introduction of direct manhood suffrage would give them a weapon with which to transform the government from an instrument of their oppression into an instrument of their liberation.

To MAKE the working class their own employers—that is the means, the only means, by which [the] inexorable and cruel law which determines wages can be abolished. When the working class is its own employer, the distinction between wages and profits will disappear, and the total yield of the industry will take the place, as the reward of labor, of the bare living wage.

The abolition by this only possible means of that law which under present conditions assigns to the workingman his wages—that part of the product which is necessary for bare existence—and the whole remainder to the employer—this is the only real, non-visionary, just improvement in the position of the working class.

But how? Look at the railroads, machine shops, ship yards, cotton and woolen mills, etc., etc., and the millions required for these establishments; then look into your own empty pockets and ask yourself where you will ever get the enormous capital necessary for these establishments, and how therefore you can ever make possible the carrying on of wholesale production on your own account!

And surely there is no fact more true, more thoroughly established, than that you would never accomplish this if you were reduced exclusively and essentially to your own isolated efforts as individuals alone.

SOURCE: Ferdinand Lassalle, "Open Letter to the Central Committee for the Summoning of a General German Workingmen's Congress at Leipzig," in *The German Classics of the Nineteenth and Twentieth Centuries*, ed. Kuno Francke, 20 vols. (Albany and New York: German Publication Society, 1913–14), vol. X, pp. 508–510, 517–520.

Just for this reason it is the business and the duty of the state to make it possible for you to take in hand the great cause of the free, individual association of the working class in such a way as to help its development, and make it its solemn duty to offer you the means and the opportunity for this association.

Now, do not allow yourselves to be deceived and misled by the cry of those who will tell you that any such intervention by the state destroys social incentive. It is not true that I hinder anybody from climbing a tower by his own strength if I hand him a ladder or a rope. It is not true that the state prevents children from educating themselves by their own powers if it provides them with teachers, schools and libraries. It is not true that I hinder anybody from plowing a field by his own strength if I give him a plow. It is not true that I hinder anyone from defeating a hostile enemy by his own strength if I put a weapon into his hand for the purpose.

Although it is true that now and then someone may have climbed a tower without a rope or a ladder; that individuals have acquired an education without teachers, schools, or public libraries; that the peasants in the Vendée in the wars of the revolution now and then defeated an enemy even without weapons; yet all these exceptions do not vitiate the rule—they only prove it; and therefore, although it is true that under certain special conditions single groups of workingmen in England have been able to improve their condition, to a certain limited extent, in certain minor branches of wholesale production, by an association based chiefly upon their own exertions, nevertheless the law stands that the real improvement of the situation of the workingman, which he has a just right to demand, and to demand for the whole working class as such, can be accomplished only by this aid of the state. No more should you allow yourselves to be misled and deceived by the cry of those who talk about socialism or communism and try to oppose this demand of yours by such cheap phrases; but be firmly convinced regarding such people that they are only trying to deceive you, or else they themselves do not know what they are talking about. Nothing is further from so-called socialism and communism than this demand according to which, if realized, the working classes, just as they do today, would maintain their individual liberty, individual manner of living, and individual compensation for work, and would stand in no different relation to the state, except that the necessary capital, or credit, for their association would be provided for them by it. But that is exactly the office and the destiny of the state—to make easy and provide means for the great cultural progress of humanity. This is its ultimate purpose. For this it exists. It has always served this purpose and always must. . . .

You see . . . that it is a mathematical impossibility to free the working class . . . by the exertions of its members as merely single individuals; that only very confused, uncritical imaginations can lend themselves to these illusions, and that the only way to this end, the only way for the abolition of that cruel law of wages to which the working class is bound as to a martyr's stake, is the encouragement and development of free, individual, cooperative associations of workingmen through the helping hand of the state. The movement for workingmen's associations founded upon the purely atomistic, isolated power of individual workingmen had only the value—and this, to be sure, is an enormous one—of showing definitely the practical way in which this liberation can take place, of giving brilliant, practical proofs for overcoming all real or assumed doubt of its practical feasibility, and, in just that way, of making it the urgent duty of the state to lend its support-ing hand to those highest cultural interests of humanity. At the same time I have already proved that the state is essentially nothing else than the great association of the working class, and that there-fore the help and fostering care through which the state made possible those smaller associations would be nothing else than the legitimate social initiative, absolutely natural and lawful, which the working classes put forth for themselves as a great association, for their members as single individuals. Once more then: free indi-vidual association of the workingmen, but such association made possible by the supporting and fostering hand of the state—that is the workingmen's only way out of the wilderness.

But how shall the state be enabled to make this intervention? The answer must be immediately evident to you all: it will be possible only through universal and direct suffrage. When the legislative bodies of Germany are based on universal and direct suffrage, then, and only then, will you be able to prevail upon the state to undertake this duty.

Then this demand will be brought forward in the legislative bodies; then the limits and the forms and the means of this inter-vention will be discussed by reason and science; and then—be assured of this!—those men who understand your situation and are devoted to your cause, armed with the glittering steel of science, will stand at your side and protect your interests; then you, the propertyless class of society, will have only yourselves and your own unwise choices to blame if the representatives of your class remain in a minority.

The universal and direct franchise is, as now appears, not merely your political principle—it is your social principle, the fundamental principle of all social advancement. It is the only means for improving the material condition of the working class. But how can they accomplish the introduction of the universal and direct franchise? For an answer, look to England! The great agitation of the English people against the corn laws lasted for more than five years, but then they had to go—abolished by the Tory ministry itself.

Organize yourselves as a general workingmen's union for the purpose of a lawful and peaceable, but untiring, unceasing agitation for the introduction of universal and direct suffrage in all German states. From the moment when this union includes even one hundred thousand German workingmen, it will be a force with which everybody must reckon. Send abroad this call into every workshop, every village, every cottage. Let the city workingmen pass on their higher standard of judgment and education to the country workers. Debate, discuss, everywhere, daily, untiringly, incessantly, as was done in that great English agitation against the corn laws, in peaceable public assemblies as well as in private meetings, the necessity of the universal and direct franchise. The more the echo of your voice resounds in the ears of millions, the more irresistible its force will be.

Establish financial committees, to which every member of the German workingmen's union must contribute, and to which your plans for organization can be submitted.

With these contributions establish funds which, in spite of the smallness of the individual amounts, would form a tremendous financial power for the purpose of agitation. A weekly contribution of only one silver groschen each from one hundred thousand members of the union would produce over one hundred and sixty thousand thalers yearly. Establish newspapers which would daily bring forward this demand and prove that it is founded upon social conditions; send out by the same means pamphlets for the same purpose; employ with the resources of this union agents to carry this same view into every corner of the land, to arouse with the same call the heart of every workingman, of every cotter and plowman; indemnify from the resources of this union all those workingmen who suffer injury and persecution on account of their activity in this cause.

Repeat daily, unceasingly, this same call. The more it is repeated, the more it will spread and the mightier will become its power. The whole art of practical success consists in concentrating all efforts at all times upon one point, and that the most important one, looking neither to the right nor to the left. Look you neither to the right nor to the left; be deaf to everything which does not mean universal and direct suffrage, to everything which is not connected with it, or able to lead to it. . . .

This is the banner which you must raise. This is the standard under which you will conquer. There is no other for you.

4. The Indifference of the Masses to Lassallean Theories

Lassalle had hoped that his ideas would soon win for him a mass following among the lower classes of Central Europe, but the General German Workingmen's Society which he founded grew slowly. The bulk of the proletariat was too ignorant, cowed, and brutalized to be interested in grand schemes of economic reform and social reconstruction. Fifty years later August Bebel described in his memoirs the indifference of most workers toward the brilliant pioneer of German socialism whose eloquence remained incomprehensible to those it was intended to inspire and convert.

THE OPEN LETTER of Lassalle [to the committee of workers in Leipzig] did not make at all such an impression upon the world of labor as had been expected, in the first place, by Lassalle himself; in the second place, by the small circle of his followers. For my part, I distributed about two dozen copies in the Industrial Educational Club. . . . That the letter should have made so little impression upon the majority of the laborers in the movement of that time, may seem inexplicable today to some people. But it was quite natural. Not merely the economic, but also the political conditions were still very backward. Professional freedom, free migration, liberty to settle down, exemption from passports, liberty to wander, freedom of association and assembly, such were the demands

SOURCE: *Bebel's Reminiscences* (New York: Socialist Literature Company, 1911), pp. 78–79.

that appealed more closely to the laborer of that time than productive associations subsidized by the state, of which he had no clear conception. The idea of association or of cooperation was just sprouting. Even universal suffrage did not seem an indispensable right to the majority. On the one hand, I have emphasized several times, political intelligence was still low; on the other hand, the fight of the Prussian [legislature] against Bismarck's ministry appeared to the great majority as a brave deed, which deserved support and praise, but no censure or derogation. A man who was politically active, like myself, devoured the reports of the proceedings in parliament and regarded them as the outpour of political wisdom. The liberal press, which then ruled public opinion far more than it does today, also took care to preserve this belief. So it was the liberal press that now greeted Lassalle's appearance with cries of rage and sneers, in a way that had, perhaps, been unheard of until then. Personal insinuations and defamations poured down upon him, and that the chief conservative organs . . . treated Lassalle objectively, because his attack on the liberals was very welcome to them, did not increase Lassalle's credit or that of his followers in our eyes. And if we realize, finally, that even today, after more than forty-five years of intense labors of enlightenment, there are still millions of laborers who run after the different bourgeois parties, it is no wonder that the vast majority of the workers in the sixties of the nineteenth century were skeptical against the new movement. And at that time no success had been obtained in social legislation, such as was secured later by the socialist movement. Pioneers are always scarce.

5. The Negotiations between Bismarck and Lassalle

Since Lassalle was unable to build a mass party which could compel the government of Prussia to found workers' cooperatives, he had to rely on personal influence and private negotiation. Establishing contact with Bismarck, he offered to provide the prime minister with proletarian support against the liberal bourgeoisie in return for a government program of economic reform. Long afterward in 1878 Bismarck explained to the Reichstag his dealings with the famous labor leader,

SOURCE: Moritz Busch, *Our Chancellor: Sketches for a Historical Picture*, 2 vols. (New York: Charles Scribner's Sons, 1884), vol. II, pp. 193–194.

insisting that he had never seriously intended to become an ally of the socialist movement.

LASSALLE HIMSELF was extremely desirous to know me personally, and, if I had time to rummage amongst my old papers, I believe I could find his letter begging me to gratify that desire, which I made no difficulty about doing. I met him and talked with him for an hour, and have never regretted doing so. I did not see him three times a week, as has been stated, but perhaps thrice altogether. It was out of the question that our intercourse should assume the character of a political negotiation. What could Lassalle have offered to me? He had nothing behind him. . . . In all political negotiations the *do, ut des* is an essential feature, even if kept in the background and not alluded to by well-bred negotiators. But when one of them is obliged to say, "Poor devil that I am, what have I to offer?" He had nothing to give me in my ministerial capacity. But he had something which was extremely attractive to me as a private person; for he was one of the cleverest and most agreeable men I ever met—a man of lofty ambition, by no means a republican, but animated by strongly marked national and monarchical feelings. His ideal, which he strove to realize, was the German Empire. This was a point of contact between us. Possibly he was in doubt whether the German Empire should be swayed by the Hohenzollern dynasty or the Lassalle dynasty; but he was a monarchist to the backbone. He ought to have thundered out a *Quos ego* to his pitiful satellites, who now claim to have been his equals; he ought to have contemptuously hurled them back into their original nullity and put it out of their power to take his name in vain. Lassalle was an energetic and singularly intelligent man, to converse with whom was highly instructive; our conversations lasted for hours at a stretch and I was always sorry when they came to an end. There was no question at all of negotiations, for I had but little to say during these interviews; he alone kept up the conversation, and did so in the delightful manner which all those who knew him will remember. I regret that his position and my own did not permit me to associate with him more intimately; I should have been delighted to have a man of such gifts and *esprit* as a neighbor in the country.

6. August Bebel Attacks the Policy of the
Prussian State

While the Lassallean socialists regarded Prussia as a potential instrument of economic justice and political democracy, the Marxian socialists were from the outset distrustful of the Hohenzollern state. To them it embodied the forces of militarism and authoritarianism which threatened the freedom of Germany. When the Seven Weeks' War broke out, Bebel helped draft a proclamation condemning the role Berlin had played in provoking a fratricidal conflict. He believed that the people of Central Europe should oppose the ambitions of arrogant Junkerdom.

TO THE GERMAN PEOPLE!

The war between German brothers has been ignited. Germany has been hurled back into the time of the brutal law of force. This gravest of crimes against the nation falls on the shoulders of that party in Prussia, which is so lost to all justice, that it wants to cap the climax by outraging all Germany after it has broken the popular law of Prussia and of Schleswig-Holstein. At the moment, when the future of Schleswig-Holstein as a state should at last have been decided by the peaceful way of German law, this party has gone to the extreme of breaking the eternal bond of the German tribes, and of pushing the enforced will of the individual into the place of public right and of the collective will. It has invaded the German countries of Hanover, [Hesse-Kassel, and] Saxony, as though they were the land of the enemy, and it threatens with the same force all German states that will not submit to it. In Prussia itself, this party incites the people to a hatred of Germany, and speaks of imaginary dangers, of humiliations, degradations, dismemberment, which are supposed to be visited against it by Germany.

For the present, Prussia is not in danger of any degradation, except such as it harbors in itself. The downfall of the war party would be the best victory for Prussia. The danger of dismemberment has been brought over all of Germany precisely by that party. By its alliance with Italy, it has endangered German terri-

SOURCE: *Bebel's Reminiscences* (New York: Socialist Literature Company, 1911), pp. 155–157.

tory in the south. In the west it has conjured up the old danger which is always threatening whenever Germany is disunited.

The German tribes, whom the policy of force of the Berlin government has called to arms against itself, do not war against the people of Prussia, do not take the field for the policies of the house of Habsburg. The nation cares as little to serve Austria as it does to serve Prussia. It wishes to be free, to be master of its own house. Having been implicated in the present disaster against its will, the nation must not, and will not, await inactively the consequences. Just as it has declined, in response to the correct prompting of its patriotism, to play the offered role of a neutral power in this fratricidal war, so it now has the duty of securing, with its full power and unanimous determination, its participation in the decision of its fates by means of a general armament of the people and a common people's parliament.

7. Wilhelm Liebknecht Questions the Efficacy of Direct Manhood Suffrage

The Marxians differed from the Lassalleans, moreover, in their rejection of direct manhood suffrage as a panacea for the ills of an industrial society. They maintained that a democratic form of franchise would be ineffectual without a democratic form of government. Wilhelm Liebknecht explained this position in a speech which he held in 1869 before a working-class audience in the Prussian capital. The Reichstag of the North German Confederation, he argued, could serve only as a forum for denouncing the capitalistic system, not as a weapon for destroying it.

I SHALL NOW DISCUSS the question: is it the duty of the democracy to send delegates to the Reichstag at all? The question of whether we shall vote or not, once the universal suffrage has been attained, is merely a question of expediency, not a question of principle. We have a right to vote—the fact that this right has been refused us does not deprive us of our natural right—and if there is any advantage to be gained thereby, let us vote. . . .

[Yet the] Social Democratic party must not, under any circumstances, or in any field, engage in transactions with its opponents.

SOURCE: Wilhelm Liebknecht, *Speeches* (New York: International Publishers, 1928), pp. 18–21, 30–31. Reprinted by permission of International Publishers Co., Inc. Copyright © 1928.

We can only transact business where there is a common basis. To do business with those who are your opponents in principle is equivalent to a sacrifice of principle. Principles are indivisible; they are either clung to in their entirety or sacrificed in their entirety. The slightest concession in matters of principle is a relinquishing of the principle. He who parliamentarizes with the enemy is fencing in the air; he who parliamentarizes compromises. . . .

"But," one of you may say, "we have the best opportunity in the Reichstag to expound the principles of the social democracy." No doubt we have an opportunity, but I very much doubt whether it is the best opportunity or even a good one.

Do you believe that the Reichstag will permit us to use its speaker's platform as a pulpit? Let us assume that a Karl Marx should desire to deliver to the delegates a series of theoretical lectures; how long and how often do you think they would listen to him? Perhaps once, through curiosity, but never a second time.

There is no possibility of our having an influence on legislation, as I have just said;—then tell me, in heaven's name, what would be the use of a presentation of our principles in the Reichstag? Do you think you would convert the members of the Reichstag? Merely to think of such a possibility would be more than childish, it would be infantile. . . .

But let us assume that the government—either because it feels it is strong enough, or because of some other calculation—makes no use of its powers, and that it becomes possible, as some socialist statesmen of imagination still dream—to elect a Social Democratic majority in the Reichstag—what would this majority proceed to do? *Hic Rhodus, hic salta!* Now is the moment for transforming society and the state. The majority will adopt a world-historic decision; the new era is born—don't you believe it! A company of soldiers will eject the Social Democratic majority from its stronghold and if these gentlemen make any objection to this procedure, a few policemen will take them to police headquarters and there they will have time enough to ponder the consequences of their quixotic aspirations.

Revolutions are not made by getting the permission of the high powers that are in authority; the socialist ideal cannot be achieved within the frame of the present-day state; it must overthrow the state in order to secure the possibility of life.

No peace with the present-day state!

Away with the worship of the universal and direct suffrage!

Let us take part with all our energy, as we have done thus far, in the elections; but let us use the elections only as a means of agitation, and let us not neglect to point out that the ballot box can never be the cradle of the democratic state. The universal suffrage will not attain its decisive and final influence on state and society until the police and soldier state has definitely been eliminated.

8. He Describes His Vision of Socialist Society

Although the Marxians and the Lassalleans quarreled regarding the means to be employed in achieving their objective, the objective itself was the same for both wings of the socialist movement. Liebknecht expounded in an article written in 1875 that the established system of property relations condemned the great majority of mankind to endless poverty for the benefit of a small and selfish minority. Only a social order in which the working class retained the fruits of its labor could put an end to the oppression and exploitation of the masses.

LET US EXAMINE the state and society as they are. All power and means of life are to be found in the hands of a small minority, and this minority naturally use their power to secure and maintain that monopoly of all advantages which domination in state and society gives, and to prevent the subject majority obtaining political and social rights.

Who exercises the political power? A scanty minority whom birth and wealth have made a privileged class. The great majority of the people are absolutely helpless, and, because helpless, also without rights, for a right to which the power of enforcement is not attached is only a picture, a play, a misleading fantasy. What meaning, for example, has the right to choose a legislative representative who can only speak but cannot exercise the slightest influence on the government of the land? The governing minority rules for itself, not for the subject majority. Between rulers and ruled there exist as little community of interest as between the plantation owner and the Negro slave. The interest of the Negro does not come in question for the plantation owner; his own inter-

SOURCE: Wilhelm Liebknecht, *Socialism: What It Is and What It Seeks to Accomplish* (Chicago: Charles H. Kerr & Company, 1901), pp. 7–12.

est is determinative for him and he handles the Negro as his interest demands. Just so in the present state. The interest of the people does not come in question, but exclusively the interest of the ruling minority.

To make the interests of the ruled subservient to the interests of the rulers is the foundation and purpose of rule—is the meaning of ruling. So long as there are rulers and ruled it must be so, for rule is by its very nature exploitation. It follows therefrom that the interests of the subject people demand the transformation of the state from its foundation, according to their interest. It must cease to be the possession of a few persons of position and class and must become the possession of citizens with full and equal rights, of whom no one rules over the other, and none will be ruled by another.

For this the social democracy strives. In place of the present class rule we will institute a free government of the people. . . .

[Social democracy] will bring into existence an organization of the state and society, which, resting on the equality of all men, will choke the source of inequality, will tolerate neither ruler nor servant and will found a fraternal community of free men. In order to make this possible the present manner of production must be brought to an end. The economic basis of society—that is, the system of wage labor—must be transformed.

The mother of all social wealth, of all culture, is labor. Whatever we are and have, we are and have through labor. We have labor to thank for everything. Not our personal labor, at least only to an inconsiderable degree, but the general social labor. It is very possible indeed—and we see it frequently enough—to enjoy the blessings of culture without personal work; but it is also absolutely impossible for the most industrious and efficient worker with the most strenuous toil to live as men of culture live without the general social labor that first created culture and without which we were beasts, not men. From this we see the communistic nature of labor, its essentially associative character, on which all state and society rests. Labor has always had this communistic character, with the ancient slave and the vassal of the Middle Ages as well as with the modern wage earner. But he did not have the product of his labor, nor has he it yet. The ancient slave worked for his master, the medieval vassal for the lord of the manor, and the modern wage slave works for the capitalist. Here is the inconsistency, here the injustice to remedy which is the object of the social democracy. The social communistic character of labor must be extended to the product of labor, the product of labor shall be the property of labor, labor no longer be the companion of misery but of enjoyment.

One can see how absurd the allegation is that we propose to abolish property. Not the abolition of property is sought but the abolition of the deprivation of property, the false property which is the appropriation of others' property; the social thievery. "Expropriation of the expropriator," Marx has called it. Above all, those who call themselves Christians have no right to cry out against this "division," for the New Testament preaches communism in the roughest, most primitive form, and the first Christian communities that had yet the "whole pure teachings" carried out "division" with the greatest thoroughness.

Let us look at present conditions. Who will deny that the majority of mankind live in the greatest wretchedness and that only a minority have the means of attaining an existence worthy of human beings? . . . The present inequality springs from this: That labor does not work for itself; that it must sell itself to the idle for wages and by them be exploited. In a word, it springs out of the system of wage labor. The present injustice is only to be abolished in this way, that labor cease to work for the idle and that instead it work for itself.

Individual labor is unproductive. Work, as we have seen, must according to its nature be communistic. Therefore we must have united labor for the advantage of every individual, united labor and united enjoyment of the fruits of labor. This it is which we would establish in place of the present system of exploitation. Socialistic cooperation in place of wage labor!

But what becomes of capital?

It remains where it belongs, with labor. There is no capital but through labor. There shall be no capital except for labor. It has been asserted by charlatans that capital creates value as well as labor—the test can be easily made. The worshiper of capital may sweep together in a heap his capital, he may gather all the capital of the earth, and after the space of a year there would not have grown a penny more of value from it, but indeed the worth of the idle mass would be considerably decreased. Capital is not merely the child of labor; it cannot grow or continue without it. Capital has in relation to labor no rights, while labor in relation to capital has the right of ownership.

The tyrannous manner of production has overturned the natural relation between capital and labor and made labor the slave of capital. Is our wage labor not slavery? Is the modern wage laborer, because he can change his master, in any regard more free than the ancient slave? Does not hunger fasten him more firmly and more mercilessly to labor than the strongest iron chain? Yet our opponents often rejoin: "The worker is in a better condition today than in the last century." Whether the assertion is true or false we leave undebated. Even if true, it would prove nothing. It is not better position the socialist worker demands, but equal position. He will work no longer for another; he insists that each shall enjoy in equal measure the fruits of labor and the blessings of culture. He has enough logic and sense of justice to lay no claim to a favored place; he will also, however, accept no inferior one.

The continuance of the present manner of production is not consistent with the continuance of society. The great capitalist production was an advance. It has, however, become an obstruction. It no longer satisfies the economic needs of society, and by society we mean not the small minority of privileged persons who are pleased to call themselves "society," but the whole people.

9. He Argues That Capitalism Must Be Destroyed

Socialism preached an unremitting struggle against the capitalistic system in order to replace it with a new form of society based on freedom and justice. It held out to exploited factory workers the vision of a promised land which they themselves might not reach, but in which their children would find a better life. The dialectical and analytical arguments with which Liebknecht sought to demonstrate the ultimate collapse of the existing economy rested on a profound personal faith that the future happiness of mankind would atone for its present anguish.

THE PRESENT MANNER of production, resting on the basis of the wage system, has as a result on the one hand the accumulation of property in the hands of a few and the corruption of these few as a

SOURCE: Wilhelm Liebknecht, *Socialism: What It Is and What It Seeks to Accomplish* (Chicago: Charles H. Kerr & Company, 1901), pp. 20–24.

result of excessive possessions; on the other hand, there is impoverishment of the masses and pauperism. The worker, in the midst of the riches which he has created, cannot satisfy his smallest necessity; privation, unhealthful workshops and factories steal his life strength, as the employer steals from him the proceeds of his labor; lingering sickness and an early death await him. He has no family life, for, since his wages do not suffice for existence, wife and child must follow him into the factory. For the budding daughter he has the prospect of the short, glittering misery of prostitution, or the long, leaden, sunless misery of the life of a proletariat's wife.

Who that groans under the pressure of these conditions unworthy of mankind will not unite with us in the call: "Down with the wage system!"

"Down with the wage system!" That is the fundamental demand of social democracy—the Alpha and Omega of our agitation. Cooperative labor and association shall take the place of the wage system with its class rule.

The instruments of production must cease to be the monopoly of a class—they must be the public property of all. There shall be no more exploiter or exploited. Production and distribution of the produce must be regulated in the interest of the whole. As the present production, exploitation and robbery must be abolished, so likewise must the present traffic, which is only fraud.

In the order of equality the worker will perform all the labor necessary for the whole body of citizens. In place of the employer and his humble subservient or rebellious wage slaves there will be free comrades. Labor will be the torture of no one, but the duty of all. An existence worthy of a human being will be provided for every one who performs his duty to society. Hunger will become henceforth not the curse of labor but the punishment of the idle.

And in order that this may be realized the people's state must exist—the state composed of all and for all, the state, which consists of the wise and just organization of society, the universal guaranteed establishment of happiness and culture, and the fraternal association of free and equal men. . . .

As with every party and class that ever opposed the ruling abuses and took for their object the removal of those abuses, so it is with the social democracy. It is slandered and abused by the selfish and deluded adherents of the maladjusted state and society; it brings disorder, class strife, destruction of property, ruin of the

family and of culture, most sensual enjoyment, the deepest degradation of woman. The truth could not be more completely and
shamefully perverted. The old society throws its crimes at us, for
on their account we have condemned it to death.

Disorder rules; socialism demands order.

War and class struggle prevail; socialism insists on peace and
harmony of interests, doing away with class struggle through the
abolition of classes.

Property is today a lie for the majority of men, a robbery for the
minority. Socialism would make property the possession of every
one. It would convert it into a truth, secure to the worker within
society the full proceeds of his labor and destroy the capitalistic
system of plunder from its foundation.

The present society separates the family—socialism, since it
removes demoralizing class rule, will give value to the rights of the
family.

State and society compete with each other to nip in the bud the
culture of men, to stunt spiritually and physically the enormous
majority of the people and to corrupt the ruling minority—socialism insists on equal and the best possible training for every individual; the practical development of their faculties for all men; the
systematic advance of art and science, and will make art and
science the common possession of the people.

Thanks to the wrong conditions of society and the state, woman
is today without rights and in countless cases is condemned to
wedded or unwedded prostitution. The intercourse of the sexes is
unnatural and immoral—socialism will bring the emancipation of
woman as well as of man. It insists on her complete political and
social equality and equal position with man. It will destroy prostitution, whether it walk ashamed under the mantle of marriage for
wealth or convenience, or whether it run shameless painted and
naked upon the street.

Enough. Beginning with real conditions; not following utopian
will-o'-the-wisps, but building on the acquisition of culture, we
strive for the abolition of the class state, class legislation and class
rule.

Our end is: The free democracy with equal economic and political rights; the free society with associative labor. The welfare of
all is for us the one end of the state and society. . . .

Although we have the nearest direct sphere of our activity in the state of which we are citizens, nevertheless we do not forget the citizens of the world and the universal brotherhood of man. And we know wherever there is a struggle for the cause of labor and the oppressed people there our cause is at stake.

We seek justice and fight injustice.

We seek free labor and attack wage slavery.

We seek the prosperity of all and struggle against misery.

We seek the education of all and fight ignorance and barbarism.

We seek peace and order and combat the murder of people, the class war and the social anarchy.

We seek the socialist people's state and attack the despotic class state.

Whoever desires these things, and struggles for them, let him unite with us and work with all his strength for our cause—for the cause of socialism—for the cause of humanity, whose victory will soon be gained.

10. A Convention of German Labor Associations Votes to Affiliate with the First International

The first significant success of Marxism in Central Europe came in 1868 with the decision of a convention of labor associations meeting in Nürnberg to affiliate with the First International. These associations had at first been democratic and reformist in outlook, but the growing class consciousness of the urban proletariat gradually radicalized them. The program which they adopted rejected the Lassallean reliance on the state by asserting that the worker must become the instrument of his own liberation and that the toiling masses of all nations must unite in the struggle against capitalism.

THE FIFTH CONVENTION of German workingmen's clubs, held at [Nürnberg], declares its agreement with the program of the International Workingmen's Association in the following points:

1. The emancipation of the working classes must be the work of these classes themselves. The struggle for the emancipation of the working classes is not a struggle for class privileges and monopolies, but for *equal* rights and *equal* duties, and for the *abolition of all class rule.*

2. The economic dependence of the workingman upon the monopolist (the exclusive owner) of the tools of production, forms the

SOURCE: *Bebel's Reminiscences* (New York: Socialist Literature Company, 1911), pp. 195–196.

basis of servitude in every form, of social misery, of intellectual degradation and political dependence.

3. Political freedom is the indispensable instrument of economic emancipation for the working classes. The social question is, therefore, inseparable from the political question, its solution by political action based upon and practicable only in a democratic state.

Furthermore, in view of the fact that all efforts of the working class, directed towards economic emancipation, have failed so far from lack of solidarity between the many lines of labor of every country, and the absence of a fraternal bond of unity between the laboring classes of the various countries; in view of the further fact that the emancipation of the workers is neither a local nor a national, but a social problem comprising all countries having modern societies, a problem depending upon the practical and theoretical cooperation of the most advanced countries, the fifth German workingmen's convention decides to join in the efforts of the International Workingmen's Association.

11. The Gotha Program of the Socialist Workingmen's Party

After the establishment of the German Empire the two wings of the labor movement began to draw closer together. It became clear to the Lassalleans that the new state could not be persuaded to work for the overthrow of capitalism, just as it became clear to the Marxians that a stubborn doctrinairism would only weaken the proletariat in its struggle against the bourgeoisie. The result was the formation of a united socialist party at a convention held in 1875 in Gotha which adopted a program combining direct manhood suffrage and workers' cooperatives with proletarian self-reliance and the international solidarity of labor.

I

Labor is the source of all wealth and all culture, and since universal productive labor is possible only through society, therefore to society, that is to all its members, belongs the collective product of labor. With the universal obligation to labor, according to equal justice, each should have in proportion to his reasonable needs.

In the present society the means of labor are the monopoly of

SOURCE: Wilhelm Liebknecht, *Socialism: What It Is and What It Seeks to Accomplish* (Chicago: Charles H. Kerr & Company, 1901), pp. 5–7.

the capitalist class; the servitude of the laboring class, which is the outgrowth of this, is the cause of misery and of slavery in all forms.

The liberation of labor demands the transformation of the means of production into the common property of society and the associative regulation of the collective labor with general employment and just distribution of the proceeds of labor.

The emancipation of labor must be the work of the laboring class, opposed to which all other classes are only a reactionary body.

II

Proceeding from this principle the Socialist Labor party of Germany seeks through all legal means the free state and the socialist society, the destruction of the iron law of wages, the overthrow of exploitation in all forms and the abolition of all social and political inequality.

The Socialist Labor party of Germany, though working chiefly in national boundaries, is conscious of the international character of the labor movement and is resolved to fulfill every duty which is laid on the workers in order to realize the brotherhood of humanity.

The Socialist Labor party of Germany demands as a step to the solution of the social question the erection, with the help of the state, of socialistic productive establishments under the democratic control of the laboring people. These productive establishments are to place industry and agriculture in such relations that out of them the socialist organization of the whole may arise.

The Socialist Labor party of Germany demands as the foundation of the state:

1. Universal, equal and direct suffrage, with secret, obligatory voting by all citizens at all elections in state or community.
2. Direct legislation by the people. Decision as to peace or war by the people.
3. Common right to bear arms. Militia instead of the standing army.
4. Abolition of all laws of exception, especially all laws restricting the freedom of the press, of association and assemblage; above all, all laws restricting the freedom of public opinion, thought and investigation.
5. Legal judgment through the people. Gratuitous administration of law.

6. Universal and equal popular education by the state. Universal compulsory education. Free instruction in all forms of art. Declaration that religion is a private matter.

The Socialist Labor party of Germany demands within the present society:

1. The widest possible expansion of political rights and freedom according to the foregoing demands.
2. A progressive income tax for state and municipality instead of all those existing, especially in place of the indirect tax which burdens the people.
3. Unrestrained right of combination.
4. Shortening of the working day according to the needs of society. Abolition of Sunday labor.
5. Abolition of child labor and all female labor injurious to health and morality.
6. Protective laws for the life and health of the worker. Sanitary control of the homes of the workers. Supervision of the mines, factories, workshops and hand industries by an officer elected by the people. An effectual law of enforcement.
7. Regulation of prison labor.
8. Full autonomy in the management of all laborers' fraternal and mutual benefit funds.

VIII
The Struggle against the Socialists

Bismarck was essentially a pragmatist in his attitude toward economic life, subordinating theories and principles to the practical needs of agriculture or industry. Yet there were important underlying assumptions in his view of the proper relationship between state and society. He believed that government had a right to regulate the interaction of classes and interests for the advancement of the general welfare. He was never a doctrinaire supporter of individualism, whether in politics or economics. The tradition of authority, deep-rooted in the landed aristocracy from which he had sprung, was reflected in his conviction that the preservation of the established order took precedence over the immunities and liberties of the citizen. This was the ideological foundation on which he was to build the first general system of social insurance in Europe. But in the period immediately following national unification the chancellor did nothing to suggest that he would eventually become an advocate of what his foes were to call state socialism. From the conclusion of the Seven Weeks' War to the abatement of the *Kulturkampf* he remained the ally of the liberal bourgeoisie in his political as well as economic policies. Recognizing that he needed the support of the middle class to defend the empire against its opponents on the right and the left, Bismarck encouraged the growth of industrial capitalism by following a course of *laissez faire* with regard to business activities and interests. The statesman who had been appointed to office to curb the ambition of the liberals became the tacit partner of his former enemies.

At the end of the 1870s, however, the chancellor's views began to change once again, shifting this time from liberalism to conservatism. He had come to distrust the motives of his bourgeois allies who seemed to be working for the gradual extension of parliamentary authority. The reverses suffered by the government in the *Kulturkampf* disturbed him, moreover, suggesting that he was in danger of becoming the captive of a doctrinaire anticlericalism which threatened to divide the nation permanently. But the most important reason for Bismarck's change of direction was the spread of radicalism in Central Europe. The sudden emergence of a labor movement hostile to all the political and economic values of the established order alarmed him. At one time he had regarded socialism as visionary and therefore harmless. He had even toyed briefly with the idea of enlisting the aid of the urban proletariat in the conflict with the liberal bourgeoisie of Prussia. But that had been in the years before the achievement of national unification. More than that, the Lassalleans with whom he had flirted in the 1860s had accepted the state and the monarchy as valid instruments of social reform. But the Marxians who were rapidly gaining strength in the 1870s rejected all the legal foundations of the existing form of government in Germany. They preached civic disloyalty, class war, and international revolution. There could be no negotiation or compromise with people espousing such beliefs. As Bismarck came to the conclusion that he must declare war against these enemies of the state, he began to abandon his alliance with the liberals. His most loyal supporters in a struggle with socialism, he reasoned, would be conservatism, traditionalism, and clericalism.

The campaign against the radical foes of the established order opened with the law of 1878 which in effect prohibited political activity by the socialists. They could no longer form associations, organize meetings, or circulate publications. The authorities assumed that the strength of radicalism derived from its ability to agitate and mislead, so that once the propagation of subversive teachings was outlawed, the lower classes would return to their traditional allegiance to crown and altar. But they underestimated the political strength of the labor movement and the ideological loyalty of the urban proletariat. The war waged by the government against the left did not destroy socialism but merely drove it underground. Its leaders went into hiding or exile, its deputies in parliament continued to preach the doctrine of class struggle, and its propagandists fanned the disaffection of the masses in defiance of the law. The number of votes cast for its candidates in elections to the Reichstag declined at first from 493,000 in 1877 and 437,000 in 1878 to 312,000 in 1881, but then it rose again to 550,000 in 1884, 763,000 in 1887, and 1,427,000 in 1890. There was irony in the fact that manhood suffrage, introduced by Bismarck as a means of defending the new order in Central Europe, proved to be a powerful weapon in the hands of its opponents. He had hoped that the lower classes would help him defeat the forces of particularism which refused to accept national unification. Instead they supported the harshest critics of the German Empire, first the clericalists and now the socialists. It was a bitter disappointment for the chancellor.

The failure of the campaign against radicalism was all the more galling because the government had not relied exclusively on a strategy of repression. Bismarck had recognized that the appeal of socialist teachings to the lower classes arose out of the economic conditions under which the urban proletariat was forced to live in the world of industrial capitalism. Hardship, poverty, and insecurity were creating a mass following for a labor movement which promised to build a new order of society founded on equality and justice. The best way to counter the subversive doctrines of the left, reasoned the chancellor, was to demonstrate to the worker that the existing political system could and would improve his material position. This was the calculation behind the decision of the leaders of the German Empire to establish a system of social security for those employed in industrial establishments. In 1883 came a law providing insurance against sickness, in 1884 against accidents, and in 1889 against invalidity and old age. For the first time in history a nation introduced comprehensive legislation to protect the urban proletariat against the vicissitudes of a capitalistic economy. The struggle against socialism forced Bismarck to adopt a program of mass welfare more important in the long run than his defeat of liberalism or his creation of an empire. Yet not even this great achievement of constructive statesmanship could halt the spread of radicalism among the lower classes. As it became increasingly clear to him that he was losing the battle against the socialists, the chancellor began to reflect gloomily on human ingratitude and to contemplate even more drastic measures against the enemies of the state.

1. Albert Schäffle Demonstrates That Socialism Is an Impossibility

To the propertied and educated classes of Central Europe the theories of socialism seemed to be either the impractical dreams of doctrinaires or the deliberate falsehoods of demagogues. The prominent economist Albert Schäffle was well aware of the hardships which the proletariat had to endure under capitalism, but he remained convinced that the solution to the problems of industrialization could not be achieved through the elimination of private ownership. In one of his books he sought to prove by a variety of ingenious arguments that a system of collective production would be incompatible with the eternal laws of economics.

I, FOR MY PART, hope . . . to be able to bring . . . striking proof that social democracy in all its democracy and in all its radicalism can never fulfill a single one of its glowing promises; and further, that each and all of the . . . points . . . over which its fanatics rave so wildly, will, if rightly considered, afford evidence of the impossibility of democratic collectivism.

It is, to begin with, a delusion to imagine that collective production could be organized and administered at all in a republic which from base to summit of the social pyramid was reared on democratic principles. It is no doubt a mistake to aver that collective production or even an entirely collective industrial system is altogether inconceivable, or must come to grief by reason of the overwhelming burden imposed on the central political power. I have myself shown that this is a mistaken view. But it is, on the other hand, quite certain that collective production, the universal panacea of the social democrats, would be wholly impossible unless the most carefully graduated authority were vested in the corporate governing organs, authority which should extend from the lowest to the highest and most central parts of the productive system. It would be impossible to allow that either from without inwards or from within outwards there should be constant overturning, changing, and all the confusion of new experiments. But if this is not to be, then a stable and self-sufficient central authority and a similarly constituted administrative system throughout the state will be absolutely necessary. And these two essentials could only for all time stand securely when based on very broad founda-

SOURCE: A. Schäffle, *The Impossibility of Social Democracy* (London: S. Sonnenschein & Co., 1892), pp. 65–74.

tion stones of some powerfully moderating elements. But then where would be your democratic republic from top to bottom and from center to circumference? Where would be your freedom and equality? Where your security against misuse of power and against exploitation? The fact is, collective production on a democratic basis is impossible. On a basis of "authority" it is possible, and even in part actually existing, but as such it is nondemocratic, and has no charms for the proletariat.

In the second place, collectivism eliminates both nature and private property as determining factors from the problem of the distribution of income. This it does by transferring the ownership of the means of production entirely to the community, and welding all businesses of the same kind—however unequal the natural efficiency of the instruments may be in the various sections—into one great "social" department of industry, worked on the principle of equal remuneration for equal contributions of labor-time. This elimination of two out of the three factors in production might be practically feasible, perhaps even just, if collective production were organized on a sufficient basis of authority. At least, experience shows that the state can without difficulty raise and maintain what is necessary for the supply of its various collective agencies, and can carry out a uniform scale of remuneration for a complicated network of officials. But under a purely democratic organization so delusively simple a method of elimination would be by no means practicable. A materialistic and greedy host of individuals, puffed up by popular sovereignty, and fed with constant flattery, would not easily submit to the sacrifices required by the immense savings necessary to multiplying the means of production. Still less would the members of such productive sections as are equipped with the instruments of production of highest natural efficiency be inclined to cast in the surplus product of their labor with the deficient production of others. Strife and confusion without end would be the result of attempting it. A social-democratic system of collective production and distribution is specially incapable of practically effecting the elimination of these factors—which furthermore would, even if effected, simply destroy the peculiar interest of the administrators of production and the industrially fertile charms of capital-profit, as well as of ground-rent and, generally, of all forms of royalty. While if it is to be carried out on a more or less decided basis of authority, it ceases at once to be democratic.

In the third place, social democracy promises an impossibility in undertaking, without danger to the efficiency of production, to unite all branches of it, and in each branch all the separate firms and business companies into one single body with uniform labor-credit and uniform estimation of labor-time. Herein it goes upon the supposition that the whole tendency of production is towards business on a large scale with local self-complete branches on factory lines. Yet this is a most arbitrary assumption. Even in trade there will always remain over a mass of small scattered pursuits that entirely escape control, some subsidiary to the arts, some connected with personal services, some in the way of repairs and mending. In agriculture the large self-complete factory system is excluded by the nature of the case. The system of the *latifundia* becomes heavier and more intolerable as the cultivation of the soil becomes more intensive and more scientific. It may well be that in the agriculture of the future there will be more and more introduction of collective administration for purposes of traction, the incoming and outgoing of produce, and for irrigation and draining, for the common use of machinery, and for operations of loading and despatch. But farming on a large scale, such as is done on the Dalrymple Farm, in the Red River district, or on Glenn Farm, in California, is not possible as a universal system. . . .

The entire sum of individual happiness, the pleasure that comes to most men in the free possession of one's own property, and of the soil inherited from one's fathers, would be exploded by social democracy for the benefit of the industrial proletariat: equality is the only thing worth having. But the peasant will hold his own, if the mountain of unproductive debt can be rolled from his shoulders, and in face of the anticollectivist proclivities of his sturdy brain, and the force of his redcoat sons, social democracy will inevitably fall to pieces at last, though it start with the most successful revolution ever achieved.

Social democracy, in the fourth place, promises to the industrial proletariat a fabulous increase in the net result of national production, hence an increase of dividends of the national revenue, and a general rise of labor returns all round. This increased productivity of industry would perhaps be conceivable if a firm administration could be set over the collective production, and if it were also possible to inspire all the producers with the highest interest alike in diminishing the cost, and in increasing the productiveness of labor. But social democracy as such refuses to vest the necessary authority in the administration, and does not know how to introduce an adequate system of rewards and punishments for the group as a whole, and for the individuals in each productive group, however necessary a condition this may be of a really high level of production. For otherwise, of course, there would be no freedom and no equality. Therefore, on the side of productivity again, all these delusive representations as to the capacity and possibility of democratic collective production are groundless. Without giving both every employer and everyone employed the highest individual interest in the work, and involving them in profits or losses as the case may be, both ideal and material, it would be utterly impossible to attain even such a measure of productivity for the national labor as the capitalistic system manages to extract from capital profit, even in the face of risk, and with varying scales of remuneration. The introduction of even stronger and more effective guarantees of universal thrift and efficiency in a partially collective system may at first sight appear to be not impossible, as I have shown at length in the third volume of my *Bau und Leben* (Structure and Life of the Social Organism). But this result is impossible if the only means of bringing it about is to be resolutely rejected and denied, namely, the free and ungrudging assignment of a larger proportion of material and ideal good to the real aristocracy of merit. Without a sufficiently strong and attractive reward for individual or corporate preeminence, without strongly deterrent drawbacks and compensatory obligations for bad and unproductive work, a collective system of production is inconceivable, or at least any system that would even distantly approach in efficiency the capitalistic system of today. But democratic equality cannot tolerate such strong rewards and punishments. Even to reward the best with the honor of direction and command is to run directly counter to this kind of democracy. The scale of remuneration in the existing civil and military systems would be among the very first things social democracy would overthrow, and rightly, according to its principles. So long as men are not incipient angels —and that will be for a good while yet—*democratic* collective production can never make good its promises, because it will not tolerate the methods of *reward and punishment for the achievements of individuals and of groups,* which under its system would need to be specially and peculiarly strong.

2. The Chancellor Accuses the Socialists of Seeking
to Destroy the Established Order

Bismarck had at first regarded socialism as vain but harmless speculation by a handful of ineffectual theorists. Yet before long the rapid
spread of radical thought among the lower classes began to alarm him.
By the end of the 1870s he concluded that repressive measures were
needed against this emerging danger to the established order. In a
speech before the Reichstag he maintained that the socialists were
planning to introduce a reign of terror in Central Europe directed
against all traditional values and institutions. The government must
therefore take firm action to protect the Fatherland from the machinations of its enemies.

I HAVE ALREADY STATED that I am ready to further any effort posi-
tively directed towards ameliorating the workingman's lot, such as,
for instance, the establishment of an association for enabling him to
obtain a larger share of industrial profits and for reducing his hours
of labor, as considerably as may be compatible with the limits
imposed by competition, and the state of the manufacture markets.
Associations of this class are no innovation in Germany. Five
centuries ago they were as active as they are now, with varying
success. But they invariably aimed at the attainment of positive
results; and the notions of infringing the rights of third persons, of
interfering with property, and of undermining belief in God and
the monarchy occurred to no man. Even during the terrible outrages of the Peasants' War, in which the most violent and ignorant
covetousness ran riot—if you will read the treaties concluded by
the peasantry with individual nobles of sufficiently evil repute, you
will find that the property of these latter was never confiscated to
an unjustifiable extent. The communist of those days did not dream
of interfering with the possessions even of their enemies. . . . As
soon as the Social Democrats shall put forward a practical scheme
for improving the lot of the working classes, I, at least, will not
refuse to consider their proposals in a benevolent and conciliatory
spirit; nor will I shrink from the theory that the state should help
those who help themselves. . . . But how do matters stand now?

SOURCE: Moritz Busch, *Our Chancellor: Sketches for a Historical Picture*, 2 vols. (New York: Charles Scribner's Sons, 1884), vol. II, pp.
209–215.

We find ourselves face to face with negation—with a resolve to pull the house down, and no suggestion on the part of anybody as to what is to replace our present roof when it shall have been torn off. We have had the advantage of sitting with Social Democrats in this House for eleven years; can you recall any one of their lengthy orations in which was to be found the faintest shadow of a positive idea or proposition concerning the future—of the program which those persons intend to carry out when they shall have battered down existing institutions? I know of none; but I also know why they do not tell us how they mean to arrange the world when they shall be its masters. It is because they do not know it themselves, not having discovered the philosopher's stone. They can never keep the promises with which they lead people astray. . . . I do not know if any of you have found the time to read Moore's "Veiled Prophet," who hid his face because, as soon as his veil was raised, he stood revealed in all his loathsome hideousness. The infuriate demagogues into whose hands a vast number of our working men, formerly so well conducted, has fallen, remind me of that Veiled Prophet of Khorassan. Their dupes have never seen Mokanna's face; should they ever catch a glimpse of it they will be appalled, for it is as the face of a corpse.

That these men of vague promises have found support amongst people dissatisfied with their circumstances, and capable of expressing their dissatisfaction with true German energy, is not to be wondered at. If you hold out brilliant prospects to people who can read, but cannot understand what they read (and, though the ability to read is much more general with us than in France and England, the capacity for practically judging the matter read is less common than in those countries); if you teach them scornfully and mockingly, verbally and in print, that all they have hitherto held sacred is nothing but humbug, lies, hollow phrases and a swindle; if you take from them their belief in God and our kingdom, their attachment to their native country, families, property, their right to transmit their earnings to their children, it is by no means difficult to bring men of restricted intelligence to such a frame of mind that they shall clench their fists and exclaim, "Curse hope, curse faith, and above all curse patience!" What remains to men thus spiritually poor and naked, but the frantic pursuit of sensual enjoyments—the only pleasures capable of reconciling them to existence?

If we ask how it has come to pass that this gospel of negation has found such favor in Germany, we must look back attentively to the time of its introduction. Up to 1870 it mattered not where the leaders of the International League resided—in London or Geneva —their real field of experiment and action was France, where they had in readiness an army capable of fighting the Commune's battles and of making itself master of the capital for a time. When they were actually the rulers of Paris, did they propound a positive program, setting forth how they proposed to utilize their power for the benefit of the poorer classes? I know of none. They did nothing but murder, burn, outrage, destroy national monuments— and if they had converted all Paris into one huge heap of ashes, they would have gazed at it blankly without in the least knowing what they wanted. All they could say was "We are dissatisfied; there must be a change; but to what, we do not know." That is where they would have stuck. Well, as soon as they had been energetically put down by the French government, they perceived that they must quit that field of experiment, as it was watched by an angry, resolute and stern sentinel. So they looked about them in Europe to see where they should set up the tents they had been compelled to strike in France. I am not at all surprised that they determined to transfer their agitation to Germany. What could be more attractive to them than a country with such merciful laws, such good-natured judges, such a strong predilection for criticism (especially in connection with its government); a country in which an attack upon a minister is reckoned a praiseworthy feat— in which grateful recognition of anything done by government passes for servility—in which socialism's bases of operations, the large towns, had been very carefully prepared by the progressists for the adoption of communistic principles—in which progressist agitation had achieved extraordinary success in discrediting the authorities and state institutions? It is a fact that the International Socialists, when they invaded Germany, found respect for those institutions destroyed in this country, where the tendency to treat them with scorn—scorn over which every Philistine chuckles, though he is glad enough to be protected from its consequences— had undergone an amazing development. In a word, they recognized the country of which they could confidently say: "Let us build our huts here!"

Every German is possessed by an intrinsic tendency toward

discontent and by boundless ambition. The baker who sets up shop does not merely aspire to become the wealthiest baker in his town; no, he wants to be a houseowner, a private gentleman, a banker, a millionaire. There are no limits to his ambition. This peculiarity of his has its good side; it is true German assiduity, which never places its goal too near, but which is also extremely adverse to public contentment—especially to that of all subordinate officials—and the consequence of which is that nearly all our subaltern *employees* are infected by the socialistic plague. Well, how were the Socialists' anticipations fulfilled in Germany? The international agitation transferred itself to that Promised Land, in which it still abides. About that time we had introduced quite new arrangements in different directions, which suddenly withdrew a vast number of workmen from the small towns and agricultural districts and imported into the cities a fluctuating population, whose productive capacity was dependent upon the varying conditions of trade and industry in the great cities. Sometimes these people got plenty of work, and sometimes not; but none of them had any inclination to return to country life. The amusements of great cities are very attractive; railway communications facilitate the movements of those who yield to attractions of that nature. . . . Then we brought in the new Press Law, which abolished the caution money and the newspaper stamp. Hitherto a certain amount of capital, carrying with it possibly a certain amount of intellectual cultivation, had been requisite and forthcoming for the creation of a newspaper; nowadays such an enterprise can be undertaken with from five to seven pounds, and there is no need of education, for all that has to be done is to copy the matter supplied by the agitators; and newspapers of this class, which appear once a week and are for that reason all the more read by and circulated amongst the operatives in small country towns—these appeals to the common man and his most dangerous instincts—this variety of agitation, in a word, was formerly not so easy. It has been materially promoted by our Press Law and by the mercifulness of our penal code; moreover, the conviction that sentence of death will not be enforced, contributes in no small degree to the commission of such hideous crimes as these attempts to assassinate the emperor. . . . Seeing, too, that the extraordinary impulse imparted to business during the years immediately succeeding the war has been followed by an utter collapse, and that many people who formerly earned a great deal of money now earn none at all; nobody can be surprised that our danger has risen to its present height, and that we now have here in Berlin between sixty and a hundred thousand men, well organized and brigaded in associations, who openly avow their resolve to fight *against* established order and *for* the program with which we are acquainted. Under these circumstances it is quite natural that manufacture, credit and trade should suffer in Berlin; for, to the apprehension of anyone proposing to invest his capital here, or to the troubled fancy of a wealthy proprietor, this organization of from sixty to a hundred thousand men presents itself as a hostile army, encamped in our midst, which has only not as yet found the opportune moment to deal with the imprudent proprietor or capitalist in question, in such sort as either to deprive him altogether of his honestly earned property, or to restrict him in disposing of it, at the very least. The fear (in which I do not share) that the ideas of Schiller's *Robbers* have been uncompromisingly adopted by our operatives, the very backbone of the people, has deeply depressed public confidence. In order to stimulate it once more I deem it necessary that the state should shatter the power of these agitators. Nowadays socialistic agitation is a trade like any other; men become agitators and popular orators as they formerly became smiths or carpenters; they take to the new business and find themselves a good deal better off in it than they did in the old one. We must defend ourselves against this class of tradesman, and the sooner we take measures to do so the more likely we shall be to finish the job without seriously prejudicing the liberties of other people or our own safety and domestic peace.

3. He Explains Why He Became an Opponent of Socialism

The chancellor admitted that at one time he too had thought of founding workers' cooperatives as a means of improving the economic position of the urban proletariat. He had even urged the king to provide financial support for an experiment in collective ownership conducted by a group of Silesian weavers. But he had always believed that large industrial enterprises could operate efficiently only under a system of private property. Besides, he explained, his cautious interest in socialism gave way to outright hostility when he heard its proponents defending the Paris Commune.

SOURCE: Moritz Busch, *Our Chancellor: Sketches for a Historical Picture*, 2 vols. (New York: Charles Scribner's Sons, 1884), vol. II, pp. 196–198.

I AM by no means yet convinced that the notion of subventioning productive associations by the state is an objectionable one. It seemed to me—perhaps the impression was conveyed to me by Lassalle's reasonings, or perhaps by my experiences in England, during my stay there in 1862—that a possibility of improving the workingman's lot might be found in the establishment of productive associations, such as exist and flourish in England. I have talked over the subject with the king, who has the interests of the working classes closely at heart, and His Majesty paid a sum of money out of his own pocket in aid of an experiment in that direction connected with a deputation of operatives from Silesia, who had lost their employment through differing from their employer in politics. . . . To attempt anything of the sort upon a large scale might entail an expenditure of hundreds of millions; but the notion does not seem to me intrinsically an absurd or silly one. We make experiments in agriculture and manufactures; might it not be as well to do so with respect to human occupations and the solution of the social question? . . . I may be reproached with not having achieved a satisfactory result; but the matter was not in my department—I had no time to attend to it—warlike complications accrued and our foreign policy became abnormally active. The merits or demerits of the notion cannot be judged by an experiment made upon a small scale; perhaps on a larger one it could not be carried out at all. Such establishments as that of Krupp, for instance, could not possibly exist under a republican *régime*. . . . It may be that the confidence of German workmen in one another and their employers is not so great as the English associations prove it to be in England. But I cannot understand why I am reproached for making the experiment above alluded to, not with public money, but with funds supplied by His Majesty out of his Privy Purse.

I now come to the question when and why I gave up troubling myself about these matters, and chiefly when my attitude changed towards the social, or rather, social democratic question. It was at the moment when Deputy Bebel or Deputy Liebknecht—I do not remember which of the two—in a pathetic appeal to the Reichstag held up the French Commune as the model of political institutions, and openly avowed the creed professed by the Parisian assassins and incendiaries. Thenceforth I clearly perceived the extent of the danger threatening us. In the meantime I had been away at the scene of war and had paid no attention to things of that kind; but the invocation of the Commune opened my eyes to what we had to expect, and I instantly recognized the fact that social democracy is an enemy against whom the state and society are bound to defend themselves.

4. The German Government Gives Its Reasons for Wanting to Suppress the Socialists

Bismarck decided in 1878 to employ repression against radical agitation by introducing an antisocialist bill in parliament. In a statement accompanying the proposed measure, the government outlined its reasons for advocating a policy of harassment and persecution. The socialist movement, so the argument went, was not content to seek a solution to the problems of industrialism within the framework of the established order. It sought rather to destroy the existing system of government and society by revolutionary activity organized on an international basis. Such a grave danger could be averted only through extraordinary means of self-defense.

THE ENDEAVORS of social democracy are aimed at the practical realization of the radical theories of modern socialism and communism. According to these theories the present system of production is uneconomical, and must be rejected as an unjust exploitation of labor by capital. Labor is to be emancipated from capital; private capital is to be converted into collective capital; individual production, regulated by competition, is to be converted into systematic cooperative production; and the individual is to be absorbed in society. The social democratic movement differs greatly from all humanitarian movements in that it proceeds from the assumption that the amelioration of the condition of the working classes is impossible on the basis of the present social system, and can only be attained by the social revolution spoken of. This social revolution is to be effected by the cooperation of the working classes of all states, with the simultaneous subversion of the existing constitutions. The movement has especially taken this revolutionary and international character since the foundation of the International Working Men's Association in London, in September, 1864. . . . It is, in fact, a question of breaking away from the legal development of civilized states, and of the complete subversion of the

SOURCE: William Harbutt Dawson, *German Socialism and Ferdinand Lassalle* (London: S. Sonnenschein & Co., 1888), pp. 251–252.

prevailing system of property. The organization of the *proletariat*, the destruction of the existing order of state and society, and the establishment of the socialistic community and the socialistic state by the organized *proletariat*—these are the avowed aims of social democracy. The well-organized socialistic agitation, carried on by speech and writings with passionate energy, is in accord with these ends. This agitation seeks to disseminate amongst the poor and less educated classes of the population, discontent with their lot as well as the conviction that under the present *régime* their condition is hopeless and to excite them as the "disinherited" to envy and hatred of the upper classes. The moral and religious convictions which hold society together are shattered; reverence and piety are ridiculed; the legal notions of the masses are confused; and respect for the law is destroyed. The most odious attacks and abuse which are levelled at the German Empire and its institutions—at royalty and the army, whose glorious history is slandered—give the socialist agitation in this country a specifically antinational stamp; for it estranges the minds of the people from native customs and from the Fatherland. The representations which are given, both by spoken and written word, of former revolutionary events and the glorification of well-known leaders of revolution, as well as the acts of the Paris Commune, are calculated to excite revolutionary desires and passions, and to dispose the masses to acts of violence. . . . The law of self-preservation, therefore, compels the state and society to oppose the social democratic movement with decision; and, above all, the state is bound to protect the legal system which is threatened by social democracy, and to put restraints upon socialistic agitation. True, thought cannot be repressed by external compulsion; the movements of minds can only be overcome in intellectual combat. Still, when such movements take wrong ways and threaten to become destructive, the means for their extension can and should be taken away by legal means. The socialistic agitation, as carried on for years, is a continual appeal to violence and to the passions of the masses with a view to the subversion of state and social order. The state *can* check such an enterprise as this, by depriving social democracy of its most important means of agitation, and by destroying its organization; and it *must* do this unless it is willing to surrender its existence, and unless there is to grow up amongst the population the conviction either that the state is impotent, or that the aims of social democracy are justifiable. . . .

Social democracy has declared war against the state and society, and has proclaimed their subversion to be its aim. It has thus forsaken the ground of equal right for all, and it cannot complain if the law should only be exercised in its favor to the extent consistent with the security and order of the state.

5. The Law against Socialism

The antisocialist bill, after receiving the approval of the Reichstag, became law in the fall of 1878. It was to remain in effect for twelve years. Its main provisions prohibited socialist organizations, meetings, and publications, imposing fines or prison terms on those who refused to comply. The established order in Central Europe, convinced that it was facing a serious threat to its vital political and economic interests, cast aside the mask of liberal reform which it had assumed after the achievement of national unification. Bismarck was now determined to pursue a policy of the mailed fist in dealing with proletarian radicalism.

1. Societies which aim at the overthrow of the existing political or social order through social democratic, socialistic, or communistic endeavors are to be prohibited.

This applies also to societies in which social democratic, socialistic, or communistic endeavors aiming at the overthrow of the existing political or social order are manifested in a manner dangerous to the public peace, and, particularly to the harmony among the classes of the population.

Associations of every kind are the same as societies. . . .

4. The [police] is empowered:

1. To attend all sessions and meetings of the society.
2. To call and conduct membership assemblies.
3. To inspect the books, papers and cash assets, as well as to demand information about the affairs of the society.
4. To forbid the carrying out of resolutions which are apt to further the endeavors described in 1, par. 2.
5. To transfer to qualified persons the duties of the officers or other leading organs of the society.
6. To take charge of and manage the funds.

SOURCE: Selections from Appendix C in Vernon L. Lidtke, *The Outlawed Party: Social Democracy in Germany, 1878–1890* (copyright © 1966 by Princeton University Press), pp. 339–345. Reprinted by permission of Princeton University Press.

5. In case the membership meetings, the executive committee, or another managing organ acts in opposition to the directives of the controlling authority issued within the scope of its powers, or in case the endeavors in 1, par. 2, are manifested after the introduction of the control, the society may be prohibited.

6. The prohibition or the imposition of control are within the competence of the state police authority. The prohibition of foreign societies appertains to the *Reichskanzler*.

The prohibition is in all cases to be publicized through the *Reichsanzeiger;* in addition, the prohibition by the state police authority is to be publicized through the designated newspaper for official notifications by the authority of the locality or district.

The prohibition is valid for the entire area of the federation and embraces all branches of the society, as well as every ostensible new society, which in reality is to be regarded as the old one.

7. With the prohibition, the society's cash assets, as well as the objects intended for the purposes of the society are to be confiscated by the authority.

After the prohibition has become final, the administrative authority designated by the state police authority must delegate the settlement of the affairs of the society (liquidation) to suitable persons and supervise the liquidation; the administrative authority must also make known the names of the liquidators.

The decision of the administrative authority takes the place of a resolution by the membership meeting provided for by the laws or statutes.

The liquidated property of the society is, without detriment to the legal claims of third parties and of the members of the society, to be utilized as provided in the statutes of the society, or in general laws.

The moment when the prohibition becomes final is to be considered the moment of the dissolution of the society (or the closing of the fund).

Appeal against the decrees of the authority is permitted only to the supervising authority.

8. The prohibition decree by the state police authority, as well as the establishment of a control is to be communicated in writing, indicating the reasons, to the society's executive committee, in case one exists within domestic jurisdiction. Against such a decree the society's executive has the right to make an appeal (26).

The appeal must be made within one week after receipt of the notice of the decree; the appeal is to be directed to the authority which issued the decree.

The appeal has no postponing effect.

9. Meetings in which social democratic, socialistic, or communistic endeavors which aim at the overthrow of the existing political or social order are manifested are to be dissolved.

Meetings for which the assumption is justified by the fact that they are intended to further the endeavors described in the first paragraph are to be prohibited. Public festivities and processions shall be treated the same as meetings.

10. Prohibition and dissolution are within the competence of the police authority.

Appeal is permitted only to the supervising authority.

11. Publications in which social democratic, socialistic, or communistic endeavors aimed at the overthrow of the existing political or social order are manifested in a manner calculated to endanger the public peace, and particularly the harmony among all classes of the population, are to be prohibited.

In the case of periodical publications, the prohibition may extend to further issues as soon as a single issue has been prohibited on the basis of this law.

12. The prohibition lies within the competence of the state police authority, and, in the case of periodical publications appearing within the Reich, under the competence of the state police authority of the district in which the publication appears. The prohibition of the further distribution of periodical publications printed abroad lies within the competence of the *Reichskanzler.*
. . .

13. The prohibition of publications by the state police authority is to be made known in writing, with the reasons of the same, to the publisher or editor, and in the case of nonperiodic publications, to the author of the same, if these persons are within the Reich.

The publisher, editor or author has the right of appeal against the order (26).

The appeal must be submitted to the authority which issued the decree within a week after receipt of notification.

The appeal has no postponing effect.

14. On the basis of the prohibition, the publications concerned are to be confiscated wherever found for the purpose of distribu-

tion. The confiscation may include the plates and forms used for reproduction; in the case of printed publications in the proper sense, a withdrawal of the set types from circulation is to be substituted for their seizure, upon the request of the interested parties. After the prohibition is final, the publication, plates, and forms are to be made unusable.

Appeal is permitted only to the supervising authority.

15. Before the decree of prohibition, the police authority is empowered provisionally to seize publications of the character described in 11, as well as plates and forms for reproduction. Within twenty-four hours, the seized publication is to be delivered to the state police authority. The latter must either order immediately the restoration of the confiscated material or issue a decree of prohibition within one week. If the prohibition does not ensue within this period the confiscation is voided and the various pieces, plates and forms shall be released.

16. The collection of contributions for the furtherance of social democratic, socialistic, or communistic endeavors aiming at the overthrow of the existing political and social order, as well as a public appeal for such contributions, are to be prohibited by the police.

The prohibition is to be announced publicly.

Appeal is permitted only to the supervising authority.

17. Whoever participates as a member in a prohibited society (6), or carries on an activity in its interest, is to be punished by a fine of not more than five hundred marks or with imprisonment not exceeding three months. The same punishment is to be inflicted on anyone who participates in a prohibited meeting (9), or who does not depart immediately after the dissolution of a meeting by the police. Imprisonment of not less than one month and not more than one year is to be inflicted on those who participate in a society or assembly as chairmen, leaders, monitors, agents, speakers, or treasurers, or on those who issue invitations to attend the meeting.

18. Whoever provides a prohibited society or meeting with a place of assembly is to be punished with imprisonment of from one month to one year.

19. Whoever distributes, continues, or reprints a prohibited publication (11, 12) or a provisionally confiscated publication (15) is to be punished with a fine not exceeding one thousand marks or with imprisonment not exceeding six months.

20. Whoever acts in violation of a prohibition under 16, is punishable with a fine not exceeding five hundred marks or with imprisonment not exceeding three months. Moreover, all that which has been received in consequence of the prohibited collection or invitation, or its value, is to devolve to the poor relief fund of the locality.

21. Whoever commits one of the acts prohibited by 17, 18, 19 without knowledge of the prohibition, but after the notification of the prohibition in the *Reichsanzeiger* (6, 12) is to be punished by a fine not exceeding one hundred and fifty marks.

The same punishment applies to those who act in violation of a prohibition under 16 after the publication of the prohibition. The concluding provision of 20 applies.

22. In addition to the punishment of imprisonment, in case of a condemnation for acts in violation of 17 to 20, a further judgment may be rendered as to the admissibility of a limitation of their right of residence against persons who make a business of the agitation for endeavors described in 1, par. 2.

On the basis of this judgment, the residence of a condemned person in certain districts and localities may be forbidden by the state police authority, only if, however, the condemned person has not resided in his place of legal residence for a period of six months. Foreigners may be expelled from the *Bundesgebiet* by the state police authority. Appeal to be permitted only to the supervising authority.

Acts in contravention are to be punished with imprisonment from one month to one year.

23. Under the conditions described in 22, par. 1, innkeepers, barkeepers, persons carrying on a retail business in brandy or liquors, book publishers, booksellers, librarians in lending libraries and proprietors of reading rooms, may, in addition to imprisonment, be forbidden to continue their business.

24. The state police authority may withdraw the license for the professional or nonprofessional public distribution of publications, as well as the license for an itinerant trade in publications from persons who make a business of furthering the endeavors described in 1, par. 2, or who have been legally sentenced to punishment on the basis of the provisions of this law.

Appeal is permitted only to the supervising authority.

25. Whoever acts in contravention of a judgment pronounced

under 23 or of a decision decreed under 24 is punishable by a fine not exceeding one thousand marks, or by arrest or imprisonment not exceeding six months.

26. A Commission is to be formed to decide upon the appeals in the cases of 8, 13. The Bundesrat elects four of its own members and five from the highest courts of the Reich or the individual *Bundesstaaten.*

The election of these five members is for the period of the duration of this law, and for the period in which they hold judicial office.

The Emperor appoints the chairman and his representative from out of the number of the members of the Commission. . . .

28. For districts or localities where the public safety is menaced by the endeavors described in 1, par. 2, the following regulations may be decreed, in case they are not already permitted by state law, with the consent of the Bundesrat for a period not exceeding one year:

1. that meetings may take place only after the consent of the police authority has been obtained; this limitation does not extend to meetings called for the purposes of an announced election to the Reichstag or to the diets of the states;

2. that the distribution of publications shall not take place on public roads, streets, squares, or other public places;

3. that the residence in districts or localities of persons from whom danger to public safety and order is to be feared may be forbidden;

4. that the possession, bearing, importation, and sale of weapons is to be forbidden, limited, or made conditional upon certain requirements.

The Reichstag must be informed immediately, that is, upon its first reassembling, about any decree that has been issued under the foregoing provisions.

The decrees are to be announced in the *Reichsanzeiger* and by whatever manner is prescribed for local police orders.

Whoever, knowingly or after public notice is given, acts in contravention of these regulations, or of the decisions based thereon, is to be punished by a fine not exceeding one thousand marks, or with arrest or imprisonment not exceeding six months.

6. August Bebel Asserts That His Party Will Continue to Function Illegally

The socialists, however, refused to be intimidated by the government's declaration of war. In a speech to the Reichstag, August Bebel stated defiantly that his party would continue its political activity illegally but successfully. The words were prophetic. The passage of the anti-socialist bill marked the beginning of a long and bitter struggle between the imperial government and the labor movement in which socialism proved that it could resist the might of the state as effectively as clericalism had done. In this test of strength the chancellor suffered the second major defeat of his political career.

I ASSURE YOU that in view of the numerous connections we possess, connections we can easily multiply three-fold or ten-fold for purposes like those now at stake, we shall sell our pamphlets not in editions of four or five thousand copies, but in editions of twenty thousand and thirty thousand copies, and not in years but in weeks or months. Furthermore, since our wares will be sold as forbidden fruit, we shall be able to ask prices yielding us such a profit as to defray the expenses of agitation from which we might otherwise have been cut off. In short, gentlemen, governments may do what they will, they cannot really put us down! For instance, can you prevent us from assembling all over the German Empire during the coming winter, in thousands and thousands of families, a few comrades at a time, let us say three, four or five of them, meeting now in one house, now in another, constituting their families as reading circles for the discussion of socialist writings, etc.? Do you know what your law will make of the German social democracy? You are forcing the social democracy, as the early Christians were forced, by means of the persecution to which you are subjecting it, to exert the utmost zeal, to resort to fanaticism, to a sort of genuine religious ecstasy. Do not doubt that the workers will fight tenaciously for their convictions; they will meet in their workshops, in the factories, in the family, in the beer gardens, on railway trains, on Sunday outings, in many places where no one can practice close surveillance over them. Each one will have his two, three, maybe

SOURCE: August Bebel, *Speeches* (New York: International Publishers, 1928), pp. 20–21. Reprinted by permission of International Publishers Co., Inc. Copyright © 1928.

ten, pamphlets in his pocket; they will visit their friends and acquaintances in the country, and in the most remote parts of the town, handing these pamphlets to them. And you will not be able to cripple this activity.

7. A Speech from the Throne Announces a Bill Establishing Accident Insurance

Repression was only one of the weapons with which the government of the German Empire fought in the war against radicalism. The other was welfare legislation designed to provide the urban proletariat with a sense of economic security. The speech from the throne which opened the Reichstag in 1881 announced that the emperor was submitting a bill to the legislature establishing accident insurance for workers in industry. It declared that the failure of the state to deal effectively with the needs and problems of the lower classes had contributed to the spread of socialism.

AT THE OPENING of the Reichstag in February 1879, the emperor, in reference to the [antisocialist] law of October 21, 1878, gave expression to the hope that this House would not refuse its co-operation in the remedying of social ills by means of legislation. A remedy cannot alone be sought in the repression of socialistic excesses; there must be simultaneously the positive advancement of the welfare of the working classes. And here the care of those workpeople who are incapable of earning their livelihood is of the first importance. In the interest of these the emperor has caused a bill for the insurance of workpeople against the consequences of accident to be sent to the Bundesrat—a bill which, it is hoped, will meet a need felt both by workpeople and employers. His Majesty hopes that the measure will in principle receive the assent of the federal governments, and that it will be welcomed by the Reichstag as a complement of the legislation affording protection against social democratic movements. Past institutions intended to insure working people against the danger of falling into a condition of helplessness owing to the incapacity resulting from accident or age have proved inadequate, and their insufficiency has to no small

SOURCE: William Harbutt Dawson, *Bismarck and State Socialism: An Exposition of the Social and Economic Legislation of Germany since 1870* (London: S. Sonnenschein & Co., 1891), pp. 110–111.

extent contributed to cause the working classes to seek help by
participating in social democratic movements.

8. The German Government Offers Its Justification
for a Program of Social Welfare

A statement appended to the accident insurance bill which the Reichstag
received a few weeks later elaborated on the justification for a program
of mass welfare. It spoke of the duty of the state to protect the poor and
referred to the ethical teaching of Christianity. Conceding that the compulsory regulation of industrial conditions contained an element of socialism, it maintained that only through a concern for economic security
could the established order retain the loyalty of the lower classes. Not
even the heavy cost of a comprehensive system of social insurance
should deter the nation from following a course dictated by expediency
as well as principle.

THAT THE STATE . . . should interest itself to a greater degree than
hitherto in those of its members who need assistance, is not only a
duty of humanity and Christianity—by which state institutions
should be permeated—but a duty of state-preserving policy, whose
aim should be to cultivate the conception—and that, too, amongst
the nonpropertied classes, which form at once the most numerous
and the least instructed part of the population—that the state is not
merely a necessary but a beneficent institution. These classes must,
by the evident and direct advantages which are secured to them by
legislative measures, be led to regard the state not as an institution
contrived for the protection of the better classes of society, but as
one serving their own needs and interests. The apprehension that a
socialistic element might be introduced into legislation if this end
were followed should not check us. So far as that may be the case it
will not be an innovation but the further development of the
modern state idea, the result of Christian ethics, according to which
the state should discharge, besides the defensive duty of protecting
existing rights, the positive duty of promoting the welfare of all its
members, and especially those who are weak and in need of help,
by means of judicious institutions and the employment of those
resources of the community which are at its disposal. In this sense

SOURCE: William Harbutt Dawson, *Bismarck and State Socialism: An
Exposition of the Social and Economic Legislation of Germany since
1870* (London: S. Sonnenschein & Co., 1891), pp. 111–112.

the legal regulation of poor relief which the modern state, in opposition to that of antiquity and of the Middle Ages, recognizes as a duty incumbent upon it, contains a socialistic element, and in truth the measures which may be adopted for improving the condition of the nonpropertied classes are only a development of the idea which lies at the basis of poor relief. Nor should the fear that legislation of this kind will not attain important results unless the resources of the Empire and of the individual states be largely employed be a reason for holding back, for the value of measures affecting the future existence of society and the state should not be estimated according to the sacrifice of money which may be entailed. With a single measure, such as is at present proposed, it is of course impossible to remove entirely, or even to a considerable extent, the difficulties which are contained in the social question. This is, in fact, but the first step in a direction in which a difficult work, that will last for years, will have to be overcome gradually and cautiously, and the discharge of one task will only produce new ones.

9. Bismarck Expresses the Wish to Conciliate the Lower Classes

In private conversation with his confidant, Moritz Busch, the chancellor explained in greater detail his reasons for advocating a program of welfare legislation. Since a man whose economic security depends on the established order will be willing to work for the preservation of that order, the state should seek to engender among the lower classes a material interest in the maintenance of the existing political system. Bismarck had always believed that the state possessed the right to regulate social conditions in the name of the general welfare, but his concern over the hardships of the urban proletariat was intensified by the growth of radicalism.

ANYBODY WHO has before him the prospect of a pension, be it ever so small, in old age or infirmity is much happier and more content with his lot, much more tractable and easy to manage, than he whose future is absolutely uncertain. Mark the difference between a domestic servant and an office messenger or court lackey; these last are much readier to do their work and display much more attachment to their service than the first, because they have a

SOURCE: Moritz Busch, *Our Chancellor: Sketches of a Historical Picture,* 2 vols. (New York: Charles Scribner's Sons, 1884), vol. II, pp. 217–219, 231–232.

pension to look forward to. In France even the common man, if he can possibly put by anything, provides for this future by purchasing *Rentes*. Something of that sort ought to be established for our working folk. People talk about state socialism, and think they have settled the matter; as if such things were to be disposed of with a phrase! Socialism or not, it is necessary, the outcome of an urgent requirement. They say, too, the bill would entail enormous expenditure, a hundred million of marks, at least—perhaps twice as much. As for me, three hundred millions would not alarm me. We must find some means for relieving the unindebted poor, on the part of the state and not in the form of alms. Contentment amongst the impecunious and disinherited classes would not be dearly purchased by an enormous sum. They must be made to understand that the state is of some use—that it does not only take, but gives to boot. And if the state, which does not look for interest or dividends, takes the matter in hand, the thing is easy enough. If the worst came to the worst, we might meet the expense with the tobacco monopoly. You need not put that suggestion forward, it is our last trump. A more comfortable future for the poor may be assured by raising taxation upon such luxuries as tobacco, beer and spirits. The English, Americans, and Russians have no monopoly; but they derive enormous revenues from taxing luxuries heavily. As the least taxed people in Europe we can bear with a good deal in that direction; and if the result enable us to secure the future of our operatives—uncertainty respecting which is the chief cause of their hatred of the state—the money will be well invested, for by spending it thus we may avert a social revolution which may break out fifty years hence, or ten, and which, however short a time it last, will assuredly swallow up infinitely larger sums than those we now propose to expend. Some of the Liberals see the force of these proposals; of course they are bound to criticize them, in order to show that they understand the question better than we do. They don't want the man who has dealt with it to have the credit of it, but would like to take it in hand themselves, for the sake of popularity. They will probably quash it in committee, as they have of late years done with several useful measures. But something must be done soon, or the socialist law will not avail us much. . . .

The state must take the matter into its own hands, . . . not as alms-giving, but as the right that men have to be taken care of when, with the best will imaginable, they become unfit for work.

Why should the regular soldier, disabled by war, or the official, have a right to be pensioned in his old age, and not the soldier of labor? This thing will make its own way; it has a future. When I die, possibly our policy will come to grief. But state socialism will have its day; and he who shall take it up again will assuredly be the man at the wheel.

10. He Emphasizes the Need to Protect the Proletariat against Privation

A lengthy and eloquent but not entirely candid explanation of Bismarck's motives in adopting a policy of social reform appeared in his speech to the Reichstag on April 2, 1881, in defense of the accident insurance bill. He talked about the need to protect the lower classes against privation; he alluded to the philanthropic injunctions of religion; and he maintained that there was a basic difference between government regulation of economic affairs and socialism. The establishment of a system of social welfare for the lower classes of Germany was to prove the most enduring achievement of his long career in public life.

OUR PRESENT poor laws keep the injured laboring man from starvation. According to law, at least, nobody need starve. Whether in reality this never happens I do not know. But this is not enough in order to let the men look contentedly into the future and to their own old age. The present bill intends to keep the sense of human dignity alive which even the poorest German should enjoy, if I have my way. He should feel that he is no mere eleemosynary, but that he possesses a fund which is his very own. No one shall have the right to dispose of it, or to take it from him, however poor he may be. This fund will open for him many a door, which otherwise will remain closed to him and it will secure for him better treatment in the house where he has been received, because when he leaves he can take away with him whatever contributions he has been making to the household expenses.

If you have ever personally investigated the conditions of the poor in our large cities, or of the village paupers in the country,

SOURCE: Otto von Bismarck, "Speeches," in *The German Classics of the Nineteenth and Twentieth Centuries,* ed. Kuno Francke, 20 vols. (Albany and New York: German Publication Society, 1913–14), vol. X, pp. 228–230, 235–237, 243.

you have been able to observe the wretched treatment which the poor occasionally receive even in the best managed communities, especially if they are physically weak or crippled. This happens in the houses of their stepmothers, or relatives of any kind, yes also in those of their nearest of kin. Knowing this, are you not obliged to confess that every healthy laboring man, who sees such things, must say to himself: "Is it not terrible that a man is thus degraded in the house which he used to inhabit as master and that his neighbor's dog is not worse off than he?" Such things do happen. What protection is there for a poor cripple, who is pushed into a corner, and is not given enough to eat? There is none. But if he has as little as 100 or 200 marks of his own, the people will think twice before they oppress him. We have been in a position to observe this in the case of the military invalids. Although only five or six dollars are paid every month, this actual cash amounts to something in the household where the poor are boarded, and the thrifty housewife is careful not to offend or to lose the boarder who pays cash. . . .

Today this bill is a test, as it were. We are sounding to see how deep the waters are, financially, into which we are asking the state and the country to enter. You cannot guard yourselves against such problems by delivering elegant and sonorous speeches, in which you recommend the improvement of our laws of liability, without in the least indicating how this can be done. In this way you cannot settle these questions, for you are acting like the ostrich, who hides his head lest he see his danger. The government has seen its duty and is facing, calmly and without fear, the dangers which we heard described here a few days ago most eloquently and of which we were given convincing proofs.

We should, however, also remove, as much as possible, the causes which are used to excite the people, and which alone render them susceptible to criminal doctrines. It is immaterial to me whether or no you will call this socialism. . . .

If the government endeavors to treat the injured workingmen better in the future, and especially more becomingly, and not to offer to their as yet vigorous brethren the spectacle, as it were, of an old man on the dump heap slowly starving to death, this cannot be called socialistic in the sense in which that murderous band was painted to us the other day. People are playing a cheap game with the shadow on the wall when they call our endeavors socialistic. . . .

[Nor will I] reply at length to the reproach that this is communism, but I should like to ask you not to discuss everything from the point of view of party strategy, or faction strategy, or from the feeling "away with Bismarck." We have to do here with matters where not one of us can see his way clearly, and where we must search for the right road with sticks and sounding rods. I should like to see another man in my place as speedily as possible, if he would continue my work. I should gladly say to him, "Son, take up your father's spear," even if he were not my own son. . . .

Alms constitute the first step of Christian charity, such as must exist in France, for instance, to a great extent. There are no poor-laws in France, and every poor man has the right to starve to death if charitable people do not prevent him from doing so. Charity is the first duty, and the second is, the assistance given by districts and according to law. A state, however, which is composed very largely of Christians—even if you are horrified at hearing it called a Christian state—should let itself be permeated with the principles which it confesses, and especially with those which have to do with the help of our neighbors, and the sympathy one feels for the lot which threatens the old and the sick.

The extensive discussions, which I have partly heard, and partly read in the parliamentary extracts of yesterday, compel me to make some further observations. The representative Mr. Richter has said that the whole bill amounted to a subsidy of the big industries. Well, here again, you have an instance of class hatred, which would receive new fuel if his words were true. I do not know why you assume that the government cherishes a blind and special love for the big industries. The big manufacturers are, it is true, children of fortune, and this creates no good will toward them among the rest of the people. But to weaken or to confine their existence would be a very foolish experiment. If we dropped our big industries, making it impossible for them to compete with those of other countries, and if we placed burdens on them which they have not yet been proved able to bear, we might meet with the approval of all who are vexed at seeing anybody richer than other people, most especially than themselves. But, if we ruin the big industries, what shall we do with the laborers? In such a case we should be facing the problem, to which the representative Mr. Richter referred with much concern, of the organization of labor. If a business, employing twenty thousand laborers and more, goes to pieces, and if the big industries go to pieces, because they have been denounced to public opinion and to the legislature as dangerous and liable to heavier taxes, we could not let twenty thousand, and hundreds of thousands of laborers starve to death. In such a case we should have to organize a genuine state socialism, and find work for these laborers, similar to what we have been doing during every panic. . . .

I am, therefore, of the opinion that a state which is at war with the infernal elements recently described to you here in detail, and which possesses among its citizens an overwhelming majority of sincere adherents of the Christian religion, should do for the poor, the weak, and the old much more than this bill demands—as much as I hope to be able to ask of you next year. And such a state, especially when it wishes to demonstrate its practical Christianity, should not refuse our demands, for its own sake and for the sake of the poor!

Bismarck was the last of the classic diplomats of Europe in the tradition of Richelieu, Kaunitz, or Metternich. The moral dimensions of war and peace seemed to him to have little importance, although occasionally he reflected piously on the evils of strife or the blessings of harmony. Basically he regarded armed might as a legitimate weapon of statecraft to be employed for the attainment of a valid object of policy. When first appointed prime minister in Berlin, he had felt that the national unification of Germany was both desirable and inevitable. In order to achieve it, he had deliberately invited military conflicts with Denmark, Austria, and France. Recourse to arms was to him the only way out of an intolerable political system in Central Europe which stood in the way of Prussia's destiny. Yet the man of blood and iron, who in the 1860s appeared to be the embodiment of ruthless militarism, did not believe in force for its own sake. He used it rather for the realization of limited goals, and once these were reached in the 1870s, he became an advocate of peace. Not that he was ever a pacifist as a matter of principle. But he concluded that just as conflict was the best way of altering an unacceptable diplomatic situation, stability was the best way of preserving a desirable one. The establishment of the German Empire, he maintained, marked the attainment of all the justifiable political objectives of his countrymen. They should now seek to consolidate what they had gained rather than covet what they had not. Here was the fundamental difference between Bismarck and the insatiable conquerors of history like Napoleon I or Hitler.

The international situation in Europe was favorable to the realization of the chancellor's aims. The period of political and diplomatic readjustment which began in 1853 with the Crimean War came to an end in 1871 with the Franco-Prussian War. Thereafter the Continent entered an era of stability without a major military conflict for more than forty years. The preservation of peace during that long time was due in considerable measure to the efforts of Bismarck. Convinced that his government had little to gain and much to lose from a new armed struggle, he labored unceasingly to maintain harmony among the Great Powers. The key to the tranquillity of Europe was, in his opinion, the isolation of France. For the Third Republic could never become reconciled to the loss of Alsace-Lorraine. The policy of *revanche* might sometimes be avowed by Paris openly, sometimes pursued secretly, but it was never far below the surface of Gallic statecraft. Its ultimate objective was the outbreak of a general war. The chancellor therefore sought to establish an international quarantine of France, convinced that without support from other states she would never dare attack the German Empire. The foundation of his diplomatic system was the collaboration of the three conservative monarchies of Central and Eastern Europe which had once formed the Holy Alliance: Germany, Austria, and Russia. Their historic attachment to the teachings of legitimism made them the logical supporters of a policy designed to preserve the established order in Europe. Early in the 1870s William I, Francis Joseph, and Alexander II entered into an informal compact to work together for the maintenance of stability in international relations.

Yet their agreement regarding ideological principles was constantly imperiled by their disagreement regarding political objectives. The decaying Ottoman Empire had become a diplomatic battleground between Russia and Austria, each eager to expand in the direction of the Balkans. The result was a series of recurrent crises in the Near East which threatened to lead to a general war in Europe. When in 1878 Alexander II seemed on the point of gaining a dominant influence over the cockpit of the Continent as the result of a successful campaign against the Turks, the other Great Powers intervened. The czarist government, alarmed by the specter of the hostile coalition which had been victorious in the Crimean War, was forced to back down. Bismarck tried to avoid taking sides in the dispute, but he only succeeded in falling between two stools. St. Petersburg in particular felt that its past favors to Germany were being repaid by rank ingratitude. Facing the danger of a military conflict between Austria and Russia, the chancellor decided that he could no longer follow a middle course. In 1879 he concluded a defensive alliance with Vienna by which the two Teutonic powers agreed to support one another in the event of an attack by the czar's armies. But Bismarck had too much respect for the strength of his eastern neighbor to accept a permanent estrangement from the Russian state. His irreconcilable foe lay beyond the Rhine, not the Vistula. In 1881 he repaired the diplomatic links among the three conservative empires, and a year later he enlarged his alliance system by concluding an agreement with Italy. The equilibrium of Europe was now restored.

The maintenance of diplomatic stability on the Continent, however, was a labor of Sisyphus. No sooner was one threat to peace averted than another would loom on the horizon. In the late 1880s there were new international complications in the Near East similar to those which had almost precipitated a general war in the late 1870s. Once again a conflict in the Ottoman Empire between the sultan and his Christian subjects led to a revolt against Turkish rule. Once again Austria and Russia found themselves on opposite sides in a dispute over the future of southeastern Europe. Once again the tranquillity of the Continent was disturbed by the perennial problem of the Balkan Peninsula. And once again Bismarck faced the danger of diplomatic isolation as a result of the competing objectives of Vienna and St. Petersburg. He reacted with characteristic decisiveness. Whereas in 1879 he had sided with Austria in order to curb the ambition of Russia, in 1887 he sided with Russia in order to check the bellicosity of Austria. In a secret agreement with the czarist government he promised to maintain benevolent neutrality in the event of an attack against the Romanov empire by a third power. The strategy was risky but successful. The international crisis engendered by the complications in the Balkans gradually subsided. Yet the system of alliances and alignments which Bismarck had constructed was becoming so delicate and complex that only a statesman of genius could make it function effectively as an instrument of peace. In the hands of the chancellor it continued to preserve the balance of power on the Continent which was the main goal of his policy. After his retirement from office, however, it toppled and disintegrated.

1. Bismarck States That Germany Needs No Additional Territory

To Bismarck war and peace were means rather than ends. Whether a state should seek or avoid military conflict, he believed, depended on its circumstances and objectives. Before 1871 it had been impossible for Germany to attain her legitimate goals within the existing diplomatic balance of power. She had therefore been justified in employing force to alter the *status quo*. But now the achievement of national unification and the acquisition of Alsace-Lorraine had satisfied all her valid political and territorial ambitions. This was the gist of an interview which the chancellor had with a Rumanian politician early in 1888.

[BISMARCK] made the following political declarations . . . "I desire that peace be maintained. I owe this to the emperor, who is too far advanced in years for any great undertaking; I owe it to the crown prince, who has been attacked by a mysterious malady, and is more seriously ill than is generally believed; I owe it to my country, which would gain nothing from a victorious campaign against Russia.

"In fact, Germany, whose boundaries are firmly established, has nothing to take from her neighbor on the east. What territory could she think of annexing? She has enough of Poland already. By seeking fresh conquests, the German Empire would only be exposing itself to perpetual warfare with Russia and France, who is simply waiting for an opportunity for avenging Alsace and Lorraine. Under these circumstances warlike proposals, no matter when they might come, would not fit in with my program." [Bismarck] furthermore declared that war will not be brought about by the allied powers. Neither Germany nor Austria will attack Russia. The attack would have to come from the Russians themselves. In discussing the probability of Russia's resorting to aggression, he said that as long as the present emperor and M. de Giers are able to dominate the situation, the mines will never be fired. Nevertheless, it is true that there exists in Russia an undercurrent of malcontent, a spirit of Panslavism, which might one day burst forth, and force the hand of the czar himself. In anticipation of such a possibility the allies must continue to maintain their arma-

SOURCE: *The Memoirs of Francesco Crispi*, 3 vols. (London: Hodder & Stoughton, 1912–14), vol. II, pp. 279–280.

ments, and be ever ready. As far as Germany is concerned, she is already in a condition to defend herself. "I am ready, and fear nothing. Nevertheless I cannot endorse the opinion of those who believe we should rush to arms today, for fear war may be declared against us tomorrow."

2. He Seeks the Preservation of Peace

Since Bismarck came to believe after the Franco-Prussian War that the major diplomatic objective of the German Empire should be not the annexation of additional territory but the retention of its acquisitions, his basic concern in foreign affairs was the maintenance of international stability. He recognized that war is the most effective means of changing the *status quo*, while peace provides the best guarantee for its preservation. This was the underlying assumption of his statecraft, as he described it in a conversation with the future chancellor Bernhard von Bülow. He was especially anxious to maintain friendly relations among the leading conservative monarchies of Europe: Germany, Austria, and Russia.

OUR POLICY is and remains a policy of peace. We have no reason to want a war, and I do not see what we should have to gain by one. The annexation of German-Austria, or the Baltic provinces, or even any Dutch or the Swiss territory, would only weaken us. And so-called prophylactic wars, that is, the policy of attacking somebody else so that he may not grow a little stronger and attack first, I consider, . . . not only un-Christian but politically foolish as well. What did Napoleon I ever accomplish with his prophylactic wars? One can always begin a war but one never knows how it may end! Three times God has given us victory. That was a great mercy. But to let it come to a fourth war, without pressing reasons, would be tantamount to tempting Providence. It is in our own interests to keep the peace. Of course we must keep our sword sharp. Our political position, power, honor and wealth we owe in the first place to the army. The army also ensures monarchical government as the only solid basis of the realm, of order and our growing prosperity. The pivot of our position, and with that of our whole policy, the point on which things turn, is our relationship to Russia. The French will only attack us if we let ourselves

SOURCE: *Memoirs of Prince von Bülow*, 4 vols. (Boston: Little, Brown and Company, 1931–32), vol. IV, pp. 556–557.

get embroiled with Russia, but then are certain to do so. As for the English, they have no reason at all for attacking us, even if they are beginning to envy our industrial and commercial progress. The Englishman is like the dog in the fable, who cannot bear that another dog should have a few bones, although the overfed brute is sitting before a bowl full to the brim. An English attack would only be thinkable if we found ourselves at war with both Russia and France, or did anything so utterly absurd as to fall upon Holland or Belgium, or block the Baltic by closing the Sound, or some nonsense of the kind, which is out of the question. For us, therefore, St. Petersburg is now the most important diplomatic post. . . . London and Paris are observation posts. In countries where, in the long run, parliament decides matters, the diplomat cannot accomplish much. In a country where things depend in the first place upon the sovereign it is different. Even the greatest autocrat never acts according to his own ideas, even if he sometimes thinks he does. He will always have a wife, a mistress, brothers, aunts, cousins, favorites, aides-de-camps and chamberlains, who influence him to a greater or a less degree. Then the diplomat can do positive and concrete work. We have, thank God, got rid of [the Russian chancellor] Gortchakov. His successor, von Giers, is not a heroic figure, but is well disposed. I consider him honest, and far preferable to Gortchakov. I look upon Alexander III as loyal too. That he is not so well-disposed toward us as his father is not a misfortune. Alexander II was steeped in the traditions of the Wars of Liberation, and for that very reason he was so sensitive about anything which he mistakenly considered to be a departure from the principles of the Holy Alliance. He was like a woman who, because she was once very much in love with her husband, goes on suspecting him all his life and continually plagues him with her jealous question: "Do you love me?" I believe that a calm and neighborly relationship is quite possible with Alexander III. . . . Nobody can know how a military clash between the three imperial powers might end. One thing is certain: The three dynasties, the three monarchs, would probably pay the penalty and the only real victor would be the revolution. Napoleon said on St. Helena, that Europe, after his fall, would be either Cossack or republican. I believe that if the Prussian and the Cossack ever come to blows Europe will become republican. The ticklish factor in our connections with Russia is of course Austria.

We cannot let Austria be overrun and shattered. But just as little must we let ourselves be dragged into war by her. To maneuver between these two crags is a matter of skill and a clear head, much the same qualities as are necessary to prevent two trains meeting in a head-on crash. The pointsman must keep his eyes open and have a steady hand. The most difficult to deal with are the Magyars, because they are so violent. They are our best support in our relationship towards the Habsburg monarchy, but, at the same time, they are those who most incline to exaggerated suspicion and imprudence. Besides, God in His wisdom has so arranged it that the peoples of the Near East, which, as we know begins on the highroad to Vienna, cannot abide one another. The Magyars and the Rumanians, the Croats and Serbs, and Turks and Bulgarians, the Czechs and Slovaks, the Greeks and the Albanians hate each other even more than they hate the German.

3. He Explains His Attitude to the Other Great Powers

Once the German Empire had been established, Bismarck concluded that the only major threat to international stability was France, for she was the only one of the Great Powers which had anything to gain from a general war on the Continent. His basic goal became therefore the isolation of the government in Paris, which would hesitate to engage unassisted in a military contest with Berlin. For this reason he sought to maintain close diplomatic relations with the other leading states, especially Austria and Russia. In his memoirs he described the broad strategy on which he had based his unceasing efforts to preserve the peace of Europe.

COUNT SHUVALOFF was perfectly right when he said that the idea of coalitions gave me nightmares. We had waged victorious wars against two of the European Great Powers; everything depended on inducing at least one of the two mighty foes whom we had beaten in the field to renounce the anticipated design of uniting with the other in a war of revenge. To all who knew history and the character of the Gallic race, it was obvious that that Power could not be France, and if a secret treaty of Reichstadt was possible without our consent, without our knowledge, so also was a renewal of the old coalition—Kaunitz's handiwork—of France,

SOURCE: *Bismarck: The Man and the Statesman*, 2 vols. (New York and London: Harper & Row, 1899), vol. II, pp. 255–258.

Austria, and Russia, whenever the elements which it represented, and which beneath the surface were still present in Austria, should gain the ascendency there. They might find points of connection which might serve to infuse new life into the ancient rivalry, the ancient struggle for the hegemony of Germany, making it once more a factor in Austrian policy, whether by an alliance with France, which in the time of Count Beust and the Salzburg meeting with Louis Napoleon, August 1867, was in the air, or by a closer accord with Russia, the existence of which was attested by the secret convention of Reichstadt. The question of what support Germany had in such a case to expect from England I will not answer without more in the way of historical retrospect of the Seven Years' War and the congress of Vienna. I merely take note of the probability that, but for the victories of Frederick the Great, the cause of the king of Prussia would have been abandoned by England even earlier than it actually was.

This situation demanded an effort to limit the range of the possible anti-German coalition by means of treaty arrangements placing our relations with at least one of the Great Powers upon a firm footing. The choice could only lie between Austria and Russia, for the English constitution does not admit of alliances of assured permanence, and a union with Italy alone did not promise an adequate counterpoise to a coalition of the other three Great Powers, even supposing her future attitude and formation to be considered independently not only of French but also of Austrian influence. The area available for the formation of the coalition would therefore be narrowed till only the alternative remained which I have indicated.

In point of material force I held a union with Russia to have the advantage. I had also been used to regard it as safer, because I placed more reliance on traditional dynastic friendship, on community of conservative monarchical instincts, on the absence of indigenous political divisions, than on the fits and starts of public opinion among the Hungarian, Slav, and Catholic population of the monarchy of the Habsburgs. Complete reliance could be placed upon the durability of neither union, whether one estimated the strength of the dynastic bond with Russia, or of the German sympathies of the Hungarian populace. If the balance of opinion in Hungary were always determined by sober political calculation, this brave and independent people, isolated in the broad ocean of

Slav populations, and comparatively insignificant in numbers, would remain constant to the conviction that its position can only be secured by the support of the German element in Austria and Germany. But the Kossuth episode, and the suppression in Hungary itself of the German elements that remained loyal to the Empire, with other symptoms showed that among Hungarian hussars and lawyers self-confidence is apt in critical moments to get the better of political calculation and self-control. Even in quiet times many a Magyar will get the gypsies to play to him the song, "Der Deutsche ist ein Hundsfott" ("The German Is a Blackguard").

In the forecast of the future relations of Austria and Germany an essential element was the imperfect appreciation of political possibilities displayed by the German element in Austria, which has caused it to lose touch with the dynasty and forfeit the guidance which it had inherited from its historical development. Misgivings as to the future of an Austro-German confederation were also suggested by the religious question, by the remembered influence of the father confessors of the imperial family, by the anticipated possibility of renewed relations with France, on the basis of a *rapprochement* by that country to the Catholic church, whenever such a change should have taken place in the character and principles of French statesmanship. How remote or how near such a change may be in France is quite beyond the scope of calculation.

Last of all came the Austrian policy in regard to Poland. We cannot demand of Austria that she should forgo the weapon which she possesses as against Russia in her fostering care of the Polish spirit in Galicia. The policy which in 1846 resulted in a price being set by Austrian officials on the heads of insurgent Polish patriots was possible because, by a conformable attitude in Polish and Eastern affairs, Austria paid (as by a contribution to a common insurance fund) for the advantages which she derived from the holy alliance, the league of the three Eastern Powers. So long as the triple alliance of the Eastern Powers held good, Austria could place her relations with the Ruthenes in the foreground of her policy; as soon as it was dissolved, it was more advisable to have the Polish nobility at her disposal in case of a war with Russia. Galicia is altogether more loosely connected with the Austrian monarchy than Poland and West Prussia with the Prussian monarchy. The Austrian trans-Carpathian eastern province lies open without natural boundary on that side, and Austria would be by no means weakened by its abandonment provided she could find compensation in the basin of the Danube for its five or six million Poles and Ruthenes. Plans of the sort, but taking the shape of the transference of Roumanian and Southern-Slav populations to Austria in exchange for Galicia, and the resuscitation of Poland under the sway of an archduke, were considered officially and unofficially during the Crimean war and in 1863. The Old-Prussian provinces are, however, separated from Posen and West Prussia by no natural boundary, and their abandonment by Prussia would be impossible. Hence among the preconditions of an offensive alliance between Germany and Austria the settlement of the future of Poland presents a problem of unusual difficulty.

4. The Text of the Dual Alliance with Austria

The greatest difficulty which Bismarck encountered in his efforts to maintain diplomatic collaboration between Germany, Austria, and Russia arose out of the conflicting ambitions of Vienna and St. Petersburg in the Balkans. Time and again they clashed over some international complication created by the gradual disintegration of the Ottoman Empire, and the chancellor would then have to engage in delicate and arduous negotiations to effect the reconciliation of his two bellicose neighbors. When the Near Eastern crisis of the late 1870s created the danger of a major war in Europe, he finally decided to conclude a defensive alliance with Austria directed against Russia.

INASMUCH AS Their Majesties the Emperor of Austria, King of Hungary, and the German Emperor, King of Prussia, must consider it their imperative duty as monarchs to provide for the security of their empires and the peace of their subjects, under all circumstances;

inasmuch as the two sovereigns, as was the case under the former existing relations of alliance, will be enabled by the close union of the two empires to fulfil this duty more easily and more efficaciously;

inasmuch as, finally, an intimate cooperation of Germany and Austria-Hungary can menace no one, but is rather calculated to

SOURCE: Excerpted by permission of the publishers from *The Secret Treaties of Austria-Hungary, 1879-1914*, vol. I, Alfred Franzis Pribam, ed. Eng. Ed. by Archibald Cary Coolidge, Tr. by Denys P. Myers and J. G. D'Arcy Paul (Cambridge, Mass.: Harvard University Press, 1920), pp. 25, 27, 29, 31.

consolidate the peace of Europe as established by the stipulations of Berlin;

Their Majesties the Emperor of Austria, King of Hungary, and the Emperor of Germany, while solemnly promising each other never to allow their purely defensive agreement to develop an aggressive tendency in any direction, have determined to conclude an alliance of peace and mutual defense.

For this purpose Their Most Exalted Majesties have designated as their plenipotentiaries:

His Most Exalted Majesty the Emperor of Austria, King of Hungary, His Actual Privy Councillor, Minister of the Imperial Household and of Foreign Affairs, Lieutenant-Fieldmarshal Count Julius Andrássy of Csik-Szent-Király and Kraszna-Horka, etc., etc.,

His Most Exalted Majesty the German Emperor, His Ambassador Extraordinary and Plenipotentiary, Lieutenant-General Prince Henry VII of Reuss, etc., etc.,

who have met this day at Vienna, and, after the exchange of their full powers, found in good and due form, have agreed upon the following articles:

ARTICLE I

Should, contrary to their hope, and against the loyal desire of the two high contracting parties, one of the two empires be attacked by Russia, the high contracting parties are bound to come to the assistance one of the other with the whole war strength of their empires, and accordingly only to conclude peace together and upon mutual agreement.

ARTICLE II

Should one of the high contracting parties be attacked by another power, the other high contracting party binds itself hereby, not only not to support the aggressor against its high ally, but to observe at least a benevolent neutral attitude towards its fellow contracting party.

Should, however, the attacking party in such a case be supported by Russia, either by an active cooperation or by military measures which constitute a menace to the party attacked, then the obligation stipulated in Article I of this Treaty, for reciprocal assistance with the whole fighting force, becomes equally operative, and the conduct of the war by the two high contracting parties shall in this case also be in common until the conclusion of a common peace.

ARTICLE III

The duration of this treaty shall be provisionally fixed at five years from the day of ratification. One year before the expiration of this period the two high contracting parties shall consult together concerning the question whether the conditions serving as the basis of the treaty still prevail, and reach an agreement in regard to the further continuance or possible modification of certain details. If in the course of the first month of the last year of the treaty no invitation has been received from either side to open these negotiations, the treaty shall be considered as renewed for a further period of three years.

ARTICLE IV

This treaty shall, in conformity with its peaceful character, and to avoid any misinterpretation, be kept secret by the two high contracting parties, and only communicated to a third power upon a joint understanding between the two parties, and according to the terms of a special agreement.

The two high contracting parties venture to hope, after the sentiments expressed by the Emperor Alexander at the meeting at Alexandrovo, that the armaments of Russia will not in reality prove to be menacing to them, and have on that account no reason for making a communication at present; should, however, this hope, contrary to their expectations, prove to be erroneous, the two high contracting parties would consider it their loyal obligation to let the Emperor Alexander know, at least confidentially, that they must consider an attack on either of them as directed against both.

ARTICLE V

This treaty shall derive its validity from the approbation of the two exalted sovereigns and shall be ratified within fourteen days after this approbation has been granted by Their Most Exalted Majesties.

In witness whereof the plenipotentiaries have signed this Treaty with their own hands and affixed their arms.

Done at Vienna, October 7, 1879.

Andrássy   H. VII v. Reuss

L.S.   L.S.

5. Bismarck Justifies the Dual Alliance

The alliance with the Dual Monarchy into which Bismarck entered in 1879 was to have far-reaching consequences for the German Empire. As the keystone of the diplomacy pursued by Berlin during the next forty years, it contributed directly to the outbreak of a world war in 1914. After his retirement from office, the chancellor sought to justify the decision to turn to Vienna rather than St. Petersburg when a choice between them became unavoidable. Yet he also emphasized that the maintenance of cordial relations between Germany and Russia was of crucial importance for the peace of Europe.

THE TREATY which we concluded with Austria for common defense against a Russian attack is *publici juris*. An analogous treaty between the two powers for defense against France has not been published. The German-Austrian alliance does not afford the same protection against a French war, by which Germany is primarily threatened, as against a Russian war, which is to be apprehended rather by Austria than by Germany. Germany and Russia have no divergencies of interest pregnant with such disputes as lead to unavoidable ruptures. On the other hand, coincident aims in regard to Poland, and in a secondary degree the ancient solidarity which unites their dynasties in opposition to subversive efforts, afford both cabinets the bases for a common policy. They have been impaired by the false bias given now for ten years past to public opinion by the Russian press. This has assiduously planted and fostered in the mind of the reading part of the population an antipathy to everything German, with which the dynasty will have to reckon, even though the czar may wish to cultivate German friendship. Scarcely, however, could anti-German rancor acquire in Russia a keener edge than it has among the Czechs in Bohemia and Moravia, the Slovenes of the countries comprised within the earlier German confederation, and the Poles in Galicia. In short, if

SOURCE: *Bismarck: The Man and the Statesman*, 2 vols. (New York and London: Harper & Row, 1899), vol. II, pp. 275–282.

in deciding between the Russian and the Austrian alliance I gave the preference to the latter, it was not that I was in any degree blind to the perplexities which made choice difficult. I regarded it as no less enjoined upon us to cultivate neighborly relations with Russia after, than before, our defensive alliance with Austria; for perfect security against the disruption of the chosen combination is not to be had by Germany, while it is possible for her to hold in check the anti-German fits and starts of Austro-Hungarian feeling so long as German policy maintains the bridge which leads to St. Petersburg, and allows no chasm to intervene between us and Russia which cannot be spanned. Given no such irremediable breach Vienna will be able to bridle the forces hostile or alien to the German alliance. Suppose, however, that the breach with Russia is an accomplished fact, an irremediable estrangement. Austria would then certainly begin to enlarge her claims on the services of her German confederate, first by insisting on an extension of the *casus foederis*, which so far, according to the published text, provides only for the measures necessary to repel a Russian attack upon Austria; then by requiring the substitution for this *casus foederis* of some provision safeguarding the interests of Austria in the Balkan and the East, an idea to which our press has already succeeded in giving practical shape. The wants, the plans of the inhabitants of the basin of the Danube naturally reach far beyond the present limits of the Austro-Hungarian monarchy, and the German imperial constitution points out the way by which Austria may advance to a reconciliation of her political and material interests, so far as they lie between the eastern frontier of the Roumanian population and the Gulf of Cattaro. It is, however, no part of the policy of the German Empire to lend her subjects, to expend her blood and treasure, for the purpose of realizing the designs of a neighbor Power. In the interest of the European political equilibrium the maintenance of the Austro-Hungarian monarchy as a strong independent Great Power is for Germany an object for which she might in case of need stake her own peace with a good conscience. But Vienna should abstain from going outside this security, and deducing from the alliance claims which it was not concluded to support.

Peace between Germany and Russia may be imperiled by the systematic fomentation of ill-feeling, or by the ambition of Russian or German military men like Skobeleff, who desire war before they grow too old to distinguish themselves, but is hardly to be imperiled in any other way. The Russian press must needs be characterized by stupidity and disingenuousness in an unusual degree for it to believe and affirm that German policy was determined by aggressive tendencies in concluding the Austrian, and thereafter the Italian, defensive alliance. The disingenuousness was less of Russian than of Polish-French, the stupidity less of Polish-French than of Russian origin. In the field of Russian credulity and ignorance Polish-French finesse won a victory over that want of finesse in which, according to circumstances, consists now the strength, now the weakness of German policy. In most cases an open and honorable policy succeeds better than the subtlety of earlier ages, but it postulates, if it is to succeed, a degree of personal confidence which can more readily be lost than gained. The future of Austria, regarded in herself, cannot be reckoned upon with that certainty which is demanded when the conclusion of durable and, so to speak, organic treaties is contemplated. The factors which must be taken into account in this shaping are as manifold as is the mixture of her populations, and to their corrosive and occasionally disruptive force must be added the incalculable influence that the religious element may from time to time, as the power of Rome waxes or wanes, exert upon the directing personalities. Not only Panslavism and the Bulgarian or Bosnian, but also the Servian, the Roumanian, the Polish, the Czechish questions, nay even today the Italian question in the district of Trent, in Trieste, and on the Dalmatian coast, may serve as points of crystallization not merely for Austrian, but for European crises, by which German interests will be directly affected only in so far as the German Empire enters into a relation of close solidarity with Austria. In Bohemia the antagonism between Germans and Czechs has in some places penetrated so deeply into the army that the officers of the two nationalities in certain regiments hold aloof from one another even to the degree that they will not meet at mess. There is more immediate danger for Germany of becoming involved in grievous and dangerous struggles on her western frontier, by reason of the aggressive, plundering instincts of the French people, which have been greatly developed by her monarchs since the time of Emperor Charles V, in their lust of power at home as well as abroad. . . .

In Hungary, in Poland, French sympathies are still lively, and the restoration of monarchy upon a Catholic basis in France might

cause the renewal of those relations with the clergy of the united
Habsburg monarchy which in 1863 and between 1866 and 1870
found expression in common diplomatic action, and more or less
mature schemes of union by treaty. The security which, in regard
to these contingencies, is to be found in the person of the present
emperor of Austria and king of Hungary is, as has been said, manifest enough, but a far-sighted policy must take account of all
eventualities which lie within the region of possibility. The possibility of a rivalry between Vienna and Berlin for the friendship of
Russia may return upon us just as in the days of Olmütz, or when,
under the auspices (propitious for us) of Count Andrassy, it once
more attested its existence by the convention of Reichstadt.

In face of this eventuality it makes in our favor that Austria and
Russia have opposing interests in the Balkan, while none such in
strength enough to occasion an open breach and actual struggle
exist between Russia and Prussia with Germany. This advantage,
however, may be taken from us—thanks to the peculiar character
of the Russian constitution—by personal misunderstanding and
maladroit policy, no less easily today than when Czarina Elizabeth
was induced by the bitter *bon mots* of Frederick the Great to
accede to the Franco-Austrian alliance. Mischief-making intrigues,
such as then served to irritate Russia, scandalous fabrications, indis-
creet utterances or acts, will not be wanting even today at either
court; but it is possible for us to maintain our independence and
dignity in face of Russia without wounding Russian sensitiveness
or damaging Russia's interests. The wanton stirring up of bad and
bitter feeling reacts today with no less effect on the course of
history than in the times of Czarina Elizabeth of Russia and Queen
Anne of England. But this reaction exerts today a much more
powerful influence upon the present and future weal of the nations
than a hundred years ago. An anti-Prussian coalition like that of
the Seven Years' War between Russia, Austria and France, in
union perhaps with other discontented dynasties, would today
expose our existence to just as grave a peril, and if victorious would
be far more disastrous. It is irrational, it is criminal by fomenting
personal misunderstandings to cut off the way of access to an
entente cordiale with Russia.

We must and can honorably maintain the alliance with the
Austro-Hungarian monarchy; it corresponds to our interests, to
the historical traditions of Germany, to the public opinion of our

people. The influences and forces under and amid which the future policy of Vienna must be shaped are, however, more complex than with us, by reason of the manifold diversity of the nationalities, the divergence of their aspirations and activities, the influence of the clergy, and the temptations to which the Danubian countries are exposed in the Balkan and Black Sea latitudes.

We cannot abandon Austria, but neither can we lose sight of the possibility that the policy of Vienna may willy-nilly abandon us. The possibilities which in such a case remain open to us must be clearly realized and steadily borne in mind by German statesmen before the critical moment arrives, nor must their action be determined by prejudice or misunderstanding, but by an entirely dispassionate weighing of the national interests.

6. The Text of the League of the Three Emperors

To Bismarck the alliance with Austria was only a diplomatic instrument designed to maintain the balance of power on the Continent. He was determined not to let Berlin become too dependent on Vienna, and as soon as the international situation permitted, he resumed negotiations with the Russians. The result was the conclusion of a new agreement among the great conservative states of Europe, the League of the Three Emperors of 1881. In order to avoid future conflicts over the complex problem of the Balkans, the signatories spelled out in detail their respective rights and obligations with regard to Turkey.

THE COURTS OF Austria-Hungary, of Germany, and of Russia, animated by an equal desire to consolidate the general peace by an understanding intended to assume the defensive position of their respective states, have come into agreement on certain questions which more especially concern their reciprocal interests.

With this purpose the three courts have appointed:

His Majesty the Emperor of Austria, King of Bohemia, etc., and Apostolic King of Hungary, the Sieur Emeric Count Széchényi, His Ambassador Extraordinary and Plenipotentiary to His Majesty the Emperor of Germany, King of Prussia,

SOURCE: Excerpted by permission of the publishers from *The Secret Treaties of Austria-Hungary, 1879–1914*, vol. I, Alfred Franzis Pribam, ed. Eng. Ed. by Archibald Cary Coolidge, Tr. by Denys P. Myers and J. G. D'Arcy Paul (Cambridge, Mass.: Harvard University Press, 1920), pp. 37, 39, 41.

His Majesty the Emperor of Germany, King of Prussia, the Sieur Otto Prince Bismarck, His President of the Council of Ministers of Prussia, Chancellor of the Empire,

His Majesty the Emperor of All the Russias, the Sieur Peter Sabouroff, Privy Councillor, His Ambassador Extraordinary and Plenipotentiary to His Majesty the Emperor of Germany, King of Prussia,

who, furnished with full powers, which have been found in good and due form, have agreed upon the following articles:

ARTICLE I

In case one of the high contracting parties should find itself at war with a fourth Great Power, the two others shall maintain towards it a benevolent neutrality and shall devote their efforts to the localization of the conflict.

This stipulation shall apply likewise to a war between one of the three powers and Turkey, but only in the case where a previous agreement shall have been reached between the three courts as to the results of this war.

In the special case where one of them should obtain a more positive support from one of its two allies, the obligatory value of the present article shall remain in all its force for the third.

ARTICLE II

Russia, in agreement with Germany, declares her firm resolution to respect the interests arising from the new position assured to Austria-Hungary by the Treaty of Berlin.

The three courts, desirous of avoiding all discord between them, engage to take account of their respective interests in the Balkan Peninsula. They further promise one another that any new modifications in the territorial *status quo* of Turkey in Europe can be accomplished only in virtue of a common agreement between them. . . .

ARTICLE III

The three courts recognize the European and mutually obligatory character of the principle of the closing of the Straits of the Bosphorus and of the Dardanelles, founded on international law, confirmed by treaties, and summed up in the declaration of the second Plenipotentiary of Russia at the session of July 12 of the congress of Berlin (Protocol 19).

They will take care in common that Turkey shall make no exception to this rule in favor of the interests of any government whatsoever, by lending to warlike operations of a belligerent power the portion of its empire constituted by the Straits.

In case of infringement, or to prevent it if such infringement should be in prospect, the three courts will inform Turkey that they would regard her, in that event, as putting herself in a state of war towards the injured party, and as having deprived herself thenceforth of the benefits of the security assured to her territorial *status quo* by the Treaty of Berlin.

ARTICLE IV

The present treaty shall be in force during a period of three years, dating from the day of the exchange of ratifications.

ARTICLE V

The high contracting parties mutually promise secrecy as to the contents and the existence of the present treaty, as well as of the protocol annexed thereto.

ARTICLE VI

The secret conventions concluded between Austria-Hungary and Russia and between Germany and Russia in 1873 are replaced by the present treaty.

ARTICLE VII

The ratifications of the present treaty and of the protocol annexed thereto shall be exchanged at Berlin within a fortnight, or sooner if may be.

In witness whereof the respective plenipotentiaries have signed the present treaty and have affixed thereto the seal of their arms.

Done at Berlin, the eighteenth day of the month of June, one thousand eight hundred and eighty-one.

L. S.
L. S.
L. S.

Széchényi
v. Bismarck
Sabouroff

7. German-Italian Negotiations Concerning an Alliance

A year later Bismarck found an opportunity to enlarge the scope of the alliance system by which he sought to ensure the isolation of Paris. The Italian government, having clashed with France over competing imperialistic claims in Tunisia, turned to Germany with a proposal for diplomatic collaboration. The chancellor regarded Rome as a weak and unreliable ally, but he also saw an important advantage in improving relations between Italy and Austria. In a memorandum of January 31, 1882, he described an interview with the Italian ambassador in which he declared that the key to Berlin was to be sought in Vienna.

THE ITALIAN AMBASSADOR declared to me today that his government desired to associate itself with German-Austrian policy and added that the king of Italy and his ministers were fully agreed on this point.

I replied that we were genuinely rejoiced at the Italian government's overture. Our policy, as he knew, was directed above all at maintaining peace, and that we were united and allied with Austria and Russia for this object. In Austria particularly the emperor and nation felt the need of peace and were working for it, and it was evident that a kind of political honor existed between us, which bound us in the important question, which he was raising, not to anticipate the decisions of our friend, the Austrian government.

Count Launay objected that he had definitely hoped for a decision from us on his government's proposal, which would otherwise be bandied to and fro. I replied that business between Germany and Italy was different from and simpler than the same would be between Italy and Austria. We shared no frontier in common, nor did the interests of the two nations clash at other points. With Austria it was quite otherwise. In the Balkans and on the Adriatic each party had competing interests, which might lead to difficulties. I did not know whether the aspirations of Italia irredenta were definitely and for ever extinct, for they had but a short time ago stood in the way of establishing good relations with Austria.

Count Launay assured me with vehemence that there was now no question of Italia irredenta, and that in all leading circles in Italy

SOURCE: E. T. S. Dugdale, ed., *German Diplomatic Documents, 1871–1914*, 4 vols. (London: Methuen & Co. Ltd, 1928–31), vol. I, pp. 110–113. Reprinted by permission of the publisher.

the desire predominated to remove all that might prejudice good relations with the neighbouring country.

He then went a step further and asked whether the understanding for a common policy with the two imperial courts, which his government desired, could not be drawn up in writing. I explained the difficulties there would be in setting out the mutual feelings of friendship, which existed, in treaty form. It would not be easy to draft anything which would express all their wishes. I would not venture to prepare such a draft as Count Launay contemplated. It was difficult to define the principles limiting the extent of such an agreement, and they might drag each one of the participants further than he meant to go or could answer for to his country. What would be Italy's position, if say, Germany, conscious that with the addition of the Italian army, the two imperial powers had increased strength behind them, declared war unnecessarily against France for some cause not now foreseen? This might seem unlikely now, but it could not be ignored that a written alliance, with the military strength accompanying it, might lead each one of the participants into temptation for his own private ends, and make excessive demands on the forces of his allies, without the excuse of being in danger. Who could say whether, under parliamentary pressure, Italian policy would sooner or later slip into complications on the north coast of Africa or elsewhere, which might perhaps have been avoided for the sake of peace, had the cabinet not been able to count on German assistance? Similar possibilities were not out of the question for Russia and Austria in the Balkans or elsewhere.

Count Launay admitted that drafting an alliance, as Italy wished it, presented great difficulties, but that he had hoped "*que je suggérerais une rédaction acceptable pour toutes les parties.*"

I replied that with the best will in the world I could only indicate the difficulties, that impeded the realization of this idea and were caused by the nature of the case.

In mentioning the advantages accruing to the participants out of a formal alliance, I had explained that it was not all countries that could offer such a guarantee for the strict observance of their engagements, and especially not those states in which the parliament was more influential than the dynasty. I gave England as an instance. It was impossible to form a lasting alliance with her, because domestic politics come before foreign and the parties, which take turns in governing the country, do not necessarily acknowledge their predecessors' engagements. The monarchy, moreover, was not strong enough to maintain its foreign policy against the party actually in power. The recent British change of ministry was an instance of this. In Germany as in Austria, it was different; although they also had Parliamentary institutions, there was a monarchy strong enough to keep the treaty promises under all circumstances. If it ever happened here that a parliament were to resist the carrying out of an international treaty, the chamber would undoubtedly get the worst of it, and the monarch would win the day, as he could rely on the nation's recognition of his rights and on a faithful army. With such allies there could be no possible danger of a change of policy occasioned by pressure at home. It was not certain whether conditions in Italy, which presented to foreigners the spectacle of ministries constantly shifting toward the Left, allowed the King similar freedom of action. Count Launay assured me that just now all parties were agreed as to the necessity of uniting with the three imperial courts. He wished to exclude all doubts as to the King's ability to rely completely on the Army. On which I pointed out that a monarch, who wore civilian dress, was not doing all that he could to identify himself with his army.

In general I met the Italian ambassador's overture in a willing and friendly spirit, so as not to discourage him. At the same time I gave him no decisive answer as to my being able to make a recommendation to the emperor. I repeatedly made it a condition that Italy should come to an understanding with Austria on the interests of both of them, and I summed up by saying that we should regard anything that Italy did for Austria, as a favor to ourselves, and that for Italy the key of the door leading to us was to be found in Vienna.

My final impression is that although I was obliged to offer many well-founded objections to the proposal of a formal alliance, Count Launay was not dissatisfied by our conversation, and will have reported to Rome in this sense.

8. *The Text of the Triple Alliance between Germany, Austria, and Italy*

Negotiations between Berlin, Vienna, and Rome culminated in the treaty of May 20, 1882, establishing the Triple Alliance. The signatories undertook to support each other in the event of an attack by France, and promised to maintain benevolent neutrality if one of them should declare war against a nonsignatory power. This agreement, which remained in effect until the First World War, enabled Bismarck to ward off the danger of a Franco-Italian entente. After the opening of the twentieth century, however, the two Latin states settled their colonial disputes and began to draw closer together.

THEIR MAJESTIES the Emperor of Austria, King of Bohemia, etc., and Apostolic King of Hungary, the Emperor of Germany, King of Prussia, and the King of Italy, animated by the desire to increase the guaranties of the general peace, to fortify the monarchical principle and thereby to assure the unimpaired maintenance of the social and political order in Their respective states, have agreed to conclude a treaty which, by its essentially conservative and defensive nature, pursues only the aim of forestalling the dangers which might threaten the security of Their states and the peace of Europe.

To this end Their Majesties have appointed, to wit, His Majesty the Emperor of Austria, King of Bohemia, etc., and Apostolic King of Hungary,

Count Gustavus Kálnoky, General, His Minister of the Imperial Household and of Foreign Affairs:

His Majesty the Emperor of Germany, King of Prussia,

Prince Henry VII of Reuss, Aide-de-Camp General, His Ambassador Extraordinary and Plenipotentiary to His Imperial and Royal Apostolic Majesty,

His Majesty the King of Italy,

Count Charles Felix Nicolis de Robilant, Lieutenant-General, His Ambassador Extraordinary and Plenipotentiary to His Imperial and Royal Apostolic Majesty,

SOURCE: Excerpted by permission of the publishers from *The Secret Treaties of Austria-Hungary, 1879–1914*, vol. I, Alfred Franzis Pribam, ed. Eng. Ed. by Archibald Cary Coolidge, Tr. by Denys P. Myers and J. G. D'Arcy Paul (Cambridge, Mass.: Harvard University Press, 1920), pp. 65, 67, 69.

who, furnished with full powers, which have been found in good and due form, have agreed upon the following Articles:

ARTICLE I

The high contracting parties mutually promise peace and friendship, and will enter into no alliance or engagement directed against any one of their states.

They engage to proceed to an exchange of ideas on political and economic questions of a general nature which may arise, and they further promise one another mutual support within the limits of their own interests.

ARTICLE II

In case Italy, without direct provocation on her part, should be attacked by France for any reason whatsoever, the two other contracting parties shall be bound to lend help and assistance with all their forces to the party attacked.

This same obligation shall devolve upon Italy in case of any aggression without direct provocation by France against Germany.

ARTICLE III

If one, or two, of the high contracting parties, without direct provocation on their part, should chance to be attacked and to be engaged in a war with two or more Great Powers nonsignatory to the present treaty, the *casus foederis* will arise simultaneously for all the high contracting parties.

ARTICLE IV

In case a Great Power nonsignatory to the present treaty should threatened the security of the states of one of the high contracting parties, and the threatened party should find itself forced on that account to make war against it, the two others bind themselves to observe towards their ally a benevolent neutrality. Each of them reserves to itself, in this case, the right to take part in the war, if it should see fit, to make common cause with its ally.

ARTICLE V

If the peace of any of the high contracting parties should chance to be threatened under the circumstances foreseen by the preceding articles, the high contracting parties shall take counsel together in ample time as to the military measures to be taken with a view to eventual cooperation.

They engage henceforward, in all cases of common participation in a war, to conclude neither armistice, nor peace, nor treaty, except by common agreement among themselves.

ARTICLE VI

The high contracting parties mutually promise secrecy as to the contents and existence of the present treaty.

ARTICLE VII

The present treaty shall remain in force during the space of five years, dating from the day of the exchange of ratifications.

ARTICLE VIII

The ratifications of the present treaty shall be exchanged at Vienna within three weeks, or sooner if may be.

In witness whereof the respective plenipotentiaries have signed the present treaty and have affixed thereto the seal of their arms.

Done at Vienna, the twentieth day of the month of May of the year one thousand eight hundred and eighty-two.

Kálnoky	H. VII of Reuss	C. Robilant
L. S.	L. S.	L. S.

9. The Text of the Reinsurance Treaty between Germany and Russia

The complicated diplomatic system which Bismarck had constructed in his efforts to preserve peace on the Continent was in constant danger of disruption as a result of the opposing ambitions of Austria and Russia in the Near East. When the League of the Three Emperors collapsed because of differences between Vienna and St. Petersburg, especially regarding Bulgaria, the chancellor hastened to repair the damage by concluding a secret agreement with the czarist government

SOURCE: Excerpted by permission of the publishers from *The Secret Treaties of Austria-Hungary, 1879–1914*, vol. I, Alfred Franzis Pribam, ed. Eng. Ed. by Archibald Cary Coolidge, Tr. by Denys P. Myers and J. G. D'Arcy Paul (Cambridge, Mass.: Harvard University Press, 1920), pp. 275, 277, 279.

on June 18, 1887. This was the famous Reinsurance Treaty by which the signatories promised not to join in any war of aggression which a third power might wage against one of them.

THE IMPERIAL COURTS of Germany and of Russia, animated by an equal desire to strengthen the general peace by an understanding destined to assure the defensive position of their respective states, have resolved to confirm the agreement established between them by a special arrangement, in view of the expiration on June 15–27, 1887, of the validity of the secret treaty . . . signed in 1881 and renewed in 1884 by the three courts of Germany, Russia, and Austria-Hungary.

To this end the two Courts have named as plenipotentiaries:

His Majesty the Emperor of Germany, King of Prussia, the Sieur Herbert Count of Bismarck-Schoenhausen, His Secretary of State in the Department of Foreign Affairs;

His Majesty the Emperor of All the Russias, the Sieur Paul Count Schouvaloff, His Ambassador Extraordinary and Plenipotentiary to his Majesty the Emperor of Germany, King of Prussia, who, being furnished with full powers, which have been found in good and due form, have agreed upon the following Articles:

ARTICLE I

In case one of the high contracting parties should find itself at war with a third Great Power, the other would maintain a benevolent neutrality towards it, and would devote its efforts to the localization of the conflict. This provision would not apply to a war against Austria or France in case this war should result from an attack directed against one of these two latter Powers by one of the high contracting parties.

ARTICLE II

Germany recognizes the rights historically acquired by Russia in the Balkan Peninsula, and particularly the legitimacy of her preponderant and decisive influence in Bulgaria and in eastern Rumelia. The two courts engage to admit no modification of the territorial *status quo* of the said peninsula without a previous agreement between them, and to oppose, as occasion arises, every attempt to disturb this *status quo* or to modify it without their consent.

Article III

The two courts recognize the European and mutually obligatory character of the principle of the closing of the Straits of the Bosphorus and of the Dardanelles, founded on international law, confirmed by treaties, and summed up in the declaration of the second plenipotentiary of Russia at the session of July 12 of the Congress of Berlin (Protocol 19).

They will take care in common that Turkey shall make no exception to this rule in favor of the interests of any government whatsoever, by lending to warlike operations of a belligerent power the portion of its empire constituted by the straits. In case of infringement, or to prevent it if such infringement should be in prospect, the two courts will inform Turkey that they would regard her, in that event, as putting herself in a state of war towards the injured party, and as depriving herself thenceforth of the benefits of the security assured to her territorial *status quo* by the Treaty of Berlin.

Article IV

The present treaty shall remain in force for the space of three years, dating from the day of the exchange of ratifications.

Article V

The high contracting parties mutually promise secrecy as to the contents and the existence of the present treaty. . . .

Article VI

The present Treaty shall be ratified and ratifications shall be exchanged at Berlin within a period of a fortnight, or sooner if may be.

In witness whereof the respective plenipotentiaries have signed the present treaty and have affixed thereto the seal of their arms.

Done at Berlin, the eighteenth day of the month of June, one thousand eight hundred and eighty-seven.

(L. S.)   Count Bismarck.
(L. S.)   Count Paul Schouvaloff.

10. Bismarck Describes to the Reichstag the
Principles of His Diplomacy

The most detailed description of the underlying principles of Bismarck's diplomacy appeared in his speech to the Reichstag on February 6, 1888, in support of an army appropriation bill. The aged statesman argued that the exposed position of his nation in the heart of Europe left it vulnerable to attack from all sides. For that reason military preparedness was an essential condition of its survival. But armed might should be used for the maintenance of peace, not the incitement of war. The chancellor concluded with the stirring declaration that "we Germans fear God and naught else in the world!"

GREAT COMPLICATIONS and all kinds of coalitions, which no one can foresee, are constantly possible, and we must be prepared for them. We must be so strong, irrespective of momentary conditions, that we can face any coalition with the assurance of a great nation which is strong enough under circumstances to take her fate into her own hands. We must be able to face our fate placidly with that self reliance and confidence in God which are ours when we are strong and our cause is just. And the government will see to it that the German cause will be just always.

We must, to put it briefly, be as strong in these times as we possibly can be, and we can be stronger than any other nation of equal numbers in the world. I shall revert to this later—but it would be criminal if we were not to make use of our opportunity. If we do not need our full armed strength, we need not summon it. The only problem is the not very weighty one of money—not very weighty I say in passing, because I have no wish to enter upon a discussion of the financial and military figures, and of the fact that France has spent three milliards for the improvement of her armaments these last years, while we have spent scarcely one and one half milliards, including what we are asking of you this time. But I leave the elucidation of this to the minister of war and the representatives of the treasury department.

When I say that it is our duty to endeavor to be ready at all

SOURCE: Otto von Bismarck, "Speeches," in *The German Classics of the Nineteenth and Twentieth Centuries*, ed. Kuno Francke, 20 vols. (Albany and New York: German Publication Society, 1913–1914), vol. X, pp. 257–258, 270–271, 274–275.

times and for all emergencies, I imply that we must make greater exertions than other people for the same purpose, because of our geographical position. We are situated in the heart of Europe, and have at least three fronts open to an attack. France has only her eastern, and Russia only her western frontier where they may be attacked. We are also more exposed to the dangers of a coalition than any other nation, as is proved by the whole development of history, by our geographical position, and the lesser degree of cohesiveness, which until now has characterized the German nation in comparison with others. God has placed us where we are prevented, thanks to our neighbors, from growing lazy and dull. He has placed by our side the most warlike and restless of all nations, the French, and He has permitted warlike inclinations to grow strong in Russia, where formerly they existed to a lesser degree. Thus we are given the spur, so to speak, from both sides, and are compelled to exertions which we should perhaps not be making otherwise. The pikes in the European carp-pond are keeping us from being carps by making us feel their teeth on both sides. They also are forcing us to an exertion which without them we might not make, and to a union among us Germans, which is abhorrent to us at heart. By nature we are rather tending away, the one from the other. But the Franco-Russian press within which we are squeezed compels us to hold together, and by pressure our cohesive force is greatly increased. This will bring us to that state of being inseparable which all other nations possess, while we do not yet enjoy it. But we must respond to the intentions of Providence by making ourselves so strong that the pikes can do nothing but encourage us. . . .

If we Germans wish to wage a war with the full effect of our national strength, it must be a war which satisfies all who take part in it, all who sacrifice anything for it, in short the whole nation. It must be a national war, a war carried on with the enthusiasm of 1870, when we were foully attacked. I still remember the earsplitting, joyful shouts in the station at Köln. It was the same all the way from Berlin to Köln, in Berlin itself. The waves of popular approval bore us into the war, whether or no we wished it. That is the way it must be, if a popular force like ours is to show what it can do. It will, however, be very difficult to prove to the provinces and the imperial states and their inhabitants that the war is unavoidable, and has to be. People will ask: "Are you so sure? Who can tell?" In short, when we make an attack, the whole weight of all imponderables, which weigh far heavier than material weights, will be on the side of our opponents whom we have attacked. France will be bristling with arms way down to the Pyrenees. The same will take place everywhere. A war into which we are not borne by the will of the people will be waged, to be sure, if it has been declared by the constituted authorities who deemed it necessary; it will even be waged pluckily, and possibly victoriously, after we have once smelled fire and tasted blood, but it will lack from the beginning the nerve and enthusiasm of a war in which we are attacked. In such a one the whole of Germany from Memel to the Alpine Lakes will flare up like a powder mine; it will be bristling with guns, and no enemy will dare to engage this *furor teutonicus* which develops when we are attacked. We cannot afford to lose this factor of preeminence even if many military men—not only ours but others as well—believe that today we are superior to our future opponents. Our own officers believe this to a man, naturally. Every soldier believes this. He would almost cease to be a useful soldier if he did not wish for war, and did not believe that we would be victorious in it. If our opponents by any chance are thinking that we are pacific because we are afraid of how the war may end, they are mightily mistaken. We believe as firmly in our victory in a just cause as any foreign lieutenant in his garrison, after his third glass of champagne, can believe in his, and we probably do so with greater certainty. It is not fear, therefore, which makes us pacific, but the consciousness of our strength. We are strong enough to protect ourselves, even if we should be attacked at a less favorable moment, and we are in a position to let divine providence determine whether a war in the meanwhile may not become unnecessary after all.

I am, therefore, not in favor of any kind of an aggressive war, and if war could result only from our attack—somebody must kindle a fire, we shall not kindle it. Neither the consciousness of our strength, which I have described, nor our confidence in our treaties, will prevent us from continuing our former endeavors to preserve peace. In this we do not permit ourselves to be influenced by annoyances or dislikes. The threats and insults, and the challenges, which have been made have, no doubt, excited also with us a feeling of irritation, which does not easily happen with Germans, for they are less prone to national hatred than any other nation.

We are, however, trying to calm our countrymen, and we shall work for peace with our neighbors, especially with Russia, in the future as well as in the past. . . .

To sum up: I do not believe in an immediate interruption of peace, and I ask you to discuss this bill independently of such a thought or apprehension, looking upon it as a means of making the great strength which God has placed in the German nation fully available. If we do not need all the troops, it is not necessary to summon them. We are trying to avoid the contingency when we shall need them.

This attempt is as yet made rather difficult for us by the threatening newspaper articles in the foreign press, and I should like to admonish these foreign editors to discontinue such threats. They do not lead anywhere. The threats which we see made—not by the governments, but by the press—are really incredibly stupid, when we stop to reflect that the people making them imagine they could frighten the proud and powerful German empire by certain intimidating figures made by printer's ink and shallow words. People should not do this. It would then be easier for us to be more obliging to our two neighbors. Every country after all is sooner or later responsible for the windows which its press has smashed. The bill will be rendered some day, and will consist of the ill-feeling of the other country. We are easily influenced—perhaps too easily— by love and kindness, but quite surely never by threats! We Germans fear God, and naught else in the world! It is this fear of God which makes us love and cherish peace. If in spite of this anybody breaks the peace, he will discover that the ardent patriotism of 1813, which called to the standards the entire population of Prussia—weak, small, and drained to the marrow as it then was— has today become the common property of the whole German nation. Attack the German nation anywhere, and you will find it armed to a man, and every man with the firm belief in his heart: God will be with us.

X
Attitudes and Values

The form which national unification assumed in Central Europe had a profound effect on the civic temper and outlook of its people. West of the Rhine a process of political liberalization generally accompanied the process of political consolidation. The emergence of England as a major power, for example, went hand in hand with the development of parliamentary government. The rise of national consciousness in France was closely related to the ideals of revolutionary liberty and the achievements of democratic republicanism. Even in the Italian peninsula, where nationalism did not triumph until the middle of the nineteenth century, a united kingdom was established in the name of the popular will and through the efforts of a liberal government. In Germany, on the other hand, political integration and military ascendancy were the accomplishments not of a new order of society but of the old forces in the state. This was the fundamental significance of Bismarckian statecraft. It succeeded in attaining within the framework of a traditional system of authority what other nations had attained through innovation and reform. The iron chancellor satisfied the demands of patriotism and defeated the hopes of democracy by making the crown, the army, and the aristocracy the instruments of political consolidation. His successes at the conference table and on the field of battle perpetuated the domination of those classes in the community which predated liberalism, industrialism, and nationalism. The German Empire rested on an unwritten compromise between an agrarian and hierarchical social tradition on the one hand and a capitalistic and individualistic economic system on the other.

The magnitude of the political and diplomatic achievements of Bismarck weakened in Central Europe the forces of reform which constituted the backbone of democracy in England and France. They were never completely crushed, but their ineffectualness condemned them to sterility. They had tried to reconstruct state and society in Germany after the Napoleonic era, only to be defeated by the stubborn resistance of the Restoration. They had tried again in 1848, when the wave of revolution which swept over the Continent seemed to offer the opportunity for creating a new civic order in Central Europe. But once again the liberals demonstrated that they lacked the strength and ability to translate their theories into realities. The last major attempt of German reformers to alter the political structure and social system of their nation came in the early 1860s during the constitutional conflict in Prussia. This time it was frustrated by Bismarck's statecraft. As a result, public opinion came to accept the view that only a strong man, bold in his objectives and ruthless in his methods, could win for the Fatherland a place in the sun. Democracy, with its eloquent theories about the rights of man and the duties of government, was all very well as a textbook abstraction. But in practice it was force, determination, and toughness which led to success. How could the broad masses of the population, sunk in ignorance and poverty, decide the difficult issues facing a statesman day after day? Only a Bismarck was fit to grapple with the complexities of administration and diplomacy. This was the dangerous lesson which Central Europe drew from the experience of national unification.

The fact that the Germans achieved political greatness not by the force of a popular movement but through the statecraft of monarchical authority reinforced among them the tradition of obedience to the established order. Civic submissiveness had deep roots in the history of Central Europe, nourished by values derived from the age of princely absolutism and enlightened despotism. The attainment of national unification in the name of the crown rather than the will of the people strengthened the belief that the state is more than the sum total of the individuals who compose it. It possesses a moral will and spiritual purpose transcending the mundane pursuit of profit and comfort which motivates the common run of humanity. It represents the noblest aspirations of the citizen, whose private welfare should be sacrificed for the collective well-being. This deification of the state at the expense of the individual was reflected in the teachings of patriotic publicists and academics inspired by the victories of conservative diplomats and soldiers. Its effect was to bolster the established system of authority. Although the worshipers of power insisted that the nation stood above parties and interests, in fact the apotheosis of the traditional political structure served to fortify and perpetuate it. Behind all the brave talk about the greatness of the Fatherland and the glory of the state stood the reality of civic domination by the crown, the army, and the aristocracy. The great triumphs which the Germans celebrated during the age of Bismarck only made it more difficult for them to shake off the incubus of authoritarian rule.

The path leading from nationalism to militarism was logical and direct. If the state possessed an importance greater than individual welfare and personal freedom, then the military establishment essential for the preservation of the state assumed a spiritual significance surpassing the mere conquest of a province or defense of a frontier. War began to seem an act of exalted self-sacrifice in which the citizen offered up his life on the altar of the Fatherland. To be sure, the Germans were not the only ones to heed the call of the martial spirit. The second half of the nineteenth century was a period when the Great Powers in general succumbed to the spell of militarism, persuaded that their security and honor depended on the maintenance of large armies and navies. The result was an armaments race in which all states participated, from democratic England to autocratic Russia. But nowhere did bellicose attitudes and values find greater acceptance than east of the Rhine. A nation which had seen the might of the sword succeed where words and ideas had failed became convinced that armed strength alone constituted the road to political greatness. It was a fatal mistake. The German Empire, swaggering, posturing, and rattling the saber, gradually turned into the bugaboo of Europe. As long as Bismarck remained at the helm, the army served as a deterrent force helping to maintain stability on the Continent. After his retirement, however, the militarism which he had tolerated and encouraged began to lead the nation in the direction of a world war. The tragedy of 1918 became the nemesis of the triumph of 1871.

1. Bismarck Explains His Opposition to Parliamentary Government

The brilliant successes achieved by the Germans under an authoritarian political system weakened their confidence in representative institutions. Many of them came to believe that while the theory of liberalism was attractive on paper, in reality blood and iron determined the course of history. Bismarck shared this view. In a conversation reported by Bernhard von Bülow, the chancellor declared that he had no desire to live under royal absolutism, but neither did he consider parliamentary government suited to the civic and historic conditions of Central Europe.

IN MY PRESENCE and in the bosom of his family, he expressed some violent opinions of his domestic enemies. He did not want in the least to govern autocratically, he said, although the reproach was daily levelled against him. Real autocracy would be very different from the present government in Germany. He was perfectly well aware that, in Germany, in the second half of the nineteenth century, absolutism and autocracy would be impossible, apart from the fact that such government had never been one of his ideals. But a parliamentary régime seemed to him just as impossible. Our parties possessed neither the patriotism of the French nor the sound common sense of the English. Under the circumstances he did not understand what benefits the German Liberals promised themselves from the "inauguration of responsible ministries of the realm," which they had lately adopted as part of their program. As long as he remained in office he would never countenance such a thing. Considering the political incapacity of the average German, the intellectual parliamentary system would lead to conditions such as had prevailed in 1848, that is to say, to weakness and incompetency on the top, and to bumptiousness and ever new demands from below.

SOURCE: *Memoirs of Prince von Bülow*, 4 vols. (Boston: Little, Brown and Company, 1931–32), vol. IV, p. 558.

2. Albert Schäffle Questions Popular Sovereignty

Doubt regarding the efficacy of democracy bred doubt regarding its wisdom. There were publicists and politicians in the German Empire who felt that while parliamentary institutions might be necessary in a

SOURCE: A. Schäffle, *The Impossibility of Social Democracy* (London: S. Sonnenschein & Co., 1892), pp. 126–130.

modern industrial society, restraints should be imposed on the popular will because most people lacked the education and the intelligence to judge civic questions correctly. This was the position of the economist Albert Schäffle. He maintained that the political effects of a mass franchise must be counterbalanced by the authority of throne, church, and aristocracy.

FOR THE LAST 21 years . . . I have desired to see a share of political life given to all adult and honest males. But I am also convinced that the political will of a nation needs yet other agents, and must be supplied with counterpoises; that a complete state organism can never result from the fluctuating decisions of the majority expressed through universal suffrage alone, and without being associated with any such efficient counterpoise; that the inevitable issue of disregarding this would be that most terrible and desolating of all despotisms, I mean mob rule. Universal suffrage . . . must neither be undervalued nor overvalued. Universal suffrage, with universal right of choice and candidature, requires either strong pillars of old authority in monarchy, army, nobility, capital, administration and the church, or to be strongly supplemented by definite corporative representation. . . . Under these conditions it will, as I believe, accomplish better than any other system the task which can and ought to be fulfilled by the vote and by the vote only: that of interesting the whole state in the government, of laying before the governing organ all its grievances and its desires, of forming a popular chamber, not only deliberative, but also with powers of regulation and administration, and independent of the ruling power, either with or without a senate, a popular house which shall have a share in legislation, a power of influencing the executive through the voting of supplies, of controlling or opposing or giving an impulse in any direction to the government, in short of warding off the perils of absolutism. On the other hand, it is unmistakeably evident that without counterpoises, universal suffrage would be dangerous, and it would in fact, be simply destructive in a state so much in need of a basis of authority as the ideal state of social democracy. It is no less evident that even universal suffrage does not and can never produce the equal freedom of all in the state, the famous "sovereignty of the people." What becomes of the vaunted freedom of the political volition of all when a million electors must constantly hand over their will for the space of three years to some popular representative who will have to handle quite unforeseen issues, while perhaps a minority of not much less than half a million is obliged to put up with this delegation of power sorely against their will? What becomes of the equality of political influence when the great majority, about four-fifths of the population, is excluded from voting by disabilities of sex and age, while of the remaining fifth, a third is regularly unable to vote; and of the rest, only two-fifteenths of the whole, a third again is eventually outvoted; and then this ultimate remainder—only four forty-fifths of the whole people—hands over its will to 400 delegates or representatives, out of whom 300 only at the very most regularly exercise their vote in the House, so that ultimately a decision may be made by 151 persons?

This is possible under universal suffrage, and more or less frequently it actually takes place. There is no such thing as the realization of the "will of the people" through universal suffrage, the individualistic "freedom and equality," the so-called sovereignty of the people. There are many kinds of political volition expressed by the people through the vote. There are many currents and countercurrents, and numberless side eddies on the wild expanse of the voting sea. But there is no simple homogeneous *will* of the people, except as expressed in its chosen organs of government, of which under a constitutional monarchy popular representation is a part and parcel. It is possible that the state machinery might be provided entirely by popular representation if certain other guarantees were afforded it. The pure popular state with collective production does not afford these guarantees. It cannot realize political freedom and an equal share of power for all. Indeed, *it is less fitted than any other kind of state to produce a purely democratic exclusive and all powerful system of popular representation*, since it more than any other demands a firm basis of authority.

3. He Tells Why Woman Suffrage Would Be a Mistake

Public opinion in Central Europe scornfully rejected the demand for woman suffrage which some radical reformers were advancing as part of a fundamental reconstruction of society. To Schäffle the political emancipation of women would only serve the interests of the socialist movement by weakening the institutions of marriage and family on which every civilized community was built.

Source: A. Schäffle, *The Impossibility of Social Democracy* (London: S. Sonnenschein & Co., 1892), pp. 130–135.

I MUST AT ONCE unconditionally allow that social democracy as a levelling and thoroughgoing radicalism is only consistent when it admits the right of *everyone* to vote and be voted for in every department. The commonwealth of social democracy cannot possibly be without the unlimited extension of female suffrage as well in politics as in industry, the entire politico-economic emancipation of the female sex. If every woman as well as every man is subject to the universal obligation to labor, that is, the obligation to industrial labor in collective production for the whole society, accompanied with distribution according to reasonable needs, if the woman is to do without the judicial sanctity of the marriage tie, if she is to hand over her children to public nurseries and public educational institutions, in short, if the family is to be no longer a small industrial, social and educational community represented by the father, but is to be broken up into its individual atoms, if individualism is to be carried to its highest pitch, then man and woman alike, both in state and industry, must be allowed full equality of rights, the most complete emancipation, and therefore naturally political suffrage and rights of candidature. The political emancipation of woman is the inevitable consequence of radical individualism, and hence, necessarily, of social democracy, which has in fact introduced it without limitation as a feature of its crypto-state—which repudiates even the name of state.

Properly speaking, children under age ought also to have a share in the state through increased voting power in their natural guardians, since they are no longer sufficiently represented by their father and mother, but are exposed to much risk in the public orphan asylums. But we do not find much movement in favor of the emancipation of children, not even of the establishment of political representation for every individual child!

Nevertheless, female suffrage, for which I formally declared myself, with certain limitations, when under the glamour of John Stuart Mill's writings, can only be absolutely accepted from the purely individualistic standpoint, and that of the loosening of family unity and stability. But those who believe that the marriage tie and family bonds can and should be and remain as a general rule indissoluble, those who do not hold that every woman *must* be a productive worker outside the sphere of the family—the great majority of women have always been in some sense *workers*—but that they all of their own free will alone may become producers and breadwinners, those who only wish to emancipate the woman in this sense, which is quite in keeping with existing conditions and moreover cannot well be prevented, such as these are not only not unavoidably committed to universal female suffrage in the political sphere, but they are in my opinion quite definitely and without circumlocution forced to refuse it.

Even if the woman has the right to vote in clubs of every kind, in labor unions and so on, in so far as she steps out over the threshold of her home, or carries on *independently* branches of business charged by the parish or the state, if she even takes a share in some future representation of labor in the organization of labor protection, even yet we should be far removed from the political emancipation of all adult women and their full equality with men in the life of the state and municipality.

It is my opinion . . . that the firm family bond between husbands and wives, parents and children, is not destined to destruction, but rather to a more perfect development: every loosening of the bond would tend only to the emancipation *of the man from the woman*, to the loss for the weaker sex of some of their strongest supports, to their abandonment by men, to a relapse into a Heterism in the highest degree derogatory to feminine dignity. But if it is true that the stability of the family bond is so indispensable for the highest development of civilization, it follows that the great majority of women as a rule are not, or at least not primarily, suited to be productive laborers outside the walls of the home. They are and will remain wives and mothers, integral parts of a stable family unity, and will still have in the man their lawful head—with due limitations imposed by custom, by private law, by administrative, punitive and corporative justice—and their protector and representative as against the world without. The majority of men will not refuse in political life the protection which they owe to the weaker sex. The woman is represented by husband, father, brothers, in the only worthy and by far the most efficient manner. Even widows and single women, some of whom there are in every family, are not without this representation. If once men grew so bad as that they would use their parliamentary superiority to oppress and enslave their wives, widows, and spinsters, and refuse them due protection in private and public legislation, in family conjugal rights, and in labor, under such a state of things universal female suffrage would not be of the slightest avail.

But this is only one side of the question, namely, its criticism from the individualist standpoint. There is the no less important social interest to be considered, the question whether the woman is not unfitted for direct participation in political life, whether the entire family life of the nation would not be ruined by politics, and the whole of politics by the atmosphere of perfumes and gallantries and coquetry, especially if the woman lived the rest of her social life among the men, if she had exchanged the life of the family for an immediately public life. To these questions the only possible answer is in the affirmative. The "eternal feminine" with the addition of the feminine in public life and even in the state, would certainly not elevate us all, but rather most certainly drag us down! The commonwealth with democratic collective production would be rendered doubly unmanageable by the emancipation of women. A refined reproduction of the supposed "maternal sovereignty" of the primeval time, or of the historical sole or joint sway of the woman in the state, evidently does not recommend itself either from the standpoint of woman's interests or from that of the social interest of the whole community.

4. The British Military Attaché in Berlin
Analyzes the German Character

The tendency of the Germans to strut and posture on the diplomatic stage irritated many foreign observers, but it was essentially an expression of insecurity rather than overconfidence. A nation which had for centuries been weak and divided in dealing with other states suddenly found itself the leading power on the Continent. Despite its new political importance, it remained touchy about real or imaginary slights by neighboring governments and peoples. This was the analysis advanced in 1885 by Lieutenant Colonel Leopold Victor Swaine, the British military attaché in Berlin.

THE GERMANS *like ourselves* are a vain people, and like the French are a very touchy people—but touchy not like the French because they are an arrogant and blustering nation, but because they are a young nation suddenly hoisted on the highest pinnacle of military strength in Europe. They owe this rapid promotion to one man. He is their God (barring of a few red caps in the Reichstag) and

SOURCE: Paul Knaplund, ed., *Letters from the Berlin Embassy, 1871–1874, 1880–1885* (Washington, D.C.: USGPO, 1944), pp. 393–394.

what he says must be right. Under Lord Beaconsfield's government they believed we were more friendly disposed toward them than we now are; consequently their disappointment at our apparent leaning toward France and their vanity is roused because they think we are hindering their extension of interests and influence outside Europe which their pet man desires to obtain for them.

The whole matter lies in a nutshell.

Germany though generally represented by us allegorically as a student drinking beer we should be making a great mistake if we consequently handled her a la student in our dealings with her.

Far from being as rough in her feelings as she appears outwardly when represented drinking and smoking, she in reality has all the delicate little vanities of a woman, and the Englishman who deals with the German should be a veritable Don Juan in his delightful and insinuating manner, and in irresistible powers of persuasion.

5. Heinrich von Treitschke Exalts the Idea of the State

Since the Germans formed a national state so late in their history, they tended to dote on it with all the exaggerated fondness of middle-aged parents suddenly blessed with an offspring. Most of them respected, admired, and even idolized the empire which they had finally succeeded in founding after so many false starts and disappointed hopes. This excessive nationalism with all its passion and fervor was eloquently expressed by the historian Heinrich von Treitschke in his lectures on the idea of the state.

THE STATE is not an academy of arts. If it neglects its strength in order to promote the idealistic aspirations of man, it repudiates its own nature and perishes. This is in truth for the state equivalent to the sin against the Holy Ghost, for it is indeed a mortal error in the state to subordinate itself for sentimental reasons to a foreign power, as we Germans have often done to England.

Therefore the power of ideas in the life of the state is only limited. It is undoubtedly very great, but ideas by themselves do not move political forces. If they are to influence public life effectively they must find support in the vital economic interests of the people. The *ancien régime* was not shattered by the ideas of the

SOURCE: Heinrich von Treitschke, *Politics*, 2 vols. (New York: Macmillan, 1916), vol. I, pp. 24–27.

French philosophers, but by the mutual interaction of various classes which resulted from the spread of these ideas.

A disturbance of social conditions followed; a middle class had arisen before which the old divisions disappeared, and here the egalitarian notions of the philosophers received support.

Undoubtedly the genuine creators of the German Empire were Bismarck and the Emperor William; not Fichte or Paul Pfizer, or other pioneers. The great political thinkers have their meed of fame, but the men of action are the real heroes of history.

In political life will power is the first essential of creative work, and therefore many builders of empire find no place in the ranks of genius. The salient characteristic of the Emperor William was not the originality of his mind, but his calm, cool determination, a much rarer quality than is commonly supposed. Therein lay his strength.

The state's capacity for justice and impartiality lies in its stern and drastic nature which touches only the exterior of men's lives. As it aims only at forming and directing the surface of human existence, it can everywhere take up an attitude of indifference towards the conflicting schools of thought in art, science, and religion. It is satisfied so long as they keep the peace.

Now if we imagine the church organized like the state we see at once why she could never remain impartial. She feels herself compelled to combat what she holds to be sin; she cannot be tolerant of it.

We have described the state as an independent force. This pregnant theory of independence implies firstly so absolute a moral supremacy that the state cannot legitimately tolerate any power above its own, and secondly a temporal freedom entailing a variety of material resources adequate to its protection against hostile influences. Legal sovereignty, the state's complete independence of any other earthly power, is so rooted in its nature that it may be said to be its very standard and criterion.

The state is born in a community whenever a group or an individual has achieved sovereignty by imposing its will upon the whole body.

We must not be misled on this point by new-fashioned teaching. Since, like all federated legal systems, the jurisprudence of the German Empire recognizes certain fictions from motives of expediency and courtesy, the senseless doctrine of first-rate and second-rate states has latterly made its appearance. This makes it salutary for us to analyze the meaning of the word "sovereignty." It is typical of the French and of their constitutional principles that they have never created any method of self-government, because they neither knew nor wished to know what it meant in practice. On the other hand they have maintained the unity of the state with spirit and determination, and it was a Frenchman who found the proper term for this idea. No doubt the Italians had already at an earlier date spoken of "sovranità," but without connecting the word with any very definite meaning. For them "sovrani" meant persons in high place, as distinguished from those below them. It was first of all in France during the Huguenot wars, when the crown had become the shuttlecock of parties, that Jean Bodin formulated the dictum, "The state is a plurality of families *avec puissance souveraine*." He was the first to use the expression in the sense in which it is now indispensable to us. Now it is the right and the duty of learning to express certain notions of universal validity in the terms of that nation's language in which they were first generated. Therefore the word "sovereign" is, and will remain, characteristic of the nature of the state, since the temporal power cannot tolerate a coordinated, and still less a higher authority in its own sphere.

6. Bismarck Gives His Reasons for Adopting a Policy of Cautious Imperialism

The outburst of patriotic sentiment generated by the achievement of political consolidation in Central Europe sometimes assumed forms which even Bismarck found excessive. The chancellor, for example, regarded overseas expansion as a useless luxury for Germany, whose vital interests were in his opinion confined to the Continent. But eventually he was forced to surrender to the ardent nationalists among his countrymen who argued that Berlin must not lag behind London or Paris in the race for colonies. He explained in a speech to the Reichstag on June 26, 1884, his reasons for adopting a policy of cautious imperialism.

As REGARDS the colonial question in the narrower sense of the words, I will explain its genesis. We were first induced, owing to the enterprise of the Hanseatic people—beginning with land pur-

SOURCE: William Harbutt Dawson, *Bismarck and State Socialism: An Exposition of the Social and Economic Legislation of Germany since 1870* (London: S. Sonnenschein & Co., 1891), pp. 149–151.

chases and leading to requests for imperial protection—to consider
whether we could promise protection to the extent desired. I have
not abandoned my former aversion to colonies—I will not say
colonies after the system mostly adopted last century, the French
system, as it might now be called—but colonies which make a strip
of land their foundation, and then seek to draw emigrants, appoint
officials, and establish garrisons. This mode of colonization may be
good for other countries, but it is not practicable for us. I do not
believe that colonial projects can be artificially established, and all
the examples which Deputy Bamberger advanced as warnings in
committee were cases in which the wrong way had been taken:
where people had wished to construct harbors where there was no
traffic, and build towns where there were no people, the intention
being to attract people by artificial means to the place. Very different is the question whether it is expedient, and whether it is the
duty of the German Empire, to grant imperial protection and a
certain amount of support in their colonial endeavors to those of its
subjects who devote themselves to such undertakings relying upon
the protection of the Empire, in order that security may be ensured
in foreign lands to the communities which grow naturally out of
the superfluous strength of the German body politic. This question
I answer affirmatively: I certainly do so less reservedly from the
standpoint of expediency, though from the standpoint of the state's
duty I do so unconditionally. . . .

My intention, as approved by the emperor, is to leave the responsibility for the material development of a colony, as well as its
inauguration, to the action and the enterprise of our seafaring and
trading citizens, and to proceed less on the system of annexing the
transoceanic provinces to the German Empire than that of granting charters, after the form of the English Royal Charters, encouraged by the glorious career which the English merchants
experienced in the foundation of the East India Company; also to
leave to the persons interested in the colony the government of the
same, only granting them European jurisdiction for Europeans and
so much protection as we may be able to afford without maintaining garrisons. I think, too, that a colony of this kind should possess
a representative of the imperial authority with the title of consul
or resident, whose duty it would be to receive complaints; while
the disputes which might arise out of these commercial enterprises
would be decided by one of our maritime or mercantile courts at

Bremen, Hamburg, or somewhere else. It is not our intention to found provinces but commercial undertakings.

7. *Heinrich von Treitschke Describes the Grandeur of War*

Worship of the state led logically to the glorification of war. The generation of Germans which had witnessed the achievement of national unification through blood and iron was inclined to believe that armed might was the necessary condition of all great political accomplishments. No one voiced this admiration for brute force more glowingly than Treitschke, who preached to his countrymen that military conflict, far from being evil, was an expression of civic courage and personal bravery.

WITHOUT WAR no state could be. All those we know of arose through war, and the protection of their members by armed force remains their primary and essential task. War, therefore, will endure to the end of history, as long as there is multiplicity of states. The laws of human thought and of human nature forbid any alternative, neither is one to be wished for. The blind worshipper of an eternal peace falls into the error of isolating the state, or dreams of one which is universal, which we have already seen to be at variance with reason.

Even as it is impossible to conceive of a tribunal above the state, which we have recognized as sovereign in its very essence, so it is likewise impossible to banish the idea of war from the world. It is a favorite fashion of our time to instance England as paricularly ready for peace. But England is perpetually at war; there is hardly an instant in her recent history in which she has not been obliged to be fighting somewhere. The great strides which civilization makes against barbarism and unreason are only made actual by the sword. Between civilized nations also war is the form of litigation by which states make their claims valid. The arguments brought forward in these terrible law suits of the nations compel as to argument in civil suits can ever do. Often as we have tried by theory to convince the small states that Prussia alone can be the leader in Germany, we had to produce the final proof upon the battlefields of Bohemia and the Main.

Moreover war is a uniting as well as a dividing element among

SOURCE: Heinrich von Treitschke, *Politics*, 2 vols. (New York: Macmillan, 1916), vol. I, pp. 65–68; vol. II, pp. 597–599.

nations; it does not draw them together in enmity only, for through its means they learn to know and to respect each other's peculiar qualities.

It is important not to look upon war always as a judgment from God. Its consequences are evanescent; but the life of a nation is reckoned by centuries, and the final verdict can only be pronounced after the survey of whole epochs.

Such a state as Prussia might indeed be brought near to destruction by a passing phase of degeneracy; but being by the character of its people more reasonable and more free than the French, it retained the power to call up the moral force within itself, and so to regain its ascendancy. Most undoubtedly war is the one remedy for an ailing nation. Social selfishness and party hatreds must be dumb before the call of the state when its existence is at stake. Forgetting himself, the individual must only remember that he is a part of the whole, and realize the unimportance of his own life compared with the common weal.

The grandeur of war lies in the utter annihilation of puny man in the great conception of the state, and it brings out the full magnificence of the sacrifice of fellow-countrymen for one another. In war the chaff is winnowed from the wheat. Those who have lived through 1870 cannot fail to understand Niebuhr's description of his feelings in 1813, when he speaks of how no one who has entered into the joy of being bound by a common tie to all his compatriots, gentle and simple alike, can ever forget how he was uplifted by the love, the friendliness, and the strength of that mutual sentiment.

It is war which fosters the political idealism which the materialist rejects. What a disaster for civilization it would be if mankind blotted its heroes from memory. The heroes of a nation are the figures which rejoice and inspire the spirit of its youth, and the writers whose words ring like trumpet blasts become the idols of our boyhood and our early manhood. He who feels no answering thrill is unworthy to bear arms for his country. To appeal from this judgment to Christianity would be sheer perversity, for does not the Bible distinctly say that the ruler shall rule by the sword, and again that greater love hath no man than to lay down his life for his friend? To Aryan races, who are before all things courageous, the foolish preaching of everlasting peace has always been vain. They have always been men enough to maintain with the sword what they have attained through the spirit.

Goethe once said that the north Germans were always more civilized than the south Germans. No doubt they were, and a glance at the history of the princes of Lower Saxony shows that they were for ever either attacking or defending themselves. Onesided as Goethe's verdict is, it contains a core of truth. Our ancient empire was great under the Saxons; under the Swabian and the Salic emperors it declined. Heroism, bodily strength, and chivalrous spirit is essential to the character of a noble people.

Such matters must not be examined only by the light of the student's lamp. The historian who moves in the world of the real will sees at once that the demand for eternal peace is purely reactionary. He sees that all movement and all growth would disappear with war, and that only the exhausted, spiritless, degenerate periods of history have toyed with the idea. . . .

When a state recognizes that existing treaties no longer express the actual political conditions, and when it cannot persuade the other powers to give way by peaceful negotiation, the moment has come when the nations proceed to the ordeal by battle. A state thus situated is conscious when it declares war that it is performing an inevitable duty. The combatant countries are moved by no incentives of personal greed, but they feel that the real position of power is not expressed by existing treaties and that they must be determined afresh by the judgment of the nations, since no peaceful agreement can be reached. The righteousness of war depends simply and solely upon the consciousness of a moral necessity. War is justified because the great national personalities can suffer no compelling force superior to themselves, and because history must always be in constant flux; war therefore must be taken as part of the divinely appointed order. . . .

War is both justifiable and moral, and . . . the ideal of perpetual peace is not only impossible but immoral as well. It is unworthy of man's reason to regard the impracticable as feasible, but a life of pure intellect is all too often enervating to the reasoning faculty. War cannot vanish from the earth as long as human sins and passions remain what they are. It is delightful to observe how the feeling of patriotism breaks involuntarily through the cosmopolitan phrases even of the apostles of perpetual peace. The prophet Joel prayed that before its day should dawn Israel might call all the heathen to a bloody reckoning in the valley of Jehoshaphat, and Victor Hugo likewise demanded that the Germans should get their drubbing first. Yet again we must repeat—the arbitrament of force is the logical outcome of the nature of the state. The mere fact of the existence of many states involves the necessity of war. The dream of eternal peace—said Frederick the Great—is a phantom, which each man rejects when the call of war rings in his own ears. It is impossible to imagine—he went on to say—any balance of power which can last.

8. Helmuth von Moltke Examines the Nature of Modern Warfare

To Helmuth von Moltke war was not so much a glorious personal adventure as a hard social reality. The architect of the successful military campaigns which Prussia had waged in the struggle for German unification believed that conflict among nations was assuming a total character as the result of technological progress and political democratization. With public opinion gaining increasing influence over the conduct of affairs of state, governments would find it more and more difficult to pursue a diplomacy of moderation and restraint.

THE DAYS are gone by when, for dynastical ends, small armies of professional soldiers went to war to conquer a city, or a province, and then sought winter quarters or made peace. The wars of the present day call whole nations to arms, there is scarcely a family that does not suffer by them. The entire financial resources of the state are appropriated to the purpose, and the different seasons of the year have no bearing on the unceasing progress of hostilities. As long as nations continue independent of each other there will be disagreements that can only be settled by force of arms; but, in the interest of humanity, it is to be hoped that wars will become less frequent, as they have become more terrible.

Generally speaking, it is no longer the ambition of monarchs which endangers peace; the passions of the people, its dissatisfaction with interior conditions and affairs, the strife of parties, and the intrigues of their leaders are the causes. A declaration of war, so serious in its consequences, is more easily carried by a large assembly, of which none of the members bears the sole responsibility, than by a single man, however high his position; and a peace-loving sovereign is less rare than a parliament composed of wise men. The great wars of the present day have been declared against the wish

SOURCE: Helmuth von Moltke, "Letters and Historical Writings," in *The German Classics of the Nineteenth and Twentieth Centuries*, ed. Kuno Francke, 20 vols. (Albany and New York: German Publication Society, 1913–14), vol. X, pp. 351–352.

and will of the reigning powers. Nowadays the Bourse has assumed such influence that it has the power to call armies into the field merely to protect its interests. Mexico and Egypt have been swamped with European armies simply to satisfy the demands of the *haute finance*. Today the question, "Is a nation strong enough to make war?" is of less importance than that, "Is its government powerful enough to prevent war?" Thus, united Germany has, up to now, used her strength only to maintain European peace; a weak government at the head of our neighboring state must, on the other hand, be regarded in the light of a standing menace to peace.

9. He Supports a Policy of Military Preparedness

Moltke, like Bismarck, believed that once national unification had been achieved, the main objective of German statecraft should be the maintenance of peace. But he also recognized that the unsatisfied political desires and ambitions of other governments made the outbreak of war a constant danger. In a speech to the Reichstag in 1880 he advocated an increase in army expenditures to ensure the defense of the Fatherland. In the arena of European diplomacy, the old field marshal declared, military weakness would be an invitation to foreign aggression.

WHO CAN DENY that Europe groans under the weight of an armed peace? It is mutual distrust which keeps the nations in arms against each other. If this distrust can in any way be removed, it will be rather through an understanding between government and government than through other means, such for instance as the Babylonian confusion of international fraternity, international parliaments, and other suggested means of like nature.

Gentlemen, all nations are equally in need of peace, and I am convinced that all nations will maintain peace as long as they are strong enough to command it. Many people look upon the government as a species of hostile power whom one cannot sufficiently curb and trammel. I consider, however, that it should be strengthened and supported in every possible way; a weak government is a misfortune for any country and a source of danger to its neighbors.

We have all of us witnessed the outbreak of wars which were wished for neither by the head of the state nor by the nation itself,

SOURCE: Helmuth von Moltke, *Essays, Speeches, and Memoirs*, 2 vols. (New York: Harper & Row, 1893), vol. II, pp. 123–125, 128–129.

but only by the leaders of parties, who had set themselves up as their spokesmen, and who had drawn after them the impressionable crowd and, at last, also the government. Cravings after annexation and longings for revenge, dissatisfaction with the state of internal affairs, the striving to draw towards one's self kindred nations which, in the course of time, have been incorporated into other state formations—all this, and much more, may also, in the future, occasion, at any time, fresh developments, and therefore it is that I am afraid that we shall still, for some time to come, have to wear the heavy armor which our historical development, and our position in the world, have forced upon us.

Historically speaking, we are of course, as an empire, only the youngest member in the family formed by the states of Europe, and an intruder is always looked upon with distrust, at any rate until he comes to be better known. As regards our geographical situation—well, gentlemen, all our neighbors are more or less, I may say, protected from rear attack; they have behind them either Pyrenees or Alps, or else semibarbarous races whom they have no cause to fear. We are placed right in the midst of all the Great Powers. Our eastern and western neighbors have only to form front in one direction, we in all directions; they can transfer, and have already in peace time transferred, a large proportion of their military forces to the neighborhood of our frontiers, whilst our regiments remain evenly distributed over the whole empire. We have no occasion to suspect any hostile intention in this. If our neighbors are really apprehensive of danger from Germany then, from their point of view, they are quite right; we must, nevertheless, take this situation into our calculations.

We have also to consider the constant growth of the armies around us. Russia had good grounds, even before the Turkish war, for adding considerably to her already strong military forces, and after the conclusion of peace she carried out and preserved this organization. Russia has created 24 new reserve infantry divisions and 24 new reserve artillery brigades, and has, in addition, formed 4th battalions for 152 regiments. The Russian press, which is now so agitated, maintained profound silence with regard to this measure, and the whole proceeding obtained hardly any notice in the foreign press.

As regards France, I have not read the article quoted from the Prussian annals. By the help of the data which are at my disposal, I arrive at quite a different result from that obtained by the former speaker. I will only give a few of the principal figures, and will spare you the details.

In the 1870 campaign France opposed us with 8 army corps; at present she possesses 19. At that time she had 26 infantry divisions, there are now 38; then there were 26 cavalry brigades, now there are 37. The strength of the French army on its first formation amounted to 336,000 men; at present, France can oppose us with 670,000 men, according to the budgetary figures. This does not include the territorial army.

I arrive at the result that France has, since 1874—that is to say, in six years—more than doubled her army. . . .

I will not take up your time with a demonstration of the great disadvantages which accrue from weak cadres in the training of the troops and more especially of their leaders. I will not detail the difficulties which weak battalions give rise to on their sudden threefold expansion in the event of mobilization. I will only remark, in passing, that our western neighbors, who are also gifted with military judgment, have not, in spite of repeated demands, seen their way to reduce the period of service in the French army; they hold that three years, which we do not even attain to, do not suffice to complete the training of a soldier. . . .

Gentlemen, it is certainly a subject for sincere regret that an iron necessity compels the German nation to impose on itself fresh sacrifices. It is, indeed, only by sacrifice and hard work that we have at last become a nation again. But what far greater sacrifices than those now demanded would follow on a hostile invasion? The eldest amongst us can bear personal witness to this. The very credit of the state depends in the first instance upon its security. What a panic would occur on our stock exchange, how all our securities would be shaken, were the continuance of the existence of the empire to be in question for a moment.

Gentlemen, let us not forget that, since the decline of the German imperial power, Germany has been the battlefield of other nations and their objective; that Swedes, Frenchmen, and Germans laid Germany waste for more than a century. Let us pass to later times. Are not the great ruins on the Neckar, the Rhine, and far into the heart of the country, lasting monuments of our whilom weakness and of the wantonness of our neighbors?

Who would further wish to recall the days when, at the dictation of a foreign ruler, German contingents were forced to march against Germany?

No, gentlemen, let us, before all things, protect the honor and safety of the empire; let us defend the long wished for, the finally attained unity of the nation; let us continue to maintain peace so long as we are not attacked, and to enforce peace even abroad, according to the measure of our strength! Possibly we shall not stand alone in this endeavor, but may find allies. There lies in this no threat to anyone, but rather a pledge for a continuance of peace in our part of the world, provided, of course, that we are strong and ready armed. With weak forces, with armies that have to be called up, we cannot achieve our object; the fate of every nation rests with itself.

10. He Sees the Constant Danger of a European War

Many Germans believed that the geographic position of their country imposed on it the need to maintain a large army. In 1873 Odo Russell, the British ambassador in Berlin, reported a dinner conversation with Moltke regarding the armaments race in Europe. The chief of staff had declared that the sea provided a natural protection for England which enabled her to achieve national security with a small military establishment. Since the German Empire was less fortunate, the cost of its defense had to be substantially greater.

Count Moltke said that while we possessed the best fighting qualities and material in the world we were not a military nation as our press and our public debates on military matters sufficiently proved —besides which our system of government and of public life were not favorable to the development of military institutions nor was freedom favorable to discipline. I asked whether he then still thought the invasion of England strategically as easy as he told me it was at Versailles in 1870?

Count Moltke replied that his frequent visits to England had left him under the impression that the invasion of England by foreign troops was quite possible and that we appeared unprepared for resistance if ever the attempt were made. Happily for us we were a peace-loving nation who could find safety in foreign alliances and he only regretted that we showed, by our commercial policy, so decided a preference for an alliance with corrupt Catholic France to an alliance with kindred Protestant Germany. He envied our

Source: Paul Knaplund, ed., *Letters from the Berlin Embassy, 1871–1874, 1880–1885* (Washington, D.C.: USGPO, 1944), pp. 91–93.

insular position which enabled us to have so small an army. The exaggerated system of standing armies in Europe, due to the attitude of France, was a public calamity and he hoped to live to see a general and simultaneous reduction of them, as war could be carried on with smaller forces as well as with millions of men, and war would last as long as humanity, God himself being favorable to war, as the Bible proved.

I said that from no one could the proposal for a general reduction of armies come with better grace than from himself. General Moltke replied that the reduction would only be possible after the war of revenge was over.

I asked whether the war of revenge could not be avoided?

General Moltke said it could not—Germany wished for peace, but France did not, nor could there be peace in Europe until the war of revenge had rendered the French harmless. The late war had left sufficient fighting power in them to keep Europe still in constant alarm and a second war was necessary to obtain the guarantees they had unfortunately not been compelled to give before Paris, that they would never again wantonly break the peace of Europe so that the other powers might disarm and place their armies on a peace footing. He did not mean that Germany desired war; quite the contrary. Germany desired peace. But the attitude and spirit of France rendered it impossible for Germany not to be ready for defense when France attacked her for the second time. Germany would have to resist the attack single-handed, he had little hope of assistance from the Italians, who with a little more decision might so easily regain the provinces France had wrested from them. Italy should not forget that she owed Venice and Rome to Germany.

I said that I noticed a very general impression among Germans of all classes that war with Russia was unavoidable, but I could not understand what they wished to fight about?

General Moltke said the impression was founded on the hatred of races, and was more encouraged by the Russian press than by the German, but Russia had proved herself too good an ally of Germany not to know that she could reckon on reciprocity. Russia and Austria he feared would come to blows in the East.

I said, Germany would then side with Austria I presumed?

General Moltke replied that Germany having no interests in the East would remain neutral, but if compelled to take an active part could only side with Russia in return for her offer to attack Austria if Austria had sided with France in the late war.

I asked what he thought of arbitration? The general replied that in his opinion arbitration was excellent for the settlement of money questions, but could not be applied to those of national honor with safety.

11. He Defends the Spirit of the Army

According to the prevailing view in the German Empire, the Fatherland required an army which was not only big and strong but disciplined and obedient as well. Most citizens regarded the officer corps, a stronghold of the conservative landed aristocracy, as a vital national institution safeguarding the greatness of the state. Demands by the parties of the left for a liberalization of the military establishment were rejected as incompatible with effectiveness on the field of battle. In a speech to the Reichstag in 1874, Moltke defended the traditional outlook and organization of the armed forces.

OUR SCHOOLS, gentlemen, do not take in the whole of our youth, and they conduct the great majority of our young men only a short way on their path through life. Fortunately when instruction, in its strict sense, ceases, education soon steps in, and no nation has, hitherto, enjoyed an education so universal in its character as that which we now secure through common liability to military service.

It has been said that the schoolmaster won our battles. Gentlemen, bare knowledge does not yet raise men to the standpoint at which they are prepared to stake their lives for an idea, for the fulfillment of their duty, for honor and for Fatherland; nothing less than education in its fullest sense will bring a man to this level. Not the schoolmaster has won our battles, but the military profession, as popular educator—the military profession, which has now, for nearly sixty years, trained the nation to bodily activity and to moral health, to order and exactness, to loyalty and obedience, to love of Fatherland and to manliness. Gentlemen, from the point of view even of domestic policy, the army, and the army in its full strength, is indispensable for the education of the nation. And how about external conditions? Possibly, a later and more fortunate generation, a part of whose burdens we already bear, may hope to

SOURCE: Helmuth von Moltke, *Essays, Speeches, and Memoirs*, 2 vols. (New York: Harper & Row, 1893), vol. II, pp. 107–108, 111–112, 114–115.

escape from the condition of armed peace which has already so long weighed Europe down. For us, no such smiling prospect is, I fear, in store. An event so great, so historically important, as the reerection of the German Empire, is scarcely to be compassed in a short space of time. That which we have wrested by force of arms in half a year we may have to protect by arms for half a century, so that it shall not again be torn from us.

This is a matter, gentlemen, about which we should cherish no illusions; since the termination of our successful war we have gained respect everywhere, but affection nowhere.

On all sides we are confronted by the distrust lest Germany, having become powerful, should, in the future, prove to be an unpleasant neighbor. Now gentlemen, it is not wise to conjure up bogies, and out of distrust and anxiety, unfounded though they may be, real dangers can arise.

In Belgium, even to this very day, you will find sympathies with France, but very few with Germany; it has not yet been recognized in that country that there is only one neighbor who can be dangerous to Belgian neutrality, and that it has only one real protector.

In Holland they have already begun to restore the line of inundations and to fortify it anew. Against whom? I do not know. I believe that in Germany the idea of annexing Holland has never even occurred to any one.

It is true that as late as the beginning of this century we captured these very lines; not for ourselves, however, but for the House of Orange. In a small, yet widely-read pamphlet, written with a view of drawing the attention of the English to the defects in their militia system, the consequences are depicted of a landing in England—not from France, not from the opposite coast, but from Germany. In Denmark, from fear of a German landing, it is considered necessary to increase the coast-defence fleet, and to fortify the points of landing on the island of Zealand. At one time we are about to conquer the Russian Baltic Provinces, at another we wish to lure away the German population of Austria. . . .

A prudent soldier stands at this moment at the head of the French government. But, gentlemen, we have all witnessed how French factions, whose field of action lies in Paris, can hurry the government and the people on to the most extraordinary decisions. What is borne to us from across the Vosges is a rabid cry for revenge for the reverses which France herself had courted.

Well, gentlemen, we have not followed our neighbor's lead in increasing the army. . . . But, gentlemen, we must not allow the intrinsic value of our army to be lessened, either by shortening the term of service, or by a reduction of the peace establishment. The first measure, if it is to have any financial value at all, leads to a militia. Wars carried on by a militia have this peculiarity, that they last much longer, and even on this ground and for this very reason involve far greater sacrifice, both of money and of human life, than all other wars. I need only remind you of the late American War of Secession, which had to be waged, on both sides, principally by militia forces. I must not miss this opportunity of communicating to you the opinion of the man who had to conduct the first American campaign, the War of Independence—the opinion of Washington—regarding a militia. You will find it given in Bancroft's excellent *History of the United States of America*. Never and nowhere could a demand have been more unpopular than that which Washington again and again submitted to Congress, the demand for the raising of a standing army. This may be a matter of surprise to you, but Washington expresses himself in the following terms: "Experience, which is trade's best guide, so completely and so decisively rejects all reliance upon a militia force, that no one who values order, regularity, and economy, and who cares for his own honor, his character, and his peace of mind, will stake these on the outcome of an undertaking which relies for its success upon militia forces."

And a little further on he writes: "Short service and an unfounded reliance on the militia are the causes of all our misfortunes and of the growth of our debt."

The war was, as you know, brought to a close by the appearance on the scene of a small corps of only 6,000 men, who were, however, real soldiers.

Gentlemen, France has twice tried a militia system. The first time that the hated army was disbanded was, of course, after the Revolution; the nation itself was to guard the newborn liberty, patriotism was to take the place of discipline, whilst the national *élan* and the masses themselves were to supersede military training. A certain halo even now hovers round the volunteers of 1791; but, gentlemen, there is also an impartial account of all this, compiled, by a Frenchman, from the official records of the French war office. I will resist the temptation of citing some very piquant passages; to do so I should, indeed, have to quote the whole book, for every page would show how useless and how costly these formations were, and what a scourge they proved to their own country. Only after thirteen years of bitter experience did the French arrive at the conviction that the army should no longer be put in the ranks of the volunteers, but the volunteers in the ranks of the army. When, therefore, such men as the first consul and other illustrious generals placed themselves at their head, then indeed these same volunteers victoriously overran the whole of Europe; but, gentlemen, they had then become soldiers. . . .

Gentlemen, the best-disposed mortal cannot live in a state of peace if it does not suit his evil-disposed neighbor.

I think, however, that we shall show the world that we have become a powerful nation and remained peace-loving; a nation which does not require war in order to acquire fame, and that does not desire it in order to make conquests. I really do not know what we should do with a conquered portion of either Russia or France.

I hope that we not only shall enjoy peace for a period of years, but that we shall also be in a position to impose peace; then perhaps the world at large will become convinced that a powerful Germany in the center of the Continent constitutes the best guarantee for the peace of Europe.

But, gentlemen, in order to be in a position to impose peace we must be armed for war, and I am of opinion that we stand face to face with the alternative—either to assume that the political aspect of Europe does not make a strong and efficient German army indispensable, or else to grant the means for the maintenance of such an army.

12. He Voices Skepticism Concerning Perpetual Peace

Since conflict seemed to be a natural condition of relations among the states of the Continent, public opinion in Central Europe viewed the idea of perpetual peace as appealing but visionary. Armed force would always remain the arbiter of political destiny. This was the opinion expressed by Moltke in 1880 in a letter to Johann Kaspar Bluntschli, an eminent authority on international law. To the professional soldier the mitigation of war was possible, but its complete elimination was only a dream of well-intentioned theorists.

SOURCE: Helmuth von Moltke, "Letters and Historical Writings," in *The German Classics of the Nineteenth and Twentieth Centuries*, ed. Kuno Francke, 20 vols. (Albany and New York: German Publication Society, 1913–14), vol. X, pp. 348–350.

You HAVE BEEN good enough to send me the manual published by the Institute of International Law, and you ask for my approval. In the first place, I fully recognize your humane endeavors to lessen the sufferings which war brings in its train.

Eternal peace, however, is a dream, and not even a beautiful dream, for war is part of God's scheme of the world. In war the noblest virtues of man develop courage and renunciation, the sense of duty and abnegation, and all at the risk of his life. Without war the world would be swallowed up in the morass of materialism.

With the principle stated in the preface, that the gradual advance of civilization should be reflected in the conduct of war, I fully agree; but I go further, and believe that civilization alone, and no codified laws of warfare, can have the desired result.

Every law necessitates an authority to watch over it and to direct its execution, but there is no power which can enforce obedience to international agreements. Which third state will take up arms because one—or both—of two powers at war with each other have broken the *loi de la guerre?* The human judge is lacking. In these matters we can hope for success only from the religious and moral education of the individuals, and the honor and sense of right of the leaders, who make their own laws and act according to them, at least to the extent to which the abnormal conditions of war permit it.

Nobody, I think, can deny that the general softening of men's manners has been followed by a more humane way of waging war.

Compare, if you will, the coarseness of the Thirty Years War with the battles of recent dates.

The introduction in our generation of universal service in the army has marked a long step in the direction of the desired aim, for it has brought also the educated classes into the army. Some rough and violent elements have survived, it is true, but the army no longer consists of them exclusively.

The governments, moreover, have two means at hand to prevent the worst excesses. A strong discipline, practiced and perfected in times of peace, and a commissariat equipped to provide for the troops in the field.

Without careful provision, discipline itself can be only moderately well enforced. The soldier who suffers pain and hunger, fatigue and danger, cannot take merely *en proportion avec les ressources du pays,* but he must take whatever he needs. You must not ask of him superhuman things.

The greatest blessing in war is its speedy termination, and to this end all means must be permitted which are not downright criminal. I cannot at all give my approval to the *Déclaration de St. Petersbourg,* that "the weakening of the hostile army" is the only justifiable procedure in war. On the contrary, all resources of the hostile government must be attacked—its finances, railways, provisions, and even its prestige.

The last war against France was waged in this way, and yet with greater moderation than any earlier war. The campaign was decided after two months; and fierceness became characteristic of the fighting only when a revolutionary government continued the war through four more months, to the detriment of the country.

I am glad to acknowledge that your manual, with its clear and short sentences, does greater justice than former attempts to what is needed in war. But even the acceptance of your regulations by the governments would not ensure their observance. It has long been a universally accepted rule of warfare that no messenger of peace should be shot at. But in the last campaign we frequently saw this done.

No paragraph learned by heart will convince the soldier that the unorganized natives who *spontanément* (that is, of their own free will) take up arms and threaten his life every moment of the day and night should be recognized as lawful opponents.

Certain requests of the manual, I fear, cannot be put in force. The identification, for instance, of the dead after a big battle. Others are subject to doubt, unless you insert *"lorsque les circonstances le permettent, s'il se peut, si possible, s'il-y-a nécessité,"* or the like. This will give them that elasticity without which the bitter severity of actual warfare will break through all restrictions.

In war, where everything must be treated individually, only those regulations will work well which are primarily addressed to the leaders. This includes everything that your manual has to say concerning the wounded and the sick, the physicians and their medicines. The general recognition of these principles, and also of those which have to do with the prisoners of war, would mark a notable step in advance and bring us nearer the end which the Institute of International Law is pursuing with such admirable perseverance.

Bismarck's success in protecting royal authority against the forces of democracy proved ironically to be the cause of his own downfall. The chancellor had devoted his great political talent to the task of making the position of the monarch invulnerable to the pressure of legislature, party, or public opinion. He had used national unification to maintain the privileges of the crown at the expense of the rights of the people. Remembering the constitutional conflict which had threatened to lead to the introduction of liberal government in Prussia, he resolved never again to expose the state to the danger of democratization. But by enhancing the power of William I he was not merely performing the duty of a loyal servant of his country's ruler. He was also protecting his own political influence against the assaults of reforming politicians and publicists who were seeking his removal from office. The achievement of national unity without civic freedom meant that he was immune to the criticism of those who opposed his methods and condemned his objectives. In the German Empire parliamentary right remained subordinate to the royal will, political parties were weak and divided, and public opinion exerted little influence over government policy. All the chancellor needed to exercise power was the approval of the emperor, and the emperor was ready to grant the chancellor's every wish. The authority of the monarch was thus overshadowed by the authority of his minister. The entire system of government seemed in fact designed to exalt the position of its brilliant architect.

Yet the invulnerability of the royal prerogative was an instrument of destruction as well as benefaction. Bismarck had created a political weapon of irresistible force which could be used against him as easily as against his enemies. But it never occurred to the chancellor that the authority of the crown, which had served to enforce his will, might also effect his downfall. He governed and dictated with a kingly haughtiness, although only the life of a thankful old man stood between him and his nemesis. When William I died in 1888, Bismarck lost the only source of his power. He continued to believe that royal appreciation of the great services he had rendered to the Hohenzollerns would safeguard his dominant position in government, but he overestimated the importance of gratitude in affairs of state. William II, the successor to the throne of Germany after the brief reign of his father Frederick III, was a man whose hunger for authority equaled that of Bismarck. Neurotic, headstrong, ambitious, and eager for fame, the new emperor became increasingly restless under the tutelage of the domineering chancellor. He yearned to emulate the achievements of Frederick the Great, yet he found himself balked at every turn by the crusty, old statesman who had become accustomed to treating even royalty with a cool disdain. It was only a question of time before the two would clash over the leading role in the determination of policy.

The conflict between emperor and chancellor arose in part out of disagreements regarding affairs of state. There was the problem, for example, of socialism, which continued to gain strength despite the repression directed against it by the government for more than a decade. Bismarck began to favor more drastic measures, perhaps even a conservative revision of the imperial constitution. William II, on the other hand, hoped to allay proletarian discontent by promises and concessions. He liked to think of himself as a great conciliator who could overcome class differences and harmonize opposing interests. His contention was that a vigorous new program of social reform would in time win the support of the urban masses for the established order. The emperor had doubts, moreover, about the chancellor's foreign policy. He felt that the system of alliances constructed by Bismarck was too complicated and cumbersome. Some day it might place the government in the embarrassing position of having to choose between contradictory and incompatible obligations. Would it not be better to simplify the diplomacy pursued by Berlin, especially with regard to Russia, before it was too late? Yet even more important than the political differences dividing ruler and minister were their personal antipathies. The conflict between them could have only one outcome. In the spring of 1890 the chancellor was dismissed, and an era in the history of Germany came to an end.

The transition from the age of Bismarck to that of William II meant a change not only in personalities and policies but in values and objectives as well. The old chancellor had belonged to the classic school of diplomacy which emphasized stability, moderation, and restraint in the conduct of affairs of state. The emperor represented the political outlook of the early twentieth century with its jingoism, imperialism, and militarism. Bismarck had believed in a balance of power maintained through the interaction of the leading states of Europe, each seeking to protect its essential interests by the methods of *Realpolitik*. William II aimed at the hegemony of Germany on the world scene without regard for the needs or ambitions of other countries, whose opposition he was ready to crush by the force of arms. Bismarck had remained within the tradition of the great opportunistic statesmen of the Continent like Richelieu, Mazarin, Kaunitz, and Metternich. William II set out on the road to daredevil diplomacy and total war at the end of which stood Mussolini and Hitler. Yet emperor and chancellor had one thing in common: a blindness to the civic and moral questions raised by the fundamental processes of industrialization, urbanization, and democratization. Accepting the values of an aristocratic and hierarchical authoritarianism, they could offer no solution to the problems of social injustice and economic exploitation except monarchical benevolence or religious compassion. The demand for the liberalization of state and society seemed to them to be heresy. The price of their incomprehension was heavy. The German Empire whose destiny they had shaped collapsed amid defeat and revolution because of their fatal inability to adapt the system of government to the vital needs of the nation.

1. Bismarck Finds Fault with William I

As Bismarck's successes multiplied, his irascibility and imperiousness increased. He clashed repeatedly not only with members of the royal family, but with the emperor himself on whose favor his position in government depended. During the Franco-Prussian War, for example, there was a sharp difference of opinion between the chancellor and his master over the procedure for bestowing the imperial crown on the Hohenzollern dynasty. In frank conversations with Odo Russell, which the latter promptly reported to London, Bismarck bitterly criticized William I for insisting on his own point of view. The statesman who always maintained that he was a defender of monarchical authority did not hesitate to oppose that authority when it conflicted with his own will.

Count Bismarck seems to delight in having someone to talk at who will listen without interruption to the torrent of his ideas and *faute de mieux* he pours them into my delighted ears.

He is most kind and hospitable, asks me often to dinner, takes me out driving with him alone, sends his carriage and a secretary to come and fetch me to sit and smoke with him and gives me long and interesting accounts of his past and present difficulties with the king, the crown prince and the royal family whom he finds it so difficult to deal with because they will have "convictions" and know everything better than himself—an unpardonable offence in Count Bismarcks opinion because it makes him "bilious."

He has been very "bilious" for the last week and has twice received me in his bedroom and on his sofa.

The king, he says, has "olympic convictions" and believes Germany to have been created for him—and not he for Germany— that the sovereigns of Germany *alone* can give him the imperial crown, and that therefore the deputation of the Reichstag who have just arrived to acknowledge the new emperor are a pack of revolutionists who are encroaching on the rights of the minor sovereigns of Germany and should therefore not be received at all—etc., etc.

After a long nocturnal altercation the chancellor told the king he would resign if the deputation was not received and took to his bed.

Source: Paul Knaplund, ed., *Letters from the Berlin Embassy, 1871–1874, 1880–1885* (Washington, D.C.: USGPO, 1944), p. 29.

The crown prince and others have since interfered and they have made it up.

I marvel at the freedom with which he finds fault with his masters and should not like to put on paper all he said in detail about them.

2. The Wife of the British Ambassador in Berlin Describes the Chancellor's Power

After the establishment of the German Empire, the authority which Bismarck exercised over affairs of state became boundless. William I regarded him as the architect of the greatness which the ruling house of Prussia had achieved, while the nation saw in him a wizard who had discovered the secret of enduring success in political affairs. He became a jealous demigod, suspicious and resentful of all who exercised independent judgment or displayed personal initiative. He was unwilling to share his power with anyone, not even with the head of the dynasty whose servant he was, at least in theory. Lady Emily Russell, wife of the British ambassador in Berlin, described to Queen Victoria in 1880 the enormous influence wielded by the chancellor.

THOSE WHO KNOW the crown prince well think that he is worried and pained to see the emperor so completely under the influence of Prince Bismarck, whose policy in regard to home questions and imperial matters he does not approve of; and he fears that the public will hold his imperial father responsible for the arbitrary and unconstitutional proceedings which the chancellor delights in.

The *initiated* know that the emperor . . . has allowed Prince Bismarck to have his own way in *everything;* and the great chancellor revels in the absolute power he has acquired and does as he pleases. He lives in the country and governs the German Empire without even taking the trouble to consult the emperor about his plans, who only learns what is being done from the documents to which his signature is necessary, and which His Majesty signs without questions or hesitation. Never has a subject been granted so much irresponsible power from his sovereign, and never has a minister inspired a nation with more abject individual, as well as general, terror before. No wonder, then, that the crown prince

SOURCE: George Earle Buckle, ed., *The Letters of Queen Victoria: Second Series,* 3 vols. (London and New York: Longmans, Green & Co., 1926–28), vol. III, pp. 169–170.

should be worried at a state of things which he has not more personal power or influence to remedy than anyone else in Prussia,
whilst Prince Bismarck lives and terrorizes over Germany from
Friedrichsruh with the emperor's tacit and cheerful consent.

Bismarck has gradually appointed a ministry of clerks out of the
government offices, who do as they are told by him, and he has so
terrified the Bundesrat, by threatening to resign whenever they
disagreed with him, that they now vote entirely in obedience to his
instructions. He now expects that at the next general election he
will, by careful management, obtain the absolute majority he requires to carry through his new taxation and commercial policy.

If Bismarck should ever die suddenly from indigestion, which his
doctors fear and predict, the difficulty of reforming the general
abuses which his personal administration has created will be great,
and will impose a hard and ungrateful task on the sovereign, who
will have to find and appoint the ministers capable of reestablishing
constitutionalism in Prussia.

3. Bismarck Criticizes the Character of William II

The accession of William II in 1888 brought to the throne of Germany
a ruler whose love of power was as great as Bismarck's. The new emperor did not share the sense of gratitude which his grandfather had
felt toward the chancellor, nor was he willing to allow a subordinate,
however talented, to determine his policy for him. A clash between the
two men became inevitable, and, given the existing system of government, the outcome was predictable. In his memoirs Bismarck left an
unflattering but not inaccurate portrait of the young monarch, con-
trasting his unstable character and overbearing personality with the
solidity and sobriety of William I.

In COMMON WITH Friedrich Wilhelm IV, the present kaiser has the
gift of eloquence and the need of employing it more frequently
than is desirable. His words flow readily; but in the choice of them
his great-uncle was more discreet and perhaps more laborious and
scientific. In the case of the great-nephew the presence of a short-
hand writer is not always desirable; but it was very seldom that a

SOURCE: Bernard Miall, trans., *The Kaiser vs. Bismarck* (New York and
London: Harper & Row, 1921), pp. 148–152. Copyright, 1920, 1948
by Harper & Row, Publishers, Inc. Reprinted by permission of the
publishers.

grammatical criticism could be brought against Friedrich Wilhelm's speeches. These latter were the eloquent and sometimes poetical expression of ideas which at that time would have been capable of stimulating men to action, had the words been followed by deeds to correspond. I very well remember the enthusiasm aroused by the coronation speech and the king's utterances upon other public occasions. If they had been followed by energetic resolutions of the same emphatic character, they might at that time have produced a powerful effect, all the more as people's feelings were not yet blunted in respect of political emotions. In the years 1841 and 1842 more was to be achieved with fewer means than in 1849. We can form an impartial judgment of those matters now that the then desirable object has been attained, and the need of 1840 is no longer present in the national mind; on the contrary, *Le mieux est l'ennemi du bien* is one of the soundest of proverbs, against which the Germans are theoretically more inclined to trespass than other nations. Wilhelm II resembled Friedrich Wilhelm IV in this, that the foundation of their policy was rooted in the conception that the king, and he alone, is more closely acquainted with the will of God than other men, governs in accordance with the same, and therefore confidently demands obedience, without discussing his aim with his subjects or announcing it to them. Friedrich Wilhelm IV had no doubt of his specially privileged position in respect of the Deity; his honest belief corresponds with the picture of the high priest of the Jews, who *alone* stepped behind the curtain.

In certain respects we shall seek in vain for any resemblance between Wilhelm II and his father, grandfather, and great-grandfather; peculiarities which were the principal features of the characters of Friedrich Wilhelm III, Wilhelm I, and Friedrich III were not to the fore in the young sovereign. A certain timid distrust of their own capacity for work had, through the four generations, made way for a certain degree of assured self-confidence, such as we have not seen upon the throne since the time of Frederick the Great; but only, I think, in the person of the reigning sovereign. His brother, Prince Henry of Prussia, seems to possess the same distrust of his own powers and the same secret diffidence as are found, on closer acquaintance, at the bottom of the characters of Kaisers Friedrich and Wilhelm I, despite all their consciousness of their Olympian rank. In the latter his profound and pious trust in God was needed as surety, in the face of his unassuming and humble conception, before man and God, of his own personality, for the steadfastness of those resolutions which he made manifest in the time of conflict. Both rulers atoned by their goodness of heart and their honest love of the truth for their occasional deviations from the current estimation of the practical influence of kingly birth and anointing.

If I seek to paint a portrait of the present kaiser after the conclusion of my relations with his service, I find in him the characteristics of his predecessors incarnated in a manner which would for me possess a strong attractive power, and result in my attachment to his person, if they were animated by the principle of reciprocity between monarch and subject, between master and servant. The Germanic feudal law gives the vassal few pretensions save to the property of the subject, except that the fealty between him and his feudal lord is reciprocal, and the infraction of this fealty by either party is reckoned to be felony. Wilhelm I, his son, and his predecessors possessed the corresponding sentiment in a high degree; and this is the essential basis of the attachment of the Prussian people to their monarchs, which may be explained psychologically, for the tendency to bestow a *one-sided* affection has no existence as an *enduring* motive in the human soul. In the presence of Kaiser Wilhelm II, I could not get away from the impression of a one-sided affection; the feeling which is the firmest foundation of the constitution of the Prussian army, the feeling that the soldier will never leave the officer in the lurch, but also that the officer will never leave the soldier in the lurch, a sentiment to which Wilhelm I conformed in respect of his servants almost to exaggeration, cannot so far be recognized as entering, in any adequate degree, into the mentality of the young sovereign; his pretension to absolute sacrifice, confidence, and unshakable fealty has increased; and the inclination to guarantee a return of confidence and security on his own part has so far failed to make its appearance. The ease with which he dismisses trusted servants, even those whom he has hitherto treated as personal friends, without explanation of his motive, does not promote, but weakens, the spirit of confidence as it has prevailed for generations in the service of the kings of Prussia.

With the transition from the Hohenzollern spirit to the Coburg-English conception an imponderable factor was lost which will be difficult to restore. Wilhelm I protected and rewarded his servants, even when they were unfortunate or unskillful, possibly more than was profitable, and in consequence of this he had servants who were more attached to him than was profitable to themselves. In particular his warm-hearted good will toward others was unchangeable, if his gratitude for services performed came into play. He was always far from regarding his own will as the sole rule of conduct, nor could he contemplate the wounding of other people's feelings with indifference. His manner toward subordinates was always that of a royal and benevolent master, and alleviated the ill humor arising in the course of official business. Ill-natured gossip and calumny, when they came to his ears, could obtain no hold upon his noble and upright nature, and place hunters whose only source of profit lay in the shamelessness of their flattery had no prospect of success with Wilhelm I. To backstairs influences and accusations against his servants he was insensible, even if they proceeded from people holding high positions about his person, and if he did take the matter imparted to him into consideration, this was done in open conversation with the person behind whose back it was meant to take effect. If his opinion differed from mine he expressed himself openly as differing from me, discussing the matter with me, and if I did not succeed in winning him over to my views I gave in when it was possible; if it was not possible I postponed the affair or let it drop for good. My independence as a political leader has been honestly overestimated by my friends, and for their own purposes by my adversaries, because I surrendered all hope of fulfilling desires to which the king had as a matter of conviction offered lasting resistance, without continuing to advocate them until they resulted in a dispute. What was attainable I took on account, and on my side it only came to a strike in cases where my personal sense of honor was involved.

4. The Differences between Emperor and Chancellor Regarding Domestic Policy

Although the basic reason for the breach between William II and Bismarck was personal incompatibility, the two also differed on questions of policy. In domestic affairs the chancellor had concluded that

SOURCE: Bernard Miall, trans., *The Kaiser vs. Bismarck* (New York and London: Harper & Row, 1921), pp. 153–155. Copyright, 1920, 1948 by Harper & Row, Publishers, Inc. Reprinted by permission of the publishers.

only ruthless repression could overcome the danger of radicalism. Since the antisocialist legislation of 1878 had failed to produce the desired result, even more severe measures would have to be adopted. The emperor, on the other hand, believed that the established order could still conciliate the working class through a program of social reform. Bismarck disagreed with the monarch's strategy of appeasement. The way to deal with an enemy, he maintained afterward, is not to mollify but to crush him.

THE KAISER ENDEAVORS, by making concessions to his enemies, to make the support of his friends unnecessary. His grandfather, at the time of his accession to the regency, endeavored to insure the general content of his subjects, without losing their obedience and thereby endangering the security of the state; but after four years' experience he recognized the errors of his advisers and of his wife, who assumed that the opponents of the monarchy would by liberal concessions be transformed into its friends and supporters. In 1862 he was inclined to abdicate rather than surrender further to parliamentary liberalism, and accepted battle, supported by the latent but decisively stronger loyal elements.

The kaiser, with his Christian, but not always (in the worldly sense) successful tendency to conciliation, began with his worst enemy, social democracy. This first mistake, which was embodied in the management of the strike of 1889, led to increased pretensions on the part of the Socialists and fresh ill humor on the part of the monarch, as soon as it became evident that under the new government, just as under the old, the monarch could not, with the best will in the world, change the nature of things and of the human race. The kaiser was without experience in the sphere of human desires and human covetousness; but that he had lost his early confidence in the judgment and experience of others was a result of intrigues by which he was confirmed in his underestimation of the difficulty of governing, not only by officious advisers, such as Hinzpeter, Berlepsch, Heyden, Douglas and other impudent flatterers, but also by place-hunting generals and aides, and colleagues to whom I was referred for support, such as Boetticher, who as minister had no other function than to support me, and even by individual members of my council, who immediately and willingly went over in secret to President von Berlepsch if the kaiser questioned them behind the backs of their superiors. Perhaps he will suffer the same disillusion in respect of social democracy as his grandfather suffered in 1862 in respect of the progressives.

This policy of making advances to, not to say running after, the enemy, had been adopted [with respect to] the Center, [with respect to] Windthorst—only to have spoken to whom was seized upon by the kaiser as one of the external causes of his breach with me—and whose official honors after my dismissal were increased to apotheosis after his death. A curious Prussian saint! It is to be feared that even these favored props of the monarchy will give way in the moment of need. At all events, the complete satisfaction of the confederates, which the Prussian monarchy and the Protestant empire might find in the Center and the Society of Jesus, will prove to be just as unattainable as that of the Socialists, and in the event of danger and difficulty we shall see results not unlike those which followed the downfall of the Teutonic Order in Prussia, in connection with the mercenary soldiers, whom the Order was unable to pay. The Kaiser's inclination to employ antimonarchical and even anti-Prussian elements, such as the Poles, in the service of the crown, gave His Majesty a temporary means of bringing pressure to bear upon parties and factions which in principle were loyal to the antimonarchical tradition. The threat that if he were not unconditionally obeyed he would turn yet farther to the Left; that he might place the Socialists, the Crypto-Republicans of the Freethinkers' party, and the Ultramontane forces at the helm: in a word, the *Acheronta movebo*, which was the distinctive trait of this running after irreconcilable opponents, intimidated the established supporters of the monarchy. They feared that "things might become even worse," and the Kaiser is today, as far as they are concerned, in the position of a ship's captain whose navigation arouses the apprehensions of the crew and who sits smoking a cigar over the powder barrel.

5. The Differences between Emperor and Chancellor Regarding Foreign Policy

There were, in addition, important differences between William II and Bismarck concerning foreign affairs. After his enforced retirement, the old statesman commented adversely on the diplomacy of his successors.

Source: Bernard Miall, trans., *The Kaiser vs. Bismarck* (New York and London: Harper & Row, 1921), pp. 155–157. Copyright, 1920, 1948 by Harper & Row, Publishers, Inc. Reprinted by permission of the publishers.

Some of this censure was simply an expression of bitterness by a fallen giant toward those who had deprived him of office and power, but there was more in Bismarck's criticism than wounded vanity. The emperor was violating a cardinal principle of his statecraft: the maintenance of friendly relations with Russia. Toward the end of his life, the former chancellor warned against the growing dependence of Berlin on Vienna, a dependence which in time was to have very serious international consequences.

EVEN IN THE CASE OF foreign countries, whether friendly or inimical or doubtful, amiability had been carried to a greater length than is compatible with the conception that we should feel secure by virtue of our own attractive force. There was no one, either in the foreign office or at court, who was sufficiently familiar with international psychology justly to calculate the effect of these political proceedings on our side; neither the kaiser nor Caprivi nor Marschall was qualified to do so by his previous experience, and the political sense of honor of the kaiser's advisers was satisfied by the kaiser's signature, independently of the consequences to the empire.

The attempt to win the liking of the French . . . in the background of which the idea of a visit to Paris may have been slumbering, and the willingness once more to allow the right of thoroughfare through the boundary wall of the Vosges, had had no other result than that the French became bolder and the Statthalter more anxious. The kaiser's announcement in the autumn of 1889 that he intended to pay a second visit to Russia in 1890—an announcement which was personally inconvenient to the Russian monarch—had disagreeable results. Our attitude toward England and Austria seemed to me equally incorrect. Instead of fostering the idea in these countries that even if the worst came to the worst we should not be lost without them, a system of gratuities was employed, which we found to be extremely costly, and which made us appear to be in need of help, whereas both our helpers needed it more than we did. England, if, owing to her lack of troops, she were threatened by France, or by Russia in India and the East, might find protection from either of these threats in the assistance of Germany. But if on our side more importance were attributed to England's friendship than England attributed to ours, then England's overestimation of herself with reference to us would be confirmed, as also the conviction that we should feel ourselves honored if, without any return services, we were allowed to burn our fingers in achieving England's aims. Even more certain, in our relations with Austria, was the greater lack of need on our part, and it is not possible to see why, at the meeting in Silesia, we should have had to buy our otherwise secure reliance on reciprocal support by the promise of economic concessions or to confirm our need of such support. The saying that fusion of economic interests—that is, the favoring of Austrian at the cost of German interests—is a necessary result of our political intimacy, has reached me from Vienna in varying forms, for ten long years, and I have turned aside the underlying expectations without a blunt refusal, but also without giving way in the slightest degree, meeting them with friendly courtesy, until they were recognized to be hopeless even in Vienna, and were abandoned. But . . . the Austrian expectations appear to have been so skillfully thrust into the foreground between the two kaisers that the natural inclination to be agreeable . . . may have been the origin of the promise on our part which Kaiser Franz Joseph had *utiliter* accepted. In the following deliberations of the Ministers, moreover, the . . . business dexterity of the Austrians would in any case have gained an advantage over our novices and free-traders.

6. Bismarck Expects a Confrontation with William II

There could be no effective collaboration between a ruler like William II and a minister like Bismarck. Sooner or later the two were bound to clash. In February 1890 Sir Edward Malet, Russell's successor in Berlin, reported a conversation with the chancellor indicating that a confrontation between him and his royal master was imminent. But Bismarck still had no idea that the result would be his dismissal from office. He continued to believe that while the emperor might in the future exercise greater influence over affairs of state, his own position remained unassailable. He was unable to conceive of a Germany in which he did not play the leading part.

PRINCE BISMARCK called on me . . . and plunged at once *in medias* as to his position with regard to the emperor and His Majesty's projected labor conference.

SOURCE: George Earle Buckle, ed., *The Letters of Queen Victoria: Third Series*, 3 vols. (London: John Murray Ltd, 1930–32), vol. I, pp. 565–567. Reprinted by permission of the publisher.

I asked the prince how he was; he replied, "I ought to be well, for my general health is good, but I am made nervous and out of sorts by the situation. I cannot approve of or agree in what the emperor is doing, and it has come to this, that I have made up my mind to resign all the offices I hold except those of chancellor of the empire and minister for foreign affairs of the empire. I shall cease to be Prussian prime minister, and resign the portfolios which I hold in the Prussian ministry (foreign affairs and commerce). I would retire altogether, but the emperor wishes me to remain, and I cannot refuse, for if I were to go now on the eve of the elections it might have an effect upon them which I desire as little now as before the present situation arose. . . . My position will be a difficult one. Herr von Boetticher as Prussian prime minister will be over me in the Bundesrat, while as chancellor I direct the policy of the empire. I doubt its working, and it will probably end in my complete retirement. The emperor is very cordial toward me, but he wishes to govern, himself. He has not realized the utility of having a screen between himself and his subjects on which the blows of unpopularity may fall without injuring him. He has no doubts. He thinks he can do all things, and he wishes to have entire credit all to himself."

I remarked that the emperor must know that he (Prince Bismarck) was regarded as a guarantee of the maintenance of peace in Europe, and that his disappearance from the scene would be regarded with something like consternation, as His Majesty had not as yet acquired the confidence of the Powers in his pacific intentions; but the prince said that His Majesty believed himself capable of managing foreign affairs quite well himself. "He is elated with what he considers to be the success of his visit to Russia and other countries. He only wants me to remain in order that I may make speeches in the Reichstag and induce it to vote money." These were the only words he uttered with some bitterness of manner. "I am glad," he said, "that seventy-five years are behind me and not before me; my work is done, but it is sad to see the edifice which I have raised brick by brick in danger of crumbling. When I was called to be minister in Prussia I found things in a state of chaos. The king wanted to abdicate. I brought him to see that it was better to share the dangers of the situation with his people than to die in dishonored retirement. He was all for peace. He wanted to surrender. . . . I made the Austrian war against his urgent wishes.

In 1870 I was obliged to have resort to a stratagem to force on war at that moment. It must have come later. It was everything to us to choose the time. The Empress Augusta never ceased to work against me. In 1877 the crisis came, and I told the emperor that he must choose between me and my enemies. He wept and besought [me] to remain. There was nothing at that time that my enemies did not say. . . . I survived all their attacks, and defeated all those who strove to destroy me."

As he went away he said, "I came to make you my call and to apologize to you for all the trouble we are going to give you, but it is not of my making."

In giving this general account of what he said I think I have not sufficiently accentuated the impression which he conveyed that the emperor deemed himself quite able to stand alone and to direct the internal and external affairs of the empire without any anxiety as to his own capacity.

7. He Explains to the Cabinet His Reasons for Retiring

The showdown between emperor and chancellor came a month later. Their disagreements, which had been mounting for some time, culminated in a crisis which could be resolved only by Bismarck's removal from office. The minutes of the ministerial session in Berlin on March 17, 1890, provide a detailed account of the events which finally convinced the chancellor that he could not continue to serve as the chief adviser of William II. Gloomily he described to his colleagues in the cabinet recent developments which left him no choice but to submit his resignation. The brilliant political career which had begun some thirty years before was now at an end.

Confidential Deliberations of the Prussian Cabinet.

Present: The president of the cabinet, and imperial chancellor, Prince von Bismarck.

The vice-president of the cabinet, Secretary of State von Boetticher.

The secretary of state of Prussia, von Maybach; Dr. Freiherr Lucius von Ballhausen, Dr. von Gossler, Dr. von Scholz, Count

Source: Bernard Miall, trans., *The Kaiser vs. Bismarck* (New York and London: Harper & Row, 1921), pp. 187–194. Copyright, 1920, 1948 by Harper & Row, Publishers, Inc. Reprinted by permission of the publishers.

von Bismarck-Schönhausen, Herrfurth, Dr. von Schelling, von Verdy, Freiherr von Berlepsch.

The Under-Secretary of State Acting Privy Councilor Homeyer.

The minister-president convened the cabinet to a confidential meeting at his official residence and advised the same that he has today addressed to His Majesty the kaiser and king a petition to be relieved of his offices, the acceptance of which is probable. He cannot but question whether he can still accept the responsibility, which is constitutionally incumbent upon him, for His Majesty's policy, since His Majesty's cooperation, which is indispensable to such acceptance, will not be conceded to him.

He has already been surprised that His Majesty has formed definitive resolutions in respect of the so-called protection of labor legislation without previously consulting him and the cabinet. He immediately expressed his apprehension that this proceeding would arouse great agitation in the country at election time, and awaken expectations in the electors which could not be fulfilled, and finally, by the chimerical nature of the hopes aroused, would operate to the detriment of the respect entertained for the crown. He had hoped that the unanimous remonstrances of the ministry might induce His Majesty to abandon the designs which he cherished; however, he had not found this unanimity in the ministry, but was forced to conclude that in several quarters it had been considered advisable to acquiesce in His Majesty's suggestion.

Again, after this he was compelled to feel doubtful whether he still possessed the secure authority as prime minister that he had enjoyed in virtue of the confidence vouchsafed him in his time by His Majesty Kaiser Wilhelm I. Now the kaiser discusses matters without him, not only with individual ministers, but even with councilors of the ministries subordinate to him. The minister of commerce has delivered memoranda to His Majesty without previously consulting him. In the interests of the unanimity of the ministry as a body he brought to the notice of the last-named minister the royal order of the 8th of September, 1852, which was unknown to him, and after he had convinced himself, in the course of the Cabinet meeting of the 2d of this month, that the Ministers generally were not all aware of this order, he had a copy of it sent to all, and in the accompanying letter he laid stress upon the fact that he applied the order only to memoranda or reports submitted to His Majesty, which aimed at the modification of legislation and the existing legal situation.

Tactfully handled in this manner, the instructions of the said order comprise no more than is indispensable to any prime minister who wishes to fill this position in a fitting manner. He does not know from what quarter His Majesty learned of this proceeding, but His Majesty commanded that the said order, by which the ministers were forbidden to present memoranda or reports directly to him, should no longer be in force. He explained that the ministers were not subjected to restraint thereby; that at most it resulted in his being present at audiences. His Majesty is then always free to decide in favor of the departmental minister and against the prime minister. The order is necessary, and least of all can he deny this now that he has just drawn attention to the matter.

This difference of opinion in itself would not have induced him to resign, still less would he have resigned on account of the labor question. In this province he has honestly done his best to support the imperial initiative, and to demonstrate, by diplomatic advocacy and by receiving the International Conference on his official premises, that he was promoting the labors of the Conference.

His Majesty the kaiser has given him a further sign of a lack of confidence in the reproach that he, without His Majesty's permission, should not have received the deputy Windthorst. He receives all deputies as a matter of principle, and after Windthorst had requested an interview he had him admitted, with the result that he is now completely informed concerning the deputy's intentions. He could not submit to His Majesty's control over his personal intercourse in and out of service.

He is confirmed in his resolution to resign all his offices now that he has today convinced himself that he can no longer represent even His Majesty's foreign policy.

Notwithstanding his confidence in the Triple Alliance, he has none the less never lost sight of the possibility that it might at some time be renounced. In Italy the monarchy does not stand upon a firm footing; the concord between Italy and Austria is imperiled by the Irredenta; and in Austria, despite the absolute reliability of the reigning emperor, a different frame of mind might supervene; Hungary's attitude can never safely be relied upon; Hungary and Austria might engage in disputes from which we should have to stand aloof; on this account he has always endeavored to avoid breaking down the bridge between ourselves and Russia; and he believes that he has so far confirmed the tsar in peaceful intentions that he has scarcely any fear of a Russian war, by which nothing could be gained even if it ran a victorious course. At most we might be attacked from that side if in a victorious war against France we sought to enforce the cession of territory by the latter. Russia needs the existence of France as a Great Power as we need that of Austria.

Now the German consul in Kieff sent in fourteen exhaustive reports, making in all a good two hundred pages, concerning the Russian situation, many of which dealt with military measures. Of these reports he (Bismarck) submitted a few of a political nature to His Majesty; others, of a military nature, to the Great General Staff, in the expectation that the latter would lay them before the kaiser, in case they were of a character to require his attention, while the rest he returned in order that they might be brought forward in the ordinary course of procedure. . . .

Concerning these reports he received the following autograph letter from His Majesty:

> The reports make it as clear as possible that the Russians are strategically fully prepared to go to war—and I must greatly deplore the fact that I have received so few of the reports. You ought to have drawn my attention long ago to the terrible danger threatening! It is more than high time to warn the Austrians and to take countermeasures. In such circumstances I can of course no longer think of a journey to Krasnö.
> The reports are excellent.
>
> [Signed] W.

In this letter the reproach is made that he has withheld reports from His Majesty and has not in due time called His Majesty's attention to the danger of war; further, the opinion is expressed, which he does not share, that a "terrible" danger threatens us from Russia, that Austria must be warned and countermeasures taken, and finally that the kaiser's visit to the Russian maneuvers, to which he had invited himself, must be abandoned.

It is not, as a general thing, incumbent upon him to lay all reports which reach him before His Majesty; he has the right to select, according to their contents, those in respect of which he thinks he can vouch for the impression which they will produce upon His Majesty. In the present instance he made a selection to the best of his judgment, and can but perceive in this letter an undeserved and mortifying lack of confidence.

Moreover, he is unable, in the face of his still unshaken opinion of the tsar's peaceful intentions, to advocate such measures as His Majesty demands.

In this connection he hears that His Majesty the kaiser, who previously approved of his proposals concerning the position to be taken up as regards the Reichstag, and the eventual dissolution of the latter, is now of the opinion that the military proposals should be introduced only in so far as one can count upon their acceptance. The minister of war has recently expressed himself in favor of the introduction of these proposals in their complete form, and if it is desired to take countermeasures against the warlike preparations of Russia, and if danger is seen to be approaching from that direction, this is all the more the right course to take.

After what has been said he assumes that he is no longer in full agreement with his colleagues, and no longer possesses a sufficient measure of His Majesty's confidence. He rejoices that a king of Prussia should himself wish to govern. He himself recognizes the disadvantage of his resignation in the public interest, and he has no longing for an idle life; his health is now good, but he feels that he is in His Majesty's way, that His Majesty wishes him to resign, and on this account he has justifiably begged for his discharge from service.

The vice-president of the cabinet declared that this communication had deeply grieved him, and, assuredly, all his colleagues. He had until now hoped that differences of opinion existed between His Majesty and the prime minister only in the sphere of domestic politics, and that therefore the procedure recently indicated by His Highness, according to which he would confine himself to the direction of foreign affairs, would prove a suitable solution. His Highness's resignation from all his offices would mean interminable difficulties, and even though he found His Highness's displeasure comprehensible, he could only urgently beg that the way to an arrangement might, if anyhow possible, be found.

The prime minister remarked that the expedient that he should resign from the service of the Prussian state and confine himself to the position of imperial chancellor was made impossible of consideration by the Reichstag and the federated governments. In those quarters it was desired that the imperial chancellor should find himself in an official position in which he would cease to lead the Prussian vote, and he could not accept a position in which he would receive instructions from the Prussian cabinet, in whose creation he had not cooperated. Consequently even this expedient, which he had recently proposed, would not be without its difficulties.

The minister of finance explained that the cabinet order of September 8, 1852, especially in conformity with the statement which the prime minister had appended in the accompanying letter, did not in any way exceed what was requisite. This could not present an insuperable difficulty. But even in respect of the difficulties in the sphere of foreign policy, he could only repeat the prayer of the secretary of state, Herr von Boetticher, that an arrangement might be sought for. For the rest, if His Highness's resignation is not, as was recently alleged, the result of reasons of health, but of political reasons, and if it affects all his offices, the cabinet will possibly be obliged to consider whether it should not join him in taking this step. Perhaps this would contribute to averting this ominous event.

The ministers of public worship and of justice remarked that with reference to the points of difference laid before them there existed merely a misunderstanding, which would be explained to His Majesty; and the minister of war added that in his presence no word had fallen from His Majesty for a long time which referred in any way to warlike developments in respect of Russia.

The minister of public works declared that His Highness's resignation would be a national disaster in respect of the security of the country and the peace of Europe, and they must seek for every means of preventing it. In his opinion in such a case as this the ministers ought to place their portfolios at His Majesty's disposal, and he at least was determined to do so.

The minister of agriculture declared that if the prime minister was convinced that his resignation was desired by His Majesty it was not possible to dissuade him from this step. The cabinet would in any case consider what it would then have to do on its own part.

The minister of commerce observed that he personally was not affected by this question, but with reference to the remarks made by the prime minister concerning the petition which he had presented he begged to be allowed to explain that this did not apply to new problems of any sort, but to His Majesty's decree of the 4th of February of this year, which he found upon entering into office, and indeed had been confined to the protection of labor legislation in general, which was touched upon in the said decree. Against the . . . order of September 8, 1852, he had nothing to say, and had not mentioned it in His Majesty's presence.

The prime minister replied that he was fully persuaded that the minister of commerce had been far from desiring to injure him in any way.

The minister of war observed that the current proposals of the minister of war were expressly excluded from the stipulations of the order of September 8, 1852, but without regard to this he had assuredly, when any important event took place in his department, kept in touch with the prime minister.

The prime minister replied that he had throughout recognized the attitude of the minister of war as his colleague, and closed the session.

[Signed] Prince von Bismarck, von Boetticher, von Maybach, Freiherr Lucius von Ballhausen, von Gossler, von Scholz, Count von Bismarck, Herrfurth, von Schelling, von Verdy, Freiherr von Berlepsch.

[Signed] Homeyer

8. William II Presents His View of the Controversy

The pathos of the circumstances surrounding the fall of the grand old man of German politics should not disguise the fact that the fault was not entirely one-sided. The emperor was neurotic and ambitious, to be sure, but the chancellor was inflexible and domineering. A few days after Bismarck's resignation, William II in a conversation with Malet tried to present his view of the controversy. He complained not only of the chancellor's unwillingness to accept his policy with regard to the socialist movement, but also of the condescension with which he was treated by the proud statesman who had created a united Germany and dominated the diplomacy of Europe.

THE EMPEROR said to me:

I should like to explain to you the train of circumstances which has brought about the present state of affairs. The chancellor had been staying at Friedrichsruh for eight months, and was ignorant of what was going on at the capital.

SOURCE: George Earle Buckle, ed., *The Letters of Queen Victoria: Third Series*, 3 vols. (London: John Murray Ltd, 1930–32), vol. I, pp. 584–587. Reprinted by permission of the publisher.

"It was not my intention to launch into a socialistic policy, but things occurred which forced this course upon me. . . . The strikes which had recently occurred in Germany had created a deep impression of anxiety, and there was a feeling in the air that, in order to prevent future disorder and even calamity arising from the state of things which had produced the strikes, something must be done. . . . Under these circumstances I had to choose between yielding hereafter, perhaps with the appearance of bad grace, to the popular movement or of taking the initiative myself. When Prince Bismarck came to Berlin on the last days of the debate on the Socialist Bill, it was evident that the government was about to suffer the defeat which eventually came; but I learnt that the Conservatives would even at the last moment be willing to vote with the government, if the government would abandon the expulsion clause in the bill, or if they would even only make an announcement that they would not press that clause during the present session, but would hold it over in order to take the opinion of the new parliament. I implored Prince Bismarck to adopt this course, but he absolutely refused. The result was, as you know, that the Conservatives and the Socialists voted together.

"About this time I spoke frequently to the chancellor about the necessity of taking up the Socialist question, but he was dead against it. One night I sat up for two hours by myself and wrote down my own views as to what ought to be done on a paper which now forms the basis of the bill, which will be laid before parliament. I gave this to the chancellor, but he treated it lightly, and I could make no way with him. . . . In the meanwhile I had been endeavoring to gain over the ministers separately to my views, but I found that they were one and all in complete subjection to Prince Bismarck, and dared not help me. Prince Bismarck did not differ with me in the view that the Socialist question must soon take an acute form, but his policy was to allow it to progress until it should be necessary to call out the troops to sweep the streets with grape-shot, and so to make short work of the whole affair. Such a policy as this might be possible, if my grandfather were still alive. The whole German people regarded him with such confidence, admiration, and respect that if he had thought it wise to allow things to come to such a pass, it would have been believed that he acted with a full sense of justice and responsibility, and he would not have alienated their affection. But for me, a young monarch, just come to the throne, to have allowed my people to be shot down in the streets, without making an effort first of all to examine their grievances, would have been disastrous to me and my whole House. It would have been said that my only idea of governing was by bayonets.

"I do not expect by the course I have taken to be able to remedy their grievances, but at least I have given a proof of my desire to do so, and my view is that although this conference may not find a solution of the difficult questions put before it, it may serve as a prelude to frequently recurring conferences, in which foreign nations shall take part, doing perhaps little each time, but producing a conviction, in the minds of the classes whose affairs they examine, that their welfare is a constant object of solicitude, and that by this means we may have some hope that we may separate the large mass of honest Socialists from those who merely use the name as a cloak to their republican or anarchical designs.

"When Prince Bismarck finally accepted the idea of a conference, I hardly like to say it, but I can assure you that he used small and undignified means to prevent its ever coming to anything. For instance, without my sanction he put into the program the question of limiting the hours of adult labor, no doubt thinking thereby to frighten your government and the French government into refusing to take part in it. In my discussions with him he treated me like a schoolboy. When I urged that I believed the ministers were really in favor of my views, although they would not venture to say so because he was opposed to them, he told me that they were all blackguards and cowards. He became so violent on occasions that I did not know whether he would not throw the inkstand at my head. The moment came when I was obliged to think of my own dignity.

"On the other hand, I was assured by the doctors that his state of mental excitement was such that it might end in a crisis at any moment. He told me six weeks ago, when I urged that he should lighten his labors, that he intended to resign the presidency of the Prussian ministry and remain only as chancellor. A short time after he told me he should resign the chancellorship as well, and a short time after that he sent to me to say that he had changed his mind and that he should resign nothing, and he began to take upon himself increased work. I finally decided that, if I wished his life to be preserved, I must relieve him of his duties. He and all his family are at present incensed against me, but I hope that in a few months they will see that they have reason to thank me.

"I cannot tell you the pain and anxiety I have gone through this winter on his account. I have always had the greatest admiration for him, and when I was prince I went through bitter moments from taking his side. I used to say to myself, 'Ah! if, when I am emperor, I could have such a minister!' for of course I never thought that I should come to the throne before I was sixty. When I became emperor I was overjoyed at having him as my minister, and I looked forward to keeping him at my side until old age should force him to retire, and now my real aim is to keep him alive for the sake of Germany and of Europe."

9. Bismarck Recalls the Days Following His Resignation

The dismissal of Bismarck removed from the political scene the leading statesman of Europe in the second half of the nineteenth century. He spent the remaining years of his life composing his memoirs, which were designed to judge the present even more than to describe the past. The account of the period immediately following the chancellor's resignation, for example, does not merely depict the events of those harrowing days. It overflows with rage against a monarch who had rewarded the architect of his dynasty's greatness with duplicity and humiliation. The only tribunal to which Bismarck could now appeal was history.

ON THE AFTERNOON of the 18th of March I sent in my resignation. . . . I took an opportunity to inform the heads of the civil and military cabinets, Lucanus and Hahnke, that the abandonment of the campaign against social democracy and the arousing of hopes that could not be fulfilled had filled me with heavy forebodings.

On the evening of the 18th the generals commanding in Berlin were sent for to go to the palace. The ostensible reason given for this procedure was that His Majesty wished to hear what they had to say of the military proposals. But as a matter of fact the kaiser addressed the gathering—which lasted barely twenty minutes—

SOURCE: Bernard Miall, trans., *The Kaiser vs. Bismarck* (New York and London: Harper & Row, 1921), pp. 113, 118–127. Copyright, 1920, 1948 by Harper & Row, Publishers, Inc. Reprinted by permission of the publishers.

and at its conclusion he told the generals, or so I was credibly informed, that he found himself compelled to dismiss me; and to the chief of the general staff, von Waldersee, he expressed his annoyance at my arbitrary methods and my secrecy in my intercourse with Russia. Count Waldersee had, with His Majesty, as a matter of departmental procedure, received the report on the above-mentioned consular reports. None of the generals, not even Count Moltke, had anything to say to the kaiser's revelations. It was not until he was on the stairs that Count Moltke said, "This is a very regrettable proceeding; the young gentleman will give us plenty to think about yet."

On the 19th of March, at the levee, my son was near Schuvalov. The latter told him, in the endeavor to induce him to stay, that if he and I did not remain the overtures which he was charged to make would come to nothing. Since these remarks might possibly influence the political decision of the kaiser, my son, in the afternoon of the following day, communicated them to His Majesty in an autograph report.

I do not know whether it was before or right after the receipt of this report; at all events, on the 20th, Adjutant Count Widel, who had been on service, went to my son, in order to repeat the kaiser's wish, which had already been announced by deputy, that my son should remain in his office, to offer him a long period of leave, and to assure him of His Majesty's absolute confidence. My son did not believe that he possessed this last, because the kaiser had repeatedly sent for councilors from the foreign office without his knowledge, for the purpose of giving them orders or to find out how the land lay. Widel granted this, and assured him that His Majesty would without doubt be prepared to redress this grievance. To this my son replied that his health was so debilitated that without me he could not assume the difficult and responsible position. Later, after I had received my discharge, Count Widel sought me out also and asked me to influence my son in the direction of remaining. I turned his request aside with the words, "My son is of age."

On the afternoon of the 20th of March Hahnke and Lucanus brought me my papers of discharge in two blue envelopes. Lucanus had been to my son the previous day, on a commission from His Majesty, in order to induce him to sound me concerning the granting of the title of duke and the proposal of a corresponding grant of money by the Landtag. My son, without reflection, declared that both would be undesired and distressing to me, and in the afternoon, after conferring with me, he wrote to Lucanus that "the grant of a title would, after the way in which I was treated in His Majesty's earliest youth, be distressing to me, and a grant of money, in view of the financial situation and for personal reasons, would be unacceptable." In spite of this the title of duke was conferred upon me.

The . . . order addressed to me on the 20th ran as follows:

My dear Prince!

With deep emotion I have perceived, from your request of the 18th, inst., that you are determined to retire from the offices which you have filled for many years with incomparable results. I had hoped that I should not be obliged to consider more closely the idea of parting with you in our lifetime. If I am none the less compelled, in the full consciousness of the grievous importance of your retirement, to familiarize myself with this idea, I do it indeed with an afflicted heart, but in the confident expectation that the granting of your request will contribute toward sparing and preserving your life—irreplaceable to the Fatherland—and your energies, as long as possible. The motives of your resolve which you have put forward convince me that further attempts to persuade you to take back your offer would have no prospect of success. I therefore respond to your wish, in that I herewith grant you the requested discharge from our offices as Imperial Chancellor, Prime Minister, and Minister for Foreign Affairs, with my good will and in the assurance that *your counsel and your energy, your loyalty and devotion*, will not fail me, and the Fatherland, in the future also. I have regarded it as one of the most merciful dispensations of my life that I had you beside me, as my first adviser, at the time when I succeeded to the government. What you have effected and attained for Prussia and Germany, what you have been to my House, my predecessors, and myself, will remain a grateful and imperishable memory for me and the German people. But even abroad your wise and energetic peace policy, which I, too, am resolved, in future and out of complete conviction, to make the pattern of my own dealings, will always be recollected with glorious approbation.

To reward your service adequately is not within my power. I must in this connection be satisfied with assuring you of my and the Fatherland's imperishable gratitude. As a token of this gratitude I confer upon you the dignity of a Duke of Lauenburg. I will also have my life-size portrait sent to you.

God bless you, my dear Prince, and grant you yet many years of an untroubled old age, illumined by the consciousness of duty loyally accomplished.

With these sentiments I remain, in the future also, in loyalty
bound, your grateful

Kaiser and King,

Wilhelm, I.R.

. . . Since then my counsel has not at any time been demanded
either directly or through an intermediary; on the contrary, my
successors appear to be forbidden to discuss politics with me. I have
the impression that in the case of all officials and officers who hold
on to their places there is a boycott against me; not only professional, but social also. This boycott found a curious official expression in the diplomatic pardon extended to my successor on account
of the discredit thrown upon the person of his predecessor
abroad. . . .

On the morning of the 21st, at ten o'clock, while my son was at
the Lehrter railway station to receive the Prince of Wales, His
Majesty said to him: "You have misunderstood Schuvalov, to
judge by your letter of yesterday; he has just been speaking to me.
He wants to visit you this afternoon and put matters straight." My
son replied that he could no longer deal with Schuvalov, for he was
on the point of sending in his resignation. His Majesty would not
hear of such a proposal: "he would grant my son all facilities, and
that afternoon or later would discuss matters with him in detail; he
must remain." Schuvalov, too, called on my son that afternoon, but
declined to make overtures, since his instructions were to deal with
my son and myself, not with our successors. Concerning the audience that morning, he told us that he had been awakened at 1 A.M.
by a military policeman, who had brought him a two-line note
from the aide-de-camp, an appointment for 8.45 A.M. He had been
greatly agitated, supposing that something had happened to the
tsar. At the audience His Majesty had spoken of politics, expressing
himself as ready to make advances, and declared that he wished to
continue the policy which had so far been followed; and he,
Schuvalov, had informed St. Petersburg of this.

To a question of Caprivi's as to a suitable successor my son
mentioned (on the 23d) the ambassador in Brussels, von Alvensleben. Caprivi stated that he was on good terms with him, and
expressed himself as against a non-Prussian at the head of the foreign office. His Majesty had named Marschall to him. In the
meantime the kaiser informed my son, whom he met at breakfast at

the dragoons' mess, that Alvensleben was also quite acceptable to him.

On the morning of the 26th my son showed Caprivi the ropes of the secretariat. The latter found the conditions too complicated—he would be obliged to simplify them—and he mentioned that Alvensleben had been with him that morning; but the more he lectured him the more obstinate he became in his refusal. My son agreed that he would make another attempt with Alvensleben that afternoon and inform Caprivi of the result. In the course of the same day he received his discharge, without having had the conversation which the Kaiser had given him reason to expect.

My son endeavored in the afternoon, as promised, in company with the ambassador, von Schweinitz, who was present on leave, to induce Herr von Alvensleben to accept the position as his successor, but without success. Alvensleben declared that he would rather abandon his career than become secretary of state, but he, nevertheless, promised not to make up his mind finally until he had spoken to the kaiser.

On the morning of the 27th the kaiser called on my son, and in the midst of repeated embraces expressed the hope that he would soon see him rested and back in the service, and asked how matters stood in respect of Alvensleben. Afterward my son reported, and His Majesty expressed his astonishment that Alvensleben had not yet presented himself; he immediately made an appointment for the latter to be at the palace at half past twelve.

My son betook himself to Caprivi and informed him of Alvensleben's attitude. He told him that His Majesty had sent for him, and he recapitulated the reasons by which he himself had endeavored to influence him. Thereupon Caprivi expressed himself somewhat as follows:

That's all too late now. Yesterday he had submitted to His Majesty that Alvensleben was unwilling, and thereupon he was authorized to apply to Marschall. Marschall had at once declared himself to be ready, with the additional remark that he had already had the consent of his grand duke for his transfer to the imperial service, and his official request to Karlsruhe was only a matter of form. If Alvensleben were to accept now there would be nothing else for him (Caprivi) to do but resign. He would report at the palace at 12.45, and remind His Majesty of yesterday's commission to Marschall.

Alvensleben, who was received at the palace immediately before Caprivi, had not been persuaded even by the kaiser. As the latter informed Caprivi of this fact, with an expression of his regret, Caprivi replied that it was very fortunate, and had saved him from a great dilemma, for he had already settled matters with Marschall. The kaiser exclaimed, briefly, "Good, then; it's Marschall." Caprivi had not awaited the result of my son's conversation with Alvensleben, but had secured the ambassador from Baden before this took place. . . .

On the 26th of March I took leave of the kaiser. His Majesty said that "anxiety for my health alone" had induced him to consent to my resignation. I replied that my health had seldom been so good of late years as during the past winter. The publication of my resignation was postponed. Simultaneously with his installation Caprivi had already taken possession of part of the chancellor's official residence; I saw that ambassadors, ministers, and diplomatists were obliged to wait on the ground floor, a coercive measure compelling me to expedite my packing and my departure. On the 29th of March I left Berlin under the compulsion of this overhasty evacuation of my residence, receiving in the railway station the military salute ordered by the kaiser, which I might justifiably have called my first-class funeral obsequies.

Index

73 74 75   12 11 10 9 8 7 6 5 4 3 2 1